LITERARY
MEMOIRS

LITERARY MEMOIRS

by
JOSÉ VICTORINO LASTARRIA

Translated from the Spanish by
R. KELLY WASHBOURNE

EDITED AND WITH AN INTRODUCTION
BY FREDERICK M. NUNN

OXFORD
UNIVERSITY PRESS

2000

OXFORD
UNIVERSITY PRESS

Oxford New York
Athens Auckland Bangkok Bogotá
Buenos Aires Calcutta Cape Town Dar es Salaam
Delhi Florence Hong Kong Istanbul Karachi
Kuala Lumpur Madras Madrid Melbourne
Mexico City Mumbai Nairobi Paris Singapore
Taipei Tokyo Toronto Warsaw

and associated companies in
Berlin Ibadan

Published by Oxford University Press, Inc.
198 Madison Avenue, New York, New York 10016

Oxford is a registered trademark of Oxford University Press, Inc.

Library of Congress Cataloguing in Publication Data is available.
ISBN 0-19-511685-2 (cloth)
ISBN 0-19-511686-0 (paper)

1 3 5 7 9 8 6 4 2

Printed in the United States of America
on acid-free paper

Contents

Series Editors' General Introduction
vii

Note on the Author, the Editor, and the Translator
xi

Chronology of José Victorino Lastarria Santander
xiii

Introduction by Frederick M. Nunn
xv

Works by Lastarria
xxxviii

Contents
xlv

Literary Memoirs
1

Series Editors'
General Introduction

The Library of Latin America series makes available in translation major nineteenth-century authors whose work has been neglected in the English-speaking world. The titles for the translations from the Spanish and Portuguese were suggested by an editorial committee that included Jean Franco (general editor responsible for works in Spanish), Richard Graham (series editor responsible for works in Portuguese), Tulio Halperín Donghi (at the University of California, Berkeley), Iván Jaksić (at the University of Notre Dame), Naomi Lindstrom (at the University of Texas at Austin), Francine Masiello (at the University of California, Berkeley), and Eduardo Lozano of the Library at the University of Pittsburgh. The late Antonio Cornejo Polar of the University of California, Berkeley, was also one of the founding members of the committee. The translations have been funded thanks to the generosity of the Lampadia Foundation and the Andrew W. Mellon Foundation.

During the period of national formation between 1810 and into the early years of the twentieth century, the new nations of Latin America fashioned their identities, drew up constitutions, engaged in bitter struggles over territory, and debated questions of education, government, ethnicity, and culture. This was a unique period unlike the process of nation formation in Europe and one which should be more familiar than it is to students of comparative politics, history, and literature.

The image of the nation was envisioned by the lettered classes—a minority in countries in which indigenous, mestizo, black, or mulatto peasants and slaves predominated—although there were also alternative nationalisms at the grassroots level. The cultural elite were well educated in European thought and letters, but as statesmen, journalists, poets, and academics, they confronted the problem of the racial and linguistic heterogeneity of the continent and the difficulties of integrating the population into a modern nation-state. Some of the writers whose works will be translated in the Library of Latin America series played leading roles in politics. Fray Servando Teresa de Mier, a friar who translated Rousseau's *The Social Contract* and was one of the most colorful characters of the independence period, was faced with imprisonment and expulsion from Mexico for his heterodox beliefs; on his return, after independence, he was elected to the congress. Domingo Faustino Sarmiento, exiled from his native Argentina under the presidency of Rosas, wrote *Facundo: Civilización y barbarie*, a stinging denunciation of that government. He returned after Rosas' overthrow and was elected president in 1868. Andrés Bello was born in Venezuela, lived in London where he published poetry during the independence period, settled in Chile where he founded the University, wrote his grammar of the Spanish language, and drew up the country's legal code.

These post-independence intelligentsia were not simply dreaming castles in the air, but vitally contributed to the founding of nations and the shaping of culture. The advantage of hindsight may make us aware of problems they themselves did not foresee, but this should not affect our assessment of their truly astonishing energies and achievements. It is still surprising that the writing of Andrés Bello, who contributed fundamental works to so many different fields, has never been translated into English. Although there is a recent translation of Sarmiento's celebrated *Facundo*, there is no translation of his memoirs, *Recuerdos de provincia (Provincial Recollections)*. The predominance of memoirs in the Library of Latin America series is no accident—many of these offer entertaining insights into a vast and complex continent.

Nor have we neglected the novel. The series includes new translations of the outstanding Brazilian writer Joaquim Maria Machado de Assis's work, including *Dom Casmurro* and *The Posthumous Memoirs of Brás Cubas*. There is no reason why other novels and writers who are not so well known outside Latin America—the Peruvian novelist Clorinda Matto de Turner's *Aves sin nido*, Nataniel Aguirre's *Juan de la Rosa*, José de Alencar's *Iracema*, Juana Manuela Gorriti's short stories—should not be read with as much interest as the political novels of Anthony Trollope.

A series on nineteenth-century Latin America cannot, however, be limited to literary genres such as the novel, the poem, and the short story. The literature of independent Latin America was eclectic and strongly influenced by the periodical press newly liberated from scrutiny by colonial authorities and the Inquisition. Newspapers were miscellanies of fiction, essays, poems, and translations from all manner of European writing. The novels written on the eve of Mexican Independence by José Joaquín Fernández de Lizardi included disquisitions on secular education and law, and denunciations of the evils of gaming and idleness. Other works, such as a well-known poem by Andrés Bello, "Ode to Tropical Agriculture," and novels such as *Amalia* by José Mármol and the Bolivian Nataniel Aguirre's *Juan de la Rosa*, were openly partisan. By the end of the century, sophisticated scholars were beginning to address the history of their countries, as did João Capistrano de Abreu in his *Capítulos de história colonial*.

It is often in memoirs such as those by Fray Servando Teresa de Mier or Sarmiento that we find the descriptions of everyday life that in Europe were incorporated into the realist novel. Latin American literature at this time was seen largely as a pedagogical tool, a "light" alternative to speeches, sermons, and philosophical tracts—though, in fact, especially in the early part of the century, even the readership for novels was quite small because of the high rate of illiteracy. Nevertheless, the vigorous orally transmitted culture of the gaucho and the urban underclasses became the linguistic repertoire of some of the most interesting nineteenth-century writers—most notably José Hernández, author of the "gauchesque" poem "Martín Fierro," which enjoyed an unparalleled popularity. But for many writers the task was not to appropriate popular language but to civilize, and their literary works were strongly influenced by the high style of political oratory.

The editorial committee has not attempted to limit its selection to the better-known writers such as Machado de Assis; it has also selected many works that have never appeared in translation or writers whose work has not been translated recently. The series now makes these works available to the English-speaking public.

Because of the preferences of funding organizations, the series initially focuses on writing from Brazil, the Southern Cone, the Andean region, and Mexico. Each of our editions will have an introduction that places the work in its appropriate context and includes explanatory notes.

We owe special thanks to Robert Glynn of the Lampadia Foundation, whose initiative gave the project a jump start, and to Richard Ekman of the Andrew W. Mellon Foundation, which also generously supported the project. We also thank the Rockefeller Foundation for funding the 1996 symposium "Culture and Nation in Iberoamerica," organized by the editorial board of the Library of Latin America. We received substantial institutional support and personal encouragement from the Institute of Latin American Studies of the University of Texas at Austin. The support of Edward Barry of Oxford University Press has been crucial, as has the advice and help of Ellen Chodosh of Oxford University Press. The first volumes of the series were published after the untimely death, on July 3, 1997, of Maria C. Bulle, who, as an associate of the Lampadia Foundation, supported the idea from its beginning. We received substantial institutional support and personal encouragement from the Institute of Latin American Studies of the University of Texas at Austin.

—Jean Franco
—Richard Graham

Note on the Author, the Editor, and the Translator

José Victorino Lastarria (1817–1888) was one of nineteenth-century Latin America's intellectual giants. During his lifetime he wrote critically on literature, history, philosophy, and, politics, was a novelist, and was a member of all significant intellectual movements of his time and place. He served in all branches of government and represented his country abroad.

His *Recuerdos literarios* contains a veritable history of Chilean letters in an isolated country carved out of the Spanish American Empire during the tumultuous years of the early nineteenth century. Less than a half century after gaining independence, Chile had established a constitutional system, achieved a measure of economic growth, and had become a leading power in South America.

In such remarkable times as those, Chileans also developed historical and literary traditions, establishing themselves as a people who valued thought as much as force as a way of settling political differences. Lastarria was at the center of all the intellectual struggles of his times. *Recuerdos literarios* reveals the intellectual depth and breadth of a man who believed in his country and in himself as representative of all that countries and individuals should be: guided by the spirit of the times but original; aware of intellectual and philosophical trends in the major centers of culture but American.

Frederick M. Nunn is professor of History and International Studies at Portland State University. He is the author of *The Time of the Generals: Latin American Professional Militarism in World Perspective* (1992) and other works on Chilean and comparative civil-military relations.

R. Kelly Washbourne is working toward a Ph.D. in contemporary Spanish-American and Brazilian literatures at the University of Massachusetts, Amherst. He is assistant editor of the *Amazonian Literary Review*.

Chronology of José Victorino Lastarria

March 22, 1817:	Lastarria is born in Rancagua, the son of Francisco Solano Lastarria López and Carmen Santander
1817–1818:	Chilean independence from Spain secured
1817–1823:	Supreme Directorship of Bernardo O'Higgins y Riquelme, followed by Conservative-Liberal factional rivalries until 1831
1831–1841:	Presidency of General Joaquín Prieto Vial
1836–1839:	War with Peru and Bolivia
1837:	Lastarria named Secretary at *Academia de Leyes y Política Forense*
1838:	Begins publishing career with textbook on geography (see "Works by Lastarria" for details on publications)
1839:	Receives law degree, begins career as Liberal Party activist, helps found review, *El Diablo Político*
1841–1851:	Presidency of General Manuel Bulnes Prieto
1842:	National University founded, "Generation of 1842" takes form
1842–1843:	Lastarria founds literary periodical, *El Semanario de Santiago*; helps found review *El Crepúsculo*, and organization, *La Sociedad Literaria de Santiago*
1843:	Serves in Ministry of the Interior, first son, Aurelio, born

1843–1846:	Serves as Deputy for Elqui and Parral
1846:	Member of faculty of Philosophy and Humanities, University of Chile, will serve as dean on several occasions; second son, Demetrio, born
1848–1849:	Founds review, *La Revista de Santiago*
1849–1852:	Deputy for Rancagua, forced to leave country in 1850 owing to civil unrest abetted by dissident Liberals
1851–1861:	Presidency of Manuel Montt Torres
1855–1858:	Deputy for Copiapó
1858–1861:	Deputy for Valparaíso
1859:	Helps found organization, *Círculo de Los Amigos de Las Letras*
1861–1871:	Presidency of José Joaquín Pérez Moscayano
1862:	Lastarria serves as Minister of the Treasury
1862–1864:	Serves as Minister Plenipotentiary to Argentina, Brazil, and Peru
1864–1867:	Deputy for Quillota
1867–1870:	Deputy for La Serena
1870–1873:	Deputy for Quillota
1871–1876:	Presidency of Federico Errázuriz Zañartu
1873:	Lastarria helps found organization, *Academia de Bellas Letras*
1874–1875:	Member of commission to codify agricultural and rural legislation
1876–1881:	Presidency of Aníbal Pinto Garmendia
1876:	Lastarria serves in Ministry of the Interior
1876–1879:	Senator for Coquimbo
1879–1884:	War of the Pacific, Chile defeats Peru and Bolivia for the second time in the nineteenth century
1879–1885:	Lastarria serves as Senator for Valparaíso
1881–1886:	Presidency of Domingo Santa María González, Lastarria and others found splinter Doctrinaire Liberal Party
1885–1887:	Supreme Court Justice
June 14, 1888:	José Victorino Lastarria Santander dies in Santiago

Introduction

C hileans take pride in their past.[1] Theirs is a rich historical and literary heritage, passed on from generation to generation since the nineteenth century through public and private educational institutions and a lively publishing industry, as well as through the build-up of folk- and elitelore. Few Chileans with the rudiments of primary or secondary education are unfamiliar with a set of heroes, events, and national accomplishments that would be the envy of any nation emergent from the western hemispheric independence movements of the 1775–1825 half century.

Soon after winning independence from Spain in 1817–1818, Chileans turned to the task of nation-state building.[2] By regional standards they did brilliantly. Struggles between Conservatives and Liberals, federalists and centralists would characterize the building process everywhere in Spanish America during much of the century—such struggles are not yet resolved in some Latin American countries to this day. In Chile they were resolved within fifteen years of independence to the degree that continued political debate within a defined polity of consensus replaced military involvement—until the twentieth century.

By 1833, conservative-centralists (the two would not be synonymous, necessarily) had control of the machinery of governance. The constitution adopted that year lasted until 1925. Never mind that there were revolts and a brief civil war, the fundamental charter of the land prevailed. The system of government that arose from the post-independence struggling of the 1820s was flexible enough to withstand rebellion, the civil war, even an ill-fated and short-lived attempt by Spain to reassert her influence on the Pacific coast of South America.

While golpe after golpe generated governmental, not necessarily political change in Peru and Bolivia, while personalist tyranny prevailed in Argentina, Chile developed political institutions, intellectual activity, and economic practices that prevailed into this century.[3] By the time the 1829–1832, 1835–1852 tyranny of Juan Manuel de Rosas ended in Argentina, Chileans were well on their way to establishing a national cultural consensus. Whereas elites in Buenos Aires had to resolve serious political problems (i.e., the form and the content of national government), Chilean elites discussed and debated politics in the same arenas they discussed and debated literature and historiography.

What Chileans accomplished was pretty much what the elites wanted done.[4] Of course, this may be asserted for any Latin American country in the past century (and for more than one in this century), but Chile's is a peculiar case. Geographic and ethnic factors contributed to the successes of the elites. Unlike other countries of the region, where distance, topography, climate, and linguistic differences hindered the nation-state building process, Chile was very lucky. In much historical literature this luck is submerged under claims of racial superiority, ingenuity, patriotism, and probity, but the historical and literary records are impressive nonetheless.

The bulk of the population of nineteenth-century Chile lived in a flat plain, the Central Valley, between the Andes and a coastal range of hills. The Central Valley, still Chile's "heartland," was bounded on the north by the fringes of the Atacama Desert, on the south by coastal waters and Indian nations. The northern frontier was peaceful enough until the 1870s, the southern contested until then with remnants of the legendary and warlike Araucanians. Chileans of the nineteenth century firmly believed that their isolation, their continual watchfulness on the southern edges of the Central Valley, the relatively rapid development of national institutions, and their successes against rival nations set them apart—from everyone.

Way off in South America, shut off from the rest of the world by mountains, the sea, and a desert, in *el rincón más apartado del mundo*, as Chileans will call their homeland, the great families and their allies built a nation. Between 1831 and 1920 there was not one chief executive who was not linked—if only through marriage—to the Basque-Castilian aristocracy.[5] This fact, along with geographic influences and a relatively homogeneous population (European and mestizo), made Chile unique in the nineteenth century. So did intellectual life.

In the pages that follow there are numerous references to the leaders and the families who made up the Basque-Castilian aristocracy. The author of *Recuerdos literarios* did not come from one of the great families. He was a provincial boy from a reputable if not influential family. Owing to the flexibility—as opposed to the openness to new ideas—of the ruling elite, there was room for him in select circles. If it had not been for social flexibility, porosity some may call it, there would have been no flowering of intellect to accompany the accomplishments in economic, military, and political realms. Lest readers wonder about the social factor, it was social stability and oligarchic rule that contributed mightily to all accomplishments.

The Basque-Castilian aristocracy was a fusion of families that represented governmental, agrarian, professional, and commercial interests. For most of the century the production of resources, and their domestic and international marketing, was in the hands of interlocked families. So was military leadership and the ecclesiastical hierarchy, and of course so would be supervision of educational institutions. Economic diversification (mining, investment, transportation, communications) only expanded this aristocracy, thus providing more opportunities. It did not serve to dilute its grip on power, only to alter the ways power was exerted and the purpose of its exercise. Intermarriage and *compadrismo* did the same. What passed for a middle sector was in essence a downward extension of aristocratic values and an expansion of the number of people who subscribed to them. This was an ideal society for intellectual activity.

Entrée into select circles might be gained through intellectual achievement, outstanding performance at school, for example. As in Great Britain, it was not unusual for something akin to a "scholarship boy" to find a niche in administrative or educational circles upon successful completion of an academic career.

Until this century's struggles to determine domestic and foreign policy based on sectoral as well as ideological grounds, relations between Church and State, the configuration of government, and the distribution of its powers were activities confined to the elites. Expansive and flexible though the Basque-Castilian was, Chile's record of achievements cannot be said to have benefited all Chileans. I do not mean to detract from such achievements, only to place them in the correct context within which *Recuerdos literarios* could be written.[6] The most significant struggles affecting nineteenth-century Chilean intellectuals were those between the executive and legislative branches of government. These were power struggles and much more.

It would be a mistake to view them simply as rivalries between liberal thinkers and reactionaries or conservatives. If there is a dominant theme woven into the fabric of Chilean political history, it is that of the rivalry between presidents and congresses.[7] Neither the writing of history nor that of literature can be separated from the intensity of political life in both Santiago and Valparaíso.

Early on in the post-independence period, those who styled themselves liberals did indeed work to expand congress's powers at the expense of the chief executive. Bernardo O'Higgins was surely a liberal—in the sense of seeking significant changes in the way Chileans governed themselves—but he was an autocrat through and through. The Constitution of 1833 enshrined a centralized, executive-dominated system (often called "Portalian" after Diego Portales, more on whom in the text). Under Manuel Bulnes (the main body of the text elaborates on this figure as well) in the 1840s, unprecedented press and speech freedoms—unprecedented for Latin America—allowed for a liberal renaissance that continued under the autocrat Manuel Montt (another figure dealt with in the text), whose conservative credentials were not enough to keep the "party" from splitting over his succession and other issues. By the time *Recuerdos literarios* was in print, the aristocracy's grip on power was being expressed through coalitions, not parties, and Liberals, not Conservatives, were in charge.

In the coalition-driven politics of the second half of the century, Liberals, Conservatives, Radicals, and Nationals (capitals are employed to specify party affiliation, not philosophical bent) jockeyed for control of congress; Liberals controlled the executive branch following the controversy over the selection of Montt's successor in 1859–1861, allied with Radicals and Nationals or Montt-Varistas (followers of Montt and his frustrated would-be successor, Antonio Varas).[8] All parties in varying configurations struggled to control the forces of change in order to preserve their own version of the status quo.

Just three years after the author of *Recuerdos literarios* passed away, the country convulsed in civil war. All party loyalties aside, the Chilean Civil War of 1891 was an executive-legislative conflict. Along the path to this bloodbath, Chileans had curbed the powers of the Church without separating it from the State, established civil registry of vital statistics, expanded the electorate and access to public education, created a system of public cemeteries and guaranteed freedom of worship (if not its public display), and decentralized the supervision of electoral processes. Each and every one of the discussions and debates surrounding these issues bore the tinge of the executive-legislative struggle.

Conservatives could be remarkably "federalist," as they would be in Argentina, say, and as opposed to what they were in Mexico. Liberals proved to be quite autocratic and zealous in defense of executive prerogatives.

Radicals appear historically to have been remarkably conservative when pondering the socioeconomic consequences of legislation and division of the powers of state. Nationals lumbered along in decreasing numbers, defending autocracy and economic progress, something that had marked the mid-century decades, back when Chilean intellectual life really began. *Recuerdos literarios* contains a good deal of both impressionistic and first-hand analysis of Chilean liberalism and conservatism, from struggles over the form of government to ultramontanism, to intellectual freedom or the lack thereof. Readers of this work will gain from it something of a nineteenth-century historiographical and literary theory base, both important in the determination of national policy back then.

Some of the themes developed in *Recuerdos literarios* apply to the political warfare of the Parliamentary Republic (1891–1920), and the interwar years (1920–1938). During these eras the executive-legislative struggle, seemingly resolved in the Civil War, renewed itself electorally, through military political action and in a socialist experiment of the early 1930s.[9] They also apply to the politics of the Popular Front era (1938–1942) and the ensuing years of Radical dominance of the executive branch, for example, until 1952. The political agendas of Arturo Alessandri Palma (president, 1920–1924, 1925, 1932–1938) and General Carlos Ibáñez del Campo (president, 1927–1931, 1952–1958), Air Commodore Marmaduke Grove Vallejo (leader of the short-lived Socialist Republic (1932), and Pedro Aguirre Cerda (president, 1938–1941) grew out of nineteenth-century controversies. It would not be too much of an exaggeration to consider the uprising of 1973, which installed General Augusto Pinochet Ugarte in the presidency, as the culmination of the executive-legislative struggle that had its origins over a century before.

While the executive-legislative struggle took form, conflict was confined to the elites. This meant that the populace would not be directly involved with political decision-making until the twentieth century. Even then popular interest and participation would expand only sporadically to the point where the system conceived in 1833 fell apart in 1973. The elites of the past century were pretty much able to formulate and implement domestic and foreign policies that made Chile one of the four major powers of the continent. Although *Recuerdos literarios* makes scant mention of foreign policy, a few lines about this important subject are appropriate to better place author and work in context.

Within a decade of the consolidation of power by conservatives in the early 1830s, Chile fought a successful war against Peru and Bolivia (1836–1839). Victory gained Chile notoriety in Europe. Internal stability (albeit enforced) increased national stature abroad. The reopening of mines and extension of the southern frontier helped expand the economy. Chile had a good reputation beyond its frontiers and self-confidence at home. Civil disorder in the 1850s was more a sign of intraelitist discontent than evidence of a potential for social upheaval. Between the writing of *Recuerdos literarios* and the death of the author, Chile defeated her Andean foes a second time, in the War of the Pacific (1879–1884), gaining an immense amount of mineral-rich territory from them both.[10] During the same five-year period, Chileans finally put an end to the wars in Araucania, consolidating the southern frontier at the expense of the stalwart indigenes who had never been conquered during the colonial period. When Chileans evince pride in their past they have some reason to do so.

Around mid-century, when Argentines were ridding themselves of Rosas and his kind, Chileans were enjoying their cultural boom. Emigrés from countries beset with post-independence strife settled in Chile. Domingo Faustino Sarmiento and Andrés Bello—both present in the pages of *Recuerdos literarios*—flourished in Chile. The National University, one of the region's best, was established in 1842 and opened its doors the next year. The famed *Instituto Nacional* finally had a complementary institution of higher learning where its distinguished young graduates could pursue further education and preparation for positions of national leadership. The "Generation of 1842," named for the University's founding, set a standard for discussion and debate in salons, societies, and in print of just what should be the essence of literature, poetry, theater, philosophy, political theory, and historiography—national culture.

It is clear from a reading of the work introduced here that these discussions and debates rarely stuck to just one topic or theme, for members of the Generation of 1842 saw learning and culture as a whole, as tools to use as well as gifts to bestow. They were not confined to subject-based disciplines.[11] Bello, Sarmiento, and their Chilean hosts proclaimed and denounced, defended and attacked, wrote and orated, published and confided. They were well read and eager to show their erudition.

The defeat of Rosas's forces at the Battle of Monte Caseros in 1852, glimmers of temporary stability in Peru, and consolidation of power by Emperor Pedro II in Brazil are all noteworthy achievements of the mid-nineteenth century decades. What was going on in Chile, if a lot less dramatic, was tantamount to cultural nation-building. It is one thing to forge a nation politically, economically, and socially out of a colonial heritage. It is quite another to establish the basis for intellectual life and for the lore that, passed from generation to generation, is disseminated among rich and poor alike, thus engendering what we call *chilenidad*.

Recuerdos literarios is one man's testament to the process of cultural nation-building. In its pages readers have found the genesis of Chilean literature and historiography. These were once inseparable. Students of both Latin American history and literature begin their studies by becoming familiar with texts from the age of discovery and conquest. History and literature blend in the letters of Columbus and Cortés, in the conquest chronicles and epics.[12] The blend had become less intense by the time Latin America broke with Iberia, so that by the time *Recuerdos literarios* appeared in print one might think they were no longer miscible intellectually. Nothing could be farther from the truth. *Recuerdos literarios* is both literature and literary; moreover, it is both historical and historic.

It is a historical work, for it portrays important goings-on in a segment of the past that is unfamiliar, even at third hand, to most people alive today. Most works of history do this sort of thing, and many segments of the past have been written about more than once. Nineteenth-century Chile is no exception, but there are few sources that treat Chilean intellectual, cultural, and literary history with the detail displayed in *Recuerdos literarios.*

It is a historic work, for it is uniquely nineteenth-century Chilean. Although Chileans were far ahead of their neighbors in terms of developing a national literature and historiographical tradition, they were not so owing to the quantity of works produced.[13] Few have been accorded the status of *Recuerdos literarios.* It is also historic because it provides us all with information on the authors and works, the figures and events, that were considered historically significant by nineteenth-century Chileans, at least the literate ones, regardless of their particular political convictions. The first section, "1836–1849," is a rich source of information for study of the political and intellectual struggles of those times.

The writing of history, like that of literature, is, more than chronicling and narrating a sequence of events, real or fictional, or sometimes, both, for elucidation or entertainment. History can be artistic and didactic at the same time. Literature, be it prose, poetry, or drama, can also be as didactic as it is creative. When nineteenth-century Latin Americans wrote history, they had purposes in mind. Some wanted to validate the break with the mother country; others lamented it or glorified the colonial experience in order to oppose too much change or justify political decisions.[14] Clio assumed both conservative and liberal guises with ease.

Latin Americans—Chileans certainly—faced the dilemmas of excolonials, and in so doing set examples worthy of examination by Africans, Asians, and Eastern Europeans who have emerged from forms of colonialism in our own century only to find cultural nation-building a largely insurmountable challenge. Nineteenth-century Chileans either had to embrace the culture of others or create their own. Chile was a sovereign state, and Chileans were an independent people. It did not discourage them to emerge from post-independence civil strife and defeat their enemies in a war, all barely twenty years after becoming independent and sovereign. Nor did stable and efficient government deter them, autocratic though it may have been, from building for the future. Chileans were a proud people—at least the activities of the literate ones would indicate so.

So *Recuerdos literarios* is no mere chronicle, no mere narrative. Nor is it simply a literary autobiography, someone's memoirs. It is a complex work. It ranges from a detailed study of conditions that encouraged the launching of the Generation of 1842, the significant intellectual movement of the last century, to a detailed study of the historiographical and literary debates of mid-century, to the later institutionalization of those debates through the creation of the *Academia de Bellas Letras*. Both the second and third sections of the book deal with these matters.

In places it is downright prolix and marked by arcane language, more anent which anon. It allows us, as we approach and endure a millennium, to experience the thought processes of a nineteenth-century Chilean intellectual, political figure, and writer. It is a window on past battles—of the mind, the pen, and the press—not the rifle and the lance. It is a chronicle, and it is a narrative; it is also an analysis and critique of literature, and an attempt to create a historical record of which the author's fellow citizens could be proud.

Prolixity is neither failure nor sin, certainly not in works from the era in question. *Recuerdos literarios* is not unique in style. It is, after all, primarily a long didactic essay in three parts, a very long essay indeed. In translation it is not so much prolix as a lesson in nineteenth-century ideation and argumentation, an example of how one was deemed virtually useless without the other. Its rendition of thought processes begs comparison with others of its time; *Civilización y Barbarie* (*"Facundo"*) for instance.[15] All students of Latin American history and literature are familiar with Sarmiento's didacticism, and his own work is pretty easy reading, owing, I have always thought, both to style and subject. *Recuerdos literarios* is a case study, by contrast, of the difficult process undertaken by an individual and his cadre of like-minded citizens struggling toward definitions: self, community, history, culture, literature.[16] *Facundo* is not an example of this, as it is an extremely effective assault on barbarism. *Recuerdos literarios*, by comparison, is a fortification against barbarism.

Chilean intellectual life was as lively in the past century as it has been in our own. *Recuerdos literarios* contains allusions to the classics, to major authors and works of the early modern and modern historical periods. These allusions are not devices used by the author solely to demonstrate his mastery of canonical works, to establish and reenforce, as it were, his intellectual credentials. References to major works—prose, poetry, and music— are commonplace in works such as this. Latin American essayists from Sarmiento to Rodó, from da Cunha to Mariátegui, and from Martínez Estrada to Paz, all introduce such documentation into their prose.[17] In the decades before the social sciences became professionalized in Latin America, there was no dearth of learned, scholarly discourse on social and cultural subjects. Neither was there any shortage of sagacity among those who debated and discussed political and economic issues. The learned individual was expected to know classics, languages, and to be familiar with the major works of Western civilization and culture.

Here such allusions and documentation serve to enhance both the historic and historical significance of the work. They serve to locate it historiographically and to set it apart from other works. Many—not all—of the allusions and references are highlighted in volume editor's and the translator's notes. Annotation of the text, as will be explained further in this introduction, has been designed to allow the work to flow.

Its flow is one of *Recuerdos*'s strengths as a representative nineteenth-century work of cultural nation-building. If it is atypical of the region, it is characteristic of Chile. The author's frequent allusions and references make it pretty clear that he was not only well read, but also that he was well versed in what to read. He was not a pretentious name-dropper, just a conscious one.

Recuerdos literarios, thus, does embody a deeply personal memoir of the author's prolific, peripatetic, and energetic life. It is also a testament to the intellectuality of a generation and the application of that intellectuality to the response to questions arising from the nation-building process. Intellectuals were deeply involved, along with generals and presidents, businessmen and landowners, in creating and sustaining the Chilean state and all its institutions. They still are. The tradition of activism that allowed intellectuals to influence the shift in government and politics via the plebiscite of 1988 has its origins in the Generation of 1842 and all the activity it spawned.

We know from the pages of *Recuerdos literarios* who Chileans of the past considered worthy of reading and emulating. We know which events they considered critical in their history, to Chile's rise to prominence on the Pacific coast of South America. We know what scientific discoveries were important to men (alas, no women were involved) bent on creating a nation-state, then fighting for change in direction of government and politics—without ever seriously contemplating a radical change in the existing social order. We know just what Chileans thought of their contemporaries in Europe and North America. At times *Recuerdos literarios* reads like a travelogue of the mind.

Historical references serve to place the work at a chronological site: nineteenth-century Chile, so far away from the centers of western cultural and intellectual life to which South Americans naturally turned for inspiration. Literary references serve to place *Recuerdos literarios* in the context of letters, better yet, belles lettres. The Chilean literati were involved in the same process in which Europeans found themselves involved from the end of the Napoleonic age until the 1890s: emerging from romanticism, entering realism, then naturalism, and flirting with symbolism and parnassianism.[18] Chileans were concomitantly struggling to establish a national tradition of letters, one that proved they were more than overseas Spaniards or slavish Europhiles. Nevertheless, intellectual, political, and philosophical references serve to place *Recuerdos literarios*, its readers, and other Chileans well within the tradition of Western thought.

Chileans wanted to be part of history—as they knew it to be defined and as they saw themselves adding to its richness. They wanted to be comfortably within the confines of Western literary tradition, yet provide their own variations on its major themes. They wanted to be recognized by others—Europeans and North Americans especially—as Chileans, a people who were in all ways the equal of others when it came to intellectual achievements. This is why French, German, British, North American, Spanish, and classical Greek and Roman authors grace these pages as much as do Chileans. *Recuerdos literarios* successfully defied the constraints of time and space in order to keep contemporary readers abreast of intellectual currents prevailing in Europe and North America. During the better part of the second half of the century, friends and foes of the author and his cadre were availed of a window on the world. Now rendered into English this work returns the gesture. It avails us of a window on nineteenth-century Chile.

Spain's former colonies in America were effectively cut off, or cut themselves off, from the intellectual currents of the mother country. Paz's assertion that independence was both a negation and an affirmation of identity is certainly validated by the cultural nation-building that went on in Chile.[19] England's former colonies, at least the thirteen mainland ones that revolted in 1776, were never cut off culturally from the mother country. Up north, independence was also an affirmation and negation process, but never to the degree that it was in South America. *Recuerdos literarios* is one of the best examples of the contrast between what went on in North America and what went on to the south in terms of a quest for national identity.

As mentioned, Chileans wanted to be unique (this was a way of justifying and maintaining a cultural status quo), and they wanted to be well within the mainstream of nineteenth-century culture (this being a way of legitimately advocating change). The dynamic of Chilean conservatism and liberalism cannot be separated from the intellectual tensions manifest in *Recuerdos literarios.* The book's author could be a good nineteenth-century Liberal and a good nineteenth-century Positivist. The fact that these two sociopolitical credos would find so much common ground in Latin America, in Brazil and Mexico, for example, does not mean that their compatibility should be considered a given in nineteenth-century Chile. The subtleties of racial prejudice, the attraction of material progress, the idiosyncratic nature of Chilean anticlericalism, and the baroqueness of the political system, as it limped through the 1860s, 1870s, and 1880s, all colored liberalism and Positivism à la Chile.

José Victorino Lastarria Santander was born March 22, 1817 in Rancagua, and died on June 14, 1888,[20] the same year Argentina's great man of letters, and Lastarria's sometime colleague, Domingo Faustino Sarmiento, would pass away. The Battle of Chacabuco, first of the major battles for independence, took place in 1817 as well. Lastarria studied at the prestigious *Liceo de Chile*, where his mentor was José Joaquín de Mora, then with Andrés Bello at the *Instituto Nacional*.[21] In 1836, where the first portion of the book begins, he received his degree from the University of San Felipe, whereupon he entered the Academy of Law. By the end of the decade, he had served on the faculty of the *Colegio de las Hermanas Cabezón* and had published *Lecciones de geografía moderna* (1838).

Of reputable origin, but not wealthy by any means, he was proud of his accomplishments from his early years and rarely missed an opportunity to affirm them. *Tengo talento y lo luzco* ("I have talent and I show it"), he is reputed to have said, establishing him among the many of modest origins who have not been able to contain their pride at having made it to the higher rungs of society or intellectual circles. Oscar Wilde, it ought to be remembered, once said (reputedly on arriving in England from Ireland): "I have nothing to declare but my genius." Lastarria's origins proved no disadvantage at all in early nineteenth-century Chile, owing to the sociopolitical flexibility that prevailed in a polity and society in formation. Nevertheless, he made no significant references to his family in any of his writings. It was as if he believed his life had begun only at the moment his intellectual ability manifested itself.

The course of Lastarria's career from 1836 forward determined the content of his memoirs. *Recuerdos literarios* is his version of what went on in literary circles—as long and as much as he was involved in them. His schooling had gained him entrée to elite circles. To this day the *Instituto Nacional* is revered as the cradle of intellectual and political leadership; at least until the mid-twentieth century, it was an advantage to have studied there as opposed to one of the private schools in and around Santiago. Lastarria's talent did show through; at the age of twenty-one he had a law degree and had begun to publish. By the time he was in his mid twenties, Sarmiento was in Chile[22] writing essays for *El Mercurio*, the country's major newspaper, published in Valparaíso, and Lastarria had a hand in getting the Argentine exile into print.

The next year, in 1842, Lastarria was in the middle of it all, with the establishment of the University of Chile, and the beginning of the literary, political, and historiographical debates of the Generation of 1842 (intitially in the *Sociedad Literaria*) he would chronicle in his memoirs. Here began the struggle to establish *Chilean* standards for belles lettres. He would be founder of reviews and periodicals, and a frequent contributor to them; founder and member of more publications and learned societies with whose activities he would be associated sporadically, owing to political activity or absences from the country. By the time he was thirty years old, he was a man of parts, well known throughout Chile and elsewhere in South America. He would also have, by this time, two sons, Aurelio and Demetrio, who would have distinguished careers of their own.

Just three years after the founding of the University of Chile he presented the first historical "paper" in Chile: "Investigation into the Social Influences of the Conquest and the Spanish Colonization upon Chile." At the time he presented the paper, he was a contributing editor of the periodical *El Siglo*. In 1846 he published a text on constitutional law. He was now a faculty member at the University of Chile.

In 1848, a fateful year in Europe that would have reverberations in Chile, he helped found *La Revista de Santiago*. The following year he began one of several terms in the Chamber of Deputies. Now in his early thirties, Lastarria was one of Chile's future leaders in the making. His militant liberalism led him to associate with the Liberal Party during his school years, back when the party was reorganizing after the political and military disasters of the 1820s and early 1830s, so he would also be a leader of the "Society of Equality" (*La Sociedad de La Igualdad*), the equivalent of a left-wing Liberal faction, often associated historically with the Generation of 1842. By the end of the 1840s, he would have served as a subsecretary in the Ministry of the Interior. Then, owing to conflicts over the succession of Manuel Montt to the presidency in 1851, Lastarria had to leave his seat in the Chamber, and the country, in 1850.

During Montt's presidency Lastarria served in the Chamber for three terms. In 1859 he helped found the "Circle of Friends of Letters" (*Círculo de Los Amigos de Las Letras*), another literary organization. One year into the presidency of José Joaquín Pérez he would serve a stint as Minister of the

Treasury, then begin a diplomatic mission as Minister Plenipotentiary to Argentina, Brazil, and Peru. By the time he was fifty, he who knew he had talent because "it showed" was a statesman as well as a politician and an intellectual leader.

In the 1870s, during the Errázuriz and Pinto presidencies, Lastarria continued to serve in the Chamber, was a founder, in 1873, of the "Academy of Belles Lettres" (*Academia de Bellas Letras*), and served in the Senate. In his sixties he would help found the Doctrinaire Liberal Party, and by the time he was seventy, he would be appointed a Justice of the Supreme Court. When Lastarria died, June 14, 1888, Chile lost one of its most significant cultural nation-builders, a member of the first rank of Spanish American intellectual and political figures of the nineteenth century.

While he was serving in three branches of government and on diplomatic missions, he continued to write, discuss, and debate: history, literature, law, philosophy, and social science. His bibliography, following this introduction, shows breadth as well as depth of interest and sophistication. *Tenía talento y lo lucía*, this is to say.

His writing established his place in history more than his years of public service, the scholarly and political writing certainly more than his attempts at prose fiction. This does not diminish him as a statesman or novelist; it merely emphasizes his accomplishments as a scholar and activist. It is in these fields that accomplished Chileans of the past century shone brightly. And Lastarria was not alone in his endeavors. He had plenty of competition, literally as well as figuratively, in the arenas of scholarly, political, and philosophical debates. He truly was an exemplary man of his times.

In political terms, Lastarria's liberalism was as pragmatic as it was doctrinaire. He was a practical man who understood the need for Liberals to wield power in order to make changes. From 1861 forward, under Pérez, Errázuriz, Pinto, Santa María, and the ill-fated José Manuel Balmaceda, the presidency was in the hands of Liberals. During this time Chile fought the second war with Peru and Bolivia, consolidated the southern frontier, successfully avoided war with Argentina, expanded exploitation of nitrate and copper deposits in the newly acquired desert north, opened up new lands in the south, created the most powerful army and navy in South America, and had an unbroken record of orderly, constitutional presidential succession—until the Civil War of 1891.[23] Lastarria would not live to see the revolt against Balmaceda, a revolt that effectively ended the period of history in which he had played such a definitional role.

During these same years, Liberals and varying coalition partners in congress were equally successful in holding the powers of the central government in check and arriving at accommodations with the Church that averted an acrimonious split between it and the state. The rise of the Radical Party in the 1860s destroyed the Liberal monopoly on opposition to Portalian politics; indeed, after Montt no one until Balmaceda would attempt to wield power as had Prieto, Bulnes, and Montt himself. The most significant result of nineteenth-century Radicalism is that it strengthened the hand of the Liberals in dealings with Conservatives and Nationals. Lastarria and his party had, with the passage of time, become moderate in comparison with the Radicals and the small Democrat Party. Chile's expanding polity, coupled with the flexible aristocracy, prevented political conflict from taking place outside the mainstream. Few of Lastarria's writings or debates of the second half of the century resemble in tone those of the heyday of the Generation of 1842. His participation in founding the Doctrinaire Liberal Party shortly before his death was a political action, not an intellectual statement.

In Chile political "gradualism" ruled until 1891; there were no challenges to the existing order from outside the educated elite strata of society. Readers of *Recuerdos literarios* should bear this in mind as they ponder the meaning of some of Lastarria's pronouncements. His writing, public service, and participation in the historiographical and literary debates of the middle and later decades of the century became increasingly part of the mainstream phenomenon. Lastarria, that is to say, continued to be a man of his times; it is not to say he was an opportunist. Whatever the issue, he had an opinion, and the issues changed as much as he did. In their publications and societies, Chilean elites mixed, mutual respect reigned, despite ideological affiliation (except during times of civil unrest), and politics was the better. This was not at all like what had prevailed in Argentina until the 1860s, but it would be comparable to what prevailed there from then until the 1890s. In the last decade of the century and the first decade of this one, politics in both countries would become more volatile. If Lastarria had been an Argentine, he could never have achieved what he did, certainly not until the 1860s. If Sarmiento had been a Chilean, he might not have been president, at least not after the 1860s.

The sophistication and intensity of intellectual inquiry and debate in Chile (a land, it bears repeating, far from the intellectual centers of Europe and North America) resemble that of London or Paris, more than that of Buenos Aires or Lima. Owing to the intense relationship of politics to letters and new ideas, what parvenus like Lastarria feasted on, after all, had to be tested. They had to be discussed, argued, published, and adapted before being deemed applicable to the process of cultural nation-building. As *Recuerdos literarios* shows, Lastarria was skilled at all these activities. In this vein, a review of comments on Lastarria's style is appropriate.

Lastarria's prose is forceful, dynamic at times, often overly formal, and heavily laden with documentation in the form of allusions to classics and to contemporary figures and works, giving it a didactic tone that is nonetheless eminently readable. His arguments are direct in formulation. Ample resort to examples in order to prove a point or buttress an opinion accompany his own arguments, set out at the beginning of a section or a paragraph. Lastarria was a stylist, as well as a man with a mission.

Nineteenth-century Chilean letters were the domain of the educated elite. This elite was knowledgeable in law and philosophy, and its members applied their knowledge to other subjects, such as history and literature, in ample measure. These fields were still in the gestation stage as academic disciplines, even though liberal historians were achieving success in the purposeful reconstruction of Chile's past, and authors and poets were consciously addressing Chilean themes. *Recuerdos literarios* testifies to the significance Chileans accorded these subjects. They were genres for debate in which skilled debaters—Lastarria being a prime example—had to devote much time and effort if they were to make their mark.

Over the course of the second half of the century, Chile's intellectuals worked out a historiographical consensus that allowed for the presence of the colonial past in Chilean history. Lastarria had argued against the positive legacy of Spain in his paper, "Investigaciones," but even he, in his maturity, came to understand that history could not exclude a past that might not justify or support the present. Lastarria had argued for "national" literature, but he, above all, understood the influence that European and North American letters had in Chile. Lastarria's book makes this obvious.

Along with others from the Generation of 1842, Lastarria came to see that it was possible to be "*muy chileno*" and still value foreign models of prose and poesy. He was also convinced of the value of the United States as a model for Chilean institutional and intellectual development. Chile's successes in diplomatic, military, and political spheres made this easier to swallow for all intellectuals. Owing to Lastarria, Chilean nationalism is multifaceted and balanced, except when it comes to national boundaries. So over the decades conservative versions of the past were not the only ones to dwell upon the centuries of colonialism. Spain did have a place in Chile's past and Liberals came to accept this. History served more than one purpose. Conflicting but mutually understandable points of view on Chile's nineteenth-century successes—because of or despite Spain's heritage, for example—characterize Chilean historiography now the way differing opinions used to characterize debate within the polity.[24]

Diego Portales could be seen as a founder of Chile's political system, as well as a ruthless autocrat by those of a liberal bent. A century after Lastarria's death, Portales would become the hero he had been in the early years of the country's history, elevated to heroic status by uniformed leaders, themselves desirous of making history the means to their ends. Even nineteenth-century progressive thinkers could acknowledge his significance, of course. Despite his autocratic ways, he could be written about in the same way the failed liberal autocrat O'Higgins could: patriots and builders first, ideological icons second. In the late twentieth century, O'Higgins would share heroic status with Portales, despite his own shortcomings as leader of all Chileans. After all, Chileans had benefited from both leaders. Success bred success in Chile: responsible government, order, hard work, probity. However much these ideals were mythologized, Liberals could appreciate them as much as Conservatives or Radicals. Lastarria certainly did; so do Chileans of today.

Interest in things Chilean, evinced by the intellectual elite, gave rise to Chilean literature. Modest in its beginnings—in terms of quality as well as quantity—prose fiction was as important to the formation of *chilenidad*, "Chileanness," as were historiography, philosophy, and law. *Martín Rivas* (1862) may be mimetic, both romantic and realistic, but it was also both *Chilean* and mainstream. Read alongside Bello's and Lastarria's works, Alberto Blest Gana's *Bildungsroman* completes the picture of intellectuality and affairs of state, of manners and customs in nineteenth-century Chile.

Whether idealized, purged of Spanish legacies, or inclusive of recognition for colonial foundations of all facets of nineteenth-century culture, reverence for the past would come to include acceptance of the conquest as a momentous, epic accomplishment. The epic poetry of Alonso de Ercilla y Zúñiga and Pedro de Oña mentioned in Lastarria's opus may not equal Dante's or Tasso's efforts in qualitative terms, but to Chileans of the nineteenth century they were as significant as José Hernández's Argentine masterpiece, *Martín Fierro* (1872), over on the east side of the Andean cordillera. The Chilean epics were, of course products of the sixteenth century, more comparable to the prose epic of Bernal Díaz del Castillo than to *Martín Fierro*. Not even a Lastarria could disown the Spanish Colonial legacy, once he had examined it from a position of intellectual maturity.

Chileans wrote epiclike pieces in the nineteenth century too. The poems included in *Recuerdos literarios* bespoke the need to historicize independence, a contentious accomplishment of historic proportions. How else could O'Higgins and the early Liberals be intellectually reconciled with Portales, Prieto, Bulnes, and Montt as forgers of all that Chile was becoming in the second half of the century. Lastarria's literary-historiographical-political testament coalesces the complex cultural nation-building process that was an integral part of life in Chile. By the time poetic works like those reproduced in Parts Two and Three were being read and awarded prizes, Chileans were looking north and south, to the frontiers waiting to be conquered, to new opportunities to spread *chilenidad*.[25] Chilean intellectual life in the nineteenth century, and in the twentieth too, I think, cannot be detached from the rest of the country's historical processes. This is owing more to the coincidence of success than to a disparity of it.

It is no coincidence that Chilean intellectuals of the nineteenth century found more than one setting in which to tie history, politics, and literature together. The halls of the National University provided them first with an academic setting, from 1843 (when the first classes were held) forward, wherein scholars could pronounce and students could respond as much as in any academic setting of the age. In the halls of academe, both figuratively and literally, Chileans would continue to provide intellectual and political alternatives to the status quo. One of Chile's most controversial administrations of this century would be brought down in part, owing to student protests that closed the University buildings, just across Avenida Bernardo O'Higgins from the presidential palace, *La Moneda*.[26] The Portalian system of the nineteenth century proved no more invulnerable to intellectual activity than did the government of General Ibáñez in the depths of the Great Depression. Even during the most repressive times of the Pinochet administration (1973–1990), purged universities proved to be places where freedom of expression was surprisingly tolerable—by standards of authoritarianism.

A second setting for cultural nation-building was the political arena, wherein intellectuals and politicians—the two were often, but not always, synonymous—could struggle vigorously in public. Liberals and Conservatives conducted politics with gusto and with a mutual respect uncharacteristic of most Latin American countries during Lastarria's lifetime. The best example of this is the protracted struggle beginning before the inauguration of Manuel Montt and ending with his aforementioned failure to impose a handpicked successor. Civil unrest marked the end of this era, but the majority of the time was spent in lively political infighting. With the advent of the Liberals to the executive palace in the 1860s, and especially after 1871, when presidential reelection ceased to be the norm, the political arena did not decline in importance as a place for the exchange of ideas. The exchange of ideas became a norm of politics.

A third setting was that of literary organizations, especially the *Academia de Bellas Letras*, focus of Part Three of *Recuerdos literarios*, wherein writers of prose and poetry joined the struggle to define history, create a national literature, and rationalize both with the perpetuation of elitist control of the republic. During the second half of the century, the *Academia* served as chief cultural arbiter of the land.

Finally, Chileans struggled to define their history and create a literature as if they were characters in a historical tale of two cities. The great families, and their businesses and banks, were associated with both Santiago and Valparaíso, the main port. Interior and coast, merchants and shippers, landowners and professionals were not divided as they were in other countries—Argentina is a prime example, at least until the 1880s.

Chilean intellectual activity was characterized, prior to 1842, by an incipient intellectual entropy. The arrival of the Argentine exiles, the presence of Bello, and the opening of the University all made possible a growth of intellectual life commensurate with expansion of the socioeconomic elite in both the Central Valley and the port city. As these lines suggest, the sound economy (over the long run), successes in foreign policy, and effective administration of domestic affairs enriched the mix all the more. Chileans had a lot of advantages and they showed.

Instead of *baqueanos, rastreadores,* and *gauchos,* essayists, poets, and novelists would define Chilean cultural identity. Rather than caudillos, men of ideas dominated politics. Chileans experienced no regional rivalries comparable to those that dominated Argentine political life. *Porteños* (referring both to residents of Buenos Aires and Valparaíso) did not have to struggle long to establish a viable government in Chile. In Argentina, of course, they were party to a long struggle with provincial bosses. Access to the central government, however, was well within the reach of Chilean provincial leaders literally and figuratively. Inter- or intraelite rivalries, like those between Santiago- and Concepción-based members of the Basque-Castilian aristocracy, never assumed the proportions in determining national policy that they would east of the Andes. Chileans fought out more in the press and in parliament than they did in the streets, until 1891, along the way to formation of their political system, their historiographical tradition(s) and their literature. Chileans fought with their neighbors more than they did among themselves. All these influences in each of the settings come through to us in *Recuerdos literarios,* here translated into English for the first time.

There could be nothing more quintessentially Chilean than Lastarria's literary testament; few could approach him in being archetypal. Arrogant and self-absorbed, yet modest when it was incumbent upon him to be so, he had no doubts about his talent. He readily acknowledged the talent of some while frequently excoriating others for their lack of it. Even though intellectual to the core, he had no trouble addressing down-to-earth political matters. Pragmatic and passionate, he participated to the fullest in every aspect of intellectual life in nineteenth-century Chile.

Patriotic to be sure, he saw no conflict of interest in opposing the autocracy that had nurtured him, or in serving in administrations that included people with whom he did not fully agree. Stylist at all times (even when mired in prolixity), Lastarria could make a point *sin andarse por las ramas* when he wanted to. At times his prose is vocal; at times reflective. Some passages of *Recuerdos literarios* sound as if Dylan Thomas or Pablo Neruda were reciting. Tense changes and intercalation remind one at times of Flaubert, Eça de Queiroz, and Machado de Assis.[27]

Lastarria's arguments sometimes read like legal briefs. He documented his cases with internal citation, only the occasional note, as would a legal scholar or a historian. Hortatory in his criticism of early Chilean publication efforts and his urging of acceptance of his own opinions, Lastarria clearly wanted them to prevail in a Chile where ideas were important. He was perpetually debating with his colleagues and was concerned with impressing them with the forms of his argument as well as with their content.

All these characteristics show up in political writings and memoirs of twentieth-century Chileans.[28] Lastarria's influence transcends literature, leading one to believe that the boundaries between literature and history and the social sciences are as demonstrably artificial as they are apparently real. So does the ability of Chileans to argue major issues with each other, then, *al fin y al postre*, to treat each other with a civility often unknown where ideological differences make the political stakes just as high.

Readers of *Recuerdos literarios* are in for a treat. Through Lastarria they enter the whirl of nineteenth-century cultural nation-state building. They come to grips with the author's conviction that the way he explains things—history, literature, pedagogy, political conflict—is the right way. Readers find themselves thrust into a sea of circumlocution, subordinate clauses packed with erudition and the wide range of allusions akin to those associated with writers of recent times. I think here of Alejo Carpentier, Julio Cortázar, Carlos Fuentes, Gabriel García Márquez, and Mario Vargas Llosa. Voyages on seas of prose should result in arrivals on pleasant shores. Readers will find this a most rewarding voyage.

Lastarria wanted to be remembered. And he is. Always considered an essential work for understanding the nineteenth-century Chilean mind, *Recuerdos literarios* is here available to English-language readers, surely a boon to students of history, philosophy, and politics, as well as literature. Some time ago one of this country's best-known translators wrote in an article entitled "But Is It Homer" that "some times a good translation can impart the essence of a book even better for us than the original, for we must remember that when we are reading the original, the words are not ours, but in the translation they are, with their baggage and impact."[29] Then again a good translation that is done in the spirit of rendering the original as truly as possible can impart that essence. The essence of *Recuerdos literarios* has been preserved intact in this translation.

Because it has been translated with the idea of conveying the essence of form as well as content (even to the point of retaining Lastarria's use of italics or emphasis in the text), it constitutes a significant contribution to the corpus of Chilean history and *bellas letras* available in English. Accompanying the text are explanatory notes contributed by both the translator and the volume editor who offers this introduction. These notes have been composed to inform the reader of the identity of major influences on Lastarria and his colleagues, to elaborate on points made in the text, or to unveil the identity of the obscure yet significant. A number of Chilean names and some of the foreign ones are not noted, for we have chosen to limit intrusions into the text to those judged most necessary to complementing Lastarria's intent and enlightening his English-language readers, not burdening them with unnecessary minutiae.

Finally, the question begs asking: "But is it Lastarria?" Yes, in form and content *Literary Memoirs*, here in an English rendition by R. Kelly Washbourne, is decidedly Lastarria.

—Frederick M. Nunn

NOTES

1. The most informative general works on Chilean history in English are Leslie Bethell, ed., *Chile Since Independence* (New York and Cambridge, Eng.: Cambridge University Press, 1993); Simon Collier and William F. Sater, *A History of Chile, 1808–1994* (New York and Cambridge, Eng.: Cambridge University Press, 1996); and Brian Loveman, *Chile: The Legacy of Hispanic Capitalism*, 2nd ed. (New York and Oxford: Oxford University Press, 1988). The reader should also consult Fredrick B. Pike, *Chile and the United States, 1880–1962: The Emergence of Chile's Social Crisis and the Challenge to the U.S.* (Notre Dame: University of Notre Dame Press, 1962). Harold Blakemore's *Chile* (World Bibliographical Series, Vol. 9) (Oxford: CLIO Press, 1988) complements the bibliographies of the general histories. In Spanish, still the handiest general source is Francisco Antonio Encina, *Resumen de la historia de Chile*, 3 vols. (Santiago de Chile: Zig-Zag, 1964).

2. *Ideas and Politics of Chilean Independence* (New York and Cambridge, Eng.: Cambridge University Press, 1967) by Simon Collier remains the best source for the

study of independence. Jay Kinsbruner's *Portales: Interpretive Essays on the Man and His Times* (The Hague: Martinus Nijhoff, 1967) is valuable for views on the immediate post-independence period.

3. Good sources for background on the nineteenth-century experience are E. Bradford Burns, *The Poverty of Progress: Latin America in the Nineteenth Century* (Berkeley and Los Angeles: University of California Press, 1980); and David Bushnell and Neill Macaulay, *The Emergence of Latin America in the Nineteenth Century* (New York and Oxford: Oxford University Press, 1988).

4. Still the best source on the political role of the Chilean aristrocracy in the nineteenth century is Alberto Edwards Vives, *La fronda aristocrática: Historia política de Chile* (Santiago: Editorial del Pacífico, 1928 and various reprintings thereafter).

5. In addition to Edwards' *La fronda*, see Frederick M. Nunn, *The Military in Chilean History: Essays on Civil-Military Relations, 1810–1973* (Albuquerque: University of New Mexico Press, 1976) for interpretations of the Basque-Castilian aristocracy's significance in Chile's emergence as a nation-state.

6. This translation is based on the 1967 printing of the second edition (1885), introduced by Raúl Silva Castro (pp. 9–16). Spanish-language readers should by all means consult Silva Castro's essay for a Chilean's perspective on the work, and especially his sharp criticism of Lastarria for his minimization of Bello's significance.

7. All previously cited works contain material on this important aspect of Chilean political history.

8. On the mid-century political struggles, see Maurice Zeitlin, *The Civil Wars in Chile (or The Bourgeois Revolutions That Never Were)* (Princeton: Princeton University Press, 1984).

9. In addition to general works already cited, see Frederick M. Nunn, *Chilean Politics, 1920–1931: The Honorable Mission of the Armed Forces* (Albuquerque: University of New Mexico Press, 1970) for views on extension of nineteenth-century political issues into the early twentieth century.

10. William F. Sater's *Chile and the War of the Pacific* (Lincoln: University of Nebraska Press, 1986) is an excellent source on this subject.

11. Intellectual currents of nineteenth-century Chile are dealt with admirably in Iván Jaksić, *Academic Rebels in Chile: The Role of Philosophy in Higher Education and Politics* (Albany: State University of New York Press, 1989); Solomon Lipp, *Three Chilean Thinkers* (Waterloo, Ont.: Wilfrid Laurier University Press, 1975); Alan Woll, *A Functional Past: The Uses of History in Nineteenth-Century Chile* (Baton Rouge: Louisiana State University Press, 1982); and Gertrude Matyoka Yeager, *Barros Arana's Historia jeneral de Chile: Politics, History, and National Identity* (Fort Worth: Texas Christian University Press, 1981).

12. On relations between fiction and history in Latin America, see Frederick M. Nunn, "*Latinoamericanidad* from *Encuentro* to Quincentennial: The 'New Novel' as Revisionist History," *Revista Interamericana de Bibliografía/Inter-American Review of Bibliography* (XLIV, 2, 1994): 219–250.

13. See Jaksić, *Academic Rebels*, Woll, *A Functional Past*, and Yeager, *Barros Arana*.

14. There is not much available in English on colonial Chile that is useful to an understanding of Lastarria's work. Jacques Barbier's *Reform and Politics in Bourbon Chile, 1775–1796* (Ottawa: University of Ottawa Press, 1980) deals well with the late colonial period. Barros Arana's *Historia jeneral de Chile*, 16 vols. (Santiago de Chile: Rafael Jover, 1884–1902) is the standard source in Spanish that deals with positive aspects of the Spanish colonial heritage that sparked so much debate in Chile.

15. In English: Domingo F. Sarmiento, *Life in the Argentine Republic in the Days of the Tyrants; or, Civilization and Barbarism*, tr. Mrs. Horace Mann (first published in English in 1868) (New York: Hafner, 1971 and reprinted since).

16. On the subject of memoirs and their value for learning about other times, other places, see Jay Parini, "The Memoir Versus the Novel in a Time of Transition," *The Chronicle of Higher Education* (July 10, 1998): A 4.

17. For good examples in English, see Euclides da Cunha, *Rebellion in the Backlands* (*Os Sertões*), tr. Samuel Putnam (Chicago: University of Chicago Press, 1944); José Carlos Mariátegui, *Seven Interpretive Essays on Peruvian Reality* (*Siete ensayos de interpretación de la realidad peruana*), tr. Marjory Urquidi (Austin: University of Texas Press, 1971); Ezequiel Martínez Estrada, *X-Ray of the Pampa* (*Radiografía de la Pampa*), tr. Alain Swietlicki (Austin: University of Texas Press, 1971); Octavio Paz, *The Labyrinth of Solitude* (*El laberinto de la soledad*), tr. Lysander Kemp (New York: Grove Press, 1961); and José Enrique Rodó, *Ariel*, tr. Margaret Sayers Peden (Austin: University of Texas Press, 1988).

18. See Bernardo Subercaseaux, "Romanticismo y liberalismo en el primer Lastarria," *Revista Iberoamericana* (Nos. 114–115, January–June 1981): 301–312.

19. I refer to Octavio Paz, *One Earth, Four or Five Worlds: Reflections on Contemporary History*, tr. Helen R. Lane (New York: Harcourt Brace Jovanovich, 1985).

20. Very good for biographical data and interfamily relationships up into the early twentieth century is Virgilio Figueroa, *Diccionario histórico, biográfico, y bibliográfico de Chile, 1800–1931*, 5 vols. (Santiago de Chile: Imprenta y Litografía La Ilustración, 1925–1931).

21. On Bello's significance in Chilean intellectual history, see Jaksić, *Academic Rebels*, and Rafael Caldera, *Andrés Bello: Philosopher, Poet, Philologist, Educator, Legislator, Statesman*, tr. John Street (London: George Allen and Unwin, 1977).

22. See Norman P. Sacks, "*Lastarria y Sarmiento: El chileno y el argentino achilenado*," *Revista Iberoamericana* (No. 143, April–June 1988): 491–512.

23. In addition to general works cited, see Harold Blakemore, *British Nitrates and Chilean Politics (1886–1906)* (London: Athlone Press, 1974); and Robert N. Burr, *By Reason or Force: Chile and the Balancing of Power in South America* (Berkeley and Los Angeles: University of California Press, 1965) for details on late-century foreign affairs. Sater's first study of the War of the Pacific, *The Heroic Image in Chile: Arturo Prat, Secular Saint* (Berkeley and Los Angeles: University of California Press, 1973) offers further evidence of Chileans' ability to mix history and politics in order to create a functional past. This would be as important in the waning years of the nineteenth century as it had been in Lastarria's times.

24. The best nineteenth-century example of attempts to salvage remnants of the Spanish heritage is the aforementioned Barros Arana's *Historia jeneral*.
25. In Part Two, "The Circle of Friends of Literature," Eduardo de la Barra's and José Pardo's odes to independence, and in Part Three, "The Academy of Belles Lettres," Manuel Boza's ode "To Eighteen September" stand out as examples of epics in the making.
26. This episode in higher-education pressure politics is described in Nunn, *Chilean Politics*.
27. On this point, see Mario Vargas Llosa, *The Perpetual Orgy: Flaubert and Madame Bovary*, tr. Helen R. Lane (New York: Farrar, Straus, Giroux, 1986), Part Two, "The Four Times of *Madame Bovary*," pp. 168–183.
28. E.g., Arturo Alessandri Palma, *Recuerdos de gobierno*, 3 vols. (Santiago de Chile: Editorial Nascimento, 1967); and Carlos Sáez Morales, *Recuerdos de un soldado*, 3 vols. (Santiago de Chile: Editorial Ercilla, 1933–1934).
29. Gregory Rabassa, "But Is It Homer," *Humanities* (October 1985): 3–6.

Works by Lastarria

Nineteenth-Century Editions

José Victorino Lastarria, *Elementos de derecho público constitucional, arre-glados i adaptados a la enseñanza de la juventud americana* (Santiago: Imprenta Chilena, 1848).

José Victorino Lastarria, *Don Guillermo: Historia contemporánea* (Santiago: Imprenta de Correo, 1860).

José Victorino Lastarria, *Cuadro histórico de la administración Montt, escrito según sus propios documentos* (Valparaíso: Imprenta i Librería del Mercurio de Santos Tornero, 1861).

José Victorino Lastarria, *Instituta del derecho civil chileno* (Ghent: E. Vanderhaeghen, 1864).

José Victorino Lastarria, *Elementos de derecho público constitucional teórico* (Ghent: E. Vanderhaeghen, 1865).

José Victorino Lastarria, *Historia constitucional del medio siglo: Revista de los progresos del sistema representativo en Europa i América durante los primeros cincuenta años del siglo XIX* (Ghent: E. Vanderhaeghen, 1866).

José Victorino Lastarria, *Investigaciones sobre la influencia social de la conquista i del sistema colonial de los Españoles en Chile* (Santiago de Chile: n. p., 1866).

José Victorino Lastarria, *Lecciones de política positiva, profesadas en la Academia de Bellas Letras* (Paris: Libreria de A. Bouret, 1875).

José Victorino Lastarria, *Recuerdos literarios: Datos para la historia literaria de la América Española i del progreso intelectual en Chile* (Santiago de Chile: M. Servat, 1878; rev. ed. 1885).

José Victorino Lastarria, *Antaño i ogaño: Novelas i cuentos de la vida hispano-americana* (Santiago de Chile: n. p., 1885).

Later Editions

José Victorino Lastarria, *Estudios literarios* (Santiago: n. p., 1912).

José Victorino Lastarria, *La América* (Madrid: Editorial-América 1917).

José Victorino Lastarria, *El manuscrito del diablo, Don Guillermo, Lima en 1850: Prólogo y notas de Luis Alberto Sánchez* (Santiago de Chile: Ediciones Ercilla, 1941).

José Victorino Lastarria and Domingo Faustino Sarmiento, *Correspondencia entre Sarmiento y Lastarria* (Buenos Aires: n.p., 1954).

José Victorino Lastarria, *Diario político, 1849–1852* (Santiago de Chile: Editorial Andrés Bello, 1968).

José Victorino Lastarria, *Portales, juicio histórico* (Santiago de Chile: Editorial del Pacífico, 1973).

José Victorino Lastarria, (ed.), *Colección de ensayos y documentos relativos a la unión y confederación de los pueblos hispano-americanos* (Panamá: Ediciones de la Revista Tareas, 1976).

A Selected List of Works on Lastarria and His Times

Santiago Arcos, *La Plata: Etude historique* (Paris: Michel Levy Freres, 1865).

Diego Barros Arana, *Historia jeneral de Chile*, 16 vols. (Santiago de Chile: R. Jover, 1884–1902).

Francisco Bilbao, *El evangelio americano: Estudio preliminar por Dardo Cuneo* (Buenos Aires: Editorial Americales, 1943).

Francisco Bilbao, *La América en peligro, Evangelio americano, Sociabilidad chilena: Prólogo y notas de Luis Alberto Sánchez* (Santiago de Chile: Ediciones Ercilla, 1941).

Alfonso Bulnes, *Bulnes, 1795–1866* (Buenos Aires: Emece Editores, 1946).

João Baptista Calógeras, *Política Americana: Resposta ão exm. sr. J.V. Lastarria, enviado extraordinário e ministro plenipotenciário da República do Chile* (Rio de Janeiro: Typographia Perseverança, 1866).

Pedro Nolasco Cruz, *Bilbao y Lastarria* (Santiago: Editorial Difusión Chilena, 1944).

Armando Donoso, *Recuerdos de medio siglo* (Santiago de Chile: Editorial Nascimento, 1917).

Ricardo Donoso, *Desarrollo político y social de Chile desde la Constitución de 1833* (Santiago de Chile: Imprenta Universitaria, 1942).

Alberto Edwards, ed., *El gobierno de don Manuel Montt, 1851–1861* (Santiago de Chile: Nascimento, 1932).

Alberto Edwards, *La fronda aristocrática: Historia política de Chile* (Santiago de Chile: Editorial del Pacífico, 1952).

Francisco Antonio Encina, ed., *Portales: Introducción a la historia de la época de Diego Portales (1830–1891)* (Santiago de Chile: Nascimento, 1934).

Luis Enrique Délano ed., *Lastarria: Prólogo y selección de Luis Enrique Délano* (México: Secretaría de Educación Pública, 1944).

Guillermo Feliú Cruz, *Estudios sobre Andrés Bello* (Santiago de Chile: Fondo Andrés Bello, 1966).

Alejandro Fuenzalida Grandón, ed., *Obras completas de don J. V. Lastarria* (Santiago de Chile: Imprenta Barcelona, 1906).

Alejandro Fuenzalida Grandón, *Lastarria i su tiempo (1817–1888): Su vida, obras e influencia en el desarrollo político e intelectual de Chile* (Santiago de Chile: Imprenta Barcelona, 1911).

Hernán Fuenzalida Wendt, *José Victorino Lastarria: Síntesis biográfica* (Santiago de Chile: "La Nación," 1942).

Luis Galdames, *El decenio de Montt* (Santiago de Chile: Imprenta de "El Imparcial" 1904).

Jorge Huneeus y Gana, *Cuadro histórico de la producción intelectual de Chile*, (Santiago de Chile: n.p., 1910).

Iván Jaksić, *Academic Rebels in Chile: The Role of Philosophy in Higher Education and Politics* (Albany: State University of New York Press, 1989).

Carlos J. Larraín, *La misión Lastarria, 1865–1866* (Santiago: El Imparcial, 1930).

Solomon Lipp, *Three Chilean Thinkers* (Waterloo, Ont.: McGill University Press, 1975).

Alamiro de Avila Martel, ed., *Estudios sobre José Victorino Lastarria* (Santiago de Chile: Ediciones de la Universidad de Chile, 1988).

Domingo Melfi, *Dos hombres, Portales y Lastarria* (Santiago de Chile: Nascimento, 1937).

Luis Oyarzún, *El pensamiento de Lastarria* (Santiago de Chile: Editorial Jurídica de Chile, 1953).

Norberto Pinilla, *La generación chilena de 1842* (Santiago de Chile: Ediciones de la Universidad de Chile, 1943).

María Luisa del Pino de Carbone, ed., *Correspondencia entre Sarmiento y Lastarria, 1844–1888* (Buenos Aires: n.p., 1954).

Joaquín Rodríguez Bravo, Don José Victorino Lastarria (Santiago de Chile: Imprenta Barcelona, 1892).

Norman P. Sacks, *José Victorino Lastarria: Un intelectual comprometido* (Santiago de Chile: n. p., 1972).

Ramón Sotomayor Valdés, *Historia de Chile durante los cuarenta años trascurridos desde 1831 hasta 1871* (Santiago de Chile: Imprenta de "La Estrella de Chile," 1875).

Bernardo Subercaseaux, *Cultura y sociedad liberal en el siglo XIX: Lastarria, ideología y literatura* (Santiago de Chile: Editorial Aconcagua, 1981).

Universidad de Chile, *Estudios sobre José Victorino Lastarria* (Santiago de Chile: Ediciones de la Universidad de Chile, 1988).

Franco Venzano Ceiesti, *El pensamiento político de don José Victorino Lastarria* (Santiago de Chile: Editorial Universitaria, 1955).

Benjamín Vicuña Mackenna, *Don Diego Portales* (Santiago de Chile: Ediciones de la Universidad de Chile, 1937).

Benjamín Vicuña Subercaseaux, *Memoria sobre la producción intelectual en Chile* (Santiago de Chile: Universo, 1909).

Allen L. Woll, *A Functional Past: The Uses of History in Nineteenth-Century Chile* (Baton Rouge: Louisiana State University Press, 1982).

Gertrude Matyoka Yeager, *Barros Arana's Historia jeneral de Chile: Politics, History, and National Identity* (Fort Worth: Texas Christian University Press, 1981).

Sady Zañartu, *Lastarria, el hombre solo* (Santiago de Chile: Ediciones Ercilla, 1938).

LITERARY
MEMOIRS

Contents

PART ONE
1836–1849

I   Motivations for and objective of this work.   3
II Organization of the Instituto Nacional and state of education in 1822 to 1826. Lonzier, Fernández Garfias, J. M. Varas, V. Marín, Vial, Gorbea, Mora's Lyceum.   6
III Historical rectification on literary reforms: Mora, Bello.   12
IV Political and social situation in 1836.   16
V   Continuation.   19
VI State of education in 1836; texts in geography, bookselling, national newspapers and publications.   20
VII Continuation: Pardo and Aliaga, Pradel.   25
VIII Writers of the age, Benavente, Gandarillas, Vicuña, Guzmán, Urízar Garfias, Marín, Egaña, Rodríguez, Bello, their publications.   28
IX Spanish literature was not represented by the national writers, as was English literature in the United States at the time of the emancipation. Political situation in 1837, its influence on intellectual development. Education project to prepare social regeneration.   35

X   Change in the political situation in 1838; representation of politi-
         cal interests in the press; the *Cartas Patrióticas* ["Patriotic Let-
         ters"], *El Diablo Político* ["The Political Devil"]; press board of
         examiners described by García Reyes.   40
XI   The youths of 1840. Mr. Bello's teachings.   46
XII   Government's stance and that of its opponents in 1840. Need for
         a new political party that serves the democratic republic; useful-
         ness of teaching political science and literary development in
         those circumstances.   51
XIII   Political progress in 1841 favors the literary movement. New books and
         pamphlets. Sarmiento, the new youth, Argentinian émigrés.   56
XIV   Activity in 1842. The *Revista de Valparaíso* ["Valparaíso Review"]
         and Vicente F. López. *El Museo de Ambas Américas* ["The Mu-
         seum of Both Americas"] and García del Río. Conditions under
         which the Literary Society is established and difficulties in inau-
         gurating it with an innovative address.   62
XV   Society news. Inaugural address.   68
XVI   The address is received indifferently by the audience. Judgment
         in *El Museo de Ambas Américas*. Sarmiento reproduces this judg-
         ment in the Valparaíso *El Mercurio*, and writes an editorial criti-
         cizing the fondness for purism and attributing our barren output
         to this flaw and to the waywardness of our schooling. News on
         the polemic to which this editorial corresponded. Assessment of
         López's inaugural address. Philological matters.   84
XVII   Historical nature of the address and of the Argentinian writers'
         judgments. In the literary movement launched by the Society,
         two parties analogous to the political ones were mapped out, and
         their controversies spread to society.   99
XVIII   Origin of the *El Semanario* of 1842, its writers. Francisco Bello,
         Núñez, Sanfuentes, Ramírez, Tocornal, García Reyes, A. Varas,
         González, Talavera, Prieto Warnes, Vallejo, Espejo, Irisarri, Chacón,
         A. Olavarrieta. Judgment of this period by the Argentinian writers.
         Debate on romanticism between *El Semanario* and *El Mercurio*.
         Sarmiento, López, Sanfuentes, Vallejo, García Reyes.   103
XIX   Continuation. Sarmiento's letter on his status vis-à-vis the na-
         tional writers. False judgments of the Argentinian writers.   112
XX   Nature of *El Semanario*. Foundation of *El Progreso*. Extraordinary
         development of the press. Conclusion of *El Semanario*.   120
XXI   Rectification of the objectives falsely attributed to *El Semanario*.
         Origin of the literary movement. *El Semanario*'s beneficial influ-

ence. Theater, Carlos Bello and *Los amores del poeta* ["The Romances of the Poet"], Minvielle and the *Ernesto*.   125

XXII   Literary competition in celebration of the anniversary of the independence in 1842.   132

XXIII   Harmony between literary and political circles. The literary movement favors the independence of the spirit and exerts a powerful influence on the emancipation of public judgment. The ecclesiastical power prepares itself for resistance and founds the *Revista Católica* ["Catholic Review"]. Division of the ruling Conservative Party. The Liberal Party begins to be outlined.   142

XXIV   Teaching of political science in 1843. The *Elementos de derecho público constitucional* ["Elements of Constitutional Public Law"] in 1846. University Report against this text, which is accepted for teaching with modifications. Teaching of literature.   148

XXV   Instituto Nacional's new plan for preparatory elementary instruction. Press movement in 1843. Founding of the University of Chile. Dean don Bello's inaugural address. Critical judgment of this address.   154

XXVI   Effects of the address on the liberal school partisans. Dean's opinions on the philosophy of history. The first historical Report submitted to the University in 1844 adopts as a philosophic system the concept of history as a natural phenomenon, rejecting theological and metaphysical conceptions on providential laws. Countering opinions from the dean and from the Argentinian writers.   162

XXVII   Failure of the philosophical system tested in the first University Report. Henry Thomas Buckle. Quinet. Letter from the latter on above-mentioned Report. Krause. Altemeyer. *Bosquejo histórico de la constitución del gobierno de Chile durante el primer período de la revolución* ["Historical Outline of the Constitution of the Government of Chile During the First Period of the Revolution"]. University Report on this work.   171

XXVIII   Rejection of the new doctrine on the philosophy of history. Debate about it between Jacinto Chacón and the dean of the University. Application of the doctrine in the book entitled *Historia constitucional del medio siglo* ["Constitutional History of the Half-Century"]. Notion of Laboulaye's opinion. Primacy of the system in the 1844 historical Report. August Comte's theory confirming that system.   178

XXIX   Progress of the scientific and literary press since 1842. The old regime found its support in public authorities and in opinion.

The literary movement begun in 1842 was the only means of achieving a regeneration of ideas. The literary newspaper titled *El Crepúsculo*, its editors. The article *Sociabilidad chilena* ["Chilean Civic Responsibility"], by Francisco Bilbao; its philosophy, its style. 187

XXX Accusation made by the article *Sociabilidad chilena*, its condemnation. Literary influence of Bilbao, his research on philosophy of history. 192

XXXI *El Siglo*, political daily. Francisco de P. Matta, Espejo. Paralyzation of the literary movement in 1846 and 1847. *El Aguinaldo* in 1848. The Revista de Santiago, its editors. Valdés, Chacón, González, Lillo, Irisarri, Briceño, Rojas, Torres, G. Blest Gana, Lindsay, Arcos, the Amunátegui brothers, J. Blest Gana, J. Bello. Reorganization of the retrograde party. The Revista de Santiago is the hub of the intellectual movement and of the organization of the new Liberal Party. 199

PART TWO
The Circle of Friends of Literature

I The conservative reaction in 1859 had reestablished the old regime, misdirecting the literary movement and paralyzing the regenerating work that the advancements had produced from 1837 to 1850. Statistical data that demonstrate the intellectual decline from 1850 to 1855. 215

II Attempts by the regenerating literary movement, the Valparaíso *El Mercurio*, the third series of the *Revista de Santiago* in 1855. Francisco Marín, Alberto Blest Gana, Varas Marín, Lira, Valderrama, Vargas Fontecilla, Santa María, G. and M. A. Matta, Barros Arana. *Revista de Ciencias y Letras* ["Review of Sciences and Letters"] founded by the regnant party, its nature. *El Ferrocarril*, influence of absorbing policy against the popular societies of primary instruction and the School of Lawyers. 219

III The political situation changes on account of the rift in the ruling party, and the intellectual movement begins to grow in 1857. Books about a bedeviled girl, political newspapers, *El País* and *El Conservador*. Development of the elements of the party in power occurring between 1856 and 1857, and attempts to reorganize the Liberal Party. The *Constitución Política comentada*.

Proyectos de ley y discursos parlamentarios. Comentarios de la Constitución de Chile by Carrasco Albano ["Annotated Political Constitution. Bills and Parliamentary Speeches. Commentaries on the Constitution of Chile"]. Political press. *La Actualidad, Correo Literario, El Ciudadano, La Asamblea Constituyente.* 224

IV Literary works from 1857 and 1858, Mrs. Marín del Solar, G. Matta, G. Blest Gana, Sanfuentes, Santa María, Gregorio V. Amunátegui, Varas Marín, Muñoz, Torres, Vicuña. The *Revista del Pacífico*, new writers, Barros Grez, Moreno, Vicuña Mackenna, Donoso and his writings. 231

V Revolutionary storm. *La Semana* and the brothers Justo and Domingo Arteaga Alemparte, their collaborators. Literary activity, new writers, Rodríguez Velasco, De la Barra, Cobo, Reyes, Zenteno, Santos, Blanco Cuartín and his poetry. 234

VI *Essay on Government in Europe* by A. Montt, judgment of this book. Need for a literary association. Founding of the Circle of Friends of Literature. 237

VII Situation of the intellectual development in 1859 and need to give it the independence of the spirit as a foundation. How the Circle serves this end, and early works by this organization. Literary competition in praise of 18 September. Award-winning compositions. 242

VIII Poetry competition held in memory of Sanfuentes. Award-winning compositions. Poetry competition in honor of the abbot Molina. Award-winning compositions. 262

IX Founding in Valparaíso of the literary society called the Friends of Education and the appearance of the second series of the *Revista del Pacífico*, edited by Jacinto Chacón. Works by the Circle members Miguel Luis and Gregorio V. Amunátegui, Rodríguez Peña, Barros Arana, Moncayo, the Blest Gana brothers, Irisarri, G. Matta, Escobar, De la Barra, Blanco Cuartín, Olavarrieta, Campusano, Santos, Varas Marín, D. Arteaga Alemparte, Rodríguez, Lira Caravantes, Pedro L. Gallo, E. Bello. Progress in national poetry, and nature of modern poetry. Scientific and sociological works by the Circle, González, Cruchaga, Miquel, Marín, Padín, Torres, J. F. Vergara, Murillo, Izquierdo, M. Carrasco Albano, Valderrama. 281

X National literature in 1864 and the assessment of the circumstances of that age. Actions of the State in public education, backing of jesuitic education, its effects. Bibliographic statistics from 1865 to 1869. The independent literary movement lacked a central gathering place at this time.   287

XI   Reinstallation of the Circle of Friends of Literature in 1869, public conferences.   294

XII   Inaugural address from the reinstatement of the Circle on the status of contemporary literature and about the nature and conditions of the literature of the South American nations.   296

PART THREE
The Academy of Belles Lettres

I   Political situation from 1869 forward. Influence of the clerical party, its doctrines, its demands after 1871.   317

II   The Church's political reaction in the face of the country's liberal opinion. The new Revista de Santiago founded by Velasco and Orrego Luco, and the Revista Médica, in 1872; nature of the first of these literary newspapers.   321

III   Ministry's reaction against public education. Spirits shaken. Organization of the Academy of Belles Lettres. Inaugural address in the founding session.   327

IV   Letter from Blanco Cuartín a propos of the inaugural address and from the Academy on national literature. Account of the publication of the following Academy documents.   338

V   Report delivered in the formal session of the first anniversary of the Academy in 1874, about its works. Report on the competition for dramatic compositions.   345

VI   Report on the official session of the second anniversary in 1875. Report on the poetry competition in celebration of the International Expo. Award-winning ballad.   355

VII   Report on the official session of the third anniversary in 1876. Report on the poetry competition in celebration of the International Expo. Award-winning hymn. Report on the competition in honor of the anniversary of the independence. Award-winning ode.   366

VIII   Report on the official session of the fourth anniversary in 1877.   389

Conclusion.   399

PART ONE

1836 – 1849

I

The attention of contemporary historians is constantly drawn to the literary movement that took place in our country in 1842,* and they rightly consider it the earliest impetus to the portentous progress made in Chilean letters in the thirty-five years that have elapsed since that memorable date.

The stimulus of that year has expanded in regular, concentric circles, as if intellectual thought were an ocean whose surface had absorbed a vertical impact. In 1812, in the Antilles sea, in the early hours of the night fell a giant meteorite, an asteroid that lit up the horizon like the sun, bursting through the atmosphere with a terrifying roar, and leaving a trail many degrees in intensity, which marked its course a quarter hour after it had plunged into the immense gulf. After a few hours, the shock wave, which had rippled in ring after ring out from the point of impact on the water, reached the fortresses of Cartagena, rising against the walls to an admirable height, and unleashing the effects of a storm on the boats. A similar effect came in the wake of

---

* I.e., the "Generation of 1842," the intellectual movement accompanying the establishment of the National University in Santiago and shaping the course of intellectual activity for the rest of the century. —Ed.

3

the phenomenon that, in a fit of patriotic ardor, was stirred up in national thought in 1842, the difference being that the waves that still continue in succession will not abate as long as said thought is not confined by the hindrances of despotism or by the enslavement of the spirit.

Yet contemporary historians have not, by and large, been exact when they describe this literary movement. The account of events is not useful, nor does it meet its objectives, if it is not exact. On the contrary, if it does not mislead future historians, it saddles them with the arduous task of uncovering the truth. An event can be seen in a different light by contemporaries, and it can be appraised, likewise, by different criteria; but facts are facts, and in narrating them, one may not alter them or attribute them to causes or people that have not participated in them, nor attribute to the undeserving the responsibility or the glory attendant to them.

And all of this is exactly what happens habitually when the origins of our literary trajectory are recalled. In lightweight works, destined to pass like the leaves of autumn, a memory may be imprinted without doing research, or even reminiscence; yet if one does likewise with a serious work, its rectification is a duty, the fulfillment of which, rather than being offensive, should be agreeable to him who has invited it.

One work of this nature, the *Historia de la administración Errázuriz*,* ["History of the Errázuriz Administration"] inspired this reflection. In the hopes of setting right its information, let us put our literary memoirs in order, with a view to testify in the judgment of the evolution of Chilean thought. In the fine outline of the movement of parties from 1823 to 1871, which serves as an introduction to the work, the author puts a popular face on the 1842 literary movement, implying that "the youthful independent society began to joyfully contemplate its own image in the early efforts of a lively, vigorous literature." This production appeared in *El Semanario*, whose publication he attributes not to its founder, whose name he forgets, nor even to its rightful authors, but to some of its collaborators and people that had no share in it, like Mrs. Marín de Solar, don Carlos and don Juan Bello, and don Francisco de Paula Matta, to whom Mr. D. Arteaga Alemparte also attributes an active role in this literary movement, which in the biography that he wrote of this interesting young man, who died regrettably in the flower of his youth, he alleges began with *El Semanario*.

Both writers, like many others, impute the movement to *El Semanario* ["The Weekly"], utterly dispensing with writers previous to this newspaper

---

* Isidoro Errázuriz, *Historia de la administración Errázuriz* (1885). Federico Errázuriz Zañartu (1825–1877) served as president, 1871–1876. His son, Federico Errázuriz Echaurren (1850–1901) was chief executive, 1896–1901. —Ed.

that had produced it; we can rest assured that neither was the former movement popular, nor was it *El Semanario's* doing. That publication was born of a preceding stimulus, without even reaching a readership sufficient to keep the publication solvent; nor could society contemplate its image in the output of a lively, vigorous literature which could not yet exist, save for in meticulous, artless articles. It is far less plausible to ascribe the impulse, calculated by the patriotism of a few, and continued steadfastly, to the memory preserved of the era of attempts at a representative system, and to the influence scientific institutions exercised prior to 1830 over young souls, as the author of the *Historia* maintains. The author is correct in asserting that our society's pulse could barely be felt, though "the dejection and prostration of a nation are never as thoroughgoing as the high priests of authoritarian dogma would have it." But he has no historical data for supporting his belief that the movement was the work of influences that by that point were nonexistent, nor the "forces or means that the nation, in its immobility, had piled up by degrees to refashion itself"; for there was neither this stockpiling nor did the society refashion itself, but on the contrary it held out for many years against any reforming, and perhaps resists it to this day.

The 1842 literary movement did not originate in social influences, nor in previous historical events, and supervened as a virtually individual reaction, which it had to produce on its own and without resources the event that it would deliver, through all manner of political and social obstacles. Had it not been thus, if social history had set the stage for the movement, the individual action that promoted it would have had an expeditious and unobstructed path. On the contrary, the event has stalled many times, and has had but a sporadic existence, until, in the span of thirty-five years, it gradually has consolidated our civic responsibility, while through the practice of freedom, the spontaneous cooperation of social elements continued its normal course. Then a society emerged that, although still young, has fairly well-defined feelings and ideas, needs and interests for seeking its expression in a nascent literature, but whose characteristic features are already clearly delineated.

Thus, it is not inopportune to look back frequently upon the age in which our literary movement began; and it is vital to ascertain accurately its historical character and the moment of its appearance. To that end we need to recall the earliest attempts made in 1826 to revise scholarship on the subject, efforts that had foundered on the reefs of old routine, which after ten years appears once again triumphant next to the colonial reaction that had grown entrenched in the backward-thinking party in 1830. The year 1836 is notable in our history for the intellectual and moral lethargy into which the political situation had thrust us. That is the supreme moment of the crisis, and there begins the convalescence of our spirit, in which, fortunately, we took some part, a fact that authorizes us to set down these memoirs.

The historians state clearly that for the current generation, which reaps the harvest of the last thirty years' efforts, it will be of no account to know what part that was; but, to be frank, the author of these memoirs cannot accept that indifference, nor should he, for even when he holds no claim to anyone's gratitude, he does have the right to reject the shroud he does not wish to wear, seeing that he is alive: the shroud of oblivion. Will one be taken amiss for wishing not to be forgotten? There is no offense in that. What is bothersome is that someone is candid enough to be omnipresent; but that candor disappears when one claims his rightful place, against those who are minded to dislodge him.

II

Taking as a guidepost the historical date that Mr. Gay* relates in volume VII of his *Historia de Chile*, the organizing efforts of all branches of government that General Freire's administration undertook in 1823 were directed preferentially to public education. The Instituto Nacional† received a yearly endowment of 25,000 pesos in order to fulfill the duties of the Instituto Normal de Preceptores ["Teacher Training School"], which attributed to it by the 10 June senatus consultum of that year, with a view to it serving as the standard in public education and as a model for all other teaching institutions yet to be founded.

---

* Claudio Gay (1800–1872), *Historia física y política de Chile*, 8 vols. (1844–1854). Sixteen additional volumes are devoted to zoology and botany. —Ed.

† The Instituto Nacional, Chile's first post-secondary institution, was established in 1813, comprising two colonial-era seminaries. The Instituto offered instruction in the humanities and free professions, pedagogy and religious preparation, and was Chile's most distinguished preparatory institution in the nineteenth century. —Ed.

The Instituto, which had been reestablished in 1819 during O'Higgins'* administration, and reorganized by Cienfuegos, the governor of the bishopric, remained in 1823 a university center, in keeping with decreed academic laws and by-laws. The Institute was divided into three sections, one for scientific instruction, the second for engineering instruction, and the third was a museum of instruments for the study of the experimental sciences; its special code of conduct, the work of don Juan Egaña,† subjected its control to the holy guidance of religious principle.

Moreover, a 10 December decree that same year created the Academia Chilena ["Chilean Academy"], which, as a main organ of the Instituto, likewise had three sections: moral and political science, physical science and mathematics, and literature and the arts.

In 1824, on the occasion of the organization of tribunals and courts and the promulgation of the Rules of Justice, special attention was paid to legal studies; the profession of lawyer became, due to the diligence with which the aspirants were trained, and the importance of government positions in the administration of justice that were obtained with that degree, the profession that gave the Instituto Nacional the supremacy with which the rules and regulations had wished to invest it, giving it the character of a university for cultivating other studies, which in fact were eliminated.

This fact was a natural result of the new organization of the administration of justice, for which public opinion had clamored with great perseverance in those days as the meeting of an urgent and supreme need. The O'Higgins administration had not been able to carry out this enterprise successfully, and although it had abolished some of many special tribunals that existed, it left standing, with slight alterations, the judicial organization and procedures from colonial times, complete with all their shortcomings and slowness. To ensure enforcement of national laws, which the lawyers tried to evade whenever convenient to their defense plan, invoking old Spanish laws, the penalty of suspension of their office was imposed upon them for cases in which they committed this misdeed, but such an objective was not reached; in order to curb raids on property, which occurred time and time again with alarming frequency, a decree by the Supreme Delegate Director, don Hilarión de la Quintana, had sanctioned the death penalty for any individual who robbed an amount in excess of

---

* Bernardo O'Higgins y Riquelme (1778–1842), independence leader and Supreme Director, 1817–1823. —Ed.

† Juan Egaña Riesco (1769–1860), a founder of the Instituto and principal framer of the Constitution of 1833. —Ed.

four pesos, and a sentence of two hundred lashes and six years of hard labor if the value was less, in which case the briefest military judgment would suffice. Shortly thereafter, the court-martial having been disbanded, it was ordered that the mayors enforce said punishments, laying aside customary formulas for criminal sentencing, with but a summary briefing that had to be submitted for review to the chamber of justice, which was obliged to settle the matter the same day.

This arbitrariness, entrenched as a normal order, was what alarmed the 1823 patriots; and although property raids had not diminished, and there were spells during which, as always happens, they proliferated with irritating and daring frequency, the legislators attached less importance to penal severity than to a judicious administration of justice that brought together procedural promptness and uprightness, safeguards sufficient to bring arbitrariness to a halt; this ran contrary to what lawmakers thought fifty years later, when in 1876 they returned to Director Quintana's system to punish robbery.

Of all the reforms that were being adopted around that time, the judicial one was the most important, for since it affected private interests most immediately, it was the one that most insistently and vigorously rallied public opinion. These circumstances, on the one hand, and the fact the new organization of the independent country was owed, and rightly, to the men of letters, more than to military men who had guaranteed independence, gave the profession of lawyer such preeminence that not only was it seen as the only and most enviable career, but also all plans advanced to establish public education on a broader, more comprehensive base were scuttled. Thus the Instituto Nacional was eventually reduced to a law school, and in lieu of the Academia Chilena, which by decree of 1823 completed its organization, the old Academy of forensic practice, which was constituted definitively on 29 January 1824 and continued in operation, as per its by-laws, until a short time ago it was disestablished and replaced by a regular University class, certainly to no advantage.

Thus stood the situation in 1826, but legal studies, Latin grammar, and philosophy, which had been their training, had not gone beyond the plan and ways in which they were done in the Colonial era; this contratemps, so contrary to the aspirations of those who had intended a reform of public education, was a death-dealing blow to its efforts. The above-mentioned historian records this fact thus: "Though the program (at the Instituto)"—he states—"was much more extensive, it still did not completely satisfy the avidity of those generous patriots. The classes labored under the lingering Scholasticism of the Middle Ages, whose teaching method was overburdened with pointless and at times ridiculous concerns; they wanted to introduce into the courses a more fitting direction, one more harmonious with the modern Zeitgeist. With this aim, the administration tried to place at the helm of the Instituto a person whose studies might have been completed with that intellectual orientation, and brought Mr. Charles Lozier, then occupied in drawing up the geographic map of Chile." General Freire's administration had brought from Buenos Aires this wise Frenchman to assume the headship of the engineering education section, which had been set up at the Instituto; but given that the scientific journey to which Mr. Dauxion Lavaysse had been commissioned had not yielded the prompt outcome that was expected, the implementation of that curricular form was postponed, and Lavaysse was replaced by Lozier.

Lavaysse was hired to study the country's natural history and to compile its statistics, indicating navigable rivers, suitable places for building factories, ports, channels, and roads—which had to be made to facilitate commerce, the means of spurring agriculture and adaptable lands for growing the basic industrial stuffs; and since the first foray he made into the north produced no immediate results, he was thought incompetent and lost his post, remaining in the country continuously until in 1829, while living in the Liceo de Mora ["Mora Secondary School"], where he had taken lodging. We students found him dead one morning in his own bed, after a few days of illness.

Mr. Lozier received on 20 December 1823 the same assignment, the task of drafting the geographic map of Chile, having for his collaborator the colonel of engineers, don Alberto d'Albe, who had been commissioned especially to marshal military figures and demarcate suitable localities for national defense. Mr. Gay considers that, in light of the Lavaysse episode, Mr. Lozier erred in committing to carrying out particulars that would require a large number of years, with no hope of executing his duties to the satisfaction of the many Chileans who feel that they can perfectly well, and in little time, perform observational tasks like the ones in question, which are invariably long and difficult, and which commonly are quite far from covering the large financial outlay they occasion. If the like-minded historian has fallen victim to similar unthinking, baseless demands, in spite of his assiduous devotion to the study of the natural history of Chile; and if the wise Pissis is in the same situation right now, a man for whom twenty-eight years have not sufficed to consummate his grand work that Mr. Lozier had undertaken in 1826, one can imagine the disillusionment into which in 1826 the governors fell, men who had imagined they would conduct in short order the scientific surveys they needed to know about their country, when after three years nothing more than the beginnings of such a formidable undertaking had gotten underway.

Therefore they scotched the project, and preferred to employ Mr. Lozier in curricular reform in order to wrest the Instituto from the grip of its peripatetic* routine and widen its sphere of action, as previously was sought through the senatus consultum that gave it the character of a standard institution of broad-based education. Don José Miguel Infante, who was the one who with the most intelligent and innovative spirit had sought to elevate public education, was responsible for the change, since as General Freire's replacement in the supreme magistracy, he reorganized the Instituto on 20 February 1826, entrusting its headship to Mr. Lozier, and empowering the new rector to make all innovations and reforms he deemed appropriate, to propose new teaching methods, and to organize its administration to the students' best advantage.

Mr. Lozier was unquestionably the most appropriate man under the circumstances to give expression to the interim Supreme Director's decree. He showed clearly that his aspirations lay in giving education a positive grounding by organizing a complete course in mathematical and physical sciences, a required course for all students, even those whose area of concentration was the legal field. These were students for whom some science classes were developed that were to a certain degree adequate to broaden their scope of knowledge. Meanwhile he made a priority of the overall reform plan, especially of the teaching methods in the humanities and law, and after early favorable results obtained in the sciences course that he himself had overseen beginning in March 1826, he organized with the most advanced students and the professors, a society for studying and disseminating elementary teaching methods unknown in the country, and which were important to circulate if curricular reform was to be taken seriously. This society, inspired by its director's enthusiasm, devoted itself assiduously to free education from its monastic rut, which rendered it sterile, and began publishing *El Redactor de la Educación* ["The Drafter of Education"], a sixteen-page literary journal consisting of translated and excerpted articles on a given topic, a publication that printed six issues up to the moment in which the innovative rector's job ended violently.

The partisans of routine, in other words, the common run of educated men, rebelled against Mr. Lozier's innovations, and their criticism and scorn spread to the students, who, freed from the whip, which had been outlawed, and from austere treatment at the hands of the schoolmasters, took for weakness the new rector's familiar, good-natured manner. Swayed by pernicious promptings, they staged an all-out rebellion against Mr. Lozier, and completely disrupted the Instituto.

Mr. Gay, regretting the reform's failure, feels that had it been adopted gradually, and not been as sweeping and large-scale, it would have reached

---

* I.e., Aristotelian teaching method. —Trans.

fruition unopposed; nevertheless he allows that: "Unfortunately Mr. Lozier's ideas with respect to education clashed head-on and excessively against deep-seated custom, habit, tradition, and memory that constituted the country's very redoubtable concerns."
Thus, they prevailed, for the student revolt gave the new president of the republic, Mr. Eyzaguirre,* leeway to repeal the Infante decree at the end of 1826, reorganizing the Instituto and placing it under the tutelage of the most rabid ambassador of colonial tradition, the Presbyter don Juan Francisco Meneses. Fortunately, he could not contain the movement begun by Mr. Lozier, destroying preparations already in place, which expedited for the partners in reform the establishment of a new course in 1827. Don Pedro Fernández Garfias instituted the teaching of Latin in the Spanish language, following the Ordinaire method; don José Miguel Varas and don Ventura Marín began to teach in the same language diverse branches of experimental philosophy. Don Andrés Gorbea took over from Lozier in teaching pure mathematics and physics.
The following year, ideas on curricular reform, which until then had not been formulated systematically, caught the public's attention when presented strikingly in the Chilean Secondary School Study Plan, which don J. J. de Mora† published; the young professors at the Instituto, with honorable emulation, were the first to galvanize efforts so that their institution did not lag behind in either the path of practical innovation, that in which the new plan had been proposed in 1829, or the Colegio de Santiago, which was founded in 1830 to rival the Liceo.
This movement died out before long with the elimination of these latter two institutions and with the triumph of the political reaction, which strengthened, organized a conservative administration, and by 1836 came to bestride all spheres of social life.

---

* Agustín Eyzaguirre Arechavala (1776–1837), a liberal thinker who served as national executive in 1826. He was overthrown in one of the many *golpes de estado* (coups) of the post-independence decade. —Ed.

† José Joaquín de Mora (1783–1864), a liberal thinker and independence enthusiast who also resided in England, Chile, Peru, and Bolivia. —Ed.

III

Before describing our society's intellectual climate in that crisis year, it would behoove us to reproduce here, by way of illustration, a rectification of the history of our literary trajectory that we published in *El Ferro-carril* ["The Railway"] on 15 February 1871, in a letter addressed to our dearest friend and disciple, Benjamín Vicuña Mackenna.*

Full of patriotism, this distinguished writer is wont to be led at times by his impetuous eloquence to deal somewhat inexactly with historical facts, an occurrence that on more than one occasion has forced us to set the record straight on matters appertaining to our own interests, not in an accusatory spirit, but for the justifiable fear that the authority of his words give license to error, which he by no means wished to sanction. The prolific writer, following certain currents of mistaken opinion that form among us in support of certain men, more out of fellow-feeling and affection than thoughtful, impartial judgment, attributed our literary reform, in one of his many works, to influences that never existed, granting to the actual reformers a role different from the one they had. This was the motive that prompted the following letter:

DON BENJAMÍN VICUÑA MACKENNA

In one of your *Letters from the Guadalete*, I read that you stated that: "in the years 1840 to 1845 everything was Spanish in Chile in matters of thought, education, books and theater; the noted Spanish man of letters don J. J. de Mora was responsible for initiating this kind of *intellectual counterrevolution* after the far-reaching upheaval in 1810, which was founded in the memorable Santiago Secondary School in 1828." Making history from this graceless reaction, you maintain that Antonio Nebrisensis and don José de Hermosilla were our sovereigns after having dethroned the Bourbons, and that their disappearance was due to the *literary revolution* begun by the illustrious Bello, contemporaneous with two seemingly insignificant events: the arrival of Argentinian émigrés and the establishment of the

---

* Benjamín Vicuña Mackenna (1831–1886), a graduate of the Instituto, liberal thinker, member of the Generation of 1842, historian, and journalist. —Ed.

Pacific steamship route. "It is impossible to hide the fact," you exclaim, "that the influence of French literature freed us from routine. Don Andrés Bello,* who had not set foot on European soil, launched this crusade with his textbooks, a battle so brilliantly furthered by his late-lamented sons. . . ."

Nothing could be further from the truth. You have made a Prussian-style invasion of your country's literary history, like those you have been in the habit of launching into your civil history; don Andrés Bello, in point of fact, is the spokesman of the intellectual counterrevolution that you assign to Mora, and the latter is one of those who, in previous years, had begun the literary crusade that you assign to don Andrés.

That literary crusade originates, Mr. Vicuña, in 1826 with Mr. Lozier, the wise French academician then at the head of the Instituto Nacional. It is true that the wise Frenchman lost his position in short order, for the pupils, accustomed to iron discipline, rose up against the rector who came to treat them with dignity and kindness, but luckily in that short time he lit the flames of the high intellects of certain distinguished youths, who, owing to their status at the Instituto, could continue the movement promoted by the noble academician. Thus in 1827, the *Nebrisensis* was banned from the Instituto, and don Pedro Fernández Garfias was beginning the teaching of Latin through Lhomond, publishing his little volume of *Terminaciones latinas* ["Latin Endings"], taken from Lhomond's *Rudimento* ["Basics"], following the Ordinaire method, his translation of language teaching method by J. J. Ordinaire, his booklet, *Nomenclatura* ["Nomenclature"], his *Manual del monitor* ["Monitor's Manual"] or analytic table of contents for Ordinaire's Latin grammar, and his *Supplement* to the second part of the Latin grammar of the same work.

At the same time, to remove the *Lugdunense* from the classroom, and the *Tractatus de Re lojica, methafisica et morali, pro filiis et alumnis Instituti Nationali Jacobo-Palitanæ erudiendis,*

---

* Andrés Bello López (1781–1865), Venezuelan savant who came to Chile in 1819, after having lived in England. Bello was the leading intellectual figure in Chile for the rest of his life. He advocated the study of history through documents and sources dating from the times being studied. He was a jurist and grammarian who championed the classics in the intellectual and cultural-definition struggles of the nineteenth century. —Ed.

scribebat Joanes Egaña,[*] don J. Miguel Varas published in 1828 his *Lecciones elementales de moral* ["Elementary Moral Lessons"], and a few months thereafter, in a joint effort with don Ventura Marín, both professors at the Instituto, brought out their *Elementos de ideología* ["Elements of Ideology"].

This change in education at the Instituto Nacional, which was not limited to Latin and Philosophy, and which included the study of literature using Hugo Blair, of natural law and peoples through Burlamaqui and Vattel, and of political economy using J. B. Say, paralleled the change don José Joaquín de Mora implemented in 1829 in the Liceo de Chile, and at the same time the modifications promoted by the French that founded the Colegio de Santiago in 1830.

In order to convince you that Mora was not the author of the Spanish literary reaction, you merely need look at the *Plan de Estudios del Liceo* ["Secondary School Education Plan"], in which for the first time in Chile the study of the humanities was divided up into five-year increments and based on the scientific surveys that don Andrés Antonio de Gorbea conducted. All the while that Latin grammar was being taught, not by Nebrija but by Mora, French, geography, history, French and Spanish literature, Spanish grammar, philosophy according to Laromiguière's immortal lessons, and mathematics were also taught, from arithmetic to differential and integral calculus, physics including optics, which in those days were not taught at the Instituto, chemistry and astronomy. Lessons in oratory and literature, grammar and geography, as well as those in law, were made through specially written texts by Mr. Mora, who, having completed his education in England, introduced Bentham's doctrines in law for the first time in America, and left far behind all Spanish recollections of literary teaching method.

Seeing as I am not of a mind to trace in this letter the history of our education, I will simply point out to you that the entire sea change of progress and emancipation of thought begins to decline with the influence of don Andrés Bello in our classrooms around 1833, contrary to what you maintain. Then Roman law appears as a requisite subject and Mr. Bello used Vinnio to teach it, perhaps because Mora had stated that: "The

[*] "Treatise on Logical, Metaphysical and Moral Matters for Instructing the Sons and Pupils of the Instituto Nacional, Written by Juan Egaña." —Trans.

preference for Vinnio in the Spanish universities demonstrates the perverse taste that reigns in their legal studies. Vinnio is an eternal disputant, a compiler of poor discretion. Heinecio is a clear, luminous and profoundly wise commentator, but restrained in the use of scholarship." Mora taught in his law class at the Liceo an exact and succinct idea of Roman law, "speaking historically, as Heinecio speaks," he would say, "not like other jurists, transporting what was then to what is today"; while Bello introduced for us the two-year course using the Instituta, in Latin and by rote, and using Vinnio's commentaries. He gave preference in civil law to Pavorde Sala, and in literature to don José Gómez de Hermosilla, and ended up stirring up that furor as a result of which everyone devoted themselves to the study of Spanish classics, and of other classics far from promoting democratic development and the emancipation of thought.

So then, Mr. Vicuña, that literary counterrevolution you found to be triumphant in 1840 is the work of don Andrés Bello and not that of Mora, and if anyone escaped it, it was none other than that Lastarria, who you assume follows in the footsteps of Mr. Bello, when, as a favorite disciple of the *Galician*, he has done nothing but work, like the latter, toward bringing that great progressive movement to maturity, a movement begun in 1828 by Fernández Garfias, Varas, Marín and Mora. Argentinian émigrés, whose influence you have fabricated, were alarmed at the time by the backward state of our education, and the genuine disciples of Bello were not, then, the only ones who defended our letters from the scorn of the emigrants, but rather the followers of Mora and the Instituto Nacional, whom Lozier's initial impetus had reached.

For the time being, then, these recollections, which are accurate and confirmed by newspaper accounts from the time, shall suffice. It is not possible, Mr. Vicuña, for a historian to come along and switch round roles, as you do, nor is it just that you come out in support of, and authorize, the falsehoods that in recent times have begun to be published about the history of our education and of our literary development, attributing the progress to men and events that if not impeding it, have not played the role with which they generously—and falsely—have been credited.

These superficial reminiscences are indeed accurate, as is born out by the narration of events that Mr. Gay makes in his *Historia de Chile* ["History of

Chile"], and which we have just reproduced, and as results from the memoirs we are about to relate, without offending against historical justice, which rests on a substantial condition: that of placing men and events in their true vantage point from which to be judged, without obscuring some men by shedding light on others, and without attributing to one the worth that inheres to another. Thereby, one may better gauge true glory, and when an illustrious man is truly possessed of it, like that of the wise author of our Civil Code,* one does not need, that one may shine the brighter, to eclipse the glory of others, to say nothing of dethroning anyone from their place in it. When that condition of historical justice is met in good faith and impartiality, criticism rests on sure footing; then it is easy to note errant judgments that the historian renders in obedience to private issues, motives, or an impassioned criterion. The only ones who can do a disservice to this condition are those who don the mask of historians to serve a sectarian interest or political faction, and since this cannot be the motive of the genial recipient of our rectification, we do not fear offending him by demanding justice.

IV

There are plants that die when the sun repairs to the opposite hemisphere, and the only ones remaining to mourn are the yellow gillyflowers,[†] the sweet hyacinth, and the mournful violets that exude subtle aromas, when a helping hand shelters them from the storm. But the gnarled skeletons of the dead plants tremble with the first rays of the returning sun, and their splendid foliage revives, vigorous and triumphant; the flowers that cry, disappear, and those that laugh, like the roses, return to life.

Yet, there is a tree with immeasurable branches, gemlike leaves, and splendid flowers, a tree called humanity, and it also has its own sun that re-

---

*   The reference is to Bello. —Ed.

†   Probably stock or wallflowers. —Ed.

vitalizes it. That sun, which is not found on distant horizons, is freedom, which radiates in every brain, and nurtures every being in the human family.

Freedom is a law, a force of our own nature, that has two manifestations: work and virtue. Through work we exercise all our faculties to master nature and place it in the service of our perfection and that of our species. Through virtue we control our instincts and guide them so that intelligence and reason prevail over them, for the purpose of serving our perfection and that of our species.

That force, which we call free will, is the sun of our life; and when it is eclipsed, we sleep, as does vegetation when the sun that gives it light withdraws. But, lo, the spring sun returns infallibly to our zone every year, bringing in its waves of light the resurrection of all nature, while the winters of humanity are wont to last centuries, and its rare springs are stormy and long-drawn-out!

Remove from a man, from a group of men, or a society, their free will, their independence of spirit, and you will be left with a tree without sap or splendor, its branches pale and denuded. Life is concentrated, its manifestations are divergent and intermittent, and do not radiate across the whole of its horizon. Work activity loses direction. Virtue's works narrow, and barely make their way from evening to evening in songs that bear the sweet fragrance of hyacinth, like those of Virgil, or in poetic illusions that carry the thorns of the rose and the poisonous nectar of the oleander, like those of Dante, or that taste of socotran aloes, like those of Cervantes.

Our society, which was born and lived in a dark winter for three centuries, had a spring-like storm that made it gain a glimpse of the sun in its life, a sun whose first light of dawn woke and opened the people's spirit. But soon the days darkened again, and for six years the ancient winter once again had the upper hand.

The 1830 reaction brought the silence of terror. Those who had tried to sketch the outlines of a democratic republic and found public law in the country, that it might govern itself autonomously, had been defeated, annihilated, excluded from political association; in their place a governing oligarchy had been created, one that was subject to the will of the dictatorship, without action or initiative, and limited in its powers to applaud and approve. Independent judgment, spontaneity, the unblemished enthusiasm of patriotism, aspiration to public life, all remained subject to a false morality and to political expediency, which justified the harsher and more arbitrary punishments meted out to rebels, or the more outrageous mockery and sarcasm leveled against those who dared have another set of morals, another opinion or another way of sizing up those expediencies, even when not offending against the interests of the dictatorship. Such a system was sanctioned by the new Political Constitution,* if its practice was guaranteed by the fidelity with which its authors executed it, with no qualms about the means, and taking refuge under that code to the point of erecting by simple dictatorial decree the scaffold against those who aspired to have rights.

In 1836 we lived in sheer terror, except for the ruling class that reigned supreme with said code, and to say nothing of those naive, self-interested souls who thrived in the shadow of absolute power, or did not feel the need for free thinking, nor the need to have rights; and since these blessed souls are always legion, all terror effortlessly has a large phalanx of *sensible* men on whom to rely.

And what of the independent of spirit, those who have not deadened their free will, nor disciplined it to the exigencies of dogma or personal interest? And what of those who live far removed from the political arena and feel, like children, that noble need for justice and equality, which makes them startled and unnerved by the presence of any irregularity, of any attack on justice? Oh! They are not many, these latter, especially in nations of our ilk, but nevertheless there are enough to maintain in all nations, in all societies, the sap of humanity, which—though it seems at times dried up by centuries of despotism—forever retains the element of regeneration. They are those who suffer under terror, and among them the haughty spirits even more so, who if they do manage to escape the cruelties of despotism, are not always spared from those of ridicule with which the despot and friends crush those who are not humbled.

Does one need a rebel spirit to not yield to such power? No. Some can have the rebellion of hatred, that of vengeance, that of offended pride: but a vigorous sense of justice and a generous heart suffice to confront the eccentricities of the despotism of social powers. Our nature has an instinct for equity, which, well cultivated, becomes the sense of what is just.

But as in societies with our history and training, this instinct receives the stimulus from developments dominated by an authoritarian morality, which goes hand-in-hand inseparably with the arbitrariness of all power; terror is in its element, like the boa constrictor in the pestilent mire of the torrid zone that raises its terrible head crowned by scaffolds, in inadequate and socially backward nations like those of our continent. There is nothing to do but weep in silence.

* I.e., the Constitution of 1833. —Ed.

V

There we were in 1836, more than a few of us, silent and crying, when the victorious reactionary opposition had consolidated its power. They alone were satisfied and calm about the state of affairs, and they had the last word on all public matters, never failing to keep their ear pricked for dissenting voices, in order to muzzle them, though they might issue from the mouths of babes. In Juan Fernández's praesidium there were schoolboys from the Instituto paying for the sins of their loose tongues, and Juan Nicolás Alvarez and other youngsters, like him, who were not reconciled to respecting the social proprieties created by the opposition, suffered persecutions on a regular basis, which unquestionably had consequences for their future. No one could stray with impunity from the structure of words and customs for which the scions of the oligarchy provided the model.

But let us not say that anyone in power was troubled by this, so long as the dominant interests were respected and the dictatorship's orders were observed. The young were allowed to play billiards in the cafes, stroll along the quay in winter and the boulevard on a summer's eve and night. Granted, every stroll was cut short by the Angelus bells. The traditions of the Colony imposed the duty of prayer twice daily, or at least the semblance of prayer, out in public, at home, in the office, amidst the most pressing tasks. At the tolling of *the hour*, which announced the moment of consecration in the parochial mass, the most devout would kneel, wherever they were, and the less pious remained standing. At the prayer bell, everyone would stop in their tracks, remove their hats, pray, and greet one another with this prescribed exchange, if formality warranted: "After you." "No, you first." "Good evening." "God willing."

The despotism of those days provided no bread and circuses, nor were there Roman-style prefects to entertain the populace and empty out their pockets. The regime let each man seek his own pastime on the condition they not make noise or lapse from the established mores.

VI

In a society of this sort, the spirit found no place to grow or find nourishment. It was paralyzed, with neither light nor horizon. It was a mandrake plant that produced its pallid, violet-hued flowers, under the thick shadow of its anxieties.

Theater had disappeared with the death of Cáceres and Morante, although when these and other remarkable actors performed, it merely provided the belated comforts of the well-to-do class. It offered on occasion some stale tragedy representative of another age's aesthetic, which Cáceres heightened with his powerful, undeveloped talent, which made one cry and cheer; more frequently Spanish comedies were staged in which Villalba's verbal levity, and later that of Moreno, dismantled the gravity of our starchy mandarins, or out-of-date French sentimentalist dramas, which scandalized the very proper theater-goers with outlandish portraits of the corruption of European customs, lubricious love affairs, which they would not have abided had their senses not been rapt by the seductive witchings of Miss Aguilar, the most elegant and witty of actresses. Still, dramatic theater in those days only presented emotional fare, and did not make one think, as it does now, about social issues, about the biting pain of mistakes and concerns that offend against truth and justice; were this not the case, the reign of opera would have taken hold ten years earlier on our stage, a genre that later, on the ashes of dramatic performance, would establish once and for always its domination.

The education of youth was still stuck in the infancy of peripatetics, which predominated in monastic education, and had just expanded its realm with the recently established Seminario de Santiago [Santiago Seminary] (1835); even when its former influence in the Instituto Nacional had begun to vanish, the new methods begun in 1827 and the zeal to complete the surveys, following the Mora Secondary School Plan, had been forgotten. The humanities course that should have been set up according to this plan was after eight years reduced to an incomplete and defective training in Latin, in Castilian and French grammar. At times one of the faculty informally had taught geographical maps, and began to hold a class in this field without the necessary resources, but geography was not a humanities course.

The writer of these lines had already begun to teach it in private schools in 1836, and in the early part of 1838 he published his *Lecciones de geografía moderna* ["Modern Geography Lessons"], which since that time has been used as a textbook and has facilitated the teaching of this subject in all educational institutions. This recollection would be unnecessary were there no need again to correct Mr. Vicuña Mackenna, who in an official report submitted recently to the University held that the first geography text to be published was the *Curso elemental de geografía* ["Elementary Geography Course"] by Godoy Cruz; the truth is he published the work nearly two years thereafter, at the behest of the Colegio de Zapata's headmasters, who could not resign themselves to accept the existence of another private institute, like Mr. Romo's, that had a text like the one we had dedicated to their students.

The first geography text published in Chile is the *Catecismo de geografía descriptiva* ["Catechism of Descriptive Geography"], which don J. J. de Mora republished. Mora's booklet, scarce by 1836, was inadequate for teaching since it was lacking and out-of-date. *Catecismo* had appeared in London in 1824, and formed part of the collection the Ackermann publishing house brought out for use by Spanish Americans; we must remember what the sensible Blanco White wrote apropos of it in number V of volume I of his *Mensajero* ["Messenger"]: that let it be known today that the *Catecismo de geografía* in 1824 and 1829 was a true novelty in Spanish textbooks, and that the honor of having published in Chile another text of this survey, which describes for the first time the geography of this and all other republics in Hispanic America, does not belong, as Mr. Vicuña Mackenna alleges in a university document, to a stranger, but to a fellow countryman.

Blanco White states, among other things, that: "I say to myself, 'congratulations,' on seeing that the Spanish language is beginning to possess elementary works of the caliber most suitable to nations in the best position to put them to use. The concision of these little works is surely their most important feature. . . . The shortage of books that to date has been suffered in Spanish America has perforce left its citizens disinclined to take on the study of deep books, to the point they are not even cracked open, but abandoned for lighter works. . . . "

According to this respectable testimonial, the Spanish language *was only beginning* to possess elementary works in 1824, and it is certain that Spain herself could not boast, sixteen years later, any other text besides the musty old tome on cosmography and the *Tratado de geografía general de López* ["López's General Treatise on Geography"], which was used in the navy at the beginning of the century; given that around the year 1845 our compatriot don Agustín Olavarrieta bought a book in a Paris bookstore, a title quite common in the Madrid shops: *Lecciones de geografía por Letrone, traducidas al castellano por don Mariano Torrente, para el uso de las escuelas pías* ["Geography Lessons by Letrone, Translated into Spanish by don Mariano Torrente, for Use in Pious Schools"] (Tenth Edition. Madrid, National

Press, 1841). It was, letter for letter, a copy of our work published in Chile in 1838, and already reproduced and taught in several South American classes. When don Antonio Varas, then assistant rector at the Instituto, first brought it to our attention, we supposed the plagiarism had been perpetrated in Chile, and we stated as much in a notice placed in the fourth edition of our *Lecciones* ["Lessons"], which the *El Mercurio* press published in Valparaíso, 1846. But later we received information leading us to believe the reproduction happened and recurred in Spain.

Nowadays there are ample elementary texts in Spanish and the Chilean schools have them to spare; but when, in 1838, the *Lecciones de geografía moderna* ["Modern Geography Lessons"] was published, a book that has served in spades the Spanish-speaking people, not only had Godoy Cruz not written his *Curso* ["Course"], as Mr. Vicuña Mackenna has it, but also geography was not taught formally, and there were no elementary books in Spanish in this field, according to our sources, apart from the *Catecismo* ["Catechism"] from 1824 and the *Manual de geografía* ["Geography Manual"] by don José de Alcalá, which was not a text, and which had just come off the Ackermann presses in London in 1837, in a volume with 372 compact pages, to compensate, in the author's words, for the lack of a work of this kind, a work that might educate speakers of Spanish.

Returning to the state of education in 1836, the branch that was taught most assiduously in the humanities curriculum at the Instituto was Spanish grammar, which until a short time earlier had been included as a mandatory course. Since we deemed inadequate the development of beginners' aptitudes, as happens even now, with the experience we were gaining at that time, hearing the lessons that were given in don Andrés Bello's literature course, we were persuaded that some preparation was needed to carry out an extensive study of the language, and published in *El Araucano*, in May of that year, an article calling for change in the methods employed at the Instituto. But the innovation introduced in education was held in such high regard that the allies of progress thought that the measure we were proposing was an attack on the valuable victory they had made, and they rejected it in articles they published in the same paper, in *El Mercurio, El Barómetro,* and *El Valdiviano Federal,* forcing us to reply in a way that would relieve them of that impression; we were far from disputing their victory, and further still from seeking a return to business as usual, as the first innovator of our education system seemed to fear, a man who was writing then in the last of the periodicals just mentioned.

This reveals that at that time, progress in academics had come to a true standstill, since the few who aspired to champion education, like in days hence, clung to like a valuable acquisition any increase the administration would authorize on the limited horizon on which public education was maintained; they feared that on the pretext of change they would be doomed to move backward.

Secondary education was, then, deficient on all fronts. Since they were limited to an incomplete education for continuing on to law school later, neither did those who did not have the good fortune to complete this field of study acquire the knowledge a citizen needs to be educated, not even the knowledge gained previously by those who completed the humanities requirements at the Liceo de Chile.

In advanced studies at the Instituto there was unquestionably a wide enough berth for developing one's intelligence and directing the spirit to a golden path. But outside of the teaching of pure mathematics, which was done wisely and sublimely to very few students, training in most other fields was done from memory, without a systematic orientation and without the least intention to inspire pleasure and love of study, which was merely sketched out. It is true that the students of philosophy and of Roman law were better initiated and supervised; but the former and the latter alike were not training in these studies for modern society and for the progress in which they ought to be participating as individuals. For in philosophy they learned a subjective metaphysics, modified by learned theologians, and in Roman law they acquired not only an antiquated doctrine and one contrary to modern progress, insofar as that legislation is completely ignorant of the Christian principle of the inviolability of the individual, but also in superimposing the divine power of the Caesars over man and society, it perpetuates personal and social bondage, and prejudices the educated man toward such ideas and against democratic institutions and habits. This course was then a recent development at the Instituto, and our objections in the press and in private gatherings did not forestall our having to study it under don Andrés Bello's tutelage, not historically as Heinecio presents it, but in the Scholastic formulas of Vinnio, and molding our modern ear to that of the Latin civilization.

The rare schools other than the Instituto that existed in the country closely followed the model, and could not alter the educational plan without opening themselves up to failure. Thus all educational institutions were quite far from serving the education of a democratic nation; and since primary education was limited to teaching reading and writing in the wealthiest population centers, it is not overstating the case to declare that at that time the education of youth was not only lacking, but also unable in all respects to produce educated men, or even to setting out on a reliable road those students who aimed to complete their schooling.

That general sterility had, however, a small oasis in private classes in Spanish literature and Roman and civil law, which at that time don Andrés

Bello was giving in his home to a small number of students; but the results were favorable neither to democratic progress, nor to the emancipation of the spirit and of letters, which, owing to the illustrious teacher's teaching method, remained enslaved to routine.

The bookstore of those days was very poorly stocked and its prices were exorbitant. Its core consisted of many ascetic books and volumes of old Spanish literature, very common works of civil law, which cost more than their weight in silver, very few history books, none in the sciences, and some treatises on juridic and political science, like Montesquieu, Fritot, Bentham, Cottu, and Vattel; Filanghieri, Becaria, Rousseau, Constant, Rivero, and Salas. Contemporary French letters was represented by *Palabras de un creyente* ["Words of a Believer"] and *Democracia en América* ["Democracy in America"].*

The press was the symbol of that social and political prostration. The party in power revealed its thought in *El Araucano* once a week, and the few who read it revered it like the word of God. *El Mercurio* in Valparaíso, echoing it at times, opened its columns up to commercial interests and to the venting of personal grudges. *El Valdiviano Federal*, forum of the old patriot don J. Miguel Infante, appeared on the odd afternoon to disturb, or rather, with the intention of disturbing, the tranquillity of the rulers; but none were keen on reading it, nor did it have a public familiar with it. Around these three lusterless, nebulous stars in the firmament of our press were wont to appear the occasional will-o'-the-wisps, giving off ominous light, then going out in silence.

In 1836 four short ascetic works appeared, of which the one with the following title could be considered the most remarkable: *Modo como los estudiantes de teología deben hacer la novena al príncipe de esta ciencia, Santo Tomás de Aquino* ["Way In Which Students of Theology Should Render Their Devotion to the Prince of This Science, Saint Thomas Aquinas"], by don José Ignacio V. Eyzaguirre; and some thirty journals constituting a record of legal pleadings, vindications, and private defenses. Literature had its only representative in the *Elogio del senador don Juan Egaña, pronunciado en la capilla del Instituto Nacional* ["Tribute To the Senator don Juan Egaña, Delivered in the Chapel of the Instituto Nacional"] by Professor don Ventura Marín, who provided, as a master of rhetoric, a model for compositions in the genre, following the classical rules of the art, in a correct style but devoid of beauty and fruitfulness, and thus lifeless and barren, like the era. Education was enriched by the text *Reglas de urbanidad y máximas de*

---

* The former is by Hughes-Félicité-Robert de Lamennais (1782–1854), the latter by Alexis de Tocqueville (1805–1859). —Trans.

moral adaptadas para la enseñanza del Colegio de Zapata ["Rules of Urbanity and Moral Maxims Adapted to Teaching at the Colegio de Zapata"] and with two translations, one of the *Curso de matemáticas para el uso de las escuelas militares de Francia* ["Mathematics Course for Use by Military Schools in France"] by Allaize, Puissant, et al., and the other of *Curso elemental de fortificación de campaña* ["Elementary Course in Field Fortification"] by Savart y Noix. These translations, printed at the State's expense, were the work of engineer colonel don Santiago Ballarna, a learned Spaniard who had embraced the cause of South American independence, and who at that time was teaching mathematics at the Military Academy, an institution founded by the conservative government* to give students pursuing a career in defense a secular rather than Scholastic education, but the teachings were nonetheless limited and unproductive.

VII

Politics in 1836 resounded intermittently in the press, in the manner of the distressing echoes of a man overboard who struggles against the waves, and who occasionally cries out for help, no one hearing his shouts, which are lost in the abyss. The conservative administration had left in force the Liberal Party's press law, and their Constitution sanctioned the freedom of press ["the right to publish opinions"]: but they reserved the right to persecute those who published thoughts that disturbed the public order; and trusting more in the vacuum the country produced around political publications, out of a lack of a taste for reading, fear, or nearly always on account of the fact the publications were ineffectual and unable to spur interest, the administration would let them appear only to watch them die of anemia, or only to kill them off if there was any life in them.

---

* The *Escuela Militar*, now known as *Escuela Militar Bernardo O'Higgins*, founded shortly after independence, functioned sporadically during the tumultuous 1820s, and was restored in the 1830s with the establishment of the Conservative Party in power. —Ed.

In 1836 six newspapers appeared. Two of them, *El Nacional* and *El Republicano*, hardly made it to their second issue. Two others, *La Aurora*, which was attributed to Benavente and Gandarillas, published eight in Valparaíso, and *Paz Perpetua a los Chilenos* ["Unending Peace for the Chileans"], which was published by don P. F. Vicuña, went as far as six, arousing a certain interest at first, which later languished due to the listless diffuseness of its style, and since by contrast it was a book published in unvarying installments that the public could ill afford. Those papers that continued publishing were *El Intérprete* and *El Barómetro*.

A few times *El Día y el Golpe* appeared, which since the previous year don Pedro Chacón y Morán had published with the collaboration of many, whose work he solicited, principally from don J. A. Argomedo, don M. A. Carmona, and the Presbyter don Domingo Frías. The editor of this very important paper was a second-rank *pipiolo*,* a man of stern and sullen countenance who seemed to show a passion for the *coup* he proposed to author, when the moment was right. He was a solitary man of some political savvy, and though lean of speech, nevertheless lived a public life, in the public eye, in the courts of law, in the printing houses, in the cafes, like the last representative of the disturbances back in '26, '27, and '28, but without offending or bothering anyone. Perhaps, owing to these conditions, the absolutist administration let him be.

El Intérprete was the most regular newspaper, the best written in prose and verse, and was published in thirty issues from June of that year until March of 1837. It was devoted entirely to the interests of the Peruvian republic, which after being conquered by Santa Cruz,† would lose its autonomy in the Peru-Bolivian Confederation, which the political boss had conceived of to build himself an empire in these Americas. The Peruvian man of letters don Felipe Pardo y Aliaga, the editor of that paper, wherein he prepared and shaped national opinion in support of the war that our dictator,‡ in order to

---

* The word *pipiolo* (novice, beginner) implies political inexperience or experimentation; i.e., in early nineteenth-century Chile a member of the Liberal Party. —Ed.

† Andrés de Santa Cruz (1792–1865), Bolivian officer who joined the independence cause in 1820. He served with José de San Martín and Simón Bolívar, succeeded Antonio José de Sucre as president in Bolivia in 1829, attempted to confederate Bolivia and Peru, and led a short-lived confederation in an unsuccessful war against Chile, 1836–1839. —Ed.

‡ Reference is most probably to Joaquín Prieto Vial (1786–1854), president 1831–1841; possibly to his *éminence grise*, Diego José Víctor Portales Plazazuelos (1793–1837), businessman, champion of conservativism, war minister under Prieto,

save Peru, had to wage against the conqueror; he did so with such skill and eloquence that he managed to elicit great sympathy for his cause and his person. A poet of satiric inspiration, former classmate of Bretón de los Herreros in Spain, where he was educated, a man of vast literary knowledge and still young, Mr. Pardo was found to be wanting, however, in democratic convictions, and belonged, for many reasons, to the party in power, whose boss honored him with his friendship.

El Intérprete provoked replies in *El Eventual*, a publication that Mr. Méndez, diplomatic minister of Santa Cruz, published five times; the former publication held running debates with *El Barómetro*, which opposed the war against the Confederation.

This paper, which published forty issues from February to August of 1836, had the goal of declaring the candidacy of General Cruz for the presidency of the Republic, an announcement it made in May, and which it tried to make ready by staying a bit aloof from issues that could displease the administration. There was frequent grumbling in the press that the administration had been turned over to the Goths* and the upstart speculators; this complaint encouraged the men to clash often with the editors of the newspapers that supported the party in power, leaving very little room for the collaboration that several of us provided it in order to treat seriously some of the issues of the moment. Thus we scarcely managed to begin our defense we proposed to make of the trial by jury of crimes of the press, a constitutional institution that *El Araucano* attacked in long editorials, which it was said were penned by don J. J. Pérez, inspired by Portales. Like this defense, there were a few thoughtful articles in *El Barómetro*, which betrayed the position its editor in chief had taken. The editor of *El Barómetro* was don Nicolás Pradel, who filled his paper with articles that served his own interests and which sparked fiery arguments, and which the administration used to provoke trials by press, in which it always found him guilty, until it had an opportune occasion to jail and exile Juan Fernández. Pradel was a restless spirit, a man given to lavish individualism, trained in law but not systematically, and possessed of an unshakable audacity. He had been the opponent of the 1828 liberals; though well-connected with the reactionary party in power, he rejected their exaggerated aspirations, advocating for the victims and defending whenever he could, with neither doc-

---

and, as such, architect of Chile's successful campaign against Santa Cruz's Andean confederation. Portales was assassinated by opponents to the war and his autocratic policies in 1837. —Ed.

* Pejorative term used in Latin America for the Spaniards. —Trans.

trine nor system, the liberal cause, and this with a coarseness that ordinarily led him to the most impassioned personal confrontations. Standing out on his own as a writer, he was renowned for his unruly nature and had no backing; had he been a committed writer, like others who with those same qualities and aptitudes make a career, he would have been a highly reputed fighter, as much feared by his adversaries as beloved of his supporters.

VIII

Nevertheless, the editor of *El Barómetro* was not a writer *in strictu sensu,* and if we leave out Messrs. Benavente, Gandarillas, and Vicuña from the very few Chileans who then customarily wrote for the public, the rest of us were not either, since we lacked substance and style; add this to the fact that in that year, excepting *El Araucano* and *El Intérprete,* there was not really a daily press or periodical that subscribed to an opinion, but rather casual and ephemeral publications that gave no inkling of literary art. The writers who had used the press as a forum for polemics or battles before 1830, and those that thereafter had fought until being defeated, all had fallen silent, the liberals because they were in exile, and the conservatives because, content with their victory, they were at rest. Don P. F. Vicuña, who was perhaps the only one of the old-school liberals to voice his opinions from time to time, was not a newspaperman but a slow, discursive thinker who reasoned with the languor of hopeless grief and who, even when arousing sympathies through the nobility of his spirit and through the moderation and fairness of his protests, he did not stand for a political opinion of any moment, one that might attract adherents or awaken the public spirit lulled to sleep by terror.

Benavente and Gandarillas had disturbed the peace of mind of their colleagues the previous year by protesting in *El Philopolita* against fanaticism and carelessness on the part of Secretary Tocornal, who, they wrote, conferred unimpeded protection of the interests of the clergy and of all retrograde elements that had emerged in support of the reactionary party. But after a short but alarming campaign, which had compelled dictator Portales to come out of retirement and return to the cabinet to shore up the opposition party by founding the archbishopric of Santiago, the bishoprics of La Serena and Ancud, the seminary council with an ecclesiastic course of study, and also requesting from Europe twenty-four priests for the Chillán school, those writers were left speechless, though not entirely. The first of them was an astute and haughty spirit, politically savvy, and though he was no man of letters nor was he well schooled, his language was correct, his style precise and vehement, and his forms betokened the art of a man of conviction and a deep, composed thinker. In his conversation he was frank, sarcastic, a natural storyteller and full of attractions that brought him respect and affection. By contrast, his associate was a man of learning, vastly knowledgeable for his time, especially in jurisprudence; but as backward as he was violent in his political ideas, which had placed him at the forefront of the impassioned conservative party writers. He was incontrovertibly the man who best wielded legal dialectics in party disagreements, and thus was a force to be reckoned with in political and historical polemics, and a skilled sophist considered capable of conjuring up a storm with his pen.

But there were other writers as well who, though they did not use the printing press in the service of political interests, had published certain books in fulfillment of official posts, or under official sponsorship. In the two years previous to 1836 the following books and tracts were published: *El chileno instruído en la historia topográfica, civil y política de su país* ["The Chilean Educated in the Topographical, Civil and Political History of His Country"] by Father fray Javier Guzmán; *Elementos de filosofía del espíritu humano* ["Elements of the Philosophy of the Human Spirit"] by Ventura Marín for use by the students of the Instituto Nacional; *Repertorio chileno para el año de 1835* ["Chilean Repertory for the Year of 1835"] by don Fernando Urízar Garfias; *Proyectos de administración de justicia y de organización de tribunales* ["Projects for the Administration of Justice and the Organization of Courts"] by don Mariano de Egaña; *Sociedades americanas en 1828, cómo serán y cómo podrían ser en los años venideros* ["South American Societies in 1828, How They Are and How They Could Be in the Coming Years"] by don Simón Rodríguez; *Principios de ortología y métrica de la lengua castellana* ["Principles of Orthology and Metrics of the Spanish Language"] by don Andrés Bello; *De la proposición, sus complementos y ortografía* ["On the Clause, Its Complements and Orthography"] by the Reader in theology and canon, don Francisco Puente.

These publications had made us vain before 1836, for the ruling class held them up as proof of the intellectual progress they had promoted. Books were being published in Chile! There were writers who dedicated themselves to far-reaching studies, and though the latter three were foreign, we considered them as our own. The philological works by Mr. Bello and by canon Puente revealed not only a profound knowledge of the language, but also principally a philosophical analysis that was so brilliant and so far-sighted that it brought glory to their authors and to the state of Spanish-language study in our country. From this point of view, no less excellent was the work of Mr. Marín, which made great strides in the methods of philosophy study in the national school, which served as a university. Through the efforts of this professor and his friend, don José Miguel Varas, who died before his time, peripatetic schooling had been given up, imparting to this type of education an experimental character, which, although ruled by a subjective and nearly always metaphysical criterion, it instilled in the students the habit of thinking completely unfettered by the rules of dialectics, which, restricting and even misleading the spirit, disable it for democratic life. One need only see how those who arrive at the public forum, court, or press after having acquired a theological and metaphysical education, under the routine of the schools still on the peripatetic system, which is an anachronism in our age, embroil and distort all discussions.

The authors of *El chileno instruido* ["The Educated Chilean"] and of *Proyectos de administración de justicia* ["Plans for the Administration of Justice"] were not writers, and even were quite inferior in style and correctness of language to the author of the *Repertorio chileno* ["Chilean Repertory"]. Father Guzmán had needed José María Núñez to write his historical memoirs for him; the latter had to give up the task, seeing as it was impossible to persuade the author to relinquish his antiquated forms and to rein in his literary taste. Mr. Egaña, who undertook the adaptation of another plan written in Spain, was very unfaithful to the original style of the model, as revealed in the titles of his work that were made laws of the Republic by the dictatorship in 1837. Mr. Egaña was an orator for his eloquence and skillful rhetorical resources, for his flair for speech and debate, for the pleasant sonority and natural fluidity of his words, and even for the magnanimity of his style and ways; but he did not use correct language, and his wordy style frequently betrayed a superficial thinker and a dialectic disputant. But this very combination of qualities made him a delightful conversationalist, full of charm, a man who kept those around him hanging on his every word, especially when he told anecdotes, an activity of which he was most fond. Don Mariano Egaña revered his father, a distinguished litterateur from the Colony and also a philosopher, who had defended his Catholic faith against the invasion of the eighteenth-century Encyclopedists, taking asylum in the ancient Greek and Roman civilizations, on whose model he wished to shape the new South American societies after their emancipation. Despite Egaña's faithful adherence to his lessons and traditions, during his trip to Europe he turned into a veritable political Anglomaniac, and took England instead of Greece as the model for his country, but without its Protestantism, in spite of the fact that his father for all his Catholicism had held with the Greek system, gods and all.

The father while alive had been a true teacher, on account of his knowledge, and with his great prestige had influenced powerfully all political organization efforts to 1823. The son, who was not vastly educated, had inherited his progenitor's great prestige and many of the eccentricities characteristic of the old man of letters. Both men, for their concerns and beliefs, for their intolerance, and for that excessive religious fervor that in no way contributes to the morality of thought, nor that of habit, were true representatives of the sixteenth-century zeitgeist prevailing in the Colony.

Accustomed as don Mariano was to the respect and consideration that accrued to one of his prestige and high position, he believed himself worthy of the right in all circumstances to speak for others and to dominate, untroubled by respect and circumspection. He would entice others pleasantly to listen to him with his witty turns of phrase and his felicitous memory, which was the greatest aid to him in adding luster to his tales. He was an extreme conservative, since in his political ideas he not only had leanings to the distant past, but also was a monarchist, a fact which he disguised by securing a strong government for the Republic, since he could not give it a king. The 1833 Constitution bears the mark of his political influence, and if it is compared to the proposal he presented to the convention which was created by the appointed commission, it is easy to see that Mr. Egaña is the organizer of personalist rule among us, and thus the inspiration for, or rather, the political mentor of the then-dictator, who needed no inspiration to strengthen the politics of hatred that led him to his tragic end.

The author of *Sociedades americanas en 1828* ["South American Societies in 1828"], don Simón Rodríguez, who is the other foreign writer to whom we have alluded, was a strange man, who in our society was out of his element, and who was considered an eccentric, a laughable man who fell short of the class of the other authors of the books published in 1834 and 1835. Rodríquez had, though, the prestige of having been the teacher of Bolívar, who honored him with his friendship and recognized him as his guiding light, who declared to him his lessons had been deeply etched in his heart and had served as infallible guideposts.

So why was Rodríguez* a laughable eccentric in our circle? Because he was a true reformer, activities placed him alongside Spence, Owen, Saint-

---

* Simón Rodríguez (1769–1854), Venezuelan tutor of Bolívar who lived in Bolivia, Peru, Chile, Ecuador, and Colombia. —Ed.

Simon, and Fourier;* and not in South American societies, which, though aged and vitiated in the ancién regime, as were the European societies that the reformers sought to revive, had been able through their emancipation to work miracles to attain their reconstitution and reform in the democratic republic.

Don Simón Rodríguez, a self-taught, independent, observant man of genius, born in a peaceful colony like Venezuela, a place simple of custom, had spent the first years of this century in Europe, teaching people to read. Overcome by the serious and insoluble social and political problems that rocked those monarchies, he had naturally joined the attractive social reform movement that came about in the second decade of the century in England and France and which continued with sectarian faith for many years. The South American reformer could not resist applying the shining hopes that the European reformers had entertained regarding the regeneration of South American societies, not noticing that the latter had already begun to seek revitalization through political reform, and trusting, like Rodríguez's great disciple, that the continent would emerge from its *chrysalis*, as the Liberator would say in his eastern vernacular, developing naturally and without violence the physiological laws of its social organization, under the protection of a political system that guarantees personal freedom and the independence of society.

Rodríguez, like the European reformers, used education to gain leverage in social reform; like an experienced founder, he adopted new practical methods for teaching reading and writing, in order that writing represent graphically the importance of an idea, by the size, shape, and placement of words and sentences, so that reading indicated relative importance through stressed inflections in voicing. But his philosophic and social system was different. With respect to the socialists that influenced Rodríguez, Luis Reybaud has said: "Here we have three eminent men, Saint-Simon, Fourier and Owen, who, almost in unison, on the same day, are struck by an idea, that of forging a new well-being and preaching a new morality. The three, using various methods, unequal in import, proceeded to go on to a better organization of labor, and proclaimed that the laws of future destinies would be: one, love; two, attraction; three, benevolence." The three, each in his own way, were moving toward joint ownership, and the

---

* Thomas Spence (1750–1814), English advocate of land nationalization and collectivism; Robert Owen (1771–1858), Welsh socialist pioneer of the cooperative principle of labor and capital relations; Claude-Henri de Rouvroy, Comte de Saint-Simon (1760–1875), founder of French socialism; François-Marie-Charles Fourier (1772–1837), French social reformer. —Ed.

better organization of labor, which was their brainchild, none of them copying or inspiring their work on another, had the goal of leveling fortunes. Rodríguez, who made assurances he was not familiar with Saint-Simon's system, nor with that of Fourier, had drawn his inspiration undoubtedly from Robert Owen's experiments in New Lanark, and making industrial internships a condition of all education, wished to motivate South Americans to love property and the habit of work, *in order to make life less difficult*, which, according to him, was the purpose of civic responsibility, which Saint-Simon also believed.

Rodríguez's system is not known except for the *Pródromo* or introduction, which he published in 1828 in Arequipa, and for the twenty-eight-page tract published in Concepción in 1834, under the aegis of don José Antonio Alemparte, the intendant of that province. The tract in question was the introduction to the fourth part of his system, in which he treats the topic of *Resources that Should Be Used in Reform* and *Methods and Ways to Proceed in Methods*.

The 1834 tract was scorned, after having brought smiles to the curious who read it. Its style was dry, aphoristic, and its clarity, the author's most highly regarded quality, virtually disappeared under the plastic forms of its language and structure, whose strangeness rankled readers. Rodríguez, moreover, was a reformer who, if he had Owen's love for his proselytes, did nothing to attract them, like Saint-Simon, nor did he show Fourier's kind benevolence, but rather crashed head-on with all accepted ideas, against social custom and harmony, neither swaying, persuading, or even flattering.

He wanted for our Americas a republican government, but by making the difference between monarchy and republic consist of having the former's purpose the well-being of a privileged class, and the latter's that of the people, he organized his administration nevertheless on a military oligarchy, whose officials must serve for life. The author excused this shocking contradiction, which of course biased all South Americans against such a system, by proposing that form of government as temporary, during which the new generation was educated, since he dismissed the present one as incorrigible, incapable of being reformed. Believing that the root of all evil lay in that *there are republics without citizens*, he wanted to create a new nation, something that seemed practicable in five years, by establishing a system of POPULAR *Education*, which assigned *useful exercises* to men and gave them a *grounded* aspiration to property ownership. Rodríguez did not want us imitating Europe, which is IGNORANT *in politics*, which never will reform its *morality* and which hides under a brilliant veil a horrid scene of *poverty* and *vice*. But neither did he want for us to ape the United States' form of government, for we were lacking nationhood, ideas on SOCIAL IN-

DEPENDENCE, and liberal ideas. Regarding the former he was right. But he was not with regard to the latter, and his error came from assuming that with his education system he would give man ideas on independence and liberal thought, to form the nation that the republican government needs. Great, doubtless, is the power of education, but never will it benefit a nation to be educated in the aspiration to property, in the useful and industrial exercises, and in liberal ideas, if the political institutions do not facilitate the development of these elements of power, of these means of prosperity, ensuring, like the institutions of North American democracy, the independence of man and society through the wholesale enjoyment of the rights that constitute personal freedom.

The particulars of Rodríguez's system are not known, nor the means it employs in reform to achieve a nation of citizens. His practices in education are indeed known; all of them were hostile to established customs and sentiments. It was said that in his school in Concepción, and in the one he had had after that in Valparaíso, he taught, concurrently with the basics of primary education, the manufacture of clay bricks, adobe bricks, candles, and other products of domestic economy. But the education he administered was far from falling in line with the beliefs, customs, morality, and urbanity of the society in which he exercised his profession. That sapped all life out of the reformer's efforts, and the oddity of his ways and habits gave him an originality that repelled adherents, regardless of the fact that for his genius and knowledge he commanded the respect of those who had dealings with him.

One of those was Mr. Bello, in whose home we saw him sometimes. One night we were both alone in Rodríguez's house after having eaten together. The spacious salon was lit by two high oil lamps, and in one corner, in an armchair closest to an end table, on which there was a lamp, Mr. Bello sat with his right arm on the marble, as if to support himself, his head leaning on his left hand, as if crying. Don Simón was standing with an impassive, almost severe, look. He had on a well-worn nankeen jacket and trousers, like those worn then by artisans. He was a lean, transparent old man with an angular and venerable face, an audacious and intelligent stare, a bald pate and wide forehead. The old man was speaking at that moment with a full, pleasant voice. He was describing the banquet he had thrown in La Paz for the conqueror of Ayacucho* and his entire staff, using ill-assorted tableware, in which for serving dishes appeared a collection of

---

* Antonio José de Sucre Alcalá (1795–1830), Venezuelan independence leader, under Bolívar, led victorious forces at the Battle of Ayacucho in Peru in 1826, first president of Bolivia, 1826–1828, assassinated in 1830. —Ed.

new earthenware chamber pots rented for the occasion from a local china shop. This story, told with the seriousness that gives one a clear conscience, was what had excited atypical hilarity in Mr. Bello, and gave him the trembling appearance of one who is crying. The narration, delivered with the emphasis and those elegant intonations that the reformer taught to paint in writing, gave the anecdote a supremely comic interest, which had utterly broken the venerable teacher's composure.

IX

But those books and these writers did not reveal the existence of a literature, and if in a way they were the faint and far-off echo of Spanish literature, with the lone exception of Rodríguez, one could not consider that the latter existed here as an instrument of our civilization, given that the South American colonies had not existed as an integral part of the mother country's society, nor could they aspire to be after their emancipation, since the institutions of its organization, into independent States, should be taking them down an opposite road.

When the United States emancipated themselves politically, they did not emancipate themselves from English literature; the latter could be of use to them, and in fact, *was* useful in their new situation, for their feelings and ideas, interests and social needs continued to be British, with the sole difference being that their civic responsibility should be better served by the new republican organization, and could be so, since the latter was no radical new development, but progress, a natural evolution of that same civic responsibility.

Thus we observe the needs of their new organization and the interests of their new political institutions were brilliantly served by politicians and men of letters of the caliber of Franklin, Washington, Adams, Hamilton, Jefferson, Madison, and Jay;* how social interest in the emancipation of the

---

*   References obviously to independence and post-independence leaders of the United States, contemporaries of prominent Chileans and other Spanish Americans mentioned. —Ed.

spirit was brought about by Paine at first, by Channing and Emerson*
thereafter; how the need to fight the concerns of the nobility and to send
morality down another path lit by poetry, was brought about by Irving,
Bryant, Cooper,[†] without any of these great writers, who founded American literature, ceasing to be an English writer; it was less the British concerns than the new politics, the new social interests, that they rejected.

Among the Chileans, Spanish literature had no representatives, and if
one or another came from outside, they did not manage to form a literary
school that could help our education, nor even the needs of the new age.
These needs, furthermore, not only were unknown, but were also negated
by the conservative reaction of 1830, and supplanted by others that began to
be taken as main and fundamental interests. They provided, therefore, the
foundation and the blueprint for prevailing public opinion.

All interest in political organization, for example, was summarized by
order, a magic word that in the public opinion represented the tranquillity
that smooths the course of business, and more, the serenity that buffers un-
certainties, reconciling peace at home and peace in the public sphere; to
statesmen and party politicians it meant the reign of arbitrary and despotic
power, or in other words, the political possession of absolute power that in
the peaceful times of the Colony, the King of Spain's minion usurped. All
political instructions and secondary ordinances, all governmental doctrines
and practices were concentrated on achieving and supporting that noble
end. Resultantly, all interests in intellectual and moral progress, which are
the backbone of personal freedom and social independence, were subordi-
nated to the same objective.

One could not have the audacity to serve such interests independently
of this goal without bringing a rebellion on oneself. The intelligent man
who would not incur the error of such an offense should hold his peace and
drift with the tide.

From our vantage point that situation openly contradicts the goals of
the American Revolution, and instead of setting out to correct our past

---

* Thomas Paine (1737–1809), philosopher, deist, political writer, born in England,
settled in North America, author of *The Rights of Man* (1791–92); William Ellery
Channing (1780–1842), United States clergyman, "Apostle of Unitarianism"; his
nephew, William Henry (1810–1884), was a resident of Brook Farm; Ralph Waldo
Emerson (1803–1882), United States clergyman and transcendentalist. —Ed.

† References clearly are to Washington Irving (1783–1859), William Cullen Bryant
(1794–1878), and James Fenimore Cooper (1789–1851), early nineteenth-century
writers who shaped the literature of the new United States the way Lastarria and
his colleagues were attempting to do in Chile. —Ed.

and educate our generation, it has shackled us at the start, reinstating the colonial system. The flow of our reading was but a trickle, and nevertheless it predisposed us against that situation in a way that became mortifying; two old books, which had been part of the estate of an English merchant's bankruptcy, were the ones which had led us to hold this conviction. *Les garanties individuelles*, by Danunou, and a history of the United States, in a thick paper-bound, well-printed volume, whose author we cannot recall. The circumstance of having been one of the three students from the English class at the Instituto enabled us to read this book, which we had pondered and read through many times, comparing the situation of the two Americas and marveling at how far we Spanish Americans have to go to place ourselves in a social organization appropriate to democratic progress, a place from which the 1836 political order distanced us to a great extent. This reading had made us appreciate also the ideas of don Simón Rodríguez for the important ones they were, and his treatise, a work met with great contempt by the populace, had steeped us in serious meditations.

We believed, as did this writer, that our Republic needed a nation of people; but to have it, it was not enough, in our judgment, to provide an industrial education to the new generation, but it was indispensable to remake our civilization, disavowing the entire Spanish past, and disciplining the current generation in the practice of freedom, through systematically and sincerely reformed political institutions. Nevertheless, political freedom was not our overall objective, as it was for malcontents at the time, but merely a part, a complement, if you will, to individual and social freedom, barring whose practice the industrial education that the reformer Rodríguez wanted, would be ineffectual, and work a simple tool of enslavement.

These ideas did not catch on. Our contacts at the Liceo and at the Instituto, which at that time we were cultivating in Mr. Bello's courses, led to contacts with liberal youths and with the aristocrats of the ruling oligarchy. The former, who had no other salvation save through violent, armed uprising against the prevailing order, rejected such ideas as cowardly proposals. The latter, who considered this order as the pride of Chile, which through it had reached the status of a model republic, disdained the ideas as simple absurdities, which smacked of folly or stupid presumption.

But our conviction was so intense that instead of weakening under so much scorn, it strengthened, and we began to implement our plan, drawing on our status as professor in Mr. Romo's school to open in 1837 a legislation course and another in literature. The purpose of these classes was to propagate our ideas, which from that point on took firmer root and progressed greatly with the study of Bentham, Constant, Montesquieu,* Fritot, and other popular writers on public law, whose valuable books represented on our shelf the honorariums of our labor and a source of wealth for the future. At twenty years of age one cannot attempt such a task without an ardent and sincere belief in the power of ideas, and blind faith in the future. Only thus can one have the courage in that situation to defy the indignation of the ruling powers and the perils of ridicule. Was there a certain vanity in this? But never has one seen vanity undertake a work of this type, nor sacrifice itself in the service of another, nor have the patience we have exercised in our humble assignment, never imagining that our conduct could authorize those who judged us forty years later to assert that all we have done for the moral development of our motherland is the excess of amour propre. That said, the truth is that the enterprise carried on, and we are furthering its progress today, forever studying the means to perfect it, to more clearly define its ends, and to make them a reality. This gives one the right to speak up loudly against those who, out of ill-will or ignorance, wish to make people forget forty years of arduous labor, or are unaware of and distort their actions in order to lessen their effects, in spite of the fact that they themselves reaped the rewards of them. And the proof that in those days we acted on our thoughts, and that today we do not ascribe to events of the past a meaning they did not have, as someone has also alleged, lies precisely in those selfsame effects of our labors, in our teachings, and in the writings that we and others penned that bear witness to them.

In 1837, the year that begun with unbridled despotism—the suspension of the rule of the Constitution, the political gallows, the execution without trial of political detainees who had fled—and that reaches the halfway-point with the military insurrection that covered in torrents of blood the tragic end of the dictator himself;† in that same year we began our dangerous enterprise of teaching society, man and his rights, the conditions of democratic organization, raising youth to the pure regions of science, and affording them a fair criterion by which they might be trained to gauge the

---

* Jeremy Bentham (1748–1832), English jurist, philosopher, and a founder of utilitarianism, author of *Introduction to the Principles of Morals and Legislation* (1789); Benjamin Constant de Rebecque (1767–1830), French writer and political figure, disciple of Mme. de Staël, author and historian; Charles-Louis de Secondat, Baron de La Brede et de Montesquieu (1689–1755), French lawyer, philosopher, author of *The Spirit of Laws* (1748); Albert Fritot (1783–1843), French legal scholar, author of works on constitutional, natural, and public law. —Ed.

† I.e., Diego Portales. —Ed.

enormous realities around them, while at the same time educating them in the art of expressing their ideas and feelings.

For our teaching, we used the Instituto Nacional texts, but the legislation text, which was so small that in approximately 150 manuscript pages it set forth the theory of civil and criminal law, and political theory merely served as a topic for oral lessons we did daily, explaining and expanding on the text with the aim of cultivating a strong spirit in the students and giving them impartial discernment and a broad-based knowledge of public law, as well as of the philosophy of civil and criminal law.

In 1838, a year which saw the continued state of siege and the resultant suspension of the rule of law, we repeated our lessons with the same love, and taught international law to another large number of students, always careful to not compromise our mission to the interests of militant policy.

The following year, the theater of our actions broadened through our being named professor of legislation and international law at the Instituto Nacional, an appointment with which the administration favored us on 23 February. That professorship, which gave us the advantage of immediately teaching sixty-three more students in the national school,* apart from the school where we had begun, amounted to a twofold victory for us, since it proved, on the one hand, that we had been able to maintain our teaching on a high level, where neither the passions nor mistrust of the moment could overtake it, and on the other hand, the exams our special students had taken in the Instituto in the 1837 and 1838 courses, had been satisfactory. The class on legislation and international law in this institution was

---

* As a fond memory, we insert here the list of those Instituto students, which contains F.S. Asta-Buruaga among its curiosities, in the same order in which he wrote it in 1839; to wit: Nicolás Villegas, J. Agustín Ovalle, J. Anacieto Montt, Francisco A. Covarrubias, Rafael Molina, Ramón Varas, Exequiel Urmeneta, José Antonio Astorga, Pedro Errázuriz, Ignacio Ortúzar, Pedro Santelices, Francisco Seco, José Dolores Sanfurgo, Miguel Campino, Daniel Novoa, Jovino Novoa, Vicente López, Francisco Bascuñán Guerrero, Alejandro Reyes, Vicente Valdivieso, José Briseño, Manuel Novoa, Rafael Cruz, Santiago Iñiguez, Antonio Pérez, José María Ugarte, Secundino Prado, J. Ramón Montt, Juan Santander, Rafael Ovalle, Egidio Díaz, Carlos Balvastro, Lindor Balvastro, Zoilo Villalón, Mariano Jurado de los Reyes, Nicolás Rodríguez, Tadeo Rojo, Diego Salinas, Vicente Gómez, Silvestre Ochagavía, Adolfo Zamudio, Eduardo Cuevas, Amador Rosas, J. Manuel Hurtado, Bernardo Villagrán, Manuel Blanco Gana, Atanasio Irisarri, José Luis Lira, Narciso Herrera, Fernando Baquedano, José Antonio Briseño, José Manuel Pizarro, J. Agustín Guerrero, Diego Serrano, Tiburcio Aróstegui, Manuel Bezanilla, Enrique Tocornal, Matías Ovalle, Francisco Gutiérrez, Carlos Riso Patrón, Fructuoso Cousiño, Pablo Ramírez, Francisco S. Asta-Buruaga.

vacant due to the illness of its worthy professor, don Ventura Marín, who shortly before had contracted it; and his replacement, the dearly departed young Felipe Herrera, had stated to us that we ought to hold a competition for his chair. At this news, after our special students' examinations, we requested of the rector, don Manuel Montt, that he sign us on to participate in the running; while we were awaiting notice, the worthy rector informed us of the nomination that he himself had received, ending the idea of opening up the professorships to competition.

X

The strained situation that had led the country to the disastrous military revolt on 3 June 1837 evolved from day to day, and this facilitated intellectual growth.

After that dreadful event, which was a bloody protest by the army and the country against the war that the dictator single-handedly had waged against the Peru-Bolivian Confederation, initiating operations with an act of piracy, which placed the country in a compromising situation, the administration, following the logic of its policy, had to disregard the protest; reorganizing the army, it invaded Peru and opened the campaign that culminated in the Treaty of Paucarpata.* We are not mistaken in affirming that this ending satisfied the majority's aspirations in Chile, but the administration disapproved the treaty, justly considering it a dishonorable failure, since the war should carry on until it brought down the monarchical framework that a military strongman had erected to his benefit in two neighboring republics. The caudillo had conquered Peru and subjugated it after defeating its armies and murdering its generals in Yanacocha and Socabaya.

The war having been justified with this noble patriotic purpose, the reactionary government appealed to the entire country, emerging from the

---

* A treaty signed in 1837 by Chilean Admiral Manuel Blanco Encalada, upon his defeat by Santa Cruz, recognizing the Bolivia-Peru Confederation. The treaty was repudiated following Chile's victory two years later. —Ed.

confines of its party; and since the country had not said a word, it was to great political advantage to urge it to join ranks with the government in defense of the national cause, since it was logical to hope that if the war was furthered with the help and support of the public, the government would change its party politics and prefer henceforth to govern with the country's backing. With this hope we became agitators, founding *El Nuncio de la Guerra* ["The Harbinger of War"] and collaborating in other papers that supported the plan to proceed with the operations, which one year later met that lofty goal with the victory at Yungay.* In fact, after that triumph, General Prieto's administration sought to become more humane, returning to the legal order. In June of that year the state of dictatorship ended, the Constitution thereby regained its dominion, and in September, the special standing courts-martial were disbanded.

The political interests assumed in the press a capacity they had not had, for in spite of the fact that the press movement in 1838 by and large had been relatively quite noteworthy, not only on account of the war, but also due to the impetus education had received in the many private institutions vying to improve it; no paper, however, had come out systematically devoted to national politics, such as *El Diablo Político* ["The Political Devil"], which appeared in June, and the *Cartas Patrióticas* ["Patriotic Letters"] in August of 1839.

The *Cartas Patrióticas*, written under the pseudonym *Junius* by D. J. Benavente, made a deep impression for the loftiness of their forms and style, and for the importance of their timely political themes, and for the liberalism and justice of their ideas. The cause of liberal reform and of the interests of the people had in those nineteen letters a worthy defense, one that stirred the public spirit and trained public opinion for the popular elections that were set to occur in 1840.

El Diablo Político was a newspaper of war, whose character led to our discontinuing collaboration with it, despite having had a hand in its founding.

One night in June we received in our house on San Antonio street, between Merced and Monjitas,† an expected visit from Juan Nicolás Alvarez and the Presbyter don Domingo Frías, who was arriving to arrange the publication of a political newspaper, using our contact with the proprietor of the Colocolo‡ printing press to have him publish the paper at his ex-

---

* The Battle of Yungay, Peru, was the final defeat of Santa Cruz's forces in 1839. —Ed.

† I.e., the center of downtown Santiago. —Ed.

‡ Named for an Araucanian chieftain. Since 1925, "Colo Colo" is the name of one of Chile's most popular association football clubs. —Ed.

pense, without the financial liability of Alvarez, who would be the editor responsible before the law. Alvarez was displeased with the patrons and the contributors sought out by his associate for the publication of *El Clamor* ["The Outcry"], whose first issue had already been prepared in the same press, and now he wished for another arrangement. Much argument ensued over the nature of the new paper, which in our judgment should be moderate, reliable, and geared toward formulating and representing the aspirations of the country against the established order. Alvarez was impetuous, ranting; he wrote in a way such that each of his political articles seemed an incendiary manifesto, and of course he could not own up to giving a bent of that sort to a newspaper that he himself proposed to edit. The nonstop persecutions, of which his fervent liberalism made him a victim, had vexed his spirit and imposed on him habits and relationships that he himself deplored. He wanted revenge, and although agreeing with us that freedom, which we could use to voice our thoughts, was a gratuitous concession by the people in power, freedom had no legal guarantee, since the Constitution itself authorized them to suspend its rule when it suited them to once again govern according to their own discretion and to enthrone a despot. Moreover, he firmly believed that the people were prepared to rise up and that he could send them revolting with a few proclamations. Father Frías did not share this perspective and thought, as we do, that it was wiser not to irritate the governors, nor make them regret having returned to the rule of law.

In the end we compromised, agreeing to make a humorous newspaper, which, arousing curiosity, would attract solidarity, without piquing our dominators, with a view to little by little raising public spirits and reconstituting the party of freedom. To that effect, he who writes these lines gave the name *El Diablo Político* to the newspaper and sought to establish its character in the verses that serve as a motto. Immediately, by consensus, we selected the materials for the first issues, having laid out and published the first one four days after that visit. *El Clamor* also appeared two days later, but we needed to retire it after number three.

El Diablo Político had the effect in our society of a fresh breeze that, suddenly and after a long lull, appears in port, bringing joy to the voyagers that awaited it with its sails at the ready. All depressed spirits were lifted. The paper was sought and read avidly, and from its inception, covered its operating costs, showing a profit. But the fiery tribune that edited it, excited by the enthusiastic reception, soon forgot its agreed-upon platform, and even in the allegories it wrote, taking on the important role with which the newspaper's title furnished it, was serious and impassioned, caustic and irritating, winning applause on the one hand, and raising the hackles of the powerful on the other.

But he is mistaken who thinks that such passion had warranted the official accusation the government leveled against the paper in February 1840, in an article that accused the government of certain murder attempts in times past. *El Diablo Político* had left out all culture, and its impudence had marginalized it, and therefore its demise, if such a stance had not been the accurate expression of the fermentation spreading in society, and the excitement produced in the liberal camp over the measures the administration adopted to ensure their victory in the elections. The accusation was, of course, a political blow designed to intimidate, proving that if the administration had been generous in allowing a certain freedom, it was not for that reason weak to restore the old dictatorship, as in fact it was through the declaration of a state of siege, which followed *El Diablo Político*'s damning judgment on that same day, 10 February 1840.

Here we have the way a friend of ours related this event in the following letter sent to us at the town where we were vacationing:

Santiago, 12 February 1840

Dear friend:

When I promised to write you of the events occurring in politics, I did not know I was taking such an onerous duty on myself as the one I presently feel: it seemed to me then that I would merely have to share some jests with you regarding developments under ordinary circumstances; but things look such that since your departure from the scene, instead of trifles, I must convey to you events with serious repercussions.

The trial of *El Diablo Político* took place on Monday, the 10th of this month. To prepare its defense the editor made some requests to the courts of justice and to the government, that they surrender the documents to prove the accusations against the government that are found in that newspaper. Of the outcome of that request to the courts, I know nothing. The petition to the government was reduced to a request for an attested copy of the writs issued against those executed in Curicó, and it was provided with the statement that only one attested copy of the preliminary proceedings existed in the ministry, a copy that any visitor could consult in the ministry itself, for whatever purposes suited him. It was known that a certain number of people were disposed to clap or hiss at speeches made in the jury. For this reason the judge indicated the criminal courtroom as a meeting place for the court, and in fact it met there at ten in the morning. The locale, as you know, has a capacity of only 150 or 200 people, whose backs, moreover, were well-protected. Nevertheless, when the prosecutor spoke there were murmurs of disapproval and the other displays of annoyance typical in such cases. The judge intimated to the bar that the jury be shown all due respect. Certain words let loose to the prosecutor on the origin of this hissing, gave rise to renewed disturbances. The Devil-editor spoke then and was applauded, whereupon the court was ordered cleared. Some shouted: "The people aren't leaving"; some did leave, however, and the allegations continued without further confrontations.

This dispute lasted from ten in the morning until twelve-thirty, at which time the jury reached a verdict. I know nothing for a fact regarding what happened in the private conference between the judges. I am told that six were in favor of condemning the Devil in the third degree and seven that he be convicted only in the first. The prosecutor had accused him of libel and sedition; but the law did not permit this official to charge these offenses, and it was decided that the dispute should fall only on the second item. The merits of the allegations are not discussed, nor the adduced arguments. Alvarez filed a charge of murder that was committed against the government in the exile of Fuentecilla and the murder-for-hire of Escanilla that the governor of Valparaíso carried out against the boat captain that carried him to exile in Peru. You will surely give me license to say that one has no need for arguments to refute such foolishness. The current government a *murderer*? They say one of the murdered, Escanilla, was in the law profession. In brief, this affair is lengthy. Onward.

The jury, which could not come to a decision until three-thirty in the afternoon, sentenced the Devil in the first degree, and when this finding circulated among the bystanders, they broke out in hurrahs and applause. Don José Miguel Infante and don Diego Guzmán spent all morning waiting at the door of the jail, but they had retreated by this time. There were roughly 300 to 400 people of all social stations when the Devil left. The tumult and the din grew ever greater, until the guard had to take up arms and drive the people back. The group headed to Alvarez's house, shouting "Long live the people, death to the ministers!", thereby rendering a kind of triumphant homage to the very man whom justice had just declared a slanderer. From Alvarez's house the group, by now a well-behaved protest demonstration, made its way to Bernardo Toro's. The ladies of the house became upset, and allowing the most respectable to enter, locked the outside door to block the rabble's entry; but the people, who will suffer no such rebuffs, clamored for the Devil to be thrown out; they broke the door down under a hail of stones and then had the good sense to disperse. Bernardo Toro threw a banquet for the Devil and his retinue.

That evening a murder plot against the life of General Bulnes was uncovered. The murderer turned up at the General's living quarters at one at night, armed with a pair of pistols; but being that he lacked the courage to consummate his crime, or that he regretted such a depraved scheme, confessed his intent, and was arrested with another accomplice. His case is proceeding posthaste. The State Council met that day and declared the capital in a state of siege. Last night the edict was published through the main avenues amidst a great throng and hoi polloi. This act, most serious given its nature, carried out in an untrafficked hour, which presaged danger to order and the suspension of laws, produced a profound effect on truth. We are, my friend, in a violent situation; the opposition organized by the entire Republic has incited a considerable percentage of the population to revolt against the government. Violence reared its head, riots, the horrible murders. . . . The government, far from backing off, threatened to operate with the resolve of an entrenched power. I don't know if last night they made some arrests, which I find probable or, rather, certain. Providence wishes to spare us the evils that threaten us, and confound with the ray of its justice those who are the source of the ills that are occurring. It is not the ruling party nor the candidate who suffers in political unrest, but the innocent people, whose name is usurped, or which heedlessly serves as a tool of vengeance and animosity. A new administration can succeed the existing one; if it is the fruit of the country's will, it will produce the country's happiness; if it is the fruit of murders and upheavals in which the respectability of judges and the most sacrosanct rights of the citizens are trampled, it will unquestionably be but a volcanic eruption, which will flood the cities with blood and shroud thousands of families in mourning. Let us harbor no illusions: it would not be the country that gained from a violent change in the status quo. I would rejoice

45

to no end were it ascertained for certain that the rancorous and ill-intentioned men that wield a remarkable influence in the business of political society were not those that placed the knife in the hands of the murderers, nor masterminded the turmoil. I take pleasure in thinking that then the state of siege would end.

My best regards.

Your dear friend. — *García Reyes*

XI

This letter is a sample of what the distinguished youth of that era thought, and on the strength of that we have saved it, more than for the historical narration it contains. Antonio García Reyes had not been a student of Mora's, nor of Bello's, as some historians have asserted: he belonged to the elite ranks of those who, having received their schooling at the Instituto since 1827, had been taken under the wing of the 1835 administration, like several others who studied with Mr. Bello, securing them positions in the ministries to train and initiate them into the interests of the ruling class.

This select youth was a sizable presence, and shone in society in 1840, putting on airs in drawing rooms, and looking down their noses at the few educated youths who, more for the connections than out of conviction, considered themselves liberals. The latter had always been under police vigilance, and the aristocracy in power regarded them as dangerous.

Undoubtedly, that sort of stylish youngster had come out of Mr. Bello's classes, where the aristocratic scions of the oligarchy had gone since 1834 to complete their studies.

Mr. Bello was the champion that the conservatives had put forth against the Liceo's education, placing him at the head of the Colegio de Santiago, when in January 1830 they made the Presbyter Meneses, who directed that institution, a minister of their new administration. In that short time that Mr. Bello stayed there, before the Colegio was eliminated, taught a course in rhetoric, following the rules of *Arte de hablar* ["Art of Speaking"] by Hermosilla, and he established the study of law-making, dictating a text composed of excerpts of Bentham and other publicists, which was adopted for teaching at the Instituto Nacional starting in 1831.

After this brief incursion into teaching, Mr. Bello only returned to it three years later, offering courses in his own house; it is in our interest to repeat here, the better to set down the situation we are recalling, what we already wrote in a book chapter entitled *Suscripción de la Academia de Bellas Letras a la estatua de don Andrés Bello* ["Academy of Fine Arts' Inscription for don Andrés Bello's Statue"]. Here is that excerpt:

> In 1834 Mr. Bello began to teach two courses in his house, one in grammar and literature, the other in Roman law and Spanish. There we would meet under the direction of the teacher, with Francisco and Carlos Bello, Calixto Cobián, José M. Núñez, Salvador Sanfuentes, Manuel A. Tocornal and Juan Enrique Ramírez, all of them agog over letters and country, the enthusiasm of youth; and with several other distinguished students, of which Domingo Tagle, the old professor of high Latin at the Instituto, is still going strong in teaching.
>
> The teaching of those branches of study was vast and comprehensive, though suffering from a certain narrowness of method, of which the teacher had not been able to free himself, under the influence as he was of the age in which he had been educated. Language study was a complete course in philology, which ran from general grammar and the history of the Spanish language to the minutia of grammar in the language; and the professor continued his old custom of writing his texts as he taught them. His treatise on Conjugation and the most interesting chapters of the Spanish grammar were painstakingly discussed in those long and pleasant meetings with his students.
>
> But Mr. Bello was extremely serious, impassive and inflexible. He never explained, he only conversed, beginning always by expounding on a matter, then making his disciples reflect on it. In his conversations he himself spoke and argued, almost always smoking an enormous Havana cigar, speaking parsimoniously, with pauses and without moving a facial muscle, except when Tagle's strokes of genius made him forget his seriousness. Then he would soften up and laugh delightedly.
>
> The classroom was his choice library, and all consulting of authors was done by the students under the guidance of the

teacher. Matters of law were debated at length, until all particulars in all cases were examined.

But this way of having students study, which can be so advantageous with a philosophical orientation, lost all usefulness with that detail-based teaching method, great, doubtlessly, for training casuist lawyers and artless literary types. Mr. Bello was a philosopher, but in teaching he adhered to certain traditions, from which in those days he did not stray, though he forswore them subsequently. Thus, for instance, he insisted, despite our protests, and despite giving us lessons in Roman law in Spanish, which today are so well known, in making us study by rote Justiniano's Instituta, and understand Vinnio's commentaries.

Mr. Bello was a philosopher, we said, not only because he proved to be so in his philosophical investigations, but also because by those years he was writing his philosophy lessons as a disciple of the Scottish school. But the experimental method of this school, which has been enough for many great writers to scale the heights of scientific knowledge of the literary art, was no help to Mr. Bello, if we are not mistaken, in extricating him from the empirical rules of that art.

This phenomenon perchance has an explanation. The experimental method, which that school applies to the knowledge of what happens in the internal world, as well as the verification of the external world, subjected to the individual observation of each, constitutes a special empiricism, which can be as vague, illusory, and controversial as Germanic spiritualism. If the presumptuous absolute theory of the *self*, seeking its criterion in virgin understanding, deeming it to be everything, and investigating the truth outside of sense perception and through pure reason, has been able to create as many philosophical schools in Germany as there are differences of opinion among philosophers, the experimental method too, surrendered to individual experience, and therefore relative in each person, has scattered down different paths the disciples of Reid and of Dugald Stewart, making them conform themselves, through an observation based on its old errors, or leading them from the illusions of spiritism to the ever-shifting compromises of the mongrel French school.

In order for the experimental method to be a dependable guideline in philosophy, as well in all branches of knowledge, it is indispensable that it adopt an empirical criterion as the basis for observation; this criterion consists, with respect to external-world phenomena, of supporting research with empirical proof, such that no fact is recognized that is not proven plainly by science; with respect to the knowledge of events in the internal world, in only acknowledging facts founded on the laws of human nature, which are that tendency that leads us to the parallel development of all our intellectual faculties, by virtue of which we choose in all acts of our lives the means on which depend our perfection and that of the species.

This was the judgment the wise teacher, like most philosophers, was lacking in those days, and the same reason he did not ascend to the philosophic truth of art, becoming bound up in the chains of empirical rules, not understanding that the fundamental strength of literature lies in the independence of spirit, guided and strengthened by the light of verifiable truth.

If art, in general, is the material translation of the state of the spirit made both suitably and beautifully, through the activity of the spirit itself guided philosophically; literature, which is the art of the word, should also be the philosophically artistic manifestation of the idea, through the word, and not the empirical arrangement of expression, in which that activity must be hobbled by rules, which have to be arbitrary, since they are not dictated by discernment born of principles, but of more or less whimsical observations, according to the ages, concerns and models adopted.

This latter practice was the one the teacher followed exactly in his literary teachings. He was a philosopher, but as a man of letters, he never gave up his rhetorical bent, and disposed of the rational principles of science, philosophical knowledge of the elements of art, and the various genres of composition, binding himself constantly, when working in those genres, to empirical laws. He was completely versed in the history of Spanish literature, like that of other countries, for he was a formidable researcher of literary history, as Barros Arana and Amunátegui are in civil history, but he never rose to the consideration of works in accordance with the social influences of the eras, in accordance with the advancements and philosophical principles verified by the facts themselves.

And what he preached was the same as what he practiced. He cultivated poetry assiduously, and admirably conceived the aesthetic situations of nature; but his inspirations translated into tangible works so overwhelmed by the demands of the poetical, that his versification, though beyond reproach and a true model of elocution, was labored and inharmonious. He cultivated literary history, but in his study of the *Poema del Cid** ["Poem of the Cid"] and in others he shows only his highly erudite side, but not the philosophical. He was very devoted to sociological didactics and even, at times, used academic oratory in great solemnity, but his work, impeccable from the point of view of grammar and rhetoric, clearly manifested that the great activity of his spirit had been sacrificed to literary and social conventions when giving tangible expression to his ideas and vast knowledge.

The influence of this teaching was immense in those days; it was practically preponderant. Mr. Bello's disciples would leave his classroom daily to spread the teacher's ideas and method; the latter did not neglect to spur on those who were already professors in the Santiago schools to propagate the study of language and literature. He was distressed at the corruptions in the Spanish language in Chile, and the inexperienced teachers were turning into raving purists, spreading the same urge among their students. From 1835 to 1842, all prominent youths in Santiago were casuist in law and purist and rhetorical in letters. The philosophic spirit pierced the mind of the students like a flash of light, while they attended courses in legislation and philosophy at the Instituto; but as soon as they reached the advanced courses and enrolled in the fashionable coteries of casuists and rhetoricians, that light died out, not to relight. The social backwardness and political situation required it to be thus, and were quite a major contributing factor to that influence's prevalence. The active spirits of society were still gestating, and the exclusive policy of the personalist government had stunted the public spirit so that they had no other open road at their disposal save that of the elegance of form.

---

*   *El cantar de mío Cid* (ca. 1140), Spain's great medieval epic of chivalry. —Ed.

XII

The return of dictatorship in 1840 was applauded by those brilliant youths, but since terror had lost all its power by 1837 with Quillota's insurrection, and was no longer a concern of good government; and since the war and its splendid outcome against the Peru-Bolivian Confederation had revived the public spirit, the state of siege on 10 February, after the first impression of discouragement, brought only indignation. The criminal proceedings and imprisonment of Benavente, Toro, and other citizens did not intimidate, and the political press confronted the strong stance the government assumed, to the point where that year no less than fifteen newspapers and ten political pamphlets appeared, several of them put out by the government itself, which also was forced to seek support in the press. That is progress.

Alongside those youths began to emerge those that we had been educating since four years previous; but while we had access to them in the courses we were teaching, we had a constant commitment to separate them from militant policy. To test the veracity of Leibnitz's dictum—"give me education and with that lever I'll lift the world"—it was indispensable to not weaken the lever.* To save ourselves from the perils in which that political situation was placing us, which each moment incited us and swept us into sympathizing with the downtrodden, who fought against arbitrary rule, our resolution to devote ourselves to the education of our youth had to be firm, in order to infuse liberal doctrines in them and make them proficient in the art of writing. We were aspiring to create citizens suitable for democracy, and able to supersede profitably the outmoded parties that maintained the political status quo, and to that end we worked at reacting against all of our social and political past and founding our future civilization under new interests and new ideas. That aspiration guided our teaching and showed in our every writing.

The Constitution of 1833 had been adapted to the circumstances of the victorious party, which intended to regularize the government, thus strengthening its power, for it centralizes all authority in the executive branch and supplies it the means of turning into a dictatorship, whenever

---

* This is a paraphrase of Archimedes: "Give me where to stand, and I will move the earth," by Baron Gottfried Wilhelm von Leibniz (1646–1716), German philosopher and mathematician. —Ed.

the interest of political stability calls for it. That was useful and highly political to a certain degree, but once authority was consolidated so that it could function regularly, no reason remained to maintain absolute power by adulterating democratic forms, nor to maintain a policy of hatred, to say nothing of returning to a dictatorship at the first sign that the country had recovered.

Nevertheless, the attempt made in 1839 by Prieto's administration to return to legal order had revealed that although the 1828 Liberal Party had been annihilated, its traditions and misfortunes served to bolster a fervent opposition that instead of discussing would recriminate, that instead of seizing opportunities in the age of legality to affirm and prepare reform, would threaten, and did not merely exercise its rights without alarming its rulers, without inducing them to reestablish the hated regime. And this latter was an imminent danger. To see it, it was enough to consider that the government was not sincerely returning to a system of laws, and did not have sufficient confidence to rise above personal attacks, nor enough faith in its might to foil any attempted rebellions with the rule of law, if they were effective.

On the one hand, we had, then, a government that loved absolutism and that was cowardly enough both to feel more comfortable in it than in a system of constitutional guarantees and to get alarmed at the slightest danger that threatened this comfort. On the other hand, we had a group of malcontents who, taking advantage of the tendencies toward a change of policy, and alleging memories of a better time, did not know how to fight within the realm of lawfulness, and was too anxious to wait for a change under the constitutional order. In both camps there were favors for the marauders: in one, the jobs, the patronage of power, the smiles and flattery of the oligarchy; in the other, the glory and popular renown, the satisfactions of valor that stands up to danger resolutely.

But the future of the democratic republic lay far from both camps, since old grudges could not be the means to their victory, nor could the ire of a pointless struggle which, kept alive by sordid ambitions and small-minded interests, could lead only to perpetuating an eccentric dictatorship, which helped preserve a musty, rotten past, or to touch off a civil war that, being unfavorable to the dictatorship, could install another that appeared no better.

In such a dangerous situation, there was no other honorable and practical way to save it, except preparing for a new party to be formed, which, unconnected with old animosities and current resentments, was able to represent true democratic interests and wisely and patiently achieve a reform of the institutions, supported in this effort by the current ones. That party should have come with the generation being educated, and we needed to guide them away from contamination by old animosities, the interests and ill-will of the moment, or the backward doctrines in vogue; also, that blind feeling that, alien to all justice, and to all rational discernment, wishes to preserve a rotten past in a nation that must regenerate, renew itself, and reform everything to complete its revolution.

That was our ambition, and on it we based our task, dispensing with participation in the parties, much more at that time, which constituted the eve before a renewal of the government, which no doubt would bring in its wake a change in the prevailing politics.

This hope, we must acknowledge, hovered in the atmosphere, and even our fellow students harbored it, however much they trusted that the conservative politics would stay afloat, to which, for reasons of principle, education, or affections, they adhered. But as far as the plans we were trying to carry out with our teaching, those friends looked on it with misgivings and several of them condemned them as dangerous. Not so Mr. Bello; to his credit we should mention that, far from reprimanding us, he encouraged us, discussing with us and dispensing advice each time we approached him for his opinion, a frequent occurrence. On another occasion we have mentioned that his spirit around that time was taking new paths, and that a progressive change in his thoughts, which took place until his final years, is one of the most remarkable features of his literary life. But he urged us to commit ourselves preferably to the teaching of literature, with a view to educating good writers.

Yet this was for us a secondary concern in the logic of our plan. We believed that political education was the basis of regeneration, because without it, it was not possible to know and love individual and social rights that constitute freedom, and less feasible still to have concrete ideas about political organization, about its forms and practices, in order to distinguish those that are adverse from those that are favorable to the democratic republic. The results we obtained from our teaching confirmed in ever greater abundance the truth of this, a truth that, moreover, should appear incontrovertible in the eyes of the conservatives, for there were several attempts that revealed the desire to have total control of the instruction given at the Instituto. When the rector of this institution was promoted in July 1840, to the position of Minister of the Interior, Mr. Egaña, who was Minister of Public Education, tapped for the headship of the Instituto the future archbishop of Santiago, don Rafael Valentín Valdivieso; and owing to his renunciation, canon Puente replaced him. The same minister later issued a brief to inquire into the texts being used in the law courses, in order to point out those that in his judgment should be preferred, mostly in the teaching of political science, as he told us more than once; after having left the ministry, he persisted, as dean of the Law School, in the same matter, and sent a circular dated 15 January 1846 to all the professors of the School, asking for reports so that the School could determine the texts.

These attempts later became an explicit reproval of political science teaching in the Instituto, since, though purely speculative, it was believed that revolutionaries were rampant at the school. When one of the young conservatives, who more frequently had argued with us over the usefulness of this teaching, became Minister of Justice, he used a military insurrection in 1851 to discharge us from our class in legislation and international law; later the study of public law was eliminated from the courses offered in the law field at the University. We do not feel that fewer revolutionaries resulted from suppressing this teaching, but it is true that the outcome proved to give, and still does, a splendid confirmation of our belief during that time, for ever since political science has not been studied, doctrine in practical politics is conspicuously absent, and gives rise not only to misguided acts, but also to pernicious errors and farcical absurdities in all political debates, both written and spoken.

Fortunately, in 1840 we still had ten years at our disposal with which to perform our task, and the results confirm in our mind that our teaching was useful, for it contributed efficiently to the progress of political ideas and to the literary development in this country. The Instituto Nacional was not the only theater of our education. We proceeded with it also in a private school that we headed at first with the indefatigable teacher don Juan de Dios Romo, and only later, in the young ladies' school the intelligent and industrious founder, doña Manuela Cabezón de Rodríguez, headed, along with her sister, doña Dámasa. In these schools we were in charge of several courses and gave preference to literature, in obedience to Mr. Bello's counsel, motivating youths with our example to write or translate, and promoting among those who were no longer students a taste for dramatic literature, which Mr. Bello wished to foster.

Making the most of the support for theater, which in 1840 was encouraging one of the best dramatic verse troupes to have visited us, we promoted among the more capable youth the task of translating for our stage the famed dramas of French literature, in which Mr. Bello himself had set the example, and was setting it still. Several of us translators followed this lead, and it contributed in no small measure to impel the good fortune with which our rendering of *El Proscrito* ["The Exile"], a drama in five acts, originally written by Federico Soulié, was performed, as well as the version the late Santiago Urzúa made of *Pablo Jones*. We made modifications to that piece, adapting it to our history, and even wrote a comedy, but lacking in talent for this difficult art, and only for promotion's sake, just as with the same intent we wrote verses, though we were not even simple versifiers, but as teachers of rhetoric, and we wrote articles of customs and manners or theater criticism, in order to train our disciples in these genres. Works by

Larra and Zorrilla, who were the Spanish models that could assist us, were already known and were gaining popularity, which later yielded profits to those who reprinted them in Chile. Everyone sketched articles of customs and manners or poetic compositions, and each outstanding drama produced generated numerous criticisms of its merits and staging, written not only by young neophytes but also those who were already established writers; this genre had the advantage of its neutrality, and the attraction that it lent to the taste for dramatic theater that had awakened.

The task was arduous, and to complete it a great deal of attention, time, and love needed to be devoted to it. Not only did we need to give political and literary instruction a philosophical orientation, to wrench the new youth from their sort of moral apathy into which the teaching methods and political demands of the dictatorship had sunk the youth involved. We needed additionally to promote, using every means available, intellectual activity, spark interest in the press, stir the spirit with new political ideas and with the incentive of political glory, inspire daring instead of routine and social conformity that contributed to furthering pusillanimity, dissimulation, and hypocrisy, which the interests of political despotism commended as virtues.

Thus did we understand our mission as a teacher, and thus we fulfilled it, running risks, facing the ridicule with which society always crushed anyone who aspired to raise their voice, incurring on us the odium of the dominant social powers, who strove to rule society and politics. That was a never-ending battle, which brought no immediate victories to gratify anyone, but rather reversals and sorrows; it gathered no wealth, but instead depleted the time and means necessary to acquire it. Neither did it have a glorious future, given that this toiler has to remember his actions to spare him from oblivion and dismiss the scorn with which those who after a third of a century look back on his sacrifices during that era, to applaud those who did nothing, to praise those who did the opposite, and to close their eyes to a name they try to efface, as if it had been them who were losing and felt offended, or as if today they were the latter's lawyers for avenging them from the agitator who had bothered them. We have never sought or courted popularity, nor have we relied on anyone's gratitude; rather we have always explained our isolation as a natural consequence of the long battle we have engaged in to defend and see our ideas triumph against all resistance, be it in the form of sentiment, routine, egotism, or the interests on which practical and capable men base themselves. For that reason we have always kept silent over the fact that the battle's reversals have placed us in the extreme that the people whom we serve have denied us even the work that provides a living for any laborer; more than once we have smiled, without anger, upon seeing those very people deny us its assistance on behalf of the liberal cause, or upon seeing its representatives deny us its cooperation and question our integrity and our liberalism, when as policy directors, we were giving them unchallengeable proof of our honest pledge to create liberal policy. But another matter is that history arrives, with its august judgments, to confirm all those omissions and errors, as it consigns with its indelible chisel the memory of that intellectual and literary movement that exacts such a price from us. Then we not only have the right to say to the historians: "That is our work"; we also have the obligation to point out our efforts, since they are a part of the honor of a name that, if it does not interest history, at least is held in regard by those who invoke it.

XIII

The political movement in 1841 was a true awakening that divides in our history the moment when one era ends and another begins. The war of the Peru-Bolivian Confederation had been the first jolt: the country lay as if shaking off the torpor, and the lively interest in the election of the chief magistrate, which engaged our hopes, wound up clearing away the sluggishness of the long sleep that the heinous despotism of a dictatorship had induced in it, a regime whose memory is cherished still by those who believe that nations come to life when they lie down to sleep under the master's heel, like a loyal dog.

The timid literary movement, which was beginning parallel to the political, was reduced to a limited circle: in those movements the press once again reproduced books that were analogous to those that had filled us with pride in 1834. Don Simón Rodríguez reappeared, producing his *Tratado sobre las luces y sobre las virtudes sociales* ["Treatise on Culture and Social Virtues"], in which he repeated his theories on reform; Mr. Marín brought out a second edition of his *Elementos de filosofía* ["Elements of Philosophy"]; Mr. Bello published a *Canto elegíaco al incendio de la Compañía*

["Elegiac Canto to the Burning of la Compañía"],* and then the *Análisis ideológico de los tiempos de la conjugación castellana* ["Ideological Analysis of the Time of Castilian Conjugation"], which Aribau appraised in the *Revista Hispano-Americana*, saying: "The point of view from which Mr. Bello considers the role the verb plays in the sentence is wholly new, and it solves part of the issues to date pending or dimly determined." The only work missing during this year was *El chileno instruido*, since for the analogy to be more complete, in place of the *Repertorio Estadístico* ["Statistical Repertory"] in 1835, the celebrated printer Rivadeneira, was then the head of the *El Mercurio* enterprise, published the *Guía de forasteros para 1841* ["Outsiders' Guide For 1841"], which he commissioned us to compose, compiling in this booklet the statistical data and illustrative information about Chile that we could then procure.

The press in Santiago published eleven political pamphlets that year, among them three that sparked intense interest: two by don Diego J. Benavente and one by don Bernardo J. de Toro, works dealing with public finance. They dealt scientifically and with a high degree of discernment with matters of finance that even now are of serious consequence; additionally it maintained, apart from *El Araucano* and *El Valdiviano Federal*, fourteen political newspapers, which revealed the fervor in public opinion brought about by interest in the three candidates for president of the Republic presented by the liberals, the conservative *pelucones*† and the conservatives from the ruling party.

Among these publications we produced one daily during the month of June, entitled *El Miliciano* ["The Militiaman"], which, backing General Pinto's‡ liberal candidacy, was aimed at illustrating for the electing craftsmen the importance of the right to vote, and the licit means that ought to

---

* Reference is to the burning of *La Compañía*, a principal central Santiago church, 8 December 1863, observation day of the Immaculate Conception of the Virgin Mary. —Ed.

† The *"pelucones"* were for a strong central government, order and authority; the *"pipiolos,"* by contrast, held French liberal and British parliamentary ideals, and supported a federalist idea of government, limited agrarian reform, and the limited power of the church. "The *pelucones*, or aristocratic 'big wigs,' colonialist and clerical-minded, attempted to turn back the clock of history and undo the achievements of the liberals who had fought for Independence; the *pipiolos* or 'upstarts' aspired to broaden the intellectual and political horizons of the country." (Solomon Lipp, *Three Chilean Thinkers*, Waterloo, Ont.: Wilfrid Laurier University Press, 1975). See also note in chapter VII. —Trans.

‡ The only serious challenge to 1836–1839 war hero Manuel Bulnes Prieto (1799–1866), president 1841–1851, was Francisco Antonio Pinto Díaz (1785–1858).

be used in its defense and in its practice. We were not militant in politics, nor did we take part in its activities; but consistent with the duty that ever since many years hence we had assumed, that of contributing to any intellectual agitation that might awaken the public spirit, that might give it firm footing on the path of lawfulness to debate and exercise its political rights, we submitted to the pleas Pedro Ugarte made to us on behalf of the liberals backing that candidacy that we join forces in helping the contending party, after its long banishment, in order to gauge the importance of the liberal ideal at that time. The daily we founded and that was published by those liberals was equal to that altruistic purpose, and Ugarte maintained in its pages all the debates that arose naturally from the conservative press's attacks.

Around that time the brilliant Argentinian émigrés were already here among us, those who the Rosas tyranny and his allies, the provincial despot and the bloody civil war that had ended with the ruin of Lavalle, and Paz and the other Unitarian bosses that had perished through liberating his country, had cast onto this side of the Andes.*

In the early days of January 1841, José María Núñez spoke to us of an Argentinian émigré, a very strange man, it seemed to him, that should make our acquaintance; out of courtesy we took steps for us to be introduced to him. He lived in the third-floor apartment of the Portal Sierra Bella, situated on Ahumada Street. It was a spacious square salon, in the center stood a little table with a small straw chair, and in a corner a small poor bed. Next to it there was a line of paper-bound notebooks, arrayed in order, as on a shelf, and placed on the brick floor, on which there was neither a mat nor a carpet: those notebooks were the installments of the *Diccionario de la conversación* ["Dictionary of Conversation"] that the émigré carted around with him, as his only treasure, and that within a few days

former military leader of the Liberals and briefly president during the 1820s, and Bulnes' father-in-law. —Ed.

* The 1829–32, 1835–1852 dictatorship of Juan Manuel de Rosas (1793–1877) forced leading Argentine liberal thinkers and *Unitarios* (i.e., centralists) to flee, principally to Chile and Uruguay. The most famous of those who sought refuge in Chile, and to whom Lastarria refers, was the intellectual Domingo Faustino Sarmiento (1811–1888), president, 1868–1874, and author of *Civilización i barbarie: Vida de Juan Facundo Quiroga. I aspecto físico, costumbres, i ámbitos de la República Argentina* (1845). This study is as fundamental to an understanding of nineteenth-century Argentina as the present work is to an understanding of the foundation of Chilean letters and historiography. Rendered in English by Mary Mann, it appeared in 1868 as *Life in the Argentine Republic in the Days of the Tyrants; or Civilization and Barbarism.* —Ed.

was ours for four ounces of gold, which he received in payment to attend to his needs.

The man really was strange: his thirty-two years seemed like sixty on account of his bald forehead, his fleshy, dangling, well-shaven jowls, his fixed but bold gaze, despite the lifeless glow of his eyes, and the whole of his head, which rested on an obese and crooked torso. But the liveliness and forthrightness of that aged young man's words were such that his physiognomy enlivened with the gleam of a great spirit, and rendered him likable and interesting. After conversing on the topic of his latest campaign, his defeat with General Lamadrid, his passage through the Andes, where he was on the verge of perishing, with all his comrades-in-arms, in a long and copious snowstorm, which lay siege to them in the las Cuevas cabin, he spoke to us with the talent and experience of a deep-thinking founder of primary education, for that most unique individual was Domingo Faustino Sarmiento, the then-schoolteacher and field soldier in the war against the Rosas tyranny, the formidable journalist, and a short while later, the future President of the Argentinian Republic. . . . That embryonic great man interested us to such a degree, that man with the talent to embellish with words his almost gaucho manners, that we were fast friends; having advised him to open a school to earn his living, we helped him found it in those very lonely apartments on the third floor of the Portal, beginning from that point to smooth away obstacles from his path toward heading the normal school for schoolmasters, which don Manuel Montt was planning; Montt was at that time the minister on whom were pinned the hopes of all of us who longed for a political change and for a more intelligent and more resolute patronage of public education.* Shortly thereafter we introduced him in that minister's house, thereby initiating a long friendship that both men maintain today, after having proved it by reciprocating services. On this visit, Sarmiento imposed upon us the company of another emigrant friend of his named Quiroga Rosas, who with his refined manners was his contrast, and with his felicitous memory to insert into his conversation everything he knew of history, of anecdotes and famous sayings, was a sort of pedant, worthy of Moratín's† brush. The young minister, who for having been rector and schoolmate of ours at the Instituto honored us by taking us into his confidence, revealed later that he had recognized the two men on

---

* Manuel Montt Torres (1809–1880), a member of Bulnes' cabinets, one of the founders of the University of Chile, president, 1851–1861. —Ed.

† Nicolás Fernández de Moratín (1737–1780) or Leandro Fernández de Martín (1760–1828) (father and son), Spanish playwrights and poets. —Ed.

sight, and had divined in Sarmiento the talent that very soon he began to use in the political press and that he used also to found the normal school.

One day in February 1841, when Sarmiento already numbered us among his friends, he read us an article on the victory at Chacabuco, whose anniversary was close at hand. The piece seemed well considered and better written, and we did not hesitate to forward it to Rivadeneira, who then was running *El Mercurio* from Valparaíso without staff and living off the correspondence his friends from Santiago, including ourselves, would send him from time to time. Sarmiento's article, which was published in the issue appearing on the 12th of the month, drew such widespread remark that Rivadeneira wrote us commissioning us to offer the author thirty pesos monthly for three or four editorials a week. Sarmiento vacillated, but after encouragement from those of us who thought well of him, became Rivadeneira's friend and writer, and then embarked on his long life as a journalist, in which he has fought so many battles and harvested as many laurel leaves as thistles.

The election of President of the Republic having been verified, the new administration organized, and peace of mind restored on a foundation of gratifying hopes and noble plans, we hazard no risk in asserting that our society began a new life. Politics took a conciliatory path that guaranteed to the populace the presence of the new Cabinet. This was lauded notwithstanding the fact that two of the ministers did no more than continue the duties they had just carried out in the Prieto administration, which showed to the end its insistence on legalizing arbitrary and backward policy, presenting in its last actions a bill establishing the interior regime that ended up consecrating the omnipotence of the Executive branch, extending its powers in a natural manner down to its lowest agents. The country did not notice this enormity, not even through the press, nor the body of liberal deputies that it had managed to put in office in 1840. Public opinion forgot that that monstrous bill, which was an ill-fated law, was signed and drawn up by the new Minister of the Interior;* it is likely that the people forgot it, won over, deceived we might say, by the law of general amnesty handed down in October for all exiles and the politically persecuted. This pardon, the peaceful resolutions made by the new President, General Bulnes, and the preference that from the first his administration gave to administrative positions, were doubtlessly the cause of the contentedness and the confidence that gave new life to society.

The distinguished youth, which shortly heretofore had been reduced to the tight circle of scions and babes of the ruling oligarchy, had received siz-

---

* I.e., Manuel Montt. —Ed.

able reinforcements with the new generation that had been brought up by us with other principles and different aspirations, and that felt their activities were stimulated by the close contact with the educated, bustling Argentine émigrés. Theater, literary gatherings, strolls, all took on life, and everywhere, mainly in the private meetings of men who had kept to some of the private drawing rooms, conversed on letters, politics, and industrial advancements.

Yet in this trade in frank and cordial relations, the sons of the River Plate's modish ease of manner and remarkable learning constantly stood out, begetting no small amount of jealousy, which they aroused and nourished, pointing up the poverty of our literary knowledge and the cowed spirit that the most distinguished of our youth owed to their routine education.

That jealousy served the author of these *Memoirs* to rouse his colleagues and disciples to study, with a view to belying these criticisms with the facts; but whether the former thought they were beyond the pale of such jealousy, and rebuffed the censures, or whether they had not the time nor the willingness to descend from their lofty perches, it is true that only the latter accepted our admonitions. Espejo, Francisco Bilbao, Javier Rengifo, Lindsay, Asta-Buruaga, Juan Bello, Valdés* helped us promote among the youths from the highest legislation courses, the formation of a Literary Society, for the purpose of writing and translating, studying and holding conferences in preparation of the publication of a literary journal that was at once a center of intellectual activity and a means of spreading ideas. Putting this arduous effort together was long and hard work, but it proceeded tenaciously, in spite of fears, setbacks, and the smiles of some of our old collaborators, who attributed our zeal to nonexistent pretensions, and who later, when the first essays by the writers we were training began to appear, applauded Zoilo, who took the trouble to mock and ridicule them, instead of encouraging them with high-level criticism. The outcome proved to bear out the fact that the reason and honor of letters lay not in the criticasters, which, lost in darkness, screeched like owls when the beginners whom they chastised with their derision became famous poets and notable writers.

Several friends tried to draw us away from the project, for they feared their friend would fail and be rendered useless from ridicule. One of them, García Reyes, attempted to present us more useful and worthy work in

* Of these members of the Generation of 1842, two of the most prominent literary figures were Juan Nepomuceno Espejo (1821–1876), journalist and pupil of Lastarria; and Francisco Bilbao Barquín (1823–1865), an organizer of the Sociedad de la Igualdad, a liberal group that opposed the ruling, increasingly fractious Prieto-Bulnes-Montt clique.

editing a legal newspaper that one of the ministers of the Court of Appeals, don Gabriel Palma, wished to found. We accepted delightedly, since at that time we took on all work that in some way worked in harmony with the intellectual movement, for which we had been rallying since 1836; after having brought the three together for deliberations, we established the *Gaceta de los Tribunales* ["Gazette of the Courts"], which appeared on 6 November 1841, and whose publication was under our authority for the first three months, and of which Mr. Palma was editor; we broke ranks after this time and left García Reyes in charge of the edition.

We could not dedicate ourselves to a legal newspaper that was aimed at influencing such a narrow sphere, and we needed to make use of the intellectual activity that had developed in order to give it new directions, and wrest it from the control of fashion, which as 1841 came to a close was decidedly supportive of articles on theater, which had tired even *El Mercurio*, which rejected them, and although we had fostered it, it was not so that this genre be the only manifestation of our literature. When the school year came back around in 1842, we continued pressing for the formation of the Literary Society, which had remained stalled since the end of the previous year, and in a matter of days all difficulties were overcome. The Society began to operate in an apartment that don Ramón Rengifo supplied on the second floor of his house; he staunchly defended the idea, and prepared a formal inauguration to make it appear honorable in the public eye.

XIV

Our Society's convalescence in 1842 was so outstanding that everywhere the symptoms of health and élan vital loomed into view. The taciturn sadness, the suspicion and fear that terror inspired before, had been replaced by openness and trust, which afford personal security. We did not have guaranteed freedom against the interests of personalist government and the whims of arbitrariness, but we were left alone, and the new administration's stance gave us the hope that we would not be disturbed in the freedom that in fact was permitted us.

That year there began, under favorable omens, an intellectual movement unknown previously, fomented and led by educated South Americans who, in flight from tyrannies and disastrous struggles, had found an amicable asylum in our company. In Valparaíso these émigrés found two literary newspapers, in the style of European journals and drawing their sustenance from serious articles, both original and translated.

This is the third time that publications of this kind have appeared in Chile, after the brief essay written by Mr. Lozier in 1826, with *El Redactor de la Educación*, and the interesting *Mercurio Chileno*, a monthly review that J. J. de Mora published in Santiago with the collaboration of don José Pasaman, from 1 April 1828 to 15 July 1829, sixteen installments totaling 772 pages.

Still, the appearance of the two new literary newspapers in 1842 did not meet the desire we nursed to have one founded and written by Chilean writers; therefore, we continued our efforts to achieve that objective.

One of them was the *Revista de Valparaíso* ["Valparaíso Review"], founded in February 1842 by Vicente Fidel López,* with the help of productions by Gutiérrez and Alberdi, all of them Argentinian émigrés. The other was *El Museo de Ambas Américas* ["The Museum of Both Americas"], published by Rivadeneira and edited by the Colombian don Juan García del Río, who as a writer in Chile had participated, writing *El Telégrafo* ["The Telegraph"], a political newspaper appearing 1819 to 1820, with don Joaquín Egaña and two others whose names we do not know.

Both publications were different in character, and the only explanation seems to be the radical ideas and tendencies in the Argentinians' literature had led to the publication of *El Museo*, which appeared after the *Revista*, as if to form a contrast; in the prospectus with which its appearance was announced on 1 April, this categorical statement was made, which implies a mission statement: "Inspired indeed by the desire to make a useful thing, and persuaded it can come about by supplanting other Spanish-language publications from abroad with this one—among them are ones that are not very well written, and others that do not offer much material of direct interest to the sons of the New World—we will cull from the immense materials that America and Europe afford us, all that we believe can interest, instruct, improve and delight; all that in our esteem tends to remove obstacles from the development of the intelligence, to banish worry, to propagate healthy principles and conservative doctrines, and to popularize the lofty conceptions issued by the intellect or the imagination of the wise men of yore, and of the wise men of now."

---

* Vicente Fidel López (1815–1903), Argentine novelist and historian who fled to Chile to escape Rosas's wrath. —Ed.

Although the *Revista* ceased publication after the sixth issue in July, López, who assumed editing duties at the *Gaceta del Comercio* in Valparaíso, which Pradel had founded in the same month of February, continued writing literary articles in this daily, so that even when *El Museo* was practically the successor to the *Revista*, the different spirit that predominated in the latter did not disappear from the realm of the press, and López and García del Río continued characterizing the two literary trends. López was a young man of twenty-five years, a son of the revolution, who in his Arabic physiognomy and in his burning black eyes revealed the seriousness of his character, the firmness of his convictions, and the torridity of his passions. Endowed with an eminently philosophical and investigative spirit, he was vastly well read, and leaned always toward contemplating the wherefores of facts, events, and principles, disdaining forms and external appearances. But his political and literary education was still not ruled by a fixed judgment that lent clarity to his decisions and his expression; that was then the general failing of all the progressive writers, for the new ideas had not yet begun a scientific evolution in the nations of the old regime in Europe and in South America. The supporters of the regime in those days were the only ones who, guided by metaphysical and religious dogma that served as their underpinnings, proceeded with apparent assurance, even when they were for reform, insofar as their interests and concerns, and their old judgment led them to serve it inconsistently and to distort it, laboring under the illusion they had a sound, clear judgment because they believed in dogma and rules, despite not questing for truth through evidence nor through philosophical induction. Those in favor of complete regeneration did not yet understand the formula for the new synthesis, which is democracy, and though without exception they wanted reform, they did not conceive of it in a set way, since they were wanting in positivist judgment; they merely attempted essays in politics and literature, not finding the straight path yet, nor the torch that should light their way and assure their progress. Thus it is no wonder that the Argentinian writers, who had ended up marveling at our intellectual backwardness, had no more found their bearings on the new path than had the Chilean liberals, though the former were bolder and more inspired, and thought themselves superior, uncorking with this belief the supreme disdain of the conservatives who were in over their heads in politics and letters, and who saw them as wayward or ignorant.

Certainly, don Juan García del Río was among the disdainful, for even when he had served the independence cause as a writer, he served it as a conservative, and so loved the old regime that together with San Martín he had been a backer of a monarchy in South America. He was a proper writer, stylish, ingenious, and so learned that he would weave a discourse around any topic, using the thoughts of different authors, like one who overlays a rich fabric in gold and silk. A man of advanced age, he retained his flexibility, the charms and elegance of youth, enhanced by the beauty of a countenance that withstood even the ravishes of old age. These qualities, his exquisite urbanity, and his talented conversation, made him king of the drawing room, and the more beautiful the women were, the more proud they felt when he was at their side.

His newspaper, which carried the motto "Floris ut apes in saltibus omnia libant," represented him; he used high-flown language, unlike the Argentinians' *Revista*, which had an unpleasant style and the harshness of the sons of the Pampa. We are not aware of why García del Río had truncated Lucretius's thought in his motto:

"Floriferis ut apes in saltibus omnia libant,
Omnia ut itidem depascimur aurea dicta."*

Whatever the reason, he took from that thought the words that squared with his literary character. It goes without saying that the men of letters in Santiago preferred *El Museo* and acclaimed it, while the youths of the new school, while not scorning it, sought out more interestedly the *Revista*, which the former did not accept, nor even read.

Thus was the situation at that juncture, when we had to appear before our society of apprentices, having writers and learned men like those as judges. But the danger lay not in their reproof, but in if we expressed our ideas with a candor that stirred up the concerns and interests in dominant political and religious powers, that reproof could be taken as the expression of a public opinion able to authorize all the hostilities of the powerful against the poor attempt we were making to ensure our intellectual development.

We had to allude to the straits in which the dictatorship had placed education, spiraling us into a downfall from which we had pulled out before it appeared; we had to reject the perverse doctrine that had social progress consist of material development and the predominance of wealth as the sole elements of political order; we had the duty to allude to the offensive scorn with which the majority of educated men had dismissed our ideas on reform and our endeavors to unite the youth and guide them down the path of political reform; we were obliged to present our new point of departure, rejecting once and for all the Spanish past, which our dominators had reestablished, and declaring Spanish literature, which our teachers and

---

* "As all things flowering offer their libations, / So too are all beautiful words imbibed." —Trans.

all us literati wished to consider national literature and take as a model, was not ours, not the literature to light our way; likewise we had to reject imitating French seventeenth-century literature, a practice which had been encouraged to the point that the official newspaper published, with recommendations and editorial praise, translations of excerpts from Racine by Salvador Sanfuentes.* We found it necessary to acknowledge what no one wanted to confess: that we did not have an education system, that our methods were erroneous, and that literary training, subjected to the routine of so-called classic rules, was far from being philosophical and from preparing us to judge literary output; this acknowledgment came to save us from the contagion of the old regime, so faithfully represented by Spanish literature and French literature from the age of Louis XIV, which made of the Pope and the emperor the two halves of God on Earth.

All that and much more did we have to say to the younger generation, colliding squarely with all the ideas and sentiments of the age; and this was a mortal danger, given that then, like in the Middle Ages, all initiatives here belonged to those two powers, and for us there was a third sovereign, which was the people, the only power that in the Middle Ages could make a new idea catch on.

Those who today have reached the golden age to which an ancient Roman would have aspired, when one can say what is thought and think about what is said; those who today can speak freely, even to the point of absurdities and distortion of principles and facts, unto defamation and insolent affronts, cannot measure the gravity of the danger to which we were exposed back in those years when we fought, teaching and espousing worthy doctrines, to hasten the advent of these happy times. And perhaps that is why they have forgotten to such an extent the address in which we set down the foundations of our literary education, which, considering it devoid of its true value, make of it not even the briefest mention when speaking of the 1842 literary movement or alluding to the history of our intellectual progress.

In our opinion, we state without boasting, that address is a historical document, and though today it seems mannered, full of vagueness, and mistaken in some incidental and passing concepts, we are going to set it down entire in these *Memoirs*, in case someone, when writing history with good will, believes, as the foreigners writing in Chile believed at the time,

---

* Salvador Sanfuentes Torres (1817–1860), a Bello student, as were most of this era's Chilean intellectuals, at the Instituto, one of Lastarria's collaborators, and a skilled translator from Latin, English, and French (e.g., works of Jean Baptiste Racine [1639–1699]) into Spanish. —Ed.

that it is "the first voice the new generation has raised," "the first one to touch on matters that national thought ought attend to," "the first word a child utters, causing a smile of jubilation on his mother's face...."

This latter metaphor, which represents the state of affairs so exactly and profoundly, and the innocent shyness of that "first word," were taken as an offense by the youths of the Literary Society, who published a stinging retort in *El Mercurio*; but a reply that appeared in the same paper, and which we believe was Sarmiento's, maintained that the address was a *new fact*, and challenged the author of that article to cite others, if it was not *the first one that had been seen*. In actual fact, it was not the first address in the genre in our country, for we had the grandiloquent address Mr. Mora delivered in 1830, at the opening of the oratory course at the Liceo, but this was a work that brings glory to Spanish literature, while our literature, being the first cry of emancipation from that literature, which was given in the old colony that lay in vegetable passivity in the foothills of the Andes, was indisputably the first voice the new generation lofted to found a literature of their own; it remained the first and the only, for at the University of Chile's inaugural address, which the following year Mr. Bello delivered, the same doctrines were not rehashed, and an attempt was made to restore the rule of the old literature from which we wished to emancipate ourselves. This counterrevolution triumphed, like for so many years the Spanish reaction triumphed in the independent Republic; and since we alone carried on with the literary emancipation movement, and do so still through roadblocks that sentiment and routine put up in our way, logically we attribute to our poor address the character of a historical document, which writers who today represent that sentiment and routine do not, nor will they, and who probably deem foolish, at least, the reproduction of that work.

We are reproducing it exactly as it appeared in a deluxe edition that Rivadeneira put out at his own expense, without omitting the words that the young students' Literary Society added to the work.

XV

The slight acquaintance with the notions of legislation theory that we have just made at the Instituto Nacional, have given us an understanding of our country's needs and its position in the scale of civic responsibility, the nature of our government and its imperious requirements, and also the character of the mission we are called to fulfill. We realized that notwithstanding the fact that the principle of popular sovereignty is recognized here, it is not yet effective; that even when the basis of our government is democracy, it is still lacking the support of enlightenment, of customs and laws. These ideas imbued in us an enthusiastic desire to be useful to our country, to coordinate efforts to obtain the goal of our revolution. And how to reach it? By educating ourselves to spread enlightenment and healthy moral ideas through the nation. To venture on such an enterprise individually was impossible: that is the origin and object of our meeting.

To date we have overcome all stumbling blocks that have been set before us. Aided by a resident of this capital, we had a place to meet, we established a fund to sustain our Society, and we drew up the standing orders, after a few conferences that have had a part in educating us, and finally we needed a President, and the voting fell to Mr. Lastarria. At his inaugural meeting, he gave the Address that we now publish together with the reply Mr. Montt, Society President during that session, gave him.

The Society's hopes have kindled with the incorporation of the President, the number of members is growing, and it trusts the youth of Santiago and other learned persons shall not deign to lend it assistance.—The Society members.*

---

* We list as follows the names of some of the members of that association, since the minutes have not been found to present the complete list: Asta-Buruaga, Francisco S.; Argüelles, M.; Bascuñán Guerrero, F.; Bello, A. R.; Bello, J.; Bilbao, F.; Bilbao, M.; Blanco Gana, M.; Chacón, A.; Chacón, J.; Espejo, J. N.; Herboso, G.; Hurtado, J. M.; Irisarri, H.; Lillo, E.; Lindsay, S.; Manterola, J. M.; Matta, F. de P.; Montt, Anacleto; Ovalle, J. A.; Pinto, A.; Ovalle, Ramón F.; Reyes, A.; Reyes, M. J.; Rengifo, Javier; Santa María, D.; Valdés, Cristóbal; Villegas, N.; etc.

> Quand nous ne sommes plus, notre ombre a des autels,
> Où le juste avenir prépare à ton génie
> Des honneurs inmortels.*

LAMARTINE.

Gentlemen:

As I introduce myself for the first time before you all, I feel deeply moved by the heartfelt gratitude you have kindled in me upon your recognizing me as one of your fellow members, with the honorable title of President of your Club; but this commotion in my breast is something more than gratitude, I should not conceal this from you; it is also fear, and shame, for I do not feel strong enough to hold up on my brow the laurel you have crowned me with: I do so without affectation. I have the greatest expectations from the enthusiasm that your dedication has awakened in me, a devotion so praiseworthy and so new in our experience. Indeed, gentlemen, your dedication is a novelty, for it leads you to form an academy to bring your intellects into contact, to be mutually useful, to show the world that our Chile is now beginning to think about what it is and what it will be. In fact, the din of arms has ceased on our soil, anarchy spread its dreadful wings and saved the Andes; peace crowned with fresh olive branches came in its place, and under its shelter our beloved country has shaken off the lethargy in which it was mired after the violent effort it made to throw off the yoke and stand triumphant before the eyes of all nations. It seems to me I see Peace looking back in pain on the past, and heaving a deep sigh upon finding nothing more than chains shattered in a pool of blood, and frightful destruction, from which it finds itself free as if by enchantment; I hear Peace saying: "The time has come when I should become worthy of the post I occupy, but I will not be able to hold on fast, the blood of my children will be forever crying out, bearing witness that nothing have I done to profit from their sacrifice if I do not fill in this depression that issues forth below me"; there ignorance lies, one hundred mouths open for me, I must destroy it, bury it forever.

---

* "When we are no more, our shade makes for the altars, / Where the just future prepares your genius / For immortal honors." —Trans.

You see, gentlemen, Chile, as well as the other sister republics, now finds herself at heights to which she was spurred by the law of progress, by that law of nature that maintains the human spirit in endless expansive movement, which at times violent, razes with its oscillations even the nations that are oldest and most attached to their past. But ours has been transported to what once was in its eyes, terra incognita; here, it has been put in danger of losing itself irremediably, for precious seeds do not take root in an infertile field: our fathers did not work the field in which they planted democracy, because they could not; they were forced to harvest it without having sown it; but the current generation, out of instinct rather than conviction, dutifully cultivates it, and it seems is headed toward bringing the task to fruition. Everyone feels they need to promote their personal interests, they undertake the task that will exalt them and that will give the nation the support it needs, in their reckoning: that of wealth; vain partnerships are devised to broaden commerce, to extract the treasures that nature hoards in the veins of the Andes, philanthropic societies emerge to protect agriculture and crush obstacles that impede their headway. But wealth, good sirs, will give us power and strength, but not individual freedom; it will make Chile respectable and carry its name around the entire globe, but its government will be tottering, and will be reduced to propping itself up on one side with bayonets, and on the other with heaps of gold; and it will not be the father of the great social family, but its lord; its servants will wait only for a chance to shake off servitude, whereas if they were its children, they would seek out the bayonets to protect their father. Democracy needs more support, the support of education. Democracy, which is freedom, is not legitimized, is not useful nor benevolent except when the country has reached a ripe old age, and we are still adults. The force we should have used in reaching this full maturity, which is education, was surrendered for three centuries to satisfying the covetousness of a backward colonial power, and subsequently employed in severing shackles, and in constituting an independent government. It is incumbent upon us to go back and fill the void our fathers left and make their work more consequent, to not leave unvanquished foes, and to continue with our feet firmly planted in the course that this century has plotted for us.

Now then, you have understood this need, you who without guidance, without refuge, drawing only on sheer valor, are congregating to educate yourselves and to educate with your labors; you who, it seems to me, have said in Chile to learned men that this thinking should have been practiced some time ago, meeting to communicate and draw up a plan of attack against social vices, to make yourselves worthy of the independence that the heroes of 1810 bequeathed to us and paid for in blood; gathering around that democracy that miraculously had been enthroned here, but on a throne whose base was eaten away by ignorance and which buckled at the slightest puff of the passions, and virtually collapses, leaving in its ruin our most cherished hopes. I congratulate you, gentlemen, and I most sincerely glory in being your fellow member, for you have done the right thing in joining to meet a social need. You all share my ideas and agree with me that Chile, all of Spanish America, will be nothing without learning. You have summoned me to help you in your literary tasks, but I should like to invite you first to reflect on what literature is in this country, on the models on which we shall propose to cultivate it, and also on the path down which we must shepherd it for it to be of benefit to the people. For, gentlemen, we should not think only of ourselves, and leave self-interestedness to those cowardly men who sacrifice everything to their passions and worries: we must think of sacrificing ourselves for the utility of the country. It has been our lot to have had an average education; well then, let us serve the people, let us light their way in their social progress so that our children find them happy, free and powerful.

It is said that literature is the *expression of society*, for in fact it is the means that reveals most explicitly the moral and intellectual needs of nations, it is the painting in which the opinions, religion and concerns of a whole generation are committed to canvas. They make up the theater in which literature displays its finery, the pulpit from which the holy minister proclaims the civilizing truths of our divine religion and the comminations and promises of the Almighty; the tribunal in which the parish priest defends the privileges of freedom and the dictates of general utility; the august seat of the defender of all that is worthy of respect in life: honor, the individual, property and citizenship; the newspapers that have become the most active agent in the intellectual movement, the safeguard of social rights, the powerful whip that flays the tyrants and muddles them in their ignorance. Literature, in sum, embraces among its copious materials the lofty notions of the philosopher and the jurist, the unchallengeable verities of the mathematician and the historian, the consolations of family correspondence, and the rapture, the delicious ecstasies of the poet.*

But what has our literature been, and what is it now? Where do we find the expression of our society, the looking-glass in which our nationality is reflected? The answer to such a query is certainly terrifying; but just as the mere little bird sallies forth boldly into flight after the fright the death-dealing blast of the hunter's gun gave him, we set ourselves in motion after suffering the terrible realization of our incompetence, when we realized that we need to build ourselves up by the sweat of our own brow. 18 September of 1810[†] scarcely has dawned for us, we are on the dawn of our own social life, and there is not a single memory that gratifies us, nor a tie that binds us to the past ere that day. During the Colonial era the light of civilization never broke on our soil. And how could it? The very nation that bound us to its heavy triumphal float remained ruled by ignorance and continued suffering the ponderous yoke of absolutism in politics and religion. When Spain began to lose the rights and guarantees of her freedom, when she began to build on a foundation of crime the cultivation of fine arts and the sciences, which were not embellished with the cumbersome adornments of scholasticism, and the Holy Office devoted its energy to persecuting unto death those who divulged truths that were not theological, then, gentlemen, the foundations for the rule of the conquistador also began to be laid. The Phillips, as fatal to humanity as to civilization for their brutal and absurd despotism; Charles II, with his imbecility and refined fanaticism; the Ferdinands and Charleses that succeeded one another, strong-willed defenders of their discretionary power and of the dread authority that the monstrous Inquisition supported, while at the same time intimidating them; these were the monarchs

---

*   Artaud.

†   September 18 is Chilean Independence Day, commemorating the day in 1810 when the municipal council of Santiago pronounced in favor of a junta to rule until the restoration of Ferdinand VII to the Spanish throne. —Ed.

under whose ominous scepter Chile traversed three centuries, in perpetual ignorance, ever oppressed and abused.* "Under the system of reasoned despotism," says a judicious observer, "which the cabinet of Madrid established in its former South American possessions, everything maintained the closest kinship: agriculture, industry, navigation, trade, everything was bound up in the trammels that the ignorance or greed of an oppressive and stupid administration dictated. But it was not enough to deprive South Americans of the freedom of action if they were not also deprived of that of thought. The dominators having been convinced that nothing was as dangerous to them as allowing the mind to develop, they sought to keep it in chains, leading us off the true path that leads to science, disparaging and even persecuting those that cultivated it." So, gentlemen, our literary ineptitude was as complete in those days as it was in our politics.

Pedro de Oña,† who according to some scholars wrote two poems of scant literary worth at the end of the sixteenth century, but which were as curious as they were strange for the day; the famous Lacunza; Ovalle, the historian, and the naive Molina, who wound up earning himself a deed of immortality with a history of his country, are the four countrymen, and perhaps the only writers of merit, that I can cite to you; but their productions are not glorious events of our literature, because they were native to another soil and they absorbed the influence of outside precepts. From 1810 until a few years ago, we cannot find a single work that can be called ours and that we can hold up as characteristic; nor can there be many writers of note, apart from several South Americans and Chileans, among which the illustrious and profound Camilo Henríquez stands out, a man whose beautiful works reveal a clear talent and a noble, enthusiastic and generous heart.‡ From recent

---

* Reference is to the Habsburg and Bourbon dynasties, 1516–1700, and 1700–1868, 1874–1931, respectively. —Ed.

† Pedro de Oña (1570–1643?), Chile's first native-born poet, author of *Arauco domado*, an episodic nineteen canto attempt to set straight the epic relation of the conquest of Chile in La Araucana by Alonso de Ercilla y Zúniga (1533–1594), Spanish poet and participant in the conquest. —Ed.

‡ Camilo Henríquez González (1769–1825), Chilean journalist and independence propagandist. —Ed.

years I cannot refrain from citing, among our press's few productions, two didactic works that will go down in the annals of our literary history, not because they are a sample of a lively national literature, but for the revolution that they launched with their ideas, and because they bear out the genius, erudition and industriousness of their authors: the *Filosofía del espíritu humano* ["Philosophy of the Human Spirit"], which is the opposite of peripatetics, one of the few sparks of enlightened reason in Chile, and whose appearance marks the age of our intellectual regeneration; the *Principios de derecho de gentes* ["Principles of International Law"], which has made us take an interested, sober look at the high dogmas of science which determine the reciprocal relationships between peoples inhabiting the earth. Various other elementary treatises have appeared, among which there are some that are vastly praiseworthy, be it for the success of execution, or for the useful reforms they sought to introduce into education. Our newspaper press, in spite of being hindered by endless obstacles that stand in the way of a nation in their early trials, does not fail to produce the occasional major work that has merited the approbation of the intelligentsia. But all these successes ought not fill us with conceit; at the most it proves that there are those of us who work for the spreading of culture, and not that we are possessed of a literature with influence and special character. The catalogue of our writers of merit is very small; we have done very little yet for literature; I venture to say that we are only just beginning to cultivate it. But it is to do justice to the strong desire that all show for education: many are the youths that longingly welcome the precepts of wisdom, and the country will falter if it does not clear the way of obstacles that thwart the benefits it can reap from such commendable zeal. There is still no education system in this country, the methods suffer from mistakes and flaws that the modern age brands with a mark of reproof and near-slanderous contempt. Therefore you see, gentlemen, the throng of educated Chileans, worthy of a better fate, jockeying at the gates of the literary sanctuary, all bound and determined to break in and pursue glory; but all are held up, either because they lack the impetus that a meticulous education and well-acquired knowledge infuse in the soul, or because dire poverty frightens them off, which always scares the imagination when the breast is bereft of hopes and inspiration. But you, I believe, feel emboldened, and thus I tell you that you still need to muster a great deal of effort to attain your goal: it will prove useful to others and glorious for you; this divine feeling and the country that gave us life deserve our sacrifices.

Never lose sight of the fact that our future progress depends entirely on the momentum we put on our knowledge at the starting point. This is the critical moment for us. We have that very natural desire that nations have, a burning desire that leads us on and deludes us: that of standing out, that of progressing in civilization, and of deserving a place alongside those ancient scientific and artistic centers, alongside those nations made old by experience, who lift their proud heads amidst European civilization. But let us not hasten to satisfy it. We have a thousand means to accomplish it; but the one most close at hand is that of imitation, which also is the most dangerous for a nation when it is blind and impetuous, when what is adaptable to the changes in nationality is not considered soundly. Perhaps this is one of the major causes of the calamitous dissension that has inhibited our social progress, spilling torrents of tears and blood on the beautiful and virginal soil of Spanish America. Oh, gentlemen, how distressing it is for young souls not to be able to build all of Rome in a day! But the great social benefits do not accrue save by dint of trials. The tools we possess could well be inefficient for attaining our happiness, but their reform cannot happen overnight; let us give in to the deliberate course of harsh experience, and the day will come when the Chileans will have a society that authors its own happiness, and in which the roots of religion and law, democracy and literature are deeply imbedded. This valuable enterprise is in our hands, and we must consider it in light of our capabilities.

But bringing these observations to bear directly on our topic at hand, how will we be able to be prudent in imitation? We must needs capitalize on the advantages that other, older nations have derived in civilization: this is the South Americans' lot. What literary models would be the most appropriate to our present circumstances? My knowledge would have to be vast, and my judgment clear and sound, to solve such an important issue; but call it arrogance or whatever you please, I must tell you that very little do we have to imitate: our literature should be ours and ours alone, it should be wholly national. Spain, with her divine religion, with her heavy-handed and indigestible laws, with her baneful and antisocial concerns, bequeathed us a literature. But that literature ought not be ours, for when the rusted chains that bound us to the Peninsula were cut, our nationality began to take on another, very different hue: "There is nothing that effects a greater change in man than freedom," states Villemain.* "What could it do, then, among nations!" We need to foment our revolution and follow it in its civilizing tendencies, on that peculiar path that gives it a character in every way contrary to what the taste, principles and trends of that literature dictate. I should give you, rather than my own ideas, the judgment of a Spaniard on the topic, a man who in our time has earned himself a reputation for his extraordinary talent, and who expresses himself thus in reference to his country: "In Spain, local causes held back intellectual progress, and with it, inevitably, the literary movement. The death of national freedom, which had already delivered such a deathly blow in the ruin of communities, added political tyranny to religious tyranny; and if in the space of one century we still maintain literary ascendancy, neither was it more than the necessary outcome of a previous impulse, nor did our literature have a systematic, investigative, philosophic bent; but in short, a *useful and progressive* one. The imagination alone should give more free range to poets than to prose writers: so that even during our golden age the number of *seasoned writers* we could name is extremely small."† In fact, gentlemen, if you seek Spanish literature in the scientific books, in the unlimited number of mystic and theological writers that that nation has in its ranks, in the theater itself, almost without fail you will find it to be backward, devoid of philosophy and oftentimes without a definite point of view. It is true that on occasions there looms up in them a trace of the rapier Spanish wit, but always in the manner of those fleeting flashes that momentarily alter the darkness of a stormy night; their beautiful productions are hidden fruits that cannot be found save by pruning

* Abel François Villemain (1790–1870), French literary critic and politician. —Ed.

† Larra. [Mariano José de Larra, pseud. Fígaro (1809–1837), Spanish playwright and satirist. —Ed.]

away the branches of the tree that contains them. This is the case with the best authors, as the quoted writer states, names that are offered more as mainstays of the language than spokesmen of their era's movement. Poetry, though, offers relevant samples of fertile and scholarly talents, of sublime passages both beautiful and philosophical; but you will need hard work and judgment to find them and to derive benefit from them.

Still, gentlemen, do not think I go so far in subscribing to these ideas on our conquerors' literature that I wind up undervaluing their beautiful and abundant language. Oh, no! The latter was one of the few precious gifts they gave us without realizing it. Some from our continent, surely weary of not finding in the old Spanish literature more than insipid and fleeting pleasures, and dazzled by the pleasant allurements of modern French letters, have thought that our emancipation from the mother country should lead us to hold their language in contempt and build on its ruins another that is more fitting, one that represents our needs and feelings. Full of admiration, captivated by what seems original to them in the Seine's books, they believe that our language does not suffice to express these ideas; they coin or introduce new words needlessly, they give to others an improper and unnatural meaning, adopt turns of phrase and exotic constructions, the latter of which are without exception contrary to the nature of the Spanish language. They thereby scorn the aforementioned utility that we could derive from a developed language, and run the risk of finding themselves forced to cultivate another new, perhaps unintelligible, one. Gentlemen, shun this bastardization, which is the result of misplaced enthusiasm.

There is much truth in the notion that languages vary in the different eras of the lives of nations, but we South Americans present a curious phenomenon in this respect: we are in our infancy in the public sphere and we possess a language that presages the advancements of reason, a language rich and sonorous in its endings, simple and philosophical in its mechanism, abundant, varied and expressive in its phrases and colloquialisms, descriptive and unique like no other.* Our progress

* Mora. [José Joaquín de Mora (1783–1864), Spanish liberal journalist, poet, and translator; resided in Argentina, Chile, Peru, and Bolivia after independence. —Ed.]

is underway, and however much we are swept up in the present day's progressive urge, we will always have in our language an easy and simple tool to use in all our work, brilliant vestments that fit all the forms our national factions take. Study the language, gentlemen, defend it against foreign expressions; and I assure you that from it you will reap a notable harvest, if you are not wanton in using it, nor so rigoristic as those who guard it tenaciously against all innovations, however necessary and beneficial they may be. It is in your interest, then, to undertake the reading of the classics, and to delve down into the history of literature, in order to appreciate them and acquaint yourselves with that poetry, which, to borrow a phrase from a critic, you will find expressive in its infancy, natural and simple, but coarse, impoverished and trivial; then serious, learned and resonant, then degenerating into affecting, pedantic and enigmatic; and finally, grand, majestic and sublime, harmonious and gentle, before ending up overblown, clamorous and nuanced. From Garcilaso you will learn to express your placid ideas and feelings with candor and affable naturalness; from De la Torre, Herrera and Luis de León you will imitate nobility, sinew and majesty; from Rioja, descriptive style and the vehemence of sententious and philosophical language. Descend to the prose writers, and Mendoza, Mariana, and Solís will teach you severity, prolificacy and simplicity of narrative style; Granada, the inimitable sweetness of their language for expressing external truths and Christian idealism; and finally, the colossus of Spanish literature will astound you with his grandiloquence and with the original wit and wisdom of his Quixote.* Study too the modern writers of that celebrated nation, and you will find in them the old Spanish Romance having turned into the language of educated reason, one able to profitably convey the loftiest concepts of philosophy and the most refined advancements of understanding in the nineteenth century.

Once you have excelled in that essential education, I believe you will be capable of absorbing the influences of French literature, that literature that dominates modern civilization, and of which one of its present-day champions has said: "Since the death of the great Goethe, German thought has once again

---

* Reference is to Miguel de Cervantes Saavedra (1547–1616), author of *Don Quijote de la Mancha* (1605, 1615). —Ed.

been shrouded in darkness; since the death of Byron and of Walter Scott, the flame of English poetry has gone out; and at this time there is no literature in the universe more afire and alive than the French. From Petersburg to Cádiz, from Calcutta to New York, no books but the French are read: they inspire the world. . . . "* We cannot decline to acknowledge this truth, but it is wise not to be blinded by its splendor: we will see how those powerful French books should inspire us. Literature in France has enjoyed three centuries of success, which have been characterized by several other schools that, while not being indistinguishable, had a certain familiar air that has caused serious blunders. It reigned supreme in the seventeenth century, which took shape, according to the respectable Villemain, under the influence of religion, antiquity, and the monarchy of Louis XIV; it reigned supreme in the eighteenth century, in which, by contrast, skeptical philosophy, the imitation of modern literatures and political reform wielded influence, in the judgment of the same scholar; finally, it has been the literature that in our time has reigned triumphant and regenerative, and which to my thinking is ruled by the vigorous and wholesome influence of Christianity, of philosophy and democracy, or in a word, by social perfectibility. The two former ages, notwithstanding their differences, have such consonance between them that we might consider them a single one; and in fact, Villemain states that those two ages have their points of contact, and that the talented features of one shared some characteristics of the other. Whatever the case may be, gentlemen, I feel that both schools are worthy of our study only insofar as they arouse the lettered man's curiosity, since they belong to the history of the progress of human understanding; but I consider nothing so inappropriate to our circumstances as the literature from those times, and consequently nothing so unworthy of our imitation. Granted the diverse causes influencing those schools, pointed out by the esteemed professor, allow me to add that there is still one more universal cause that acts as a link to bind them; such is that air of tiresome affectation that prevails in them, in keeping with the disciplined taste of those eras, according to the customs, ways and esprit de corps that united the courtiers and others on the level of the French

* Hugo.

court of the day. That taste dictated a harsh and imperious criticism, self-important criticism, if you will, which condemned irremediably all fits of fantasy, however natural, when they did not please the king and the ladies of the court, and enslaved the spirit, forcing it into religious skepticism, and into the courtesy and frivolity of convention. All the great spirits from those two centuries were swept up in that influence, and paid blind tribute to it in their output. Not even the austere and profound Montesquieu could escape contagion: the author of *El espíritu de las leyes* ["The Spirit of Laws"], that immortal work, also wrote the *Cartas persianas* ["Persian Letters"]. The literary republic then was an absolute monarchy that stretched its moral predominance to all of Europe, and into our day: it did more, invading the regions of the New World, and it propagated those overblown and chimerical principles of political regeneration. It is curious to research the causes of a marvel of such proportions, but my goal does not allow me to tarry on it.

Nevertheless, the times have changed, time with its bronze hand has come to awaken men, to make them more rational and positivistic, to lead them down a more spacious path. Modern literature follows the impulse that imparts social progress to it, and has turned out more philosophical, to set itself up as interpreter of the movement. "Criticism," writes the judicious Artaud, "has become freer, now that the authors are addressing a larger, more independent public, and thus it should take another banner; its currency is *the truth*; the rule of its judgments, *human nature*: instead of going only as far as external form, it should fix only on inner substance. Instead of judging the works of the poet and the artist exclusively on their adherence to certain written rules, the general comparability of the classics, it will endeavor to sound the innermost depths of our literary works, and to arrive at the idea for which they stand. The critical truth will confront continuously literature and history, commenting on one through the other, and evaluating works of art by the state of society. It will judge the works of the artist and the poet by comparing them to the model of real life, with human passions and the variable forms with which the various states of society can invest them. It should take into account, when making such a survey, the climate, the appearance of places, the influence of governments, the uniqueness of customs and everything that can give a nation an original physiognomy; in this way criticism becomes contemporaneous with the writers it judges, and momentarily adopts the ideas, customs, concerns of every country, the better to get inside its spirit. . . . " In this definition that you have just heard, gentlemen, you have in living color the delineated features of modern French literature, features that have been adopted discernibly in Spanish literature and later will be seen in South American letters. France has raised the banner of literary rebellion, she has freed her literature from the rigorous and narrow rules that before were seen as immutable and sacred; she has paid in the coin of *truth* and has indicated *human nature* as the oracle it should consult for its decisions: in this it deserves our imitation. Let us found, then, our fledgling literature on independence, on freedom of the spirit; let us scorn those doltish critics that seek to dominate everything, their dictates are more often than not suitable to bind knowledge in chains; let us shake off those shackles and give wing to our fantasy, which is as vast as nature. Let us not forget nevertheless that freedom does not exist in licentiousness; this is the most dangerous pitfall: freedom likes to alight only where truth and modernity dwell. So, when I tell you that our literature should be founded on the independence of the spirit, it is not my intention to inspire aversion for the rules of good taste, for those precepts that can be considered the very expression of nature, from which it is not possible to stray save by working against reason, against morality and against everything useful and progressive there could be in the literature of a nation.

I should tell you, then, to read the works of the most important French authors, not so that you copy them and transfer them without good judgment to your works, but so that you learn to think from them, so that you become completely conversant with that philosophical coloring that typifies their literature, so that you can follow the new path and depict nature vividly. The former would only be good for maintaining our literature in a state of borrowed existence, always hanging on the exotic, on what least befits us. No, gentlemen, we must be original; we have in our society all the resources to be so, to turn our literature into the true expression of our nationality. If you ask me what I mean by all this, I will reply with the sensible writer I have just quoted you, that the nationality of a literature consists in its having a life of its own, in its being particular to the nation that possesses it, faithfully preserving the imprint of its character, that character that it will reproduce with a success commensurate with the degree to which it is of the people. We need literature to not be the exclusive patrimony of a privileged class, that it not close itself off in a tight circle, because then for its subtleties it will wind up yielding to a pusillanimous taste. On the contrary, it should give vent to all feelings of human nature and reflect all the affections of the multitudes, which definitely are the best arbiter, not of the procedures of art, but indeed of its effects.

I cannot resist the desire to share now the ingenious thoughts with which this same author develops his doctrine. "One can think of literature," he writes, "as being like government: both should have their source in the very bosom of society, in order to withdraw from it continuously the nutritious juice of life. It is necessary that the free circulation of ideas bring the public into contact with the writers, just as it is necessary that active communication connect the powers to all social classes. In this way, the needs, opinions and feelings of the greatest number at any moment can be made room for, made manifest and flow back over those who perform the exalted mission of enlightening spirits or of guiding general interests. Poor literature! Woe be to the governments that place themselves outside the nation or that at minimum lead but the privileged classes and belong only to a reduced number! Internally stirred by a set of ideals that it no longer holds, the human race continues ever onward, the academies and governments remain stationary, backward: soon a time arrives when spiritual leanings and generally adopted opinions no longer are in line with the institutions and with habits, then it is necessary to reestablish everything: this is the age of revolutions and reforms. Literature should, then, speak to an entire people, represent it entirely, just as governments should be the summary of all the social forces, the expression of all needs, the representatives of all superlatives: only on these conditions can a literature be truly *national*."

Follow these precepts, which are those of progress and the only ones that can set you down the road to the goal of our aspirations. No peoples on earth have a more urgent need to be original in their literature than the Spanish Americans, because all their modifications are particular to them and they have nothing in common with those that constitute the originality of the Old World. South American nature, so prominent in its forms, so variegated, so new in its beautiful ornamentation, remains virgin; it has still not been interrogated; it waits for the spirit of its children to exploit the inexhaustible lodes of beauty it supplies. What resources these treasures offer to your application to the social and moral needs of our nations, their concerns, their customs and feelings! Its example only presents you materials so abundant that they would suffice to take up the life of an entire generation; now our religion, gentlemen, contains on each page of its sacred books a treasure capable of gratifying your ambition. Begin, then, to benefit from such substantial wealth, to fulfill your mission of utility and progress; write for the nation, educate it, combating its vices and fostering its virtues, reminding it of its heroic events, getting it used to revering its religion and institutions; thus will you tighten the ties that bind it, you will make the people love their country and accustom them to see freedom and the public sphere as forever one. This is the only path you should follow to consummate the great work of making useful and progressive our national literature.

I do not have the presumption to give you counsel, since neither my knowledge nor my aptitudes entitle me in any way for that: I will settle for presenting you my ideas in this brief outline, supporting them on the opinion of the wise writers I have cited: thus you have listened to them more attentively. I cannot but accompany you on your tasks, to share in the glory you are going to earn yourselves as you attempt the task of regenerating our literature. We will help one another mutually: for the mere fact of gathering we have pledged to a sacred commitment to society; let us overcome all obstacles to honor it, and may future generations and the present one not accuse us of having missed the opportunity offered us to raise our country up to the grandeur for which its resources have prepared it.

REPLY FROM THE PRESIDENT, DON ANACLETO MONTT

Sir:

Enlivened by the keen desire to be useful in some way to our country, we gathered to make every endeavor to achieve that.

Our first step was the drawing up of regulations that curbed injustice, avoiding disorder, and that regulated the progress of society resolutely and durably. I know you have read these rules. In it you have seen (as your address makes clear) that our objective is to study literature while deepening the truths that our teachers have taught us, and acquiring new ones. But this work was too onerous for our weak abilities and we had no choice in seeing it through but to seek the patronage of some of our illustrious compatriots. And who better than you could we find? You, who so many times have shown your love, and that now you pledge your commitment to our progress? You, sir . . . ?—But I am unable to continue, so as not to give offense to your modesty.

Let me simply say that our gratitude will be equal to your contributions, the latter of which will follow us throughout life, and in it you will find us always willing to pay homage to you.

XVI

This address was read in the formal session that the Literary Club held on 3 May 1842, and a few days later was published separately. The Club members greeted it with marked interest, but the public stayed deeply silent. Not even the official newspaper nor any other said a single word. That has happened to us often. Books we have published have been reviewed in the foreign press, without the Chilean papers making any mention of them. The *Historia constitucional del medio siglo* ["Constitutional History of the Half-Century"], among other histories, was first announced in *El Comercio* in Lima on 29 January 1853, and only one month later was there brief mention of it in a bimonthly review *El Mercurio* put out to inform of other publications by Mr. Bello and a few other writers, but without devoting a special article to him, as did *La Libre Recherche* in Brussels, a worldwide review edited by Pascal Duprat. That proves that our works have not matched the prevailing ideas in our readership, or that perhaps they have run afoul of their concerns, and thus we have had to think of it so as not to lose heart.

But if this is an explanation that, like any other, has managed to satisfy us, we have never been able to make sense of two other facts that, when our works were published, we noticed several times, and in 1842, after the address appeared, grieved us deeply: the silence of our own friends and colleagues, neither congratulations nor an encouraging word from them; and afterward the adversaries' efforts to carry out extensive investigations to try to catch us in plagiarism. This shortcoming of those who, forever questing to be original, do not understand the important role played in backward nations by the writers who reproduce others' ideas, who generalize them or popularize them, vexed many at that time, who were hell-bent on discrediting our address, discovering some instances of plagiarism in it.* We have no regrets in having committed them, nor will we ever shrink from reproducing foreign ideas that have become engraved on our memory, forgetting their authors, because we try to teach the truth, without affecting erudition, or worrying about claiming authorship of the quotes for ourselves; and without that itch that certain writers have who are so enamored of their fame as original writers, that never fail to put after their book title, though the book may be a monstrosity, that it is an original work by such-and-such author.

The silence with which the address was met and the meticulous search for plagiarism lasted for many days, until don Juan García del Río reported on it in issue 7 of *El Museo de Ambas Américas*, corresponding to 21 May. His article was entitled *Establecimiento de una sociedad literaria en Santiago* ["The Founding of a Literary Society in Santiago"], and was very favorably disposed to our enterprise, which was an open door to the Literary Society, and it should have straightened out that plagiarism tangle, since he denounced none and that very learned writer, from whom we received unexpected solace, praised us extensively. We did not have the honor of knowing him at that time, and entertained no hopes of even attracting his notice, since we had not succeeded in catching our friends' attention.

García del Río's judgment, after many reflections on the importance of literary societies, in the interest of intellectual progress, yielded the following passage:

---

*   Over the years there have been numerous accusations of plagiarism or liberal adaptation of foreign works by Iberians and Latin Americans. The Portuguese novelist and essayist, José Maria Eça de Queiroz (1843–1900) suffered unjustified accusations that he had based his anti-clerical novel *O Crime do Padre Amaro* (1876) altogether too freely on Émile Zola's *La faute de l'abbe Mouret* (1875). Federico Gamboa's *Santa* (1903) has been viewed as a Mexican version of Zola's *Nana* (1880). The Zola cases are typical: French writers in particular were idolized by Iberians and Latin Americans, so imitation was commonplace, outright plagiarism rare. —Ed.

It is certainly very satisfactory for all those with an interest in the happiness and glory of Spanish America, to find countries, to record acts that redeem so much calamity, so much disorder, so much vilification, as we have witnessed in the last thirty years. It is flattering to patriotism and even to the national pride of the sons of Chile to work diligently, in the shadow of peace, to improve its welfare, making strides in agricultural projects, devoting themselves to industry, to the arts, to commercial speculations; refining customs, propagating education, fomenting, or rather, creating the spirit of, association. While the youth of other countries, as Mr. Chevalier observes, have lost the feeling of due respect to their elders, and that, exasperated by discontent, have reached the point of scorning experience, and fancy themselves superior to men seasoned in the governance of human affairs, it is comforting to see that the Chilean youth, by contrast, convinced that without intellectual energy there is neither health, nor urbanity, nor glory, nor prosperity, nor civilization; persuaded that the "sublime delights of the intelligence constitute the noblest power of man, and raise him up to the throne of truth on the strength of talent," they rush to seek out that energy, venerating the men who lit the beacon of reason and morality, to save us from the political storm and lead us safely to the port of peace and prosperity. It is an eminently laudable, patriotic act that a spontaneous association of youths who, driven by such grand motives, "without guidance," as Mr. Lastarria notes, "drawing only on sheer valor, are congregating to educate [them]selves and to educate with [their] labors; [they] who, it seems to me, have said in Chile to learned men that that should have been practiced some time ago, meeting to communicate and to draw up a plan of attack against social vices, to make [them]selves worthy of the independence that the heroes of 1810 bequeathed us and paid for in blood; gathering around that democracy that miraculously had been enthroned here, but on a throne whose base was eaten away by ignorance and which buckled at the slightest puff of the passions, and virtually collapses, leaving in its ruin our most cherished hopes." What educated men have not in fact done, what the youth of Santiago has just done, to the greatest glory for themselves and the greatest hopes for the future, should serve as a stimulus, lest the felicitous impulse thus given to the cultivation and diffusion of knowledge stall on this point. The propagation of primary education throughout the Republic, the progressive improvement in the scientific education system, the establishment of private agencies that promote these useful ends, and lastly, that of a National Academy to serve as the copestone of the majestic edifice of civilization, should be the focus of the government's attention and act as an incentive to individual efforts. . . .

After this sincere and spontaneous support from such heights, after this generous approval of our literary venture, which was presented as an example to government action and that of private individuals, the distinguished writer continued transcribing and commenting lauditorily on those passages of our address that involved the contradiction and the respectful assault on outdated ideas and prevailing concerns among the men of letters that then shaped opinion.

Immediately the Valparaíso *El Mercurio* on the 22nd reprinted the *El Museo* article, and as if to present the nascent literary movement from a new point of view, Sarmiento devoted that day's editorial to refuting this opinion: that, just as in politics there is a legislative body, there ought to be a body of scholars that legislates linguistic matters, establishing laws to which the people's speech ought to be adapted. After the writer demonstrated, among other facts, that people are the ones who shape languages, and that writers should not busy themselves with forms before ideas, that they might have a literature that represented society, he exclaimed:

"See here! Here we have countries like those of South America, which lack for literature, science, art and culture, just recently learning the basics of knowledge, and already they have ambitions to develop a polished and correct style, which can only be the flower of a mature and complete civilization! And when civilized nations disassemble all their scaffolding to build other new ones, whose forms are not yet plain to them, here we are, clinging to the old forms of a language exhumed yesterday amidst the rubble of political and religious despotism, and newly returned to the life of modern nations, to freedom and progress!"

And then, agreeing that the Argentinian writers, as he said, were turning Spanish into a Gallic dialect, he added:

> But these literati have written more verses, the true manifestation of literature, than tears have fallen over that sad country; and we with all the consolations of peace, with the profound study of admirable models, with the possession of our pure language, we have not been able to do a single one; we seem para-

lyzed with eyes to see, and sound judgment to criticize and to admire with our mouths open what others do, yet without the breath or ability to lift a finger to imitate them. To what could one attribute such a phenomenon? To the soul-chilling weather? To the imagination-dulling atmosphere? Now there's a fine solution! . . . That is not it, it is the perversity of education that is happening, it is in the influence of the grammarians and the respect for the admirable models, the fear of violating the rules, that has caused the Chileans' imagination to seize up, which causes them to squander their beautiful dispositions and generous spirits. There is no spontaneity, there is a prison guarded by inflexible culteranismo* at the door and sparing no blows of his rifle butt on the poor devil who fails to report to him in fine fettle. But change studies, and instead of focusing on forms, on the purity of words, on the roundedness of phrasing, on what Cervantes or fray Luis de León said, acquire ideas, from whatever source, nourish your thought with the thoughts of the great luminaries of the day; and when you feel that your ideas in turn are awakening, cast your inquisitive gazes over our country, over the people, the customs, the institutions, the current needs, and then write lovingly, courageously, what is within your power to do so, whatever you please, for it will be good in content, though the form be nonstandard; it will be impassioned, though betimes incorrect; it will please the reader, though it infuriate Garcilaso. . . . As far as we are concerned, if the law of ostracism were in force in our democracy, in time we would have requested the exile of a great writer living here in this country, for no other reason than being excessive and having exceeded what our nascent civilization requires in the arcana of the language, and having given a taste to our youth for study of the externals of thought, and of the forms in which it is evolving in our language, to the detriment of ideas and of true education. . . . †

* A highly Latinate, metaphorical style using tortured syntax and recherché images, common at the end of the sixteenth century and beginning of the seventeenth. Its maximum practitioner was the Spaniard Luis de Góngora (1561–1627). Sarmiento uses the term somewhat broadly to denote contemporary Chilean writers' pretensions to refinement. —Trans.

† Mark well that what Sarmiento indicated in this passage as the cause of our literary impotence was the misdirection of our education, which had made us slaves to

Sarmiento broached a subject that we had only insinuated in our address. We had maintained that Spanish literature was not ours, nor should it be, but we had recommended the study of the language, since it is a valuable tool that we already possessed and that we could use and perfect, but without speaking of that vice called purism that motivated us in the perverse inclinations of our studies.

routine school rules, binding freedom of thought to inflexible forms and to artificial conformities against which he could not transgress without peril. This was the fact that struck the foreign literati who arrived in the country in 1839 and 1840, that the educated youth, who represented the men of letters, did not have a liberal, to say nothing of democratic, education, and who turned writing all their literature into being loyal custodians of purity, and dauntless admirers of the Spanish classics, taking Gómez de Hermosilla as their ideal author, whose narrow judgment was gospel, almost a dogma, for them.

If this was the fact, according to the testimony of impartial witnesses of the day, who raised their voices to fight it; if our efforts in teaching since 1837 were aimed at reacting against that fact, and we censured it in our 1842 address as antithetical to our democratic progress and to our literary future, establishing that: we did not have an education system, that the methods suffered from mistakes and flaws unworthy of the era, for which we were lacking full knowledge and motivation; that Spanish literature was not ours, nor did we have anything to gain from it; that we should found our literature on the independence of spirit, scorning foolish criticism, whose chains enslaved our understanding; and that we should learn to think of modern authors, to study philosophically our civic responsibility and be able to represent it in a national, popular literature, taking truth as our currency and human nature as our oracle; if, moreover, then, as now, we had evidence that that universally noted fact was the result of the teaching that don Andrés Bello performed since 1833, since we had been his disciples; how could we not counter with our testimony in 1871 our friend Vicuña Mackenna's assertion that Mora truly had authored this *intellectual counterrevolution?*

It is known that Vicuña Mackenna had said in one of his *Cartas del Guadalete* ["Letters from the Guadalete"] that from 1840 to 1845 everything was Spanish in intellectual matters, education, books, theater; that Mora was the one responsible for this species of *intellectual counterrevolution*, imposing Nebrija and Hermosilla on us as our sovereigns, after having dethroned the Bourbons; and that their disappearance is owed to the *literary revolution* begun by the illustrious Bello. We find fault with this assertion for its inexactitude, and history bears out our claim that the emancipation and reform of education had begun with Lozier and his disciples, with Mora and his, and that that literary revolution attributed to Mr. Bello, the intellectual emancipation movement, had begun its decline starting in 1833 with the latter's influence in our classrooms.

But here the historian who has written the most on the 1842 literary movement, always omitting our efforts, our initiative, and passing over our name, don M.L.

But Sarmiento was not writing thus out of caprice, letting himself be carried away in *his adventurous education to be a heretic in literature, politics, and religion*, nor did he declare that it was folly to study the national language, as Mr. Amunátegui alleges, in his *Juicio de las poesías de Sanfuentes* ["Judgment of Sanfuentes's Poetry"], inserted in a work awarded a prize by the School of Philosophy and Humanities in 1859. Nor did he attribute a

Amunátegui, steps forward to correct us; and to do us such a great honor, applauding this writing generously and kindly, implies to us literally that we have charged "a thinker of the stature of Bello with having assumed the role of despot of a *reaction intended to strengthen and reestablish the intellectual regime of the Spanish colonies*." We have not committed such an affront to the memory of the wise teacher, and we believe with Mr. Amunátegui that such an intention would have flown in the face of the most irresistible and imperative drifts of Mr. Bello's spirit, that that had been against the grain of his nature. What is more, we did not even commit this affront to the conservative dictatorship of the time, which Mr. Bello served. The only matter we have established is what the facts confirm, to wit, that in 1830 the reform of our education begun previously, ground to a halt, that the teaching of Spanish literature and Roman law under Mr. Bello's authority starting in 1834 turned out rhetoricians instead of literati, and casuists instead of jurists, and chapter XI of these *Memoirs* provides the explanation for this phenomenon, in our judgment, to determine historically, without incriminating Mr. Bello, whose progressive spirit we acknowledge, what sway his teaching held against the emancipation of our thought. Twixt this and what is imputed to us, to correct us, there is an enormous difference.

And how has Mr. Amunátegui contradicted that the fact that the Argentine writers of 1842 attest to it, and that he himself has acknowledged it in other writings, is not the work of the influence that Mr. Bello had in his teachings during the dictatorship? Has he proven that this fact was the work of Mora, as Vicuña Mackenna alleged, or that it stemmed from the Instituto Nacional's teaching? No: reasoning falsely that we have offended the memory of the teacher, imagining him to be reactionary and determined *to reestablish the Colony's intellectual regime*, he sings us the teacher's praises for the hundredth time, and proceeds to provide the following proofs:

1st. "That Mora was more superficial and Bello more profound in his teaching; that both and several others strove to emancipate us from ignorance and from the concerns of the *old regime*; for it would have been impossible for a single man to take on such an arduous and extraordinary labor." Leaving out the parallel between the two teachers, which is entirely arbitrary, and recognizing their service, like all those who have worked to educate us, all that does not prove that teaching Spanish literature and Roman law, as Mr. Bello did, tends to emancipate us from the *ancien regime*, that is to say, of the regime of absolute power and the incompetence of man and society: if this had been the case, their disciples would not have been essentially conservative, and would not have presented, as men of letters, the phenomenon to which we and the Argentine writers attest.

too-profound survey of the language to our poetic impotence, nor did he wish to exile don Andrés Bello *for being a great connoisseur of the Spanish language*, as Dr. Valderrama alleges in his interesting *Bosquejo histórico de la poesía chilena* ["Historical Outline of Chilean Poetry"], a memoir submitted to the University in its formal session in January 1866. It is necessary to rectify these errors, which appear in this official work, doubtlessly because their authors had a share, eighteen and twenty-four years later, in the passions that shook the grammarians in 1842, or because they did not see the many declarations that the editor of *El Mercurio* made, mostly in his 5 June editorial, establishing categorically that what he was attacking was not the study of the language, but the pretension to link thought to form; that he accused us of not having poetry, not due to *incompetence*, but due to the *harmful*

2nd. "That Bello was a foreigner and poor, modest and forbearing, and that he was the target of the most virulent and unjustified attacks." Mr. Amunátegui paints Bello for us in a sorry situation, one that would heighten his distinction as a teacher of youth, if, fighting against such disadvantages, he had reacted against the old regime and given a liberal teaching that freed the students from the errors and the reaction that bolstered the dictatorship in that era. But he forgets that, though foreign, poor and modest, he was the servant, the philosopher, the *prompter*, as they called him, of that dictatorship; that therefore the oppressed attacked him, like they attacked the dictator and his underlings, without those attacks offending them, nor did they lessen their power and domination in the slightest. He forgets also that Mr. Bello's same personal circumstances forced him to not teach contrary to the political interests he served, and those circumstances, far from proving that the fact of our literary underdevelopment was not the offspring of his teaching, confirm the truth that Mr. Amunátegui intends to rectify.

3rd. Finally, our rectifier makes plain that Bello was an experimental philosopher, that he had completed his education in England, alongside illustrious teachers; he copies for us the articles he wrote in *El Araucano* to promote moral instillment in the nation, through education, to advocate for the organization of primary education, for its expansion, for the study of natural history and sciences, etc. We join in his praise, and all the teacher's works, with which we already were acquainted, as well as his subsequent efforts for our intellectual progress, of which we have given testimony in the article we wrote for the book that the Academy of Fine Arts devoted to his memory, render him venerable to us and clinch our gratitude. But in no way do those grand services prove that his influence as a teacher during the dictatorship would not have triggered the counterrevolution that reigned in those years; Mr. Amunátegui himself contributes to confirming this fact by recalling the polemic that Mr. Bello engaged in against the illustrious reformer Infante, when he imposed the study of Roman law upon us, and grew determined to perfect that of Latin, studies that could have been worthy of the acclaim Mr. Amunátegui offers him, but to us they have never been of use as tools of progress.

trends in our education, and that it was somewhat disloyal and *quite coarse to imply* that when one indulged in the waggishness to speak of the ostracism of the director of those harmful studies, *that he had really wanted to rid himself of a great writer, for whom personally he had only respect and gratitude.*

In fact, Sarmiento had not written that out of caprice, nor out of hatred of the language in which he wrote and which he then studied with interest, but rather having recommended in an editorial the *Ejercicios populares de la lengua castellana* ["Popular Exercises in the Spanish Language"], which *El Mercurio* began to publish, and which we think was the work of don Pedro Fernández Garfias, in which appeared a catalogue of words in the way in which we were using them faultily, and the way in which they ought to be corrected, one of our grammarians addressed an article to him, asking for him to abstain from producing publications of that ilk, *before he wound up spreading abroad a very base impression of our education*, and accusing the *Ejercicios* of gross and unforgivable mistakes and of downright foolishness, all in the understanding that they were Sarmiento's work. A few days later, the same editorialist renewed his charge against the *Ejercicios*, upbraiding the Argentinian writers for their ignorance of the admirable models of *our rich literature* (the Spanish), charging them with having caused the language to degenerate into a *Frenchified Spanish*, and hailing *licentious-romantic freedom* as *the urge for novelty*, or by exempting themselves from the work of studying the language, and defending the theory that it fell to the grammarians to assume the dictatorship of language matters, a matter referred to in the article Sarmiento published when transcribing the *El Museo* piece on our address.

In those attacks our educational distemper appeared to be a burning issue, and made us loath to endorse any innovation. We withdrew into the stronghold of an overzealous nationalism, like Spain of yore, from whom we did not wish to part company, making her literary glories our own, however much we had freed ourselves from her political sway; at the same time we rejected our fellow Spanish Americans as foreigners, since they did not write Spanish purely. Purism, of which we considered ourselves loyal custodians, is a true vice that stirs one deeply, when the discipline of our intelligence imprisons us in a narrow horizon and instills in us a love of detail; and it inflames the passions all the more when the one writing has no independence of spirit for thinking, for then the sterile activity of the intelligence reduces the whole literary art to forms that are artificial, mannered, and purely conformist to forms either societal or sectarian, as happened to those who had been educated under the harsh rule of the conservative dictatorship, which had ensured the success of the Spanish reaction in our country. All of them had been shocked at the revolutionary propositions in our address, but since these had been absolved by a great writer like García del Río, they consigned them to oblivion, and directed their ardent condemnation against the editor of *El Mercurio*, who indirectly appropriated them, blowing them out of proportion and taking their criticism to greater lengths, but without offending or insulting—we must acknowledge—as his adversaries insulted him.

The polemic continued this way for some time yet, after that editorial with which *El Mercurio* had run the transcription of the article from *El Museo de Ambas Américas*, and now fewer than twenty articles about it appeared in that newspaper, until Sarmiento put a stop to it in a truly ingenious way. He brought together in one article titled *La cuestión literaria* ["The Literary Matter"], using verbatim opinions by Larra on all contested points, and presented them as original, forming a summary of sorts of what *El Mercurio* had stated and supported. As no one noticed that that article had been cribbed, the editorial board at *El Mercurio* took it on itself to expose it, demonstrating that everything they had maintained was the same that the popular Spanish writer had opined in different writings, from which the summary had been excerpted. From this demonstration, they concluded that it was a fact that young Spain, through the words of that celebrated critic, has scorned, and stronger still, denied, the existence of a literary model in Spain. "Like us," they added, "and before us, he has pronounced a divorce with the past, and gotten across the need to set off on new roads to reach a regeneration of ideas and of literature; like us, he has declared the inability of a decrepit language to express new ideas; like us, in short, he has recommended freedom in language and literature, like in politics. Those who so prejudicially and scornfully attack our principles can rectify with this reading the clearest of his ideas and come away convinced that in language and literature we lag behind Spain by at least a century, and that they have set out to rehabilitate Spanish, at the same time when its legitimate speakers have forsaken this fruitless task."

Grammarians involved in the debate must have been surprised to notice that all that Sarmiento had told them were the selfsame thoughts of the Spanish writer they touted so highly, since they stopped arguing.

A few days after that 22 May editorial with which Sarmiento stirred up so many sensitive issues; and when our fellow countrymen remained always reserved, which the writers who are wont to cast a backward glance at that age still so carefully remain this very day on the topic of our inaugural address to the Literary Society, to applaud those who did not take part in the movement, and more than anything those who opposed it, another of the Argentinian émigrés registered his opinion about the address in Valparaíso's *Gaceta del Comercio*. In the 31 May issue, V. F. López published the following editorial, which we should reproduce, for it also has historical importance:

This is the first time that we have devoted ourselves to our task of writing for the public with complete satisfaction, for we do so under the influence of genuine ideas, and on a matter of importance that seems certain to hold seriously the country's attention.

A few days ago a writing entitled *Discurso de incorporación* ["Incorporation Address"] by J. V. Lastarria became available to the public, addressed to a literature society in Santiago, etc., and as much for the theories that predominate in this treatise as for the goal that inspired it, we think it a summons to initiate a major movement that will shake the national literature from its swaddling clothes and imprint upon it the *free and progressive impulse* literature has in Europe and in some other parts of this continent as well.

The publication of Mr. Lastarria's address is in this Republic something more than the printing of a writing. We classify it as a *social event*, without seeking to discount in the least the high praise these words imply.

This address is the first voice the new generation has raised; that generation to whom time and the necessary intensity of things have given different principles from the ones their fathers had, and which has witnessed spectacles in the formative years that the latter did not. In this work is manifested the awareness that the youth of today are called to a new task, a silent but productive assignment, one that is solid but lacking in brilliance; to study, in short, which is the slow and peaceful route that lead nations that are traveling toward *education* and *democracy*. Mr. Lastarria is the first among the young Chileans who with his ideas and studies has raised the issues that ought occupy national thought: and he has raised them beautifully and clearly; but let us state frankly that we might have wished to see more depth to his address, in order to extrapolate from society the causes and laws of intellectual development in this country. We should have liked to have seen him rise to the heights of his intelligence and stylistic graces, and get to the bottom of the nation's past, to root out in them the progressions in ideas, interests and customs, and to explain to us in his speech the new needs that the Society in Santiago have produced, through the successive development of national history, thus clarifying the causes that in the present situation make him and the youth think and do things that before now were not done. It is to be hoped that Mr. Lastarria do this from here on, and that he not distance the light of his intelligence from these matters, which are vital in the current state of civilization. We have seen that the author conceives of how very necessary it is to not let go of the chain that links the past to the present, for if it were let go, we would wind up losing our way in the vast breadth of Earth. Nonetheless, we do not think as he does, that the anarchy he so bemoans and which he sees as a barren age, an aberration, has not contributed at all to shaping national thought and to nurturing the seeds from which today he himself and those in his circle show the fruits. We should have liked to have seen him explain how it is that we arrived at the present developments, proceeding through previous situations, for attributing the current state of affairs, as the author does, to magic and luck strike us as unbecoming to his pure philosophical talent.

The young writer begins by depicting his situation upon finding himself called to head the development of that germ of science and knowledge that was founded in his country under the name Sociedad de Literatura ["Literature Society"]. He seems possessed by the idea that what appears here is a fertile novelty; and that this novelty is the product of the law of social progress, which has brought *new science* to the fore in the history of humankind: that science, which belongs to our century, is called *philosophy of history*, and consists of connecting *what is to what will be.*

It is a joy for us to be able to place Mr. Lastarria's words side by side with those of another young Spanish American in a perfectly identical situation to the one that prompted the speech in question. They are: "Could we not know why and for what end we have joined the revolutionary movement? I am of a mind that advancing would be of no account if we did not ascertain whence we came and where we are going. Here you have, then, our revolution in the presence of philosophy, which obstructs it with its eternal *why* and *what for?*" That is what Mr. Lastarria says as well to his fellow citizens. That is the important matter that this young man presents, for the national spirit to work on, enveloped in the most beautiful stylistic forms. His writing is the first step taken in issues of great importance; it is like the first word a child utters with his beautiful and comical lips, eliciting a jubilant smile on his mother's face. The country ought to have smiled with delight upon hearing the young writer's words.

One could scarcely provide a more consoling and holy spectacle in the thinking man's eyes than the constant confirmation by the history of humankind of those truths that great men impart, truths that first are presented to us like a handful of ideas collected in a book, and as time passes, become stable and divine laws; these ideas from time to time fall on a nation, like baptismal water on a new convert's forehead, to open the doors to them onto an immortal posterity, and to implant the laws of the spirit over the laws of matter. When Leibnitz said: "The present, child of the past, is pregnant with the future," he could have also added: "I have handed down the fundamental code of humankind." His words are repeated today by the movement of the entire world, which perhaps does not recall them, but acts in accordance with them. The new generations are on a never-ending pilgrimage toward the future, because they are pregnant with it, and are traveling a path that for stretches widens, and new men, races and nations are scattered over it, each in their turn. The time has come too for us Spanish Americans to take our place in the ranks of civilization; and Mr. Lastarria's address is ample proof.

But to consider this writing in the best light, we have to turn our gaze to the background of our situation, to examine the meaning of our history, the development of our ideas, foregone situations through which we have passed; to confront all this with the speech we are concerned with here and to express our definitive judgment on it. We shall do this under the following title: *Cuestiones filológicas suscitadas por el discurso del señor Lastarria* ["Philological Issues Raised by Mr. Lastarria's Address"].

In *Cuestiones filológicas* ["Philological Issues"], López begins by filling the lacuna he noticed in our address, surveying rapidly but enraptured and with sound judgment, European influences on Spanish America, to unearth the laws of our intellectual development; as he vividly traces the importance of our revolution, he laments that we had declared that great age in our history the *age of anarchy*. Yet we had not committed such a sin, and what gave rise to this criticism was a certain amphibologia* in the passage

---

* A grammatical ambivalence or ambiguity. —Trans.

in which we alluded to the end of the dictatorship and the civil war, when we had thought we had made our idea clear in stating that *anarchy had spread its dreadful wings and saved the Andes*, to mean that the civil war had broken out over on the other side after 1837,* which in no way were we confusing with the glorious South American epic.

Another lesser mind led the critic to find that we were making a certain poorly considered separation of *wealth* and *education*. He did not know that, following the example of Napoleonic despotism, the despotism that ruled over us in Chile had formed a treacherous current of opinion supporting the development of material interests and the oligarchy of wealth, and naturally he did not understand that we were advocating moral and intellectual progress when we said that in that type of development, individual freedoms were not won, and that the government that sought its support in it would be forever tottering as long as it did not understand that democracy needs additional support, that of education.

The allusion we were making to the indifference with which *men of learning* had viewed our conviction to accomplish through association the regeneration of ideas and educational reform, motivated López to write brilliant pages wisely explaining the historical antecedents leading to the advent of that society, and excusing our fathers for not having done a bit more, for he felt our allusion incriminated the founders of our independence. He was not aware of the particular fact to which we were alluding, and thought we had committed that unjust error by having omitted historical study, the lack for which he reproached us. By way of explanation of this reproach, among other reasons, he said: "The ideas from which literature draws its sustenance are of two kinds: progressive, new, revolutionary; and traditional, old, retrogressive. Currently, there is a battle on in Europe that proves this, as there is and has been here, though on an infinitely smaller scale. Then in literature there are two camps; if one of them is progressive and the other is not, one of the two is not socialist, and not being socialist, cannot attain Mr. Lastarria's aspirations, which are to have them work for the utility of the country. Here we must serve the country by making one of the literary trends triumph over the other, the progressive over the retrogressive. There is no happy medium. That is the incontrovertible truth we penned in one of our previous articles written to note the lack of social and historical antecedents in the address, Chilean antecedents, not *Greek, Roman, Dantesque*, as they would have it that I said. But if they had explained to us the antecedents and allowed our literary needs to be extracted from them, we would have known which was in our opinion the true social literature."

* I.e., in Argentina; may also refer to civil disorder in Bolivia. —Ed.

The distinguished critic was forgetting that we did not set out to deal with the issue from that point of view, and that it was enough for us to indicate to the youth that we had no literary antecedents, nor models to follow, that our literature remained to be developed, that it should be the expression of our democratic society, when this had a life of its own, and that it should have truth for its currency, human nature for its oracle, the independence of the spirit for a foundation, in order to think and produce freely and not make a standard of judgment of the rules, which before were seen as unchangeable and holy.

In another article in the *Gaceta* on 17 June, the recommendation we made about the study of the Spanish language met with a frontal assault. It was argued that Spanish was a tool that we had the good fortune to receive in our social infancy, a tool already fashioned by the progress of reason, and which we could adapt to fit all forms that thereafter our national factions would take. The writer believed he spotted a contradiction between this idea and the repudiation we made of Spanish literature, for the critic assumed that literature is style, and that style is the same thing as language, unaware that the literature of an age can be composed of many different styles, and that since these are the particular ways that writers have of manifesting their thought, language is the tool that is used to represent their way of thinking and producing. "We do not believe," stated the critic, in reply to others, "that those profound and beautiful words with which Mr. Lastarria repudiates the alliance of our nascent and future literature with the old Spanish literature, can be put forward to us as an objection. Few are the times South America has been so truthfully and penetratingly written about, but despite this we have deliberately refused to see in these words an objection to our previous observations, for quite soon we will find others that to our mind contradict them. . . . But at the same time he tells us that our address augurs the progress of reason. We know not how to combine these two mutually exclusive proposals, for we think that if it is true that Spanish literature is retrogressive and antisocial, it is important that that address, which is not only vocabulary but style and literature also, herald the progress of reason; and we will add further that if the former is true, the Spanish language certainly has not worked any of the modern sciences with its own tools; mathematics, politics, philosophy, industry, chemistry, etc., cannot include among its vocabulary any words or colloquialisms that satisfy them; the Spanish language has not had the least part in recent words that all these sciences have newly reformulated."

XVII

To understand the historical character we attribute to the address and the judgments of it the Argentinian authors made, we must take into account the antecedents of that moment, which we have recorded by describing in broad strokes the situation in which we were placed by the dictatorship, education and the principles that men of letters who formed opinion had been heir to, and the concerns and political interests that the ruling class, the oligarchy, represented.

Let those who wish to judge that historical moment contemplate the impression that ideas like those of the editor of *El Mercurio*, which we have reprinted before, and like the following, spoken in a lordly tone, would make on such men: "We think this address a summons to initiate a major movement that will shake the national literature from its swaddling clothes and imprint upon it a *free* and *progressive* impulse." "We classify it as a *social event*." "The author is the first of the young Chileans to raise issues that ought occupy national thought." "Here it is necessary to serve the country by making one literary trend triumph over the other, the progressive over the retrogressive." "We believe that if Spanish literature is retrogressive and antisocial, it is impossible that *speech* herald the *progress of reason,* and we add further that the Spanish language has not shaped any of the modern sciences." "How will we achieve a thoroughly Spanish and national expression in literature? . . . By using our time to create a language that represents it and not by reducing ourselves to imitating the style of writers who had nothing to do with the order of ideas that prevail amongst us and that hold great allure for us." We omitted many other passages that were somewhat more offensive in those days, such as this one: "We feel we have laid the groundwork of that address and of that Society in a clear and genuine manner, without needing to have written *volumes* on the Greeks and Romans and other such *nonsense* as that." And this other one: "Here is where youth has to run up against a formidable obstacle, to wit: the ideas, customs and traditions *harmful to the old education.*" These quotes suffice to appreciate the outburst that these ideas produced in the servants of the Spanish reaction, which was victorious in our society and in the political order; likewise in the jurists and rhetoricians that dreamed of having a *national literature*, and that, believing they had saved the language of Castile from the calamity of Spanish domination in South America, they could not but take fright at such literary developments.

This, to say nothing of the *Revista de Valparaíso* having had a hand in subduing the prevailing spirit by publishing in May an article on López, on *classicism and romanticism*, at which many years later both Amunátegui* would still become indignant; and by reprinting in July an article on Alberdi,[†] entitled *Algunas vistas sobre la literatura sudamericana* ["Some Views of South American Literature"], in which ideas like the following slip out: "Let us then cast some reflections on the law that they wish to impose on us in literature. This law is the one that generally is characterized today by the title of Mechanics, for comprising all the material and external conditions of style, and which is, according to M. de Yac, the one with least force in constituting a democratic literature; its role is practically nil in the age in which each literature is making its first national appearance, as M. Nisard repeatedly observes in remarks gleaned from the history of all the primitive literatures, etc.; it is a law by which Homer, Shakespeare, and Dante would be defeated in a literary competition by a fifteen-year-old student of rhetoric. Let us leave Spanish American talents to their own devices...."

Argentinian writers, it is true, made *no bones of their superiority*; but it is not accurate to state that they treated us disdainfully or with insulting provocations. If the reactionaries felt insulted in their political and social beliefs, and in their literary concerns, those of the liberal opinion, not even the young liberals, never took umbrage. In the literary movement the Literary Society originated, two parties were designed analogous to the literary ones, and resultantly it is not accurate to state that the movement had only one center, as Mr. I. Errázuriz asserts in his *Historia*. Errázuriz is also the author of the concepts we have just rectified. "In the realm of production and of the most important studies," states this historian, "the Venezuelan Andrés Bello, critic, humanist, poet, intellectual, and educator of the highest order, was the center of a movement active during the early years of General Bulnes' administration. . . . Throughout this entire movement, which took place within known limits and *under the watchful eye of a leader* who loved letters and sciences, but who also was a heartfelt adherent to the established political order, there was seemingly no danger or cause for alarm in the eyes of the rulers. . . . What did it matter to the system of government that Portales founded and that Montt was destined to further and formulate legislatively, what did it matter to the prevailing political code, what did it matter to the aggregate of beliefs and traditions on which the

---

* Miguel Luis Amunátegui Aldunate (1828–1888) and Gregorio Víctor Amunátegui Aldunate (1830–1898), distinguished writers, teachers, and journalists. Both were products of the Instituto. —Ed.

† Juan Bautista Alberdi (1814–1886), Argentine statesman and philosopher, architect of the Argentine Constitution of 1853. —Ed.

power of the State and that of the Church rested, that the young adepts of the budding national literature should, in *El Semanario de Santiago* and in *El Crepúsculo*, pitch battles in their own ranks between the classicals and the romantics, and that they should set out stepping lively in the footsteps of Horace and Victor Hugo? . . ."

None of this is accurate. Mr. Bello no longer conducts the private classes he held during the age of the dictatorship, for he had given up teaching the old courses five years previously, courses in which he had educated the youths that now are included among the front ranks; and he was far from being the center of the literary movement and of having it under his watchful eye as leader, since on the one hand, he had expressed a somewhat poor impression the address with which we began that movement made on him, and on the other, being scandalized by the Argentinians' ideas, he influenced the movement to speak for the founding of *El Semanario* in a way that later we will relate, and spurred its classical disciples to go against the torrential current of the literary revolution. As for how much it mattered to the administration and to the beliefs and traditions of the State and the Church that the youths were pitching battles between classicals and romantics, the demise of *El Crepúsculo* illustrates the answer clearly, an episode we will recall in its proper place.*

Those beliefs and traditions, to which Mr. Bello, the administration, and the conservatives belonged, were outside of the literary movement we were championing and spearheading, and formed the crux of one of the literary parties, the strongest one, the prevailing one, for the other, in which the Argentinian émigrés participated, was just emerging and stood only for new ideas that were neither understood nor appealing, and which even today fight to make room for themselves.

The battle lines between the two parties were drawn in all arenas: in literary gatherings, in coteries, in the theater, for the literary question was the event of the day, and it was argued whether we had literature and writers, whether Spanish literature was ours, and all the rest, the *cult of beauty* of Mr. Bello's school glutting its fury against every word and phrase from the Argentinian writers, with raillery that left far in its wake that which the author of the *Art of Speaking* employed against Balbuena's Bernardo. In the salons frequented by the youths, much music, art, and literature were done,

---

* Will it be taken as an insult to Mr. Bello that we assert that he was neither the *center* nor the *leader* of the 1842 literary movement, as Mr. Errázuriz alleges him to be? We would be afraid to oblige Mr. Amunátegui with our agreement to write two more columns in *La República* to be persuaded that what he states to us personally is not true and that we attest with the facts and impartial testimonies we cited.

as the French say; the fair sex enthused over poetry, and their enthusiasm encouraged the Chilean youth to compete in brilliance and wit with the Argentinians, to which occurred in no small measure what the Cat endured in the Catfight,* for the reason Lope de Vega† offers when he exclaims:

> ¡Oh, cuánto puede un gato forastero,
> Y más siendo galán y bien hablado,
> De pelo rizo y garbo ensortijado!
> Siempre las novedades son gustosas,
> No hay que fiar de gatas melindrosas . . .

> Oh, the power of a strange cat,
> Greater still if gallant and well spoken,
> With dashing, curly wavy hair!
> Novelties are forever a delight,
> One must not trust the finicky tabbies . . .

From times previous to these exciting moments, as we said, the Argentinians, using the familiar form of address, uninhibitedly vented their opinions on the wretched state of our literary education, on the backwardness of our top writers, on the sway that the habits, traditions, and feelings of old colonial life still held. They, who were coming from the battlefields, from the tremendous clash of ideas and swords in which the River Plata was engaged, had just observed, as onlookers and even as participants, the electoral war of 1841, and had seen as a curiosity characteristic of the burning debates over language and grammatical purity, which, next to the most insolent diatribes and repugnant offenses, of which *Guerra a la Tiranía* ["War On Tyranny"] and *El Porvenir* ["The Future"] had fanned the flames. These were the newspapers that supported the conservative candidacy for President of the Republic, under the leadership of writers like Vallejo, Tocornal, and Ramírez. It was somewhat inexplicable to them, on account of the ridiculousness of this press disdaining and fighting their liberal adversaries for not writing Spanish well. What would they say today upon beholding the progress in which, after thirty-five years, this method has made, a method that the conservative press uses to discuss principles!

---

*   Possibly a reference to Bello's fondness for cats. —Ed.

†   Lope Félix de Vega Carpio (1562–1635), renowned Spanish poet and playwright. —Ed.

The rather farcical frankness of those men of war had incited the enmity of all proponents of *Order*; and since the latter were those who shaped and led opinion, there soon developed a wholesale aversion to the Argentinians apropos of the literary debate, and the literature question assumed the proportions of a national issue, which spared the author of the address, who had sparked the movement, the reproof with which those who commended and generalized his ideas were saddling him.

The Argentinians, though, were quite at home in society, though they often went boldly against the grain; for, as always happens with the odium of one nation for another, individuals escape the aversion that weighs upon the whole. Their education, the ease and elegance of their ways, and their habitual liberality, which contrasted with the national formality, lent their personal dealings a certain charm; frequently this congeniality was expressed by saying in praise of someone that *he did not seem Cuyan.**

The literary issue turned into one of nationality. Due to the belief that Chilean honor would be offended were the Argentinians to support the reform begun by the author of these *Memoirs*, and in supporting it, they were to reprove as a sign of backwardness the retrogressive ideas that reigned in the intellectual order, an aspiration emerged: to show that there was talent in Chile and that her men of letters could compete with its detractors. This hope, which appealed to patriotism, aided us and the few youths who followed up on our initiative for other reasons and for other ends, for it had been some time since we had planned to do a literary publication, to prove neither talent nor literature, but to continue our movement and to complete our new education.

XVIII

The organization of the Literary Society and the stir the inaugural address caused, as well as the debate that rages on, facilitated the fulfillment of our aims; and of course we devoted ourselves to preparing the

---

* Cuyo is an Andean region of Argentina, and here is used synecdochically to stand for the country. —Trans.

publication of a *literary weekly*, to bring to light the compositions that the Society deemed most worthy, and above all to insert translations done with the purpose of propagating new ideas and fomenting good taste and the cultivation of art. We relied on the cooperation of Nuñez, who took it on himself to exploit contemporary French literature, and that of Francisco Bello,[†] who would introduce English literature, with which he was quite familiar. Both men shared our literary ideas and our hopes, above all the latter man, with whom we had been close since years prior, having done our law studies which his father had supervised, and canonical law, which we took on privately through a Devoti compendium written in Latin, since in the years around 1836 at the Instituto Nacional, the *Enquiridion*[*] which served as our text, or syllabus rather, had seemed extremely deficient and flawed.

Francisco Bello had an eminently British classical education, and used to study Spanish literature, not with the love and veneration that our other peers professed, but with a certain detachment born of the difference of ideas and biases between the civilizations represented by it and English literature. Francisco was a lymphatic, almost consumptive young man, pale and dull in countenance, beautified by jet-black hair and by large ebony eyes, whose melancholy revealed that he dreamed of his early death. He was unassuming and cold, took no part in political interests or ideas, spoke always in a low voice, joking melancholically as was his wont, a practice he enhanced with his acute perception of all deformity, and with his felicitous memory of the witticisms of the English and Latin writers. He had already written his Latin grammar as professor at the Instituto, and as such was forever lamenting that a Literary Society we professors at that institution had organized had been so short-lived; and he urged us to impart consistency to the youths whose education had been turned over to us. For this reason he had joined our project at *El Semanario*.

But one day Bello called us on behalf of his father to talk about that project. The interview with the teacher was long and of great mutual interest. This was the first time that he was taken into the 1842 literary movement, and he did it advising us that we not create an exclusive single-party newspaper with a single literary doctrine, for we should appear united, when our first duty was to avenge our literary honor, to demonstrate our collective intellectual progress and to affirm it; thus could the new movement that our address initiated be well served, without breeding distrust,

---

[*]   Not to be confused with Desiderius Erasmus's *Enchiridion militis christiani* (1503), eponymous example *par excellence* of the genre. —Ed.

[†]   Son of Andrés Bello. —Ed.

without alienating the support and cooperation of so many distinguished intellects; our labors and those of our fellow youths would not suffice to run the publication worthily, such that it rival *El Museo* and *Revista de Valparaíso*; and above all because a newspaper with literary leanings, under the circumstances, was accustomed to political dangers, and more than this, the danger that we could not manage and moderate youthful impetuousness, which perchance could stir up storms.

This last reason was ultimately confirmed two years later with the failure of *El Crepúsculo*; and at that time it stopped us dead in our tracks, and was a factor in our not pressing the discussion of the others, and in our resolving to follow Mr. Bello's counsel, for the very reason that what we most feared, what we had always sought to avoid, was jeopardizing, in the dangers of politics, our role in teaching and the reformist movement we wished to found. Indeed, we visualized instantly neutralizing the influence of the conservative writers that were his disciples, and that he, quite struck by the need to defend the national honor, proposing to him that we commit, suggesting that we also create an alliance with the most outstanding youths from the Instituto, a proposal he accepted without hesitation.

This was a very critical moment for us. For six years we had been tenaciously pursuing in our teaching a truly revolutionary plan against the dominant political doctrines, against the routines and concerns that guided youth's intellectual development by affixing it to the sentiment and the practices of the backward Spanish civilization, which we thought baneful to our democratic future, and against the literature that stands for that past. We had a true passion for this plan, which encourages us still, but then we understood that we could not carry it out by force, that we should do what we did later, battle head on, for we had no facts on which to base our judgment, since we took stock of our personal powerlessness, which would not have happened had our plan been the brainchild of a youthful hauteur.

Ah, if that had been the motive, better conditions and very promising happiness would have motivated us to do the opposite, and our faith in the grand future of Chile would have forsaken us a thousand times, faced with so many difficulties, so many contrasts, disappointments, sorrows, and poverty, as we have found in a society incapable of appreciating our efforts, and overridden by a powerful conservative spirit, which its ruling powers maintained at all costs. Even the writer's modest fame, which then we had reached, damaged our lawyering profession, which was not enough to live off, for it was said that we did not know law by understanding letters; just as later our fame as a heretic has deprived us of clientele, forcing us to seek out in industry and other occupations the work that our countrymen have denied us as penalty for our reform efforts.

What has befallen us is simply the fair punishment, the natural sanction, for having been false to the moral precept that dictates we first fulfill our duties to ourselves and our family before those we have to our country and to humanity. And for the same reason we resign ourselves to that law of our nature, we reject the penalty that, with neither the right nor plausible motive, our contemporaries wish to exact on us in omitting our name when alluding to the literary movement that we served at great cost, and when they speak of *El Semanario*, attributing it to those who are not due credit, perhaps because they assume and maintain erroneously the idea that that newspaper was the catalyst of that movement; the truth is that the paper came out later in support of the movement, in a certain sense, as betokened by the history of its origins that we are narrating. This history may seem long-winded, but to our way of thinking it is of great interest, as a war maneuver can be to military men who are permitted to submit their record of service.

Relying on Francisco Bello and José María Nuñez, with Juan N. Espejo and the cooperation of the other Literary Society youths, Mr. Bello associated us with Salvador Sanfuentes, Juan E. Ramírez, and M. A. Tocornal, and we requested and received the support of A. García Reyes, A. Varas, M. González, Manuel Talavera, and Joaquín Prieto Warnes, to whom we entrusted theater criticism. Talavera took it on himself to provide us the collaboration of J. J. Vallejo, who was residing in Copiapó and who at the time was publishing his ways and manners articles in Valparaíso's *El Mercurio*.

The editorial board was organized with the main writers, excluding collaborators, who later were Hermógenes de Irisarri, Jacinto Chacón, and A. Olavarrieta; it was agreed to meet once a week at the Instituto Nacional, having held the first meeting in the room that Núñez had there, and the others in Varas's.

The editorial board's first decision gave *El Semanario* the character of a general interest newspaper, and not exclusively literary, as we had proposed; it fell to us to oversee the publishing and assume responsibility before the law and the printer, therefore the newspaper's proprietorship was our lot. García Reyes worked with interest at helping us with the publishing.

El Semanario appeared on 14 July 1842, registering a number of subscriptions that did not cover its costs. López, who ended production that very month on the *Revista*, received him at the Valparaíso *Gaceta* and delivered harsh criticism of a shallow poem by Prieto Warnes in the first issue, entitled *Un suspiro y una flor* ["A Sigh and a Flower"]; and Sarmiento, in *El Mercurio*, hailed him loftily, regretting that it was stated in the prospectus that this daily was of passing interest, and concluding after lengthy considerations on the mission of Spanish American writers, with these words: "If all our youth were convinced of these humble truths, we would not see at every turn the scandal that our journalistic polemic provokes with the *irritation* that a new idea excites, and the insults and vexations that rain down upon whomever generated it, or whoever calls into question the truth of *certain doctrines* greeted by youth as inconclusive."

Sarmiento understood that the conservative youths that were a part of *El Semanario* were incensed by the new ideas that their compatriots had just put forth, apropos of our address to the Literary Society, and he went ahead and admonished them. But *El Semanario* ignored the admonition, publishing in their second issue an article by Sanfuentes on romanticism, in which vivid allusions were made to the ideas that López had published on the issue in the *Revista*. Sanfuentes reminded us in that article that the word romanticism had been much used in this country without anyone understanding what it really meant, and that at that time it was passé. He did not blindly pledge his allegiance to the flag of rigid classicism; but, demanding that the Romantic school not use its freedoms *unnecessarily*, condemning it whensoever it did not obey the customs of each age, each time, and that, instead of presenting us with faithful depictions of life, gave us freaks or prodigies, he criticized the dramatic works that were recommended as romantic, among them Victor Hugo's *Ruy Blas*.* "With romanticism in Chile," he would say, "what is happening is what has always happened and always shall with those writings full of bombastic phrases, but lacking utterly in common sense, phrases with which false merit frequently seeks to find the hard road of glory." Later he would add that the *servum pecus* of the Romantic school had been the same as that of the days of Horace, "for it is this scoundrel's destiny for life to never approach his models in the good, and to outstrip them always in the bad," as is bespoken by the overdrawn premises of some dramas, "and infinite other absurdities, which heap that many more insults upon morality, good taste and sound criticism." He concluded by praying for the passing of "the influence of the school that has threatened to invade everything and for them to replace it with a new one, neither classical nor romantic, nor as outlandishly free as that of Victor Hugo, nor as obsequiously slavish as that of La Harpe.†"

Two days after publishing this article in *El Semanario*, on 23 July, *El Mercurio* ran a *Carta a un amigo de Santiago* ["Letter to a Friend of Santiago"],

---

* Opening in 1838, the play is a hybrid of melodrama and political commentary. An 1872 revival featured Sarah Bernhardt. —Trans.

† Probably Jean-François de Laharpe (1739–1803), French poet and literary critic. —Ed.

written by Jotabeche, in which the latter laughed at romanticism, "at this fashion," he said, "that is the cheapest that they have sold us from Europe, with a port of call at San Andrés on the River Plata, where the national *intelligentsia* welcomed it with open arms," and adding other jibes at the Argentinian writers, he referred in these terms to López's writing: "Prepare to receive this sacrament of penance in reading the *Revista de Valparaíso* article on romanticism and classicism, and let me know if the Spanish in which it is written is the Spanish that we speak or some newly arrived Spanish; for hand to God! we have not been able to make head or tail of it, though to that end a committee of the garrulous was dedicated."

Such attacks were unjustifiable, not even in the interest of defending literary doctrines or language purity, for all in all they were naught but the violent outlets of the irritation brought about by our literary emancipation that we promoted, and which was supported with a certain disdainful pedantry by the River Plata writers. The two writers that led them were ambassadors of the old school, though the first was a disciple of Bello and the second of Mora, and though both men had differing characters and tendencies.

Sanfuentes, peace-loving and moderate by nature, was the reverse of Vallejo, who had a restless, protean and ardent spirit. The former had received a classical education that he broadened by studying with relish the works of the Latin, Spanish, and French writers, and with more fondness than inspiration, cultivating poetry; while the latter had done frivolous studies of the humanities in the Liceo, and had no other favorite book than the collection of articles by Larra, cultivating the genre that had brought this writer to fashion, a genre for which he had a vocation on account of his sharpness and wisdom, his natural good taste and jovial disposition. Both men were conservatives, but of a different stripe. Sanfuentes believed that *peluconismo*, or rather, the political system that rendered everything unto authority, had made his age, and that the country needed another progressive regime that made self-modifications in the democratic sense; he was on a course to be a sincere liberal politically, though he remained conservative literarily, though moderately so: meantime Vallejo, who in his first outing had come to serve in the Prieto administration, was a radical partisan of the omnipotence of authority, and thus had supported the conservative candidacy for the presidency, and was willing to support, as he did later, any strong government, though all political freedoms be relinquished, provided that they leave us the personal freedoms, which were the crux of all their liberalism, and provided it not be considered a personal freedom to think and write how he did not.

Both writers took as romanticism what to their eye was madness or folly, be it in thought or language; but actually they could not fail to be acquainted with the school that bore that name, nor could they sincerely believe that the fantastic, the absurd, and the bizarre in form and content were ailments unique to this school, for all of the above were found in the classicist school, as evidenced by the Grotesques of French literature depicted by Théophile Gautier, and the infinite examples found in the Spanish classics, beginning with the Histories of Bernardo del Carpio, of Judit, of the Cid Campeador, and several others, written by Manuel José Martín; and ending with certain miscarried labors that those writers ought to know intimately.*

So we state that they could not help but know the Romantic school, as much for the fact that Mr. Bello had begun to write his studies on Hugo, as attested by the imitation of The Harpies that *El Mercurio* had just published on 19 June, as for the fact that by those days the prologue the celebrated poet added to *Hernani*, a romantic drama, was quite common in our country.†

Hernani was staged here a few months later in a translation by don Rafael Minvielle, and is today admired in the Comédie Française; M. Pérrin just had these words to say about it: "A half century has passed over this, a most feverishly contested work at first, one which unleashed so many storms. Today it has entered the serene region of masterworks. It has in turn become a classic, for posterity has begun for it, and here it is halfway to its first centennial. Within fifty years, in the time of the glorious commemorative years, *Hernani* will be produced, like the Cid and the Horaces are produced, all three from a single family, brothers in the masculine nobility of their sentiments, brothers for the incomparable splendor of their language."

The author of that monument of the new school, in the aforementioned prologue stated:

> Romanticism, a term so often ill defined, well-considered is nothing but *liberalism* in literature, and this is its true definition. This truth is now understood, more or less, by all decent spirits, whose number is large; and soon, since the work is well underway, literary liberalism will be no less popular than political liberalism. Freedom in art, freedom in society, such is the twofold purpose toward which all honorable and logical souls should head with synchronized step; such is the double link

---

* Théophile Gautier (1811–1872), French Parnassian writer and literary critic. Bernardo del Carpio, ninth-century, semi-legendary Spanish heroic figure, comparable to El Cid, Rodrigo Díaz de Bivar. —Ed.

† "Hernani" premiered in 1830, causing a furious literary debate between classicists and romanticists. It was the inspiration for Verdi's "Ernani" (1844). —Ed.

that that will join, excepting very few intellects (who too will be enlightened), all the very strong and patient youth of today; youth, and at its head the flower of the foregoing generation with those wise elders who, after an initial moment of distrust and of examination, recognized that what their offspring are doing is a consequence of what they themselves did, and literary freedom is the child of political freedom. This is the century's principle and it will prevail. However much those *ultras* of all sorts, classicist or monarchist, assist in rebuilding a piece of the old regime, society and literature, the country's every advancement, every intellectual development, every step of freedom will cause all they have built up to fall. So definitely, their reaction efforts will have been useful. In revolution, all movement serves to gain ground. Truth and freedom have that excellent quality, for all that is done for them, or against them, is equally useful to them. After such lofty things our fathers accomplished and which we have seen, here we are broken out of the old social mold. How could we not break out of the old poetic mold as well? To a new nation, new art. . . . And the public wants this freedom as it should be, reconciling itself with the State's order and with art in literature. . . . Let the principle of freedom carry out its business, but let it do it well. In letters, as in society, we will have nothing of ceremony, nothing of anarchy: laws. Neither red heels nor red caps . . .*

That was essentially just what we had proclaimed, as did the Argentinian writers who backed us, while the national writers said nothing. Why are the latter now rising up against the former, attacking them as representatives of romanticism and taking all that is absurd as such? Could it be because they were explaining the new doctrines incorrectly? Honestly, neither he who writes these lines, nor the Argentinians, invoked, nor proclaimed, romanticism as our own: we took from it the basis of freedom, to affirm the independence of the spirit. But we invoked truth as our currency; as our oracle, human nature carefully observed and well understood, declaring that freedom was not licentiousness, and that if it was to free us from the narrow Scholastic rules, that it impose those of art, the rules of good taste. And this was indispensable within the logic of the idea that we adopted as a starting

---

* Reference is to the association of red with revolutionary and authoritarian causes. Rosas and the conservative-minded Federalists in Argentina would be the case in point for nineteenth-century Chileans. —Ed.

point: to wit, that literature, being the expression of society, for us could be neither Spanish nor French nor monarchical, nor classicist, but Chilean, South American, democratic, national, in the sense that its object was to represent the needs, interests, aspirations, and feelings of everyone; for it should not remove itself from the nation, nor become the instrument of the privileged classes: it should address the entire nation, represent it as a whole.

V. F. López, in his article in the *Revista*, had sought to trace the historical genealogy of romanticism, attempting to investigate philosophically its trends, its aims, its aspirations; but taking his inspiration from his French readings, he had, like his inspirers, stumbled upon the difficulties of the old language for expressing new ideas, exotic ideas that still had not been well studied, original principles that still had not been well defined, as happens with all sciences that have not entered their true evolution, with all theories that have not been proved by a long battery of observations. But all of this was far from being absurd, to the extreme of unsettling the peace of the classical writers, and of hurting the delicate feelings of writers who had no other distinction than that of molding the geniality of their spirit to the forms of a certain model. That could be unpleasant, shocking, for its novelty, and be far from the common sensibilities; but it was not fair to represent it as a collection of tasteless pieces dedicated to the execretion of those who did not understand it, as happened in those exciting moments.

It is indeed understood that at that juncture, when the literary issue had turned into a nationwide jealous row, that writing in the *Revista* had been jeered, and with it, romanticism, confusing under a single anathema the new literary school and the work of one of its adepts. But it is a wonder that twenty-four hours later, there would be repercussions from that impassioned outpouring on writers like Messrs. Amunátegui, who had taken part in the struggle, and who speak of López's article in Vallejo's biography, which they published in 1866, recalling it as *a curious event* in the short literary history of Chile, for: "It was," they state, "one of the first cases of *metaphysical imbroglios*, of which we later had to endure so many repeat performances, in which the *greatest platitudes* and even *idiocies*, artless and illogical, wanting in clarity and respect for grammatical rules, with hollow, high-flown phrasing that bring back to life a new breed of culteranismo, but one as unbearable as that of Góngora and his disciples."

To justify such ideas, these writers cite some passages from López's writing in which are noticed allegories in poor taste or dark ideas, alongside others that, read in good spirit, are not deserving of censure. But since we do not hazard to consider that they have judged them with narrow and backward-thinking criteria in literature, we would rather think they have formed their opinions under the influence of Sanfuentes's and Vallejo's writings, both men of which were in the struggle; for otherwise they would not have insisted on maintaining that an article like López's, which today is nothing more than a still-undigested essay on a new doctrine, is *in its entirety more senseless than the particulars they cite, a collection of heresies against fine language and sound reason*, and that its author stood out among the *corrupters of public taste*.

XIX

Vallejo's Letter was published in *El Mercurio* on 23 July, and though it did not contain condemnations as sharp as those we have just quoted from his biography, which was written a quarter century later, it produced a distressing impression on Sarmiento, the editor of that newspaper; but like Sanfuentes's writing, published in *El Semanario* on the 21st, coming from a loftier source, leaving aside that Letter, Sarmiento unleashed a firestorm against him in a series of articles written with the ardor and savage daring with which this remarkable writer has characterized his polemics.

In an article on the 25th he wrote: "We wish to know for what end was this "Romanticism" article written in *El Semanario*, and to see what sort of writings are applicable to that bit about 'full of bombastic phrases, but lacking utterly in common sense, phrases with which false merit frequently seeks to find the hard road of glory.'" On the 26th he praised López's writing, reproducing his ideas, expanding on them and explicating them with sound judgment, comparing them with those expressed by Sanfuentes; and he asked *El Semanario*, "Why could they not make head or tail of it? Because it was hard? Because either it was a web of falsehoods or else the Romanticism article that we criticized is trifling indeed." On the 27th he made room in his columns for a judicious installment that reproached the *Gaceta del Comercio* for its acerbic criticism of *El Semanario*'s first issue, and its attacks on the same article by Sanfuentes; but on the 28th he revisited the issue in an editorial, reiterating the *Revista* doctrines and encouraging *El Semanario* to discuss them, or to "give up those gestures of scorn with which they reply to everything, and that well serve the purpose of hiding presumptuous vanity, like the knowledge they do not deign to manifest. . . ."

On that same day Sanfuentes had replied in issue number three of *El Semanario* with an article mocking the *El Mercurio* attacks; the latter, ruled by an overexcitement that swelled in proportion to the agitation that it itself produced in the opinions it was fighting, published another more incendiary editorial on the 29th, from which we excerpt this paragraph:

> Granted that proverbs act as literary rules, we will declare that we have not forgotten that other one: *he who says what he wants to, hears what he does not want to.* So, just tell us then, for we are waiting to see where this abscess bursts. Contempt and disdain? Hah, that is our favorite dish! Reasonings, ideas, intelligence? We will analyze them. Language errors? So much the better, we will prove to them that in matters of the philosophy of language they do not know the half of it; that they do not have their own style, that they shall not ever have it, and that, as long as they seek to represent national literature, we shall not see a scintilla of thought, nor of spontaneity. It could be that once we have them all worked up, and the fury and vehemence of literary debate have subsided, we come in with the calm that truth imparts, to put in evidence the ways in which those works they call classics, and which are nothing but behind-the-times works, influence public opinion and all those who think of the country's future; the ways in which the lack of philosophy in those studies, or rather, of that philosophy that studies history, humanity, and the course of civilization, influences opinion and is in evidence in party trends, in the direction of politics. We will show why that younger generation is unmoved by all feelings of freedom, without personal attacks or defenses; why they do not sympathize with the cause of liberal principles; why they are not moved by them, why they live for nothing, stand for nothing; why they make a farce of the asylums of San Andrés del Plata, where the principles that they stand for, play tricks on human heads. Then we will see in whose name the political inquisition has been launched, and has drowned light, freedom, fashion, romanticism, and all those bagatelles, in blood. . . . Write another article on romanticism and see right away where you end up. . . .

This violent attack on the spirit, trends, education, and doctrines that were assumed uppermost in the *El Semanario* editors, could not help but wreak the havoc caused by those first rounds a shameless press fires on the virgin sensibility of novice writers. But this was not a literary debate, though the *Gaceta del Comercio* sought to instigate it with more art and conceit than *El Mercurio*, and it was necessary to put a definite end to a diatribe that, if it could give Sarmiento the chance to prove what he promised, it imperiled our peers' dignity and affected our responsibility as editor to the public and to our own conscience, inasmuch as he had proposed to us it would be a responsible and noble newspaper. Moreover, *El Semanario* ought not partake in the quarrel the purists had with the Argentinian writers who were helping us promote literary development: that rendered them unable to serve the movement. Sanfuentes, as sensitive as he was noble, though he was affected in a way that left a painful impression on us, agreed, and wrote a quick article rectifying the *Gaceta* and declaring that they were in agreement on many of the newspaper's ideas; however, García Reyes, who was more vehement than *El Mercurio*'s editor, and equally or more capable of holding his own in a contest, was not reconciled to end the matter without an article that he wrote, in which the least severe item was his declaration to not continue the debate, expressed thus: "The editors of *El Semanario* are not so spineless that an iridescent plume on a peacock would give them a fright, nor would the vacuous writings of science and prudence, replete only with stupid presumption and glib mountbankery: with the certainty of triumph, they would enter a sustained debate in which they would have to contend with a hollow ghost; but this debate would be a scandal, a disgrace that they are not up to incurring.... *El Semanario* will move ahead on its course: when a gentleman takes the floor, he will give an attentive reply; when the challenger is a man of influence, he will scorn to join battle with him."

Both articles were approved by a majority vote from the directorial board to be published in the newspaper's next issue, number four, to put the debate on our side to an end. But we are left with the doubt over whether *El Mercurio* greeted this declaration in a spirit of forbearance, and having found Sarmiento that same night of the agreement, we held a fiery interview in which, without disrupting the friendship we had, we took him to task and called him to reason. Sarmiento was brave, and therefore generous: he knew how to restrain his drive when a noble interest surfaced, such as that of spurring and guiding intellectual development, without the deviations of passion. The proof is in the following letter we received the following day, which we have kept as a memory that accords him honor:

Dear Lastarria:
The few words we exchanged last night have filled me with regret and I must say, distress as well; and as I cannot see you

until tonight, I make use of this medium to render you my explanations, which perhaps will justify my conduct in the current debate, and though they do not achieve that end, they will at least account for the behavior in question. Long ago have I renounced the friendship of the educated youth of Santiago. Be it for their not believing me worthy of deserving it, or that I have not warranted the least right to aspire to it; be it, in sum, that absorption in my life's habits has not allowed room for such relationships to be established, I certainly have not had aught other friends besides you among the intelligent youth, at least one I had reason to believe sincere. You, then, who have had close dealings with me, have been in a position to judge, if I am not mistaken, the purity of my heart, and my heartfelt sympathies for the Chilean youth and the liberal interests of the country. Very well: a literary debate arises now and I rise to the occasion, and if you wish, I degenerate it, using a causticity and acerbity that are manifested on every page I write, in every word I set forth. The issue is *romanticism*, and I made light of it in *Nona Sangrienta* ["Bloody Nones"], and on every opportunity I have had to do so. Today I defend it with a true fervor. Whence was born this most keen interest? Remember that during the political debate, many felt that my efforts were responsible for the fact that the issues of the day lost the almost inevitable acrimony, when interests that affect mankind to so great an extent are aired. And in fact I never gave offense to anyone, and if any gave offense to me, I took them to task and saw to it they came to reason. But then it was a question of the interests of a party whose cause had been embraced and not ours: being an enduring truth that I have never impugned the ill-bred figures of whom I have been the target. Notwithstanding these antecedents born of my natural character and my aversion to everything but the discussion of principles and public facts, I reveal today an entirely opposite tendency, a tendency for which you revile me, which my friends recognize and which I myself confess. Again I say, whence issues this phenomenon? Whence? I will tell you, and if it does me no justice, you will take pity on me for having gone astray, in my unavoidable stance. You remember that matter of the debate over the Spanish language, a debate I did not kindle, and which I forsook when I found myself engulfed in affronts and made the butt of mordent jests. Observe that I can say what Louis XIV said of the State: "*El Mercurio* is me"; because even the beasts of the field know I edit it. I held my tongue then, and swallowed my mortification in silence. *El Semanario* appeared, and you saw the restrained judgment I rendered of its first issue and how I abstained from condemning one word of those written therein; despite the expression "*written by Chileans*," you should have understood it as everyone did, as a reference to my person; despite there having been in that first publication ideas that could give me grist for justified criticisms; despite, in short, that I was apprised of the personal antipathy of a vast number of its writers. But the second issue appeared and in it I find an article, *Romanticism*. Written, for what? for whom? Did it explain romanticism? What antecedent motivated such an article? When they announced their newspaper they offered issues of less ephemeral interest than the works in *El Mercurio*: when they criticized the little piece *El español y la francesa* ["The Spaniard and the Frenchwoman"], a matter unworthy of taking up space in a newspaper, *El Semanario* saw *personified Gallecisms, crossbred language, Frenchification.* When they speak of *romanticism* without coming to the point, they are speaking of *certain bombastic writings* they admired at first, but that later are spurned, and indifference gives way to scorn. Jotabeche writes and the promised scorn in fact arrives. On whom? On *El Mercurio*, or rather, on me. One would need be a mole, then, to not see the plan of the articles, and the links that unite them; no matter if *El Semanario* names me or *El Mercurio* does, so that the whole world understands that I am the wounded one, that I am the representative of romanticism, of gallecism and of crossbred language. Moreover, do they think I am not aware that a great number of youths among the writers in their conversations use the most offensive and irritating expressions against me? Am I not aware that everywhere they speak of my *ignorance*, of my pure *charlatanism*, of how preoccupied I am with my status, and of the disdain that my ideas, my language and my writings merit? Do they think I am not aware that verses are hammered out to call me an eccentric writer? That they cultivate scorn, and are fattened in pitiless hatred? And that not even do they deign to answer me? Do they think it possible, then, that a man forever endure, suffer and stay silent, though he already feels the hand clutching his hair to drag him through the slime; to stir up universal scorn; to be put on public display as a wretched charlatan and ignoramus? But I will not subject myself voluntarily to the humiliations that they present me. Concerned with these notions, I joined the fray against the Romanticism article; not for the literary issue, but insofar as it concerns my reputation, which they wish to tarnish; and resolved to defend myself, I vowed to wound unto death, mercilessly, unrestrained, using the same weapons that by word of mouth and by pen have been used against me. Do they speak of *charlatanism*, of *presumption*, of *ignorance*? I will, if I can, have those arrows fall on other heads than my own, and if I cannot, I will yield, but not humbly. Does it pain them when I wound the self-esteem of those who write? Oh! judge then who ought suffer more, whether they who are on their own soil, and are legion, or I who am alone and who they seek to humiliate at every turn with the above-quoted words and with such from abroad; I who need to purify myself of this final stain to have some right to public consideration; I who need a small reputation like a dominium utile!

Are those youths actually persuaded that I am a wretched charlatan, a *transcriber*, as they say, an ignoramus? Fine, then, I will disabuse them of their error insofar as I am able, or they will become convinced of their mistakenness. Let them write about speculative matters.

But, dear friend, after all this rancor and these preparations for war are said and done, what is there in essence? What is it that divides us? My pretensions? But I appeal to you who knows me, to my previous writings, to my character, to all my friends, to clear me of this charge, which is the one I least wish to accept. Pretensions, I! I who have always lent an ear to everyone and allow myself to serve as an example to all my friends, without complaint, ever without argument, without clinging to dogmatic views. At the heart of the matter, my friend, lies a deplorable misunderstanding, which I have not caused, and in my view, a bit of jealousy, and a great deal of clannishness in those youths, perhaps on my part as well. Is it necessary to trample me underfoot because I have not the least regard for the Spanish writers, nor their style, nor their well-bred language? For could there not be a man who is a maniac in one respect, and sane in others? Am I then to be a charlatan, an ignoramus? But one must moderate oneself in words of that sort when writing, for the word *sings*.

Above all there is a great evil and it is born of the fact these youths gather, communicate, get one another riled up, applaud themselves and support one another's prejudices and opinions, and can wind up deceiving themselves to the point of thinking I am to blame for everything and not them. You know that the misdeeds committed among many weigh quite little on the conscience of each individual; and it is enough that they speak as one to think themselves on the side of justice.

I have spent so much time on all this, because I think too highly of you to be indifferent to your esteem: the same does not hold for those who attribute to me all the vices of an evil man and the waywardness of a mind devoid of common sense.

I had promised you an explanation of my conduct and I believe I have given it to you in the foregoing. When we see each other again you will help me with your judgment, and happy will I be if I manage to convince you I am your friend forever, an indiscreet friend, if you think me thus, but never a disloyal one, as they try to persuade you.

I have run out of paper and this is the limit.

Yours.—Sarmiento

On 31 July *El Mercurio*'s editorial board explained its stance in the polemic, a *grosso modo* like its writer did in the preceding letter, and invited *El Semanario* to declare a truce. But the García Reyes article, which appeared in issue 4 of that newspaper, would have rekindled the feud, had we not made use of our personal relations to pacify Sarmiento, giving him assurance that *El Semanario* would thenceforth respect the free actions of the Argentinian writers who, at all events, might help us to drive forward the literary movement in progress, and to propagate liberal ideas. Sarmiento then brought a close to the polemic on 8 August, alluding to that article in a jesting tone, and calling his adversaries to moderation with friendly reflections and sly threats, like a gaucho would do in making peace after a fight.

Thus went the so-called *romanticism polemic*, which is always quoted, alleging that in it the principles of clashing systems were debated. It was simply a burning reflection of the petty nationalistic jealousies fanned by the literary debate that had been caused by our address delivered to the society of youths that had congregated to study; determined to quash those jealousies, not to have *El Semanario* reflect them again, and to have this role maintained in the realms of thought and the public interest, not stooping to the contests of verbal abuse that had so debased our press on other occasions, and whose trial had been as painful for us as for our noble countrymen, we placed especial care that similar confrontations not recur thenceforward. Yet our collaborator Vallejo refused to follow such a plan, answering our private admonitions by calling us *cuyanos*, Argentinized writers, and other gaieties that he took to using in his familiar dealings with us, and believing he satisfied us with his faculty of pruning down his writing as we saw fit, a faculty that we did not hazard to use and whose employment would certainly have been blocked from us by Tocornal and Talavera, who held and defended Vallejo's position. Thus he continued in his correspondence to *El Semanario*, waging harsh war on the River Plata writers, for he had much to avenge, and not as his biographers so kindly allege, that he did so as an enemy of the *corrupters of the public taste, and of a style and doctrines that offended his good sense, and on behalf of the repugnance he felt against the romanticism of López in literature and Chacho in politics.*

Meanwhile López and Sarmiento, Piñeiro, Frías, Peña, all those *corrupters of the public judgment*, all his writer compatriots, cultivated fellow-feeling and relationships with the editors of *El Semanario* and all the studious youth, in the interest of intellectual and liberal development, with which they wished to cooperate; and for however much *El Semanario* would publish Vallejo's jibes and the letters and rebuttals with which two of the writers supported him, Sarmiento only directed against this writer his retorts and diatribes, always respecting the peace he had made when putting an end to the aforementioned debate on romanticism. That conduct, which honored him greatly, placed us under the obligation to repay him, and finally, seizing the moment of the declaration of a wish to end the press war, a statement which the Argentinians made in *El Progreso*, considering their nationality lost after the Arroyo Grande disaster,* we ended the publication of the Jotabeche correspondence. Additionally, we announced in issue 29 of *El Semanario* that in response to that plea to forget, the publication of another Letter that the former had sent to continue hostilities was omitted.

After so many years of calm, we are strengthened in our conviction that beyond being unjust, the ill-will that was raised against the Argentine émigrés was too puerile, only because their writers, who have continued to be great writers in their country and in Spanish America, came to help us in our literary movement and make us see how far behind our literary education was. How much more justifiably will we not marvel now that there is still persistence in justifying those animosities to posterity, from the very

---

* The Battle of Arroyo Grande, fought 5 December, 1842 in Argentina's Entre Ríos province, pitted the forces of Uruguayan gaucho leader Fructuoso Rivera against those of Rosas's ally Manuel Oribe. Oribe won and proceeded to lay siege to Montevideo, the Uruguayan capital. —Ed.

writers that have gained the most from those who stirred up the bad blood! It has fallen to us too, on more than one occasion, to be an émigré in neighboring republics, and not having been as useful as the Argentines were here, we have seen that we Chileans had them beat for arrogance, and that it was true what was said by *El Progreso* in 1842 in the peace declaration to which we have alluded, speaking of the emigrations for civil causes, which carry their national spirit to foreign soil: "Setbacks irritate it and make it more powerful, and not a few times incite animosities or damaging prejudices."

XX

Since the time *El Semanario* broke free of that irritating debate, which disturbed its tranquillity for its first four issues, it had no other; it continued on its way until 2 February 1843, the day on which it finished with its issue 31, having dealt nobly, and with a keen interest in accuracy, with all the issues that at that time concerned public opinion, keeping its readership informed of the parliamentary debates and administrative works, and serving as a forum for the literary productions that then began to surface, not unlike the first flowers of spring, timid, isolated, and lacking the shelter of the leafy foliage they forerun.

El Semanario itself, in its issue 24, seeking to chart the course the press should follow under the country's circumstances, vis à vis *El Mercurio*'s and another leaflet's accusation they leveled for not limiting themselves to politics, expounded at length on the object of their labors in an article that we ought to excerpt in these memoirs so that it be known today what the paper's role was, which always is recalled without knowledge of it.

> If by politics—it said—we are to mean the discussion of party interests, the open contesting or systematic defense of those who exert authority, by all means we should declare that it has not been our purpose, nor will it ever be, to take up politics. For too long the newspapers have been in this country the manual tool of party ire and rancor, the battleground on which

wild passions that spawn governmental confrontations apply the heinous tactic of raining down malicious suspicions, false accusations, sarcasm and venomous taunts on enemy factions. An era of scandal that one cannot call to mind without sorrow. . . . It will not be *El Semanario* who resurrects it. We do not belong to *any of the factions* that have divided the Republic, and we do not recognize *a government we can support*, nor an opposition party to fight. A nobler, purer, more selfless end should occupy the mind of the citizenry, that of promoting the improvement of our social conditions. The eagerness to instigate quarrels, to overthrow one government only to replace it with another one as partial and short-lived as the first, contribute nothing to this goal. . . . Democracy in our day and age is not aimed at governments to ask them for freedom, prosperity, wealth. . . . Nor does it seek to impose the law on them and subject the cabinet to the accords struck by lodges and private guilds. It puts its energy into educating the masses, in seeing that they overcome their vices and pernicious habits, in rising above the obstacles that block the development of the constituent parts of their happiness. . . . When education has spread widely, when the general welfare, which is the work of civilization and of laws, has made the people strong and powerful enough, then public opinion will doubtless triumph, and democracy's authority will be erected on indestructible foundations.

Resolved in these principles, we have endeavored to alter the directions of governmental quarrels, which have engendered so little practical utility, and to point them toward other aims with a more solid end. Civilization in the provinces naturally consumed *El Semanario*'s attention, and in its columns are found articles in which there are attempts to delve into the causes that maintain the greater part of these provinces in a lethargic state, and the means to place them on the path to betterment. We have paid special attention to the profitable enterprises that have begun cropping up in our midst, be it by extolling the savings banks and motivating the citizens to protect such an advantageous enterprise, or by fostering the effort that plans to supply pure water to the city of Santiago, or by proposing the system that ought to be adopted for setting up a police force in the streets and for providing for their maintenance and improvement, or explaining the prospectus of the industrial and colonization interests that so vitally affect the commonweal. We have recommended the foundation of a civilian widows' and orphans' fund that provides a means of support for the families of deceased workers, and requested the reform of the laws that regulate the preferencing of credits in proceedings, whose deleterious influence on the morality of trade it is pointless to ponder. The Santiago police force has been the object of our constant requests. And save for the difficulties that the position of censor entails, we have engaged in stirring the ardor of the authorities to repress certain vices, and in correcting with ridicule our society's flaws. But since the improvement should be expected rather from the generations that lift themselves up free of preoccupations and hardened customs, our main energy has been directed toward education, and several articles that have appeared from the first to the latter issues under different forms and titles attest to this. In these articles, as in those devoted to theater and pleasant literature, we have sought to spread liberal ideas, but devoid of the rigor of systems and of the exaggeration that usually renders them dangerous; we have wished to show them applicable to practice, instead of presenting them in the form of general and absolute theory. In the survey of the plans for founding a new University, the freedom of the literary republic was defended, which to a certain extent was compromised by one of the provisions of the law. In several works in prose and verse the concerns of the aristocracy were battled against, and in general we missed no chance to spread ideas of moderation, tolerance and order. Our newspaper is not, then, a battering ram meant for demolition; discussion and examination are more to its taste, as is addressing the citizens, rather than attacking the leaders. . . . Not for that reason have we indifferently considered the administration of nations, nor the defense of institutions. So far from that, we have been the only ones who, for some time now, have remembered their obligations to subordinate officials, and take active part in the issues on our public law.

In fact, *El Semanario* addressed and discussed all issues submitted to the legislative houses in its time, and most especially the reform of the election law, and that of public education, about which it published, in the issues subsequent to the one in which they wrote that review, interesting studies and arguments. Its activities in the press were undeniably beneficial, for they eliminated the occasional newspapers, which had appeared by chance until then to deal exclusively with current politics; leaving commercial interests to the Valparaíso dailies, it set the example of a reliable newspaper that was pledged to address independently all other general interests, preferring those that are related to intellectual development, like public education, belles lettres, and dramatic theater.

The *Revista de Valparaíso*, for part of that year, and *El Museo* for all of it, were devoted to these latter issues; in September *El Mercurio* began, in its Sunday issue, a literary section to reproduce the most notable works from the European literary movement. "From the abundance of light," this newspaper stated on that occasion, "that contemporary Europe scatters, only pale glimmers reach here for lack of earnest agencies; and the state of infancy in which our book business still is found adds also to the fact that not many productions circulate in this country, and perhaps the ones most analogous to our needs, from European literature. After having seen something of Hugo, of Dumas, of Scribe, and having read a passage out of Cousin* or some other writer, one would think one knew, perhaps, the entire intellectual activity of the French press; and after having enough Bretón de los Herreros,[†] one will think he holds all of Spanish literature in the palm of his hand." And to make the European literary movement known, *El Mercurio* later made interesting transcriptions of biographies, speeches, and articles on literary criticism, theater, and music.

Two or three new newspapers appeared in 1842, only to fade soon, but 10 November was a red-letter day for the press, because *El Progreso* was born, which is the first Santiago daily founded for the purpose of steadfastly serving the general interests. Withal the serious press enjoyed an unprecedented development: no less than thirty leaflets on topics of general interest to Chile and other South American republics were published, and approximately twelve important works, most of them reproductions of literary works and texts like Larra's *Fígaro*, Blair's[‡] compendium of the *Retórica* ["Rhetoric"], and others; but among them there were two books relating to the contemporary history of Bolivia and the Argentinian Republic, two original dramas, *Los amores del poeta* ["The Romances of the Poet"] and *Ernesto*, and the interesting *Análisis de los métodos de lectura conocidos y practicados en Chile* ["Analysis of the Reading Methods Known and

---

* Augustin-Eugène Scribe (1791–1861), prolific French playwright, author of serious and comic operas; Victor Cousin (1792–1867), French philosopher and leader of the "Eclectic" school. —Ed.

† Manuel Bretón de los Herreros (1796–1873), prolific Spanish playwright. —Ed.

‡ Hugh Blair (1718–1800), English author of *Lectures on Rhetoric* (1783). —Ed.

Practiced in Chile"], which Sarmiento published as headmaster of the Escuela Normal de Preceptores ["Teacher Training School"], which had also been incorporated that year. On the main works from among these, *El Semanario* published some articles and specially devoted to the latter a critical homage befitting the importance of the issue.

This progress in the press revealed a new situation, the expression of analogous advancements in society's speculative and active endeavors. Society at that time was beginning a life different from its previous one, owing to the hopes the new administration inspired. The new politics founded on legality and devoted to reestablishing security in public administration, and the confidence it awakened, not only breathed life into material interests, which were the principal aspiration of the conservative government's political platform, but also favored intellectual development *in a liberal sense*, a new social turn of events promoted outside the circles of power and the politics we pursued in the previous few years, and furthered with altruism and perseverance. Thus alongside the business concerns that arose to broaden the domain of general industry, and of the associations that were attempted in order to foment local interests as well as those of the colonization and cultivation of wastelands, the literary societies appeared, which, following the example of the one instituted in Santiago on 3 May, were forming to promote intellectual progress. The 11 August *El Semanario* gives notice of the *Asociación Instructiva* ["Teaching Association"] formed in Concepción by the most respectable citizens to foster education; and later it announced another literary society formed in Santiago by lawyers for the purpose of conducting a philosophical study of history. Contemporary writers rightly mark that memorable year of 1842 as the dawning of our literary movement, and indicate it as the first year of a new era.

Why then did *El Semanario* meet such an untimely end? Messrs. Amunátegui, in Vallejo's life story, assert that the reason for its brief existence was having promptly seen their writers overwhelmed by public and private posts; and that is not the cause, given that out of those writers, only one was named, during the time the paper was being published, to a public post, that of rector of the Instituto Nacional, which was conferred to Varas;* for it cannot be considered that Sanfuentes had been graced with a position from the promotion he received then as a ministry official. The true reason was that, over and above *El Semanario*'s failure to respond to our old plan, on account of its compromise, it imposed two encumbrances

---

* Antonio Varas de la Barra (1817–1866), former rector of the Instituto, served in various cabinet posts, and was touted unsuccessfully as successor to Manuel Montt in 1861. —Ed.

on us that made its publication bothersome: that of procuring the materials needed for the publication of each issue, and that of having to pay the expenses, for, according to the press's accounts, the product did not cover publishing costs. It was not that the paper lacked interest, but that, in spite of being widely read and acclaimed, there was no one to protect it from the custom of reading free, as was the style of the day. Moreover, since the capital had a great daily like *El Progreso*, it was more profitable to eliminate that paper and replace it with another that was exclusively literary, as we had planned previously; since *El Museo de Ambas Américas* also closed operations in December 1842. It is true that Mr. García del Río* likewise had abandoned his profitable enterprise due to a lack of circulation and patronage, as he states in his farewell article; but we believed that it was possible to test in Santiago the publication of a lower-cost literary paper, and with more assistants than those who helped that distinguished writer, who declared that he had had to write 230 of the 251 articles comprising the three volumes of *El Museo*.

XXI

The narration of these particulars has its importance, for it serves to rectify several mistaken judgments, including the one most common among historians, the one that imagines that *El Semanario de Santiago* was a specifically literary newspaper and geared toward showing Sarmiento that our country was *capable of producing poets*. Thus the university Memorial on *Chilean Poetry* affirms almost officially, declaring triumphantly that Sanfuentes and Irisarri, Vallejo and García Reyes in no time demonstrated in that paper how unfounded were the Argentinian's charges.

Before *El Semanario*, these charges had been refuted and argued, for the literary movement had made its first advancement with the polemics that critical judgments of the Literary Society's inaugural address provoked, and

---

* Juan García del Río (1794–1856), an associate of Bolívar and Bello, publisher of *El repertorio americano*. —Ed.

those that, apropos of the revolution born with this address, *El Mercurio*'s editor had published. It is true that said newspaper allowed those polemics to drag out, but fortunately it did bring them to a timely end, to focus peacefully and nobly on general interests that the paper set out to serve. It also fomented intellectual progress, without being an exclusively literary publication geared toward proving the country was capable of producing poets, and without proposing to demonstrate that the impotence for which we were reproached was not the work, as Sarmiento and the other Argentinian writers maintained, of the wayward direction of our education and of the fear of trespassing against the rules of Scholastic routine, which drove away beginners. That direction was already more liberal and more appropriate to the independent development of the spirit, and this fear had begun to dissipate, however much Vallejo and some others still fought to shore it up with the weapon of ridicule and mockery, in lieu of helping bring the country's capabilities to the fore. *El Semanario*'s mission was more extensive and larger, for, as the agency of communal interests, it lent an air of distinction to journalism, an honorable, intelligent tone that the press that intends to represent public opinion and educate it ought have; as a servant of intellectual progress, it furthered its development in public education, in the Literary Society, and in the theater, which were the great hubs in which the literary movement was at work, a movement already afoot, not minding the charges the Argentinian writers had hurled at us, not *against the country*, but against the ambassadors of routine, who had tried to nip that healthy movement in the bud, scared that they were seeking to overthrow the rule of the old traditions.

El Semanario steered clear of this battle, and publicized all the literary compositions, sometimes essays from the new school, other times productions from the old, like *El campanario* ["The Bell Tower"], a legend presented by those who had elicited those charges as proof of the country's poetic capability, not realizing that in it there is no creativity, nor inspiration, nor art, and that due to its dull, labored versification it lent itself to victorious criticisms, which those accused of offending the national honor abstained from making, proving that they aspired only to work together for our literary progress. Thus likewise they respected the experiments by the youths who were being initiated in the secrets of the poetic art, and it is obvious to us that López, among other Argentinian writers, encouraged and corrected the beginners, at the same time the supposed defenders of the country's honor censured them with bitter jests, which could have caused them to lose heart had not we been there at their side to cheer them on. Who were the ones then that were determined to have people believe that the country was incapable of producing poets, those who proclaimed the fact they did not exist, attributing the absence to our education's having turned us into purists and rhetoricians instead of teaching us to think freely, or those bent on reinforcing that barricade of fear with their mocking criticisms, and on maintaining the education system that drained the life from us?

El Semanario should follow no other course: if according to our original aim, it had been the exclusive organ of the literary revolution begun in the Society of youths, it would have formed a common front with the Argentinian writers accused of offending the national honor, and with all those who, like them, assisted that movement, acknowledging that our impotence was brought about not because a *too-profound survey of the language* was conducted, but because in this survey and in the others, our spirit had ended up in the chains of certain routines and certain comforts antithetical to the freedom of thought. But since that paper was to have another nature, from the influence Mr. Bello's writings had on the organization, it of necessity could not be the forum of the purists and classicists either, to be used against the Argentinian writers, and instead of intending it to prove the country was capable of producing poets, it was set to the task of overcoming the lifelessness for which we were reproached, destroying the floodgates that held back thought in stagnation. To that end, shunning all parties and schools, avoiding all disputes, accusations, and fruitless battles, *El Semanario* opened up its columns to everyone, so that beginners could publish their works fearlessly, side by side with established writers who, as Amunátegui expresses accurately, *knew not what to say before*; for actually they could not say it without danger of being flanked on the one side by the language purists cutting them to the quick with scorn and disdain, and on the other, conservative politics that threw Juan Fernández, like Pradel, either into jail, like Benavente and Toro, or subjected them to police persecution, like Juan Nicolás Alvarez.

That is why the promissory essays by Irisarri, by J. Chacón and A. Olavarrieta, the first sketches by Ovalle, Espejo, Lindsay, Rengifo, and other youths that aspire to wear Apollo's wreath are included alongside Sanfuentes's polished rhymes.

What we proposed to do was educate writers, and without distinction or picking and choosing, we summoned everyone who wrote in prose or verse, however well they could, for we were repeating the counsel that Sarmiento had given to the younger generation in his 22 May article, when, taking on himself the embittered scorn of the purists, he had exclaimed: "Change studies, and instead of focusing on forms, on the purity of words, on the roundedness of phrasing, on what Cervantes or fray Luis de León said, acquire ideas, from whatever source, nourish your thought with the thoughts of the great luminaries of the day; and when you feel that your thought in turn is awakening, cast your inquisitive gazes over our country, over the people, the customs, the institutions, the current needs, and then write *lovingly, courageously, what is within your power to do so, whatever you please*, for that will be good in content, though the form be incorrect; it will be impassioned, though betimes nonstandard; it will please the reader, though it infuriate Garcilaso. . . ."

Oh, today's writers do not know the patience needed to attain that freedom in apprenticeship, and the historians of the day do not even suspect how great was the violence with which those great writers treated those who dared attempt this freedom; today we enthusiastically praise those great writers, scorning or harshly judging those who stood up to the violence by educating writers and wresting the national spirit from the lifelessness in which those great men kept it! If only such unpremeditated judgments had had no other effect than that of falsifying our literary history, reaching the point of engendering in our age the false conviction that only the literary purists are worthy of remembrance, those writers who antagonized or at least stood in the way of the 1842 literary movement, while those who promoted it are deemed unworthy of ranking alongside the latter, or are thought outlandish writers, nonsense-peddlers or heretics! In the end, those facts admit of corrections, and those who take the trouble to investigate them or to corroborate the testimony of the author of these notes, shall be able to write the true story: the irreparable harm lies in the fact that those judgments that were launched and repeated so long after the facts, and in cold blood, without the heat of the battle for an excuse, and giving unjust and open offense to the Argentinian writers who aided the movement, have played their part effectively in kindling the ire with which these writers treat us today.

Be that as it may, the literary movement, for which our teaching since 1837 paved the way, as well as our activities and the example with which we had stirred it, was organized around a center and formulated in a manifesto in 1842, and led from that time on in such a way that not only those that attacked it would have a hand in its fulfillment, but also those who looked askance at it and were offended by the brusqueness with which the Argentinians lent it their support, and was served in this connection by *El Semanario;* that movement, we assert, was by the beginning of that year an event. The facts naturally wound up confirming and furthering it.

In August Carlos Bello arrived from Copiapó, an original drama in hand, which he submitted, after reading it to some friends, to the theater company for it to be performed. The theater was then a crux of true social activity. Everyone was concerned with the worthiness of the plays put on there, and that of the remarkable actors Casacuberta, Fedriani, Jiménez, Rendón, Mdme. Miranda, Mdme. Montesdeoca, the Samaniegos, and Mdme. Fedriani, who performed the masterworks of Victor Hugo, Scribe, Dumas, Delavigne, Larra, Bretón de los Herreros; everyone clamored for buildings to be erected in Santiago and Valparaíso that were suited to the importance of this element of civilization and progress. *El Mercurio*, supporting this call in its 10 June editorial, and explaining why they considered theater *a part of our social organization*, among other reasonings made the following one: "There is practically not a single work by Bretón de los Herreros that does not proclaim a principle, that does not attack a concern; and these principles maintained in Spain, and those concerns attacked there, are the same principles we proclaim here and the same concerns we have to address. The Spanish theater, like the French theater, works to destroy all class concerns, all tyranny, be it public or domestic, to enshrine in its place the individual freedom of one sex and the other, and to have an influence and status in society commensurate with their real value. For this and a thousand other points of contact with the dramatic literature of France and Spain, which follows its steps on the path to regeneration, with our needs, the theater is a veritable school for us, a school that through the senses and the heart ideas reach us that we need for the same regenerating work on our practices." ...

This was the expression of public opinion in Valparaíso and Santiago in that era of real success for the dramatic arts in Chile. This success was due to the talents of actors who popularized the most distinguished productions of European ingenuity, to the publications *El Mercurio* and *El Semanario*, which inspired the taste for and the interest in this genre of literature, and to the translations of French dramas that were done here, not waiting for those rendered by Spanish translators to arrive. But until that time no national talent had emerged that could satisfy the widespread desire to see a drama that was a homegrown production.

Carlos Bello was at the forefront of fulfilling this desire, and though he had been born English, he was taken to be Chilean and ranked among the most outstanding of the Santiago youth. Possessed of physical beauty, heightened by a certain British standoffishness that did not prevent his being every inch the gallant gentleman, by virtue of his urbane manners and amiability he was universally well liked and won the favor of the ladies. This Adonis was struck with the fortuitous inspiration to return to the capital after a long absence, in search of his fortune in the Copiapó lodes, bringing back an original drama entitled *Los amores del poeta* ["The Romances of the Poet"] to secure the glory of his name, already writ large by his father and older brother, and to increase the prestige that he himself had won in society as a stylish man, a daring industrialist able to take part in the much-talked-about enterprises that in those days sent Chañarcillo's fame ringing far and wide.

The whole of Santiago high society was moved by the announcement of the production of *Los amores del poeta*, which took place on the night of 28 August before a restless, enthusiastic house that was so crowded that it did not fit in the spacious stage storehouse that served as our theater. The author scored a splendid success, and the description that *El Semanario* and *El Mercurio* made of him on 1 September repeated his glory throughout the country. The article by this latter paper, which was attributed to García del Río, was excellent and far superior to the former's. It is written with the love and tactfulness characteristic of the celebrated writer. In his view, the play was the first step national talent had taken in the difficult theatrical arts, it was the prologue to the nascent literature written in this genre, but regretted that the work was set in France and not in Chile, a tribute that, unwittingly, we would be paying for quite some time yet to the literature of that nation, devoting it the most flowery of our thoughts, when they would scorn even our éclat, and when this earth has flowers too that, though a bit wild, could, if well chosen, be used to weave very beautiful and attractive wreaths. That was the reason that, in such a simple composition as that drama, the exposition had to be so drawn-out and dull, for it had to set a broad scene, to then hurtle toward a denouement that could not wait.

As for the work's merits, the article stated that the plot was limited, void of all action, but rich in details, in lofty feelings and deep emotions; for in matters of feeling, and feeling truly and nobly, the author gave evidence of enviable gifts. "The language," he added, "has all the naturalness and the artistic fluency that are appropriate to the drama, and all the harmony of prose poetry. On the strength of its beauty in style and imagery, which like burning glasses focus in one luminous point all the rays of an idea; on the strength of charming and fascinating us with the most beautiful thoughts and ideas that startle and delight, the young Bello has managed to keep us in our seats, eyes riveted, short of breath and slack-jawed, not noticing that the characters moved little, that the early scenes lagged on, notwithstanding that the appearance of the coronel gave the first act a certain dramatic tincture, which until then the play had not had. The power of charming lies!"

The rehearsal not only had been a success, but also productive. After forty days, on 9 October, in an equally enthusiastic and crowded venue, *Ernesto* was staged, an original drama that don Rafael Minvielle had composed in a very short period of time. This Spanish man of letters, who had been serving the Republic in the revenue office since six years previous, had taken an active part in the newspaper business, and was a part of the literary movement in conjunction with the purists who aspired to maintain it within the traditions of Spanish literature, and above all to defend the purity of the language against the eccentricities of the Argentinian writers, who had supported our categorical repudiation of that musty literature that runs contrary to the new trends and new destinies of our Society. But Minvielle was not an adversary of literary emancipation in the sense of the modern French school, and thought, as did his countrymen Ribot* and Larra, that Spanish literature could and should no longer be classical. The same writer had figured among the national translators of modern French dramas, and had given our stage the translation of *Antoni*, and three months after that brought us *Hernani*.

Minvielle, like C. Bello, read his drama to a score of literary people, which met in Joaquín Prieto Warnes's salons, and after this blessing of sorts, staged it. The author of *Ernesto* entered, we do not know if deliberately, in the new evolution of modern dramatic literature, leaving sentimentality behind and setting up, in the way of a main theme, a situation that we could consider political, a premise whereby the Spanish military have forsaken the flag of their king to fight for South American independence.

"This play," stated *El Semanario*, "written with a style that is correct and elegant, vehement and impassioned at times, brought tears to the eyes of many of the young ladies in attendance, and was vaunted on numerous occasions. . . . At the top of this article we stated that don Rafael Minvielle had tackled an arduous and delicate subject matter, and in fact, for a first effort, a political issue clips the wings of fancy and strews the path with difficulties. Don Rafael Minvielle has overcome some of these difficulties, but there are other ones inherent to the issue itself that he has not managed to surmount."

That newspaper's critics, agreeing with the spectators' opinion, found that in *Ernesto* there was a good deal of reasoning, that too much was discussed, that action came to a standstill, and that the courtship of Ernesto and Camila, which ought to have been the main event of the drama, was reduced one episode due to the importance given the discussion of whether or not the hero had been a traitor when he followed his liberal convictions in embracing the cause of independence. But it is true that neither *El Semanario* nor the public would have noticed all that if they had taken an interest in the issue that served as the drama's theme: the flaw lay in that the topic was not a social issue that sparked great interest, but a particular situation that never managed to captivate the nation enough that its intellec-

---

* Théodule-Agustin Ribot (1823–1891), French historical and portrait painter. —Ed.

tual interest, so to speak, outstripped that of the emotions, nor was it set forth and sustained in those riveting poetic forms that in *Los amores del poeta* had made one forget the weak plot.

Both dramas, moreover, had appeared at a time unfavorable to the success of national art, for they were performed in the moments when the public had fallen for the exquisiteness of French art, so admirably portrayed by the most outstanding actors of our stage. Thus, though they fulfilled an aspiration, they proved nevertheless that the task of composing original works in this genre that could appeal to taste and hold their own compared to the European ones, was extremely difficult, and disheartened the most industrious, and which therefore mired the cultivation of art. That was the moment in which a powerful stimulus was needed lest despair get the upper hand. There was none other than the applause of the public, which was not possible to win save with the help of circumstances not everyone, like C. Bello and Minvielle, could bring together. There was no dramatic company that, holding themselves to certain standards of success, rewarded authors with part of the earnings collected from the staging of a rightfully acclaimed work. There was no other way to capitalize on that attempt to cultivate dramatic composition than through the protective actions of the authorities to stimulate it; but neither the government nor the municipality understood this duty, and not only passed up this felicitous opportunity, but, in spite of fresh efforts made later by many literati, they ignored dramatic theater until it wasted away, then replaced it with lyrical theater, which never took the place of the civilizing influences of the former.

XXII

Another fact that substantiates that in the same era the literary movement that had begun before *El Semanario* was already an event, and which the newspaper served as its agency, is the competition that the Literary Society held to do its part to celebrate the anniversary of the Republic in 1842. We promoted this competition to give incentive to young writers, and since among them preference was given to the study of metrics, compositions in verse were much more copious than those that vied for the prize for prose. This was natural, for youth is poetic, and its strongest inclination is that of expressing its feelings in verse. Far from standing in the way of this proclivity, we fostered it, hoping to find among the versifiers those who had the privilege of combining the gifts that Horace cites as characteristics of the bard, in these verses, which then were uppermost in our mind, for our memories of school were still fresh:

> "Ingenium cui sit, cui mens divinior; atque os
> Magna sonaturum de nominis hujus honorem." *

Of the many poetic compositions that were submitted, only four were deserving of consideration by the jury the Society had elected to award the prize. The others were consigned to oblivion. Of those written in prose, only one was accepted.

On 17 September, in a formal meeting of the Society, we gave the reading of the jury's report, amidst a profound silence that betrayed the anxiety and interest with which the whole auditorium awaited the decision. When the winners were announced, the Society applauded the decision as the expression of justice, with charming fellow-feeling between winners and losers. All the authors were young boys: Santiago Lindsay, who won the poetry prize, was barely twenty years old; Ramón F. Ovalle, the author of the second piece, was sixteen, and Francisco Bilbao, the author of the third, was roughly the same age; Javier Rengifo, author of the fourth, and Juan Bello, who garnered the prize for prose. The prize-winning compositions were published in *El Semanario*, and also in the jury's report, which Carlos Bello drafted, and which we transcribe below to bring full circle the image we are giving of that memorable affair.

REPORT FROM THE COMMISSION CHARGED WITH JUDGING
THE MERITS OF THE COMPOSITIONS

Since the Commission does not have the necessary time to perform a thorough analysis of all the compositions submitted to its judgment, it limits the survey of them it is prescribed to perform to those that stand out for their excellence; in passing it will indicate some of the charms and flaws of those that occupy the second rank, and give a quick glance over those that it

---

* "Of which his spirit and mind be of the divinest; and the / Honor of his name will resound from a noble mouth." —Trans. (with Jorge López Cortina).

feels ought to be placed lower. As a matter of course it establishes two principles as a basis or standard for its decision: talent and artistry together earn first place: when talent competes with artistry, the latter defers to the former.

In reference to the various forms in which thought can be expressed in verse, we will say merely that our endeavor was to find that nobility of conceits, and judgment and sensitivity that constitute the immovable essence of poetry, which at times pours its inspirations into variable rhyming stanzas, other times it molds them into the difficult eight-line form, still other times it lets them flow in the cadenced *silva*.* It is our opinion that the repeated allusions to mythology, handled ad nauseam in Herrera and Lope's day, and their tiresome invocations to the muses, that indispensable prelude of yore, are considerable flaws in taste and cannot be suffered today. They have been replaced to best advantage by the autopsy, to coin a phrase, that the modern poet performs on the human heart, by the philosophy which, by forsaking the scowl that oft clouds his noble features and is bedecked in images, imparts luster to his poetic creations.

Seeing the compositions in verse in light of this theory, and lacking the happy concordance of talent with artistry, we have chosen from among the works the one in which the most poetic graces stand out, as well as a fertile and brilliant imagination, the seat of new ideas and intrepid thoughts. In our estimation, these endowments are brought together in the composition that has as its epigraph:

"El sol brilla en el cielo, Chile en la América del Sud."
["The sun shines in the sky, Chile in South America."]

The plan the author has dreamed up seems fortuitous, and fairly well developed. We are presented with the flotilla—"which seeks the terra incognita that the great Columbus conceived"—on the verge of abandoning its task, and avenging the supposed deceit on the person of their leader:

---

* The *silva* is a poem of either hendecasyllables, or more commonly, variably alternating hendecasyllables and heptasyllables, of unequal strophic length, and with end rhymes not strictly patterned. —Trans., following *Princeton Encyclopedia of Poetry and Poetics.*

"Mas en este instante fiero
Un hombre de mar avisa,
De lo alto de un mastelero
Que ya tierra se divisa."

"But in this momentous instant
A seaman gives word
From atop a masthead
That he now spots land."

    The gloomy portrait of the New Continent crushed under an oppressor, which in the name of the religion of Christ, but pushed by covetousness, lays waste, robs, and kills with impunity. Whereupon bravely, with a passion equal to the topic, the work depicts the uprising that Caupolicán headed. From the shores of the Bío-Bío he issues a resounding challenge, to which the Castilian replies with dignity:

"But where are you headed, wretched Iberian?
Do you not see the snow-capped peaks of those mountains?
Do you not know that they are the gateway to Chile?
And Arauco the unconquered, which is a nation of Chile?
Do you not hear a noise that sounds far off
And is very like a lion's roar,
When it yearns vehemently for the chance
To see in its clutches the prey to which it aspires?

For that far-off noise
The Bío-Bío makes,
And means, tyrant,
I challenge you to a duel.
To an eternal duel
And I swear by my life
That the fall shall be quite fatal for you
From my mace.

And the thrust of my lance
And the stone-blows from my *sling*
Shall be the vengeance
Of betrayed America.

And I have no fear of your horses,
For to my *lariat* they will fall,
And my arrows will douse
Your infernal rays.
. . . .
But, Castile, do not accept
The terrible duel from Arauco;
Never more may your accursed hands
Rebel against the heavens;
Holy God, do not allow it!
. . . .
I, the proud Castilian,
As brave as the Cid,
Am I not to concede to a Spanish American
Who incites me to fight?

I who saw Numancia in flames,
And Sagunto, destroyed,
Who saw them dying bravely
But never saw them defeated.

I who have trod the nape
Of the savage Mohammedan,
Like Francisco the First,
With his France and his fleur-de-lis.

I who have seen you shine
throughout the world, Castile.
Am I, God alive, to taint
Your banner with such a blemish?
. . . .
But where are the banners
Of the Hispanic monarchy?
Where were its coats of arms?
There lies a cold tomb,
Holding its champions."

We have read this passage time and again, stopping now on
the daring allocution of the Indian, now on the proud response
by the Spaniard and pausing also on the 5-line stanzas in which
the success of the battle is prophesied, for with a single stroke

he informs us how in fact it ended. Overlooking any rhythmic imperfection, we qualify this stretch as beautiful, lively and worthy of its subject; there is naturalness and bravery in it. What more appropriate expressions than those that flow from the mouth of Castille's veteran? What more opportune memories for a soldier of Phillip II than the feats of the Catholic Kings and Pavía's glorious expedition? After the battle, we are brought to an age in which

> "Todo es desolación, todo exterminio."
> ["All is desolation, all extermination."]

And lastly he depicts with some novelty our emancipation, with its reversals of danger and glory. In moving on from this composition, we recommend the author exercise more care in versification. He will find poorly cadenced verses marked in the margins; and there are examples of others that are supremely harsh: we underlined as much in this composition as in several others the employment of words that in addition to not belonging to the language, express no new idea, and that having equivalents, should be discarded as useless. We should impress our reservations on the spirit of the author, for we descry in his work a true vocation for poetry.

We chose for second place the *silva* that begins thus:

> "Epoca triste de silencio y llanto."
> ["Sad age of silence and crying."]

There is simplicity in the structure, facility and correctness in the verse; nevertheless there are vast passages in which the life and luster of the poetry are in short supply. The following strophe is one of the ones that we enjoy most:

> "Sacred country, hear our voices;
> Remember now your first-born sons,
> Remember their valor and their battles,
> The staunch and fearless warriors
> Who sooner suffered death
> Than for an instant endure seeing you
> Lashed down by the chains that bind you.
> Break them, then, for they are surely rusty;

Bathe in the blood of that wild tiger;
Let ours come that ran first,
Like torrents down spacious riverbeds,
One thousand times it shouts *independence or death*;
Let the shout be heard the world wide
And let the bee buzz into the ear
of the cruel Iberian tyrant" . . .

Next to obscure passages, we have found some profound and even philosophical thoughts in the composition that has these verses on its first page:

"The dark mystery rested,
Between worlds that the haughty ocean divided.
God in a ray of light illuminated it,
And rapt, these worlds beheld each other.
And Columbus was the bearer of the ray
Of divine light, which encompasses so much,
For here on Earth, human thought
Is the gleam from the light of God."

This other passage seems to us to be also most worthy of recalling, speaking to Spain:

"You would hold time fast
But time does not backward go.
It moves on, and dissolves
What stands opposed to its goal.

For time is the tool
with which God crowns his work,
It is a breath of air that makes up for
A nation that has stopped dead.

Vain are your efforts;
Time does not stop,
And sooner or later
To the evil man comes his evil hour.

You would hold time fast,
For you see that if it runs, it lights

The cross's ray, and rends
In twain the chains.

For if man understands
Man dying on the cross,
You will see him digging
A grave for your power."

There are deep thoughts here, rendered in a tone that suits them, and they above all have a daring to them. It is regrettable that a meter was chosen that leaves the ear unsatisfied. When the author gains a bit more experience in poetry and becomes used to overcoming its difficulties, we will enjoy fine works from his pen; meanwhile we bid him farewell with the recommendation he take more care in and bring more clarity to the development of his concepts.

We missed in the *Canto al 18 de septiembre* ["Song to 18 September"] the inspiration we found in the previous compositions: the pitfalls of a challenging meter perhaps have bogged down the flight of fancy, though to be sure the fluidity of verse gives one reason to suspect that few stumbling blocks of this sort have been in the way of the author in the course of his work.

"Three centuries the enslaved Chilean
suffered the servitude of a tyrant,
And in chains was tied at the feet
Of the lion of Iberia, of the Spanish colossus,
Of that lowly despot that bathed
In the blood of the defenseless South American,
Who always loved, in spite of the violence,
His never-forgotten independence" . . .

The second quintet of those we copied is of great merit; it is a most felicitous inspiration:

"The Chilean on this day
Proclaimed his freedom,
And on it the atrocious tyranny
Forever fled
My adored country.

. . . .
And you, sun, shining star,
Witness to so many feats,
You emerged in the east
Opaque to Spain,
Shining your way to Chile.
. . . .
Your beautiful September day has been
Like the gaze of that grandiose God
Who has turned dark *nothingness* into *everything*,
And the terrible He can make beauteous."

With these four fairly good verses we bring to a close our copious quotes. If the committee has seen flaws in each of the four
works it mentions, it has also seen in all of them beauty from
which their weaknesses are far from detracting. It is, additionally, hugely difficult, if not impossible, to score a bull's-eye as a
matter of course in a genre of composition that, at the same
time that it makes room for the violent impulses of youth, casts
off everything that can temper the passions of the reader once
excited. Works of this genre call for a sustained style and there
is no need to mention how arduous it is in works of some length
to fulfill this requirement.

Out of the speeches in prose we have chosen as deserving of
the prize the one that has as its epigraph a fragment whose first
verse is:

"Una hora Dios ha fijado."
["God has fixed a time."]

There is fluidity of style, fantasy has its place, and the images it presents are felicitous and fairly well developed. We
shall not dally on the occasional discordant epithet, and we believe we see in this piece, and for the first time during our examination, the harmony that talent and art produce.

Outdoing it in dazzle of imagination, but suffering at every
turn from serious flaws, there is a composition that we assign
to second place; it begins: "Cheers, cheers, my country." How
much talent and how much imagination wasted for lack of the
basics of the art! There are ill-developed metaphors, but that

sparkle even so; there are ideas that, well expressed, would suffice to create an energetic, beautiful speech.

The Commission believes that what was stated about the prose pieces is sufficient for their due appreciation, and reminds those who have glided down this easier, well-trampled road, that if they grab a laurel on equal footing with the poet, it is without the sleeplessness that is the price of long works: with less work and thus with less glory.

Our task was done, and we gladly exchange the harsh tone of judge and censor for another more agreeable, more candid one. We have been pleased to see the literary works from the younger members in this Society. It is true that there is no shining perfection in them of the sort that is the offspring of an assiduous cultivation of letters and which lends its beautiful and delicate proportions to the first fruits of talent; but instead there are traces of genius, new and profound ideas, valiant passages, colored by the rainbow of fancy. Could anything more be expected of the contenders in their first outing?

We will take this opportunity to issue a word of encouragement, which coming from us perhaps will not be ignored. The spirit has received a jolt in these latter years: education is beginning to yield its fruits, and stimulates in youth the noble desire for knowledge and to flaunt that knowledge. Each generation has its task, its obligation to fulfill: to others fell the lot of weakening a colony and forging a country; it was necessary to set it aright then on its course, and now that it continues at a steady pace, and has now made the strength of its arm felt, it is the new generation's responsibility, the youth's, to make the eyes of this country sparkle with the beneficent light of intelligence.

Santiago, 14 September 1842.—*J.V. Lastarria.*
—*A. García Reyes.*—*C. Bello.*

XXIII

When *El Semanario* finished in February 1843, peace reigned among all literary and political circles, and even the nationality battle with the Argentinians had disappeared. The latter, having well-nigh abandoned hopes that the cruel tyranny that separated them from their country would end soon, fraternized with the people that gave them comfortable asylum, worked diligently, and took an active role in all matters both public and of social progress that concerned their newly adopted country.

This quite sudden change seems inexplicable, when the better part of the previous year had been spent in a true struggle that shook Santiago and Valparaíso high society, turning up in the heated discussions in the press and in all displays of mood that took place, sometimes in the literary gatherings and in personal dealings, other times in the shows and public meetings. That phenomenon is all the more remarkable as much for the fact that the truce was established as for the fact it suddenly continued to at least 1850, with very brief interruptions, characterizing the intellectual development at work throughout that entire era, and which transforms our society. All contemporary historians take this transformation into account, and deem it our society's initiation into modern life.

In our judgment, the phenomenon is easily explained. The literary movement begun in 1842, the reasoned discussions and loud debates that originated in and were cultivated by that initiative, and the boost that the *Revista de Valparaíso* and *El Museo de Ambas Américas* gave the movement on the one hand, and *El Semanario*, *El Mercurio*, and the *Gaceta del Comercio* on the other, these latter papers following the independent and noble direction that our newspaper impressed on journalistic expression of thought, brought as an immediate result the complete emancipation of the spirit, and achieved and guaranteed the widest freedom of judgment and of the word in all circumstances and to all effects. This social evolution had occurred at a great remove from all pressure by the State and the Church, the only two powers that could have quelled the movement, or steered it toward its interests, had it so aspired. It did not do that, and from its abstention the evolution came to pass with complete independence. Intellectual and moral progress could in this way take wing to advance on a par with all the other material advancements that had come about for a long time in national life. The rights that constitute individual freedom were in fact won, and society, satisfied with its possession, did not notice that such a valuable conquest was not guaranteed by law, nor did it have any other surety than the goodwill of the rulers.

The natural outcome of such an evolution was the social liberation of religious, political, and literary concerns and traditions. The emancipated public spirit turned freethinking in religion, liberal in politics, and romantic, or rather, independent in literature. Critics replaced the old-school submission to precepts, and since it was not yet sufficiently demonstrated, welcomed, and applauded novelty of all stripes, in the social as well as the domestic realm, in politics as in religious beliefs.

We have stated previously that this new social event had been promoted outside of the realms of power, and although we can assert that in 1843 it was given life by the confidence that the Bulnes administration's policy inspired, we should also point out that at the beginning of that year, ecclesiastical power began to make ready its resistance, founding the *Revista Católica* ["Catholic Review"] in April, a weekly *religious, philosophical, historical, and literary* journal that was dependent upon the papal Curia and headed by the future bishops Valdivieso and Salas, who additionally were organizing the Instituto Nocturno ["Night School"], from which in Chile have emerged ultramontanism and jesuitism. The clergy understood that social emancipation was but dawning, and that it was still time to eclipse it, or at least take charge of it, bolstering the feeling that served as the lifeblood of the traditions that began to collapse.

We should also make mention of the fact that in Conservative Party regions a rift began to form, one that had existed in a latent state since the 1841 presidential election, prompted by the old liberals' (the *pipiolos'*) adherence to that party. This rift had its representatives in the very heart of the cabinet: some thought that conservative politics should be changed toward reform, in order to stay ahead of the demands of public opinion, to preserve the immunities of power, avoiding conflicts and disturbances, following the example of the Tories in England, who so frequently made concessions to those demands; others aimed at not having the absolute rule of power slacken, and at carrying on the political traditions that the all-powerful *pelucón* party dictatorship had maintained. These latter individuals tended naturally to form the center of the recalcitrant party, which no longer ruled since its former dictatorship had relaxed, and which nevertheless aspired to reconstitute and recover its predominance; likewise, the former had a tendency to form a new Liberal Party which ought to have been weak and uneven, since in it were to be included in the first ranks the conservatives that adopted reform as an expedient for preserving the traditions of power, alongside the old-school liberals and the younger generation, who wanted downright reform of political institutions to safeguard the democratic republic.

Political history shows the gradual development of all these background events, from the moments to which we are referring until 1851, and straightaway presents all its political and social consequences.

We needed to present in perspective as we did that facet of our political history, the better to explain in these *Memoirs* our role in intellectual development during that whole era. Understanding the circumstances of the moment, we directed all our efforts from 1843 on to taking part in organizing the new Liberal Party, so that the ferment of divisiveness might fade, or at least so that in that party neither the ideas nor the interests of that splinter group of conservatives that were beginning to weigh in as *moderate* liberals, would hold sway.

To achieve this noble end, or at least this end, we needed to define, propagate, and foster love of the true democratic doctrine, which the majority still did not know then, and establish the new party's political interests upon the need for well-defined political reform, in the democratic sense, that it might serve as the groundwork for civil reforms.

Our entrance into politics widened our sphere of action in carrying on with and serving such an uphill task. In that year we had managed to come out ahead in the deputy elections as a popular candidate in Elqui and Parral;* and in July we accepted the high clerkship of the Ministry of the Interior, with the assurance that our unforgettable friend don Ramón Luis Irarrázaval, head of that department, aspired with all the sincerity of his noble character and with deliberate conviction to modify the politics of his former party toward liberal reform. It was necessary to take the opportunity to assist the leader of the new politics in his new undertaking, and support him in his far-reaching goals. These latter were pursued with rigorous logic in the interior administration,† as the facts attest; and if they did not prevail until liberal politics triumphed in the government, it was because the traditions of absolutist politics predominated in the ruling class and in society itself. This is the truth that is reflected in the excerpt from the Report from the Interior submitted to the 1844 Congress, which the author of the *Historia de la administración Errázuriz* ["History of the Errázuriz Administration"] transcribes in part, making the triumph of the old politics depend not on the situation that passage from the Report describes, but on the inferiority of the leader of the new politics. "Irarrázaval

---

* The River Elqui mouths at La Serena-Coquimbo, to the north of the capital. Parral is a town between Santiago and Constitución in the Central Valley. —Ed.

† The Ministry of the Interior is in charge of internal affairs: government administration, elections, public order. —Ed.

has the disadvantage," states the historian, "and the flaw from which some of the best rulers of his age suffered and even by which they were victimized, the lack of training for public life and for the tasks of governing and lawmaking, and of this in large part consisted his inferiority with respect to Montt; but his independent and flexible spirit could sympathize with the cause and interests of the people and with liberal tendencies. In his 1844 Report, a much more thorough and detailed exposition than most of the documents of its kind, we find phrases that, upon reaching us across time, sound like cries of anguish wrenched from the ruler by the twofold and terrible awareness of the enormity of his power and the incompetence of the country" (p. 206, *H. de la A. Errázuriz*).

We, who wrote that exposition in a way superior to most of the documents of the era, serving our great end and in the certainty that the Minister of the Interior understood what we were having him sign, took care to describe the social and political situation, which, "in spite of having consolidated the healthy rule of law and having made the enjoyment of personal safeguards a habitual event, through the new politics," still rendered useless the government's eagerness to complete our political regeneration, and threw up roadblocks of all sorts to any reform, and powerful resistance to the constitution of our democratic system. No one who studies the history of the age and who sees how even today much of that situation endures, and how our form of democratic government still remains unconsolidated, can doubt that that was the truth. This suffices to explain the outcome of that attempt at liberal politics; we need not assume that he who made it was not trained for public life, when it so happens that that generous soul Irarrázaval had had no other life than the public one, since from earliest youth he had practiced the functions of governing and lawmaking.

But we are not seeking to make our memoirs political, but to indicate in general that, concurrently with our activities in public education, we performed the role we had in politics, attempting to have the new Liberal Party proclaim and maintain the principles of a true democratic doctrine and focus its party interest on the need for political reform. It is enough for now to recall that whenever, in the era to which we are referring, we had a hand in some way in the writing of Executive documents, we recorded events and principles like those that drew the attention of the historian in the 1844 Memorial, and like those in the Memorial from the Interior submitted in 1848, in which the foundation of the system adopted by the government is proclaimed to be the idea that "domestic tranquillity would be worth precious little without the possession of the rights the Constitution grants us," and like those that serve as the foundation of the bill on municipal organization submitted to the 1847 Congress by Minister Vial, at whose behest we drafted it.

Thus too, as political writers, writing for *El Progreso* at the close of 1843, and editing and writing for *El Siglo* with M. González and J. Chacón from October 1844 to mid-1845, and thereafter writing for various other papers, we always proclaimed and spread the democratic doctrine and maintained the need to remake our political organization, until in a document of a certain notoriety we formulated definitively the *Bases de la Reforma* ["Foundations of Reform"], which Federico Errázuriz signed as well, proponent that he was of the declaratory project of the need for constitutional reform.

In our post as deputy was where we most zealously served the great purpose of founding the new Liberal Party, so that in it the ideas and interests of the conservatives not prevail, since with this goal we managed to organize a majority in the 1849 Chamber, in which the principles and interests of the new party prevailed, impelling to reform even the conservatives and moderates who formerly dominated in organizing the new Liberal Party. But since these efforts and victories could not have solid footing without intellectual development in a democratic sense, which we had been urging and serving since 1836, we had not neglected *primary school*, which is the cornerstone of all intellectual progress, and as soon as we appeared in the 1843 Chamber, we submitted the first bill to be framed for the regulation of Primary education, which was referred, with our approval, to the University, wherefrom, after two years of work on it, it was returned to the Chamber, and was discussed and approved in the 1849 sessions.

The ensuing political vicissitudes came to confirm the truth that it was impossible to organize a true Liberal Party without spreading and asserting the democratic doctrine; for in peoples like the Spanish American, which by no means were prepared for self-rule, changes in ideas needed to come in order to instill new political habits; and since the democratic doctrine disappeared from teaching and its principles did not have the sanction of the law and administrative acts, nor the respect of the rulers, naturally there would be a resurgence of the old civic responsibility and situations like the one the 1843 Memorial described ought recur, when the formation of the new Liberal Party gets underway.

So it happened that, the conservative reaction having been victorious since 1851, which ended intellectual development in the democratic sense, just as was done before through our efforts, the Liberal Party which had not yet consolidated, by degrees began forgetting its doctrines, and losing the faithful conception of reform, which formerly was its article of faith and its great party interest. Liberal hopes remained up in the air, thanks to the interests, personal affections, the conventions, and the transactions that the circumstances of the given moment had made prevalent; the party, which on occasion has represented those hopes, has carried on without cohesion, lacking any fixed principles and devoid of a political interest that would give it unity; it sought its strength and support in personal commitments or in factitious groups and coalitions: the deadly result of the lack of a political doctrine, since there is no party possible, there is not that collective feeling that gives life to the parties, when there is a lack of a system of interests founded on clear ideas and on defined principles that attract and associate, as truth associates.

Such is the danger we sought to stave off when, with a constant, passionate devotion that can resist all opposition, we consecrated our efforts to consummate that literary revolution, which consisted in giving youth a liberal, democratic education, and we strove to have the liberal idea and democratic principles prevail in all public acts and documents on which we could have any influence. Separated from our task, the incipient Liberal Party having been defeated and disbanded, the movement to organize it stalled; and every time we have returned to political action, seeking to link the interests of doctrine and of this party's interest, we have not found it where it belongs, try as we might to find it. But never has this absence been more painful than in the previous era, in which, as a cabinet member, we sought to establish democratic policy in the autonomy of national representation, fixing the true liberal doctrine in the Memorial, in speeches, in all documents and bills from the Ministry of the Interior in 1877, principally in those concerning the reform of the interior and municipal administration and the election law, logically connecting administrative acts and facts to thought and doctrine. The liberal press and affiliates of the party that bears this name were silent toward these developments. The liberal doctrine taken to the regions of power and proclaimed and practiced from there were not worth their examination, nor even their attention, despite the fact that the media that represent the liberal idea are ordinarily quite solicitous in lavishing praise on even the most insignificant resolutions made by their friends in power. Perhaps ages hence a historian will stumble across those documents, and will gaze at them, marveling at their oddity, as was the case with 1843 Memorial from the Ministry of the Interior, whose exposition seems a bit strange for its era. Could the principles to which we are seeking to align our government in 1877 seem peculiar and strange to the present age?

But let us renew our literary memoirs.

XXIV

Since it was in teaching where we could serve our plan most efficiently, we introduced a substantial change in the legislation course we taught in the Instituto Nacional in 1843. The old text gave greater latitude to the theory of civil and penal law, reducing that of public law to generic introductions of a few matters, without formulating a true political doctrine; and though we cleared up this part in our explanations, it did not suffice to give a well-rounded idea of constitutional science. From that year on, the legislation course dealt mainly with this science, and leaving the basics of civil law to the coursework in natural law, we began then to arrange two separate texts for our course, one of them in constitutional law and the other in the theory of criminal law.

The reasons for this change, which was consistent with a new course plan in law that we proposed to don Mariano Egaña, dean of the Law School, are set forth in the preface entitled *Objeto y plan de esta obra* ["Purpose and Plan for This Work"], which we added to our *Elementos de derecho público constitucional* ["Elements of Constitutional Public Law"], whose first part appeared in print in 1846. The following year we also published the *Teoría del derecho penal* ["Theory of Criminal Law"], which is an excerpt of the works of Bentham.

The *Gaceta de los Tribunales* ["Tribunal Gazette"] on 14 August 1846 and Valparaíso's *El Mercurio* on the 19th of the same month announced the publication of *Elementos de derecho público constitucional* ["Elements of Constitutional Public Law"], calling attention to the fact that our text had not lost sight for a moment of the idea that education ought not be mixed up with the issues of the day. "The younger generation," it stated, "should not partake of the errors inherent to our age of transition, and no greater service can it render it than saving it from our worries, to forge the beautiful age that awaits the South American countries. Lastarria's goal is a praiseworthy one, met in the course of his work: would that all our countries' men who in some way are in contact with the youth fully comprehend the destinies they are called to fulfill. Mr. Lastarria's work is confined to making manifest the principle of law in all matters relative to social organization, clearly, precisely, methodically, as any work meant for use as a teaching text requires. . . . "

But these sentiments were not shared by the Priest Iñiguez, from whom the Law School at the University requested a report on the quality of that textbook. He found it obscure, inexplicable, Protestant, and at the same time atheistic and heretical, and meriting severe censure. As this review has never been published, though it ought be included in the official annals of our literary history, we insert it here:

DEAN OF THE LAW SCHOOL

In fulfillment of the University of Santiago's request, I have read the first part of the *Elementos de derecho público constitucional*, authored by J. V. Lastarria, which has been given me to render my decision on its usefulness in the teaching of youth: and naturally I regret to observe that the author has adopted a theory that based on the name alone should have been considered unworthy of his talents and devotion. It is true that he adds some brief corrective measures, but not enough, and always the heart of the doctrine remains with all the vices in its authors' sophistry and Protestantism. I cannot touch on all the points I deem deserving of censure, but I will merely indicate what to my mind stands out.

The first item that strikes one is the unintelligible definition of law, which seems made up to obscure and confound the clearest notions human reason forms. It is conceived of in these terms: "the just expression of the whole of internal and external conditions, dependent upon freedom and necessary to the development and fulfillment of the end assigned to men by his nature, is what is meant by law." In this definition we can perceive neither the principle of law, nor its author, nor the formal reason to oblige commitment, nor from it can one discern just from unjust. This definition seems to be that of the law that the atheists recognize, and its acceptance would spell the triumph of atheism.

The purpose of law, according to the author, "is man, because law has its raison d'être in the need for developing the intelligent person, and relates to the fulfillment of his rational purpose." If one asks the author what purpose this development and this fulfillment have, he will not be able to explain it without discovering the gap in his theory. He speaks many times over the course of the work about man's rational purpose, of the destiny he must fulfill, of the noble purpose that the social body is inclined to reach in its development; but nowhere is it explained what this purpose is, nor are the yardstick and the norms that should lead man to obtain this purpose determined and fixed: one only finds abstraction, obscurity and confusion on the subject.*

But the strangest part is the sanction he assigns to law and to natural law. It is none other than the one the atheists espouse and accept. "The sanction they call natural, which consists of the penalties and pleasures that affect man physically or psychologically, the social or sympathetic sanction, which refers to the individual who suffers or enjoys consequent to domestic or personal relationships." And lastly the popular, that of human vengeance and public opinion, which comprises the good and ill that can befall us from society's decision on our conduct." If natural law has no other sanction than the one proposed here, one ought not speak of law. Society and religion are through: man can mock with impunity all the laws of the supreme legislator. I do not know how the author gained his bravery to assert such an idea.

If these are the preliminary foundations of the theory, I find it useless to continue and observe the conclusions drawn from these principles: but I ought not omit mentioning something on this single chapter, section 3, first §, which treats the relations between Church and State: all the ideas it contains are Protestant and somewhat more. He states that religion is subject to the actions of law, that is, to political power in all externals, and reduces religion to the conscience as if to its original state; thus the need and obligation of the state religion in the individual and in the nation are not known.† Thereafter he speaks of the Church as a purely human association: he affects ignorance of its supernatural and divine institution, he subordinates it to the State in its observation, "grants it the right to intervene to indicate to the Church its duties and faculties with respect to the other spheres of public life"; thus he is of the opinion that nations are not bound to Him who holds all power on heaven and earth, that for them the laws of the Gospel were not handed down and that man is within his rights to adjust and revise the work of God. Finally, the author even asserts that it is the State's prerogative to

---

* Nevertheless, this point is explained with total clarity in paragraph II, chapter 1, and in section I of chapter 2.

† The opposite is explained in paragraph I, only chapter of the third section.

watch that religion not spread beyond the confines of the temples meant for its practice. This is the utmost one can say in a Catholic culture. A writing in which such ideas are set down is far from deserving the approval of any Catholic: and so, instead of believing it useful to youth, I deem it pernicious and deserving of the most severe censure. This is my judgment."
—Santiago, 9 January 1847.—*José S. Iñiguez.*

The political circumstances at the time the book was subjected to the Law School's scrutiny, in mid-1846, were favorable to the backward-thinking, sectarian ideas and tendencies expounded in the report. One year previous, the conservative reaction had emerged victorious once again.

At the beginning of 1845, the liberal idea and the goal of organizing a new party that served it, following the principles and interests that had cleared a path in the first four years of the Bulnes administration, no longer had their representative in the cabinet, which was organized with the elements and men that maintained the political traditions of the conservative dictatorship. From the start they affirmed their aspiration in the government, yielding to all the ultramontane clergy's exegencies, bolstering the strength of this power, and ignoring the liberal demands of public opinion, which certainly were quite moderate, since in politics they were nothing more than a democratic reform in the administrative order, by means of an amendment to the interior administration law.

At the same time that the reaction was strengthening, the remains of the old *pipiolo* party reappeared on the political scene, alarming the conservative circles, even those most given by their moderation to the goal of organizing a new Liberal Party. Our efforts had fallen short of achieving this organization, for even in the Central Election Society, which was formed by adopting our *El Siglo* program, the old Liberal Party had prevailed, and had constituted as the organ of its outdated interests the *Diario de Santiago*. We moderate liberals had no part in that battle of old antagonists, in which the true democratic idea did not appear, and whose purpose could be none other than the total victory of the conservative dictatorship. We closed down *El Siglo*, and being already distanced from the public posts in which we had worked for the organization of the new party, we saved our energy for a better occasion, jointly with all the new-school liberal youths. None of these helped the conservative government to rehabilitate the spent influence it began to set in motion, spreading the alarm, sowing fear, and calling out for help in the name of *order* to all the conservatives who had dispersed or changed in the early days of the Bulnes administration. In mid-1846, those worn-out connections, the bogus conspiracies, imprisonments, states of siege, had served their end marvelously; the government found in its camp many brilliant youths who, impassioned with *order*, returned obediently to the yoke of a strong government and the rule of conservative ideas.

It was not strange, then, that our *Elementos de derecho público constitucional* had been condemned at that time by a father of the Church and member of the Conservative Party, who had just restored, though fleetingly, his politico-religious interests. With all this restoration, he had not been effective enough to stem the tide of intellectual development, which, as we stated earlier, had grown strong in the concord of all the literary and political coteries, which had been in force in 1843. This accord for intellectual progress still existed, and the Argentinian writers who had aided it in 1842, continued serving it, though they had taken part in politics in the conservative ranks, like many other national writers who, having added their part, had not renounced their literary background.

Thus we have a reason why, despite the university report, our public law text had been adopted by the rector of the Instituto Nacional, and that this adoption was officially supported later by the *Gaceta de los Tribunales*, which, relating in their 24 June 1848 editorial the Memorial that that official had read in a formal ceremony, writes as follows: "Mr. Lastarria's work," it states, "ordered adopted by the rector of the Instituto Nacional, is in our opinion proof of the independence and the appreciation of true merit: of independence, inasmuch as Mr. Lastarria's text had been rejected in the Law School by a too-cowardly and unenlightened member; and of appreciation, for the outline Mr. Lastarria presents in his legislation course is, as the rector of the Instituto Nacional states very well, a compilation of doctrine based on a vast and shining theory, where pure reason prevails, and where all social interests are reconciled admirably."

In the end the text was also adopted by the University, but with a few slight modifications indicated by other Law School proxies, Messrs. A. Bello and G. Ocampo, changes which were spelled out in the second edition of the work by means of this

NOTICE

The differences in this edition from the first edition are on pages 5, 25, 30, 33, 63, 64, 79, 88, 89, 185, 186, and 187, on which are contained the modifications with which the work has been adopted for study.

The University having taken two and one-half years to issue its report on this work, the author has been dissuaded from publishing the *Second Part*, as much to avoid similar difficulties as for the fact that, his observations not being integral to the Constitution of the State, for the students to constantly pursue the positive study of constitutional law, it is enough to make the former code available to them, not losing sight of the principles explained in this First Part.

The commentary on the Constitution, which had constituted the Second Part, will be published separately under more favorable circumstances. Santiago, December 1848.

Actually, the University's administrative conditions and the spirit that then reigned in it were not favorable circumstances for the stance we had taken in fostering liberal education, however much we found support outside that body. Thus we continued teaching our commentaries on the Political Constitution, though we did not bring them to light until much later, and our theory of criminal law, which, though in print, we did not submit to the University. We had no incentive to do so, since this learned institution had gone so far as to convey to us on more than one occasion that the prizes that the law confers on professors who write textbooks had not been established for the author of those works. Then, and to this very day, were a professor to submit what we have written, his reward would be the doubling of his years of service. But for us was reserved a dereliction: the condemnation of the liberal ideas we were championing.

In literary education, also in 1843, we introduced substantial changes. Mr. Bello was then teaching Roman law to a few students, following his own lesson plans, and literature using *Arte de hablar en prosa y verso* ["Art of Speaking in Prose and Verse"] by Gómez Hermosilla, which was perennially his preferred text, irrespective of Mr. Amunátegui's many remarks to the contrary; having urged us to offer a literature course to the many youths who had requested admission to his class, Mr. Bello being unable to meet this demand, we yielded to their requests, organizing a private class at the Instituto Nacional. Lacking textbooks and not wishing to use Hermosilla's, though the students could consult it, since it was the most common one at the time, without incurring detriment, we embarked on an oral course, introducing for the first time the teaching of the history of Spanish literature, using copious lessons we wrote for the occasion and of which we have preserved only fragments today. We conformed otherwise to the *Lecciones sobre la retórica y las bellas letras* ["Lessons on Rhetoric and Belles Lettres"] by Hugo Blair, translated from the English by Munarriz, from whose worthy treatise a poor compendium had been taught for many years in that same establishment.

Yet, though we did not manage to see our plan to fruition, since we had to accept, four months after beginning, the head clerkship of the Ministry of the Interior, we entrusted its completion to V. F. López, who, sharing our ideas, presented the brilliant exams that proved to bear splendid witness to the advantages of innovation. Then López wrote his *Curso de bellas letras* ["Course in Belles Lettres"], which he published and from which he later taught, and which, though not a faultless text, stood head and shoulders above the Spanish works known here.

In the introduction to that book, López, explaining his plan, surveyed the known texts, and rendering due praise to Blair, let loose a barrage of justified condemnation of Hermosilla's and Gil de Zárate's texts. The numerous Hermosilla adepts, which still prevailed, were outraged, as were the reverent adherents of Spanish literature, who could not yet believe that this literature was really ours.

XXV

B ut let no one think that progress in education was limited to courses under our purview, for the literary movement, which in 1843 underwent unimpeded development, was at work mainly in the public education administered at the Instituto Nacional and the several private schools that were being founded to take advantage of the extraordinary crowd of students that flocked daily to the places of education, proving that the entire society was taking part in that healthy movement.

That year, the Instituto newly organized elementary or preparatory education in the scientific professions, in keeping with the decree of 25 February, which stipulated that in the six years of the program, one study the following fields in the order it established: 1. Latin, Spanish, English, and French languages; 2. drawing; 3. arithmetic, algebra, geometry, and trigonometry; 4. religion; 5. cosmography, geography, and history; 6. elements of natural history, physics, and chemistry; 7. rhetoric, and 8. philosophy; establishing as well an academy of literary exercises for sixth-year students, who had to take Latin literature with written exercises, intellectual and moral philosophy, and the history of Latin America, especially Chile.

This new plan, which had been pondered and discussed beforehand among the Instituto professors, was aimed not only at suitably training those who were devoted to advanced studies, but also mainly to give those that did not pursue scientific professions a more extensive and practical education than the one they used to receive over six years under the 1832 plan, studies centered on Latin, Spanish, French, and geography. But this outcome, which was sought with the desire to propagate an education that enabled the citizen to use his practical know-how in real life, was going to depend entirely on the methods and the application given to the new plan, limiting theoretical studies to the essentials, restricting learning by rote, and giving the fullest development possible to the exercise and practical applications of scientific knowledge. Thus was the plan carried out at first; but unfortunately, later the custom of providing extensive development for rote studies was inaugurated, mainly in history, and of turning scientists to the learning of vast, impracticable theories; so, at the time that major innovation in 1843 failed, and the instruction one acquires in the preparatory course prepares one for practically nothing, neither to he who is devoted to a scientific profession nor to the citizen who limits his education to the humanities, believing that with it one gains the skills to live in modern society.

The movement in the press matches the aspiration, culminating in that very remarkable year in our literary chronicles; for out of twenty-four fairly wide-ranging works, twelve are didactic and entirely devoted either to teaching or to the spreading of knowledge.

But the most important event that bears witness to that aspiration is the establishment of the Universidad de Chile, which had been created by law on 17 September 1842, and was inaugurated formally on 17 September 1843, in the main hall of the old Universidad de San Felipe, which then was used as the boardroom of the Chamber of Deputies, in spite of still having its old decorations, among them the portraits of Saint Thomas Aquinas and that of his contradictor, the subtle Escoto, that of Aristotle, and that of the master of sentencing, Peter Lombard,* in addition to others, and that of Heraclitus crying, and Democritus laughing, who faced one another from opposite sides of the main entryway as if to suggest that in that place there was reason to laugh and also to cry.

* Saint Thomas Aquinas (1225?–1274), Italian theologian, Dominican Scholastic philosopher, author of *Summa Theologica*, and commentator on *Sententiarium Libri Quatuor*, the compilation of patristic opinions by Peter Lombard (1095?–1160 or 1164); John Duns Scotus (1266?–1308), Scottish Franciscan Scholastic, commentator on Lombard and critic of Aquinas. The prominence of such portraits indicates that the teachings and the disputations of these great Catholic thinkers made for intellectual debate of a high level. —Ed.

The establishment was performed by the President of the Republic, in the company of his ministers, committees from both legislative Houses, and the courts and other civilian and military bodies, and attended by eighty-six members that the administration had named to the five schools, and the twenty-two doctors that remained from the Universidad de San Felipe, several of which turned out in gown and tassel, old style. After a brief address by the Minister of Public Education and one that the new rector, don Andrés Bello, read, the entire assembly moved to the Cathedral, where the *Te Deum* was sung with great pomp, and thereafter all went to the governor's hall, where the ceremony ended. This was a true civil celebration, which helped commemorate the thirty-third year of our independence.

Mr. Bello's address was awaited with great interest, for despite the fact that everyone forgot the previous year's antagonism and polemics, excited to serve intellectual development, the old-school literati expected the words of the wise master would condemn the subversive ideas that had begun the movement, while we of the new school flattered ourselves with the certainty that those words would be favorable to us. And this certainty was not unfounded, for the new rector, our old teacher, had already taken a position in our ranks, becoming a collaborator of *El Crepúsculo*, which we had begun to publish three months previously.

But the master lent a hand to everyone, without giving satisfaction to either of the two bands, building his work on both enemy trends. He stated rightly that all truths are touching, and just as one cannot keep a structure standing over the two rivers that for stretches run together in opposite directions in the heights where Petrópolis is nestled, that city of gardens that delights the Rio de Janeiro aristocracy, neither could one keep up the great portal of the University on similar foundations.

The rector introduced his address with a testimony of recognition of the University for its establishment. "As for me," he said, "I know only too well that those distinctions and that confidence I owe much less to my aptitudes and strengths than to my former zeal (this is the one quality I can attribute myself without pretension), to my former zeal for spreading healthy principles, and to the laborious dedication with which I have pursued some branches of study, uninterrupted throughout all ages of my life, not left undone in the middle of serious tasks"; and as if to emphasize the unity of his healthy principles, as he rejected the muted echoes and old-fashioned orations that look on the cultivation of letters and sciences as a danger, added: "morality (which I do not separate from religion) is the very life of society: freedom is the stimulus that gives healthy vigor and fertile activity to social institutions."

Afterward, founding and demonstrating the proposition of his address, which comprised three topics—moral and political influence in the letters and sciences, the administration of literary organizations, and the special tasks that university schools should perform in the present state of the Chilean nation—, he split his loyalties between the age's two schools of literary opinion. The old school found its defense in many opinions in the address. The wise master stuck to the transcendental philosophical conception of the unity of truth, which the Unitarian school proclaimed in harmony with the unity of nature, which so many philosophers from Democritus on, have taught: "all truths are touching," he stated; but soon leaving the scientific order, after having insinuated that the progress of civilization, the longing for social improvements, and the thirst for freedom were owed to literature, he went on to place the beliefs that have no other support than faith alongside the truths that can be proven scientifically; he exclaimed: "All truths are touching, and I extend this assertion to religious dogma, to theological truth. . . . I believe there exists, and it can do no less than exist, a narrow alliance between scientific revelation and that other universal revelation that speaks to all men in the book of nature. If misguided understanding has abused its knowledge for the purpose of impugning dogma, what does this prove save the condition of things human? . . . " This union of scientific evidence and dogmatic belief perhaps was a reminiscence of Leibnitz's theodicy, in which German philosophy, moving from metaphysics to theology, sought to conciliate the realm of nature with that of grace. Be that as it may, after the new rector made manifest his adherence to that conjunction, which he so many times had attempted and never achieved, to proclaim a confessional morality, a confessional science, and also a confessional literature, whose pleasures make of the letters, "after the humble and contented religious resignation, the best preparation for the hour of misfortune," it came as no surprise that he demand a confessional education. After establishing that "the fostering, above all of the religious and moral education of the nation, is a duty that is incumbent on each member of the University for the fact of having been received in its heart," he asserted that the foremost of the body's objectives, and the most far-reaching one, was the fostering of ecclesiastical sciences, and added these assertions: "If the cultivation of the ecclesiastical sciences matters for the functioning of the sacerdotal ministry, it matters as well that there exist among young intellectuals, among all the youth that partake of literary and scientific education, an adequate knowledge of dogma and of the annals of the Christian faith. I do not think it necessary to prove that this should be an integral part of the general education indispensable to all professions, and even for all men who wish to occupy a position in society higher than the lowest."

And as if to link these essentially conservative traditions to the old dictator's political doctrine, which had social progress consist of material progress and the predominance of the oligarchy of the rich, which we had fought, the eminent man of letters stressed the idea, as if in passing, that the subsistence and welfare of the working classes derived from the wealth of the fortunate class, instead of acknowledging that the origin and support for that welfare lie in work and in saving. Insightfully explaining the hypothesis that primary education owes its advancements to the cultivation of its advanced studies, he stated: "Literary and scientific education is the source from which elementary instruction draws its sustenance and its vigor, in the manner in which in a well-organized society the wealth of the class most favored by fortune is the wellspring from which the working classes' subsistence and the nation's welfare are derived."

In thus validating with the authority of his teaching profession the principles upon which the old school based the cultivation of letters of sciences, the wise rector did not wish to forget the study of Roman law, which was the great innovation that he had introduced into public education.* "The

---

* Despite Mr. Bello's conscientious and spirited adherence on such a solemn occasion to a system of public education that is diametrically opposing the emancipation of the human spirit, Mr. M. L. Amunátegui, who knows and has worked with that address so many times, affirms in the last elegy that he wrote of Mr. Bello that he was the one who most had served against that system in Chile. "*Intellectual emancipation,*" he states in his articles in *La República* in April 1878, "like political emancipation, was too vast and complicated a work for it to be accomplished by a single individual. Nevertheless, Bello's share in this task was one of the most considerable, one could say *the main one.*" Mr. Amunátegui, in his efforts to present his hero as a liberal and progressive teacher, even in his teachings in the time of the dictatorship (1834–1837), when he professed and practiced the system he proclaimed in 1843, an age in which he was already more transigent and even more liberal, he had no qualms about warping history, nor about giving the most random and flexible explanations of the master's facts and opinions. One clearly discerns that behind those efforts lies a clear purpose, for under the pretext of rendering one more tribute to Mr. Bello and of defending him from imaginary attacks, he published, these *Memoirs* having just appeared, his long work on the *Influencia de don A. Bello en los orígenes del movimiento intelectual moderno de Chile* ["Influence of don A. Bello on the Origins of the Modern Intellectual Movement in Chile"], with the purpose of contradicting the author of the *Memoirs,* whose name he had omitted scrupulously in all his writings on literary history, denying him the place he has had in the intellectual emancipation, in the liberal reform of public education. Mr. Amunátegui is a partisan of the outdated system, and defends himself as he justifies Mr. Bello, and wishes to play the leading role in this reform of intellectual emancipation, for the author of this writing even would consent to do what the wise master did, when he invoked his former zeal (*this is the one quality I can attribute myself without pretension*), his former zeal for the spreading of knowledge and of sound principles. This

University, I venture to tell you," he exclaimed in convincing tones, "will not yield to pressures that it condemn the study of Roman law as useless and pernicious; I believe, on the contrary, that it will provide it a new stimulus and give it a broader grounding." But he no longer defended this study as he did in 1834, stating that "the private law of the Romans, in opposition to their public law, is the good one, it is ours, and there are scarcely a few matters in it that need simplifying or improvement, since the reforms introduced by the emperors made it greatly superior to the *Roman Republic's code of iron* and have been adopted by most of the civilized nations of Europe." In the address he defended it because according to the testimony of Lerminier, who he assumes to be an equalizing democrat, and that of Leibnitz, that study is the best apprenticeship in juridic and forensic logic; and in response to the objection that it also is an apprenticeship of a doctrine contrary to all democratic progress and to the principle of the inviolability of the individual, the family, and of society, he added that we needed to purge legislation of the sovereign people, from which we are descended,

is the reason why, in this difficult task, Mr. Amunátegui has had to distort everything, denying Mr. Bello's influence on the misdirectedness of our studies in 1834, failing to mention the principles that the latter proclaimed at the University's establishment in 1843, while seeking to paint him as a servant of intellectual emancipation; he does so by recalling some of his progressive ideas on other matters, such as literary criticism and even on theater criticism, and by transposing to a previous age the ways of thinking the master had after 1843, in the age in which he was entering the progressive movement, modifying his old ideas, and even becoming liberal. We are not attempting to understand Mr. Amunátegui's motive, but his goal is clear, and we will not shrink from presenting it just as it appears in the plan that he has enacted to achieve it, for we believe we have the right to reject a systematic attack against an honor that is ours, without diminishing another's. Why does Mr. Amunátegui not render his homages to the great merit that Mr. Bello has as a founder of our literary, juridic, and public law studies, a merit that we have acknowledged gratefully and praisingly in our *Recuerdos del maestro* ["Memories of the Teacher"]; and he seeks to attribute to him, furthermore, merits that are not his, that of the main protagonist of our intellectual emancipation, that of initiator of the liberal reform of our education and of the modern literary movement? Why? We have said as much before, and we are not inclined to repeat it, leaving all at liberty to say what they will to that distinguished writer, as with those that helped Mr. Bello in the task of telling to their liking the history of our literary progress. We do so without changing the facts, or distorting the documents: if each one's part played in that movement seems different from them, we have not had the will to censure nor accuse anyone. We recognize and respect the worth of all, and we repeat with Victor Hugo: "Truth and freedom have that excellent quality: that everything done for them, and against them, is of equal service to them."

"from the stigma it acquired under the damaging influence of despotism; we must clear up the inconsistencies that detract from a work to which so many centuries, so many alternating interests holding sway, so many contradictory inspirations have contributed. We must accommodate it, bring it back into the fold of the *republican institutions*."

After such contradictory defenses of the study of Roman law, the rector, always demonstrating the topics of his address's proposal, and undoubtedly thinking he had said enough in support of conservative doctrines, met, though reservedly, the aspirations of the new school. Upon listing the special tasks of the School of Humanities, of "that literary department that through the contemplation of ideal beauty and through its reflection on works of genius, refines taste and reconciles bold fits of fancy with the unprescribable rights of reason," he did not make a single allusion to Spanish literature nor to the *admirable models*. This in itself was significant, since he desisted from considering that literature ours. Later, replying to the charges that in the previous year's literary polemic he had been led down the wayward path of our studies, he vindicated the reputation as purists and theorists those of his school had earned in those heated discussions. "I shall never," said the teacher, "advocate the excessive purism that condemns all novelty in language; I believe, on the contrary, that the multitude of new ideas that daily pass from literary intercourse into general currency, demand new words to represent them. . . . But one may broaden the language, one may enrich it, adapt it to society's every requirement, and even to those of fashion, which commands an incontestable authority over literature, without adulterating it or vitiating its constructions, without distorting its spirit." And then he added: "Art! Upon hearing this word, though taken from Goethe's very lips, there are probably those who will place me among the supporters of conventional rules, which for a long time usurped that name. I solemnly protest such a meaning; and I do not think my background justifies it. I do not find art in the sterile precepts of a school. . . . But I believe that there is an art founded on the impalpable, ethereal relationships of ideal beauty; I believe there is an art that guides the mind's eye in its most fiery raptures; I believe that without that art, fantasy, instead of fleshing out in its works the model of beauty, miscarries with sphinxes, enigmatic and freakish assertions. This is my literary faith. Freedom in everything; but I do not see freedom, but rather licentious intoxication in the imagination's orgy."

Protesting thus against the misdirection that had been attributed to his teachings, the master adhered to the new school and as a writer joined forces resolvedly with the romantics. *Freedom in everything* was his watchword. But how was the old school to reconcile freedom of the spirit with the basis the rector adopted before in the cultivation of letters and sciences?

Fearing this conflict, he explained that he desired "freedom, as a counter-point on the one hand to the servile meekness that welcomes everything unexamined, and on the other, to the intemperate dissoluteness that rebels against the authority of reason," an authority that, according to the judgment he had just issued, could only be found in the union he had forged between scientific evidence and dogmatic faith, considering every challenge to dogma an error in understanding and a misuse of knowledge.

To connect his literary background, which he so candidly defended for himself, with the stance that at the time he had assumed as a new-school collaborator in *El Crepúsculo*, he alluded affectionately to the young poets that were then a part of it, exhorting them enthusiastically and excusing the faultiness of their poetry. "But correctness," he said, "is the product of study and time; who could expect it from those who, in a moment of exaltation at once poetic and patriotic, rushed headlong into that new arena, determined to prove that in Chilean souls too that divine fire burns, of which an unjust prejudice had thought them deprived? . . . " The rector omitted the true events leading up to the literary movement, which he applauded; likewise he omitted above all that the reproach to our poetic lifelessness had been flung in the debate that happened *after* the movement had begun, and that the author of said reproach had asserted many times that he did not think Chilean souls were lacking that divine fire, and did not attribute the life-lessness to a lack of capability, but to the misdirection of our studies, which had made us slaves to purism and conventional rules, observations that the teacher as director of those studies strenuously rejected.

These inexplicable omissions have become law in our history, for all those who have written about that literary movement had omitted what the rector omitted, and attributed it, as he did, to the desire to give the lie to a supposed prejudice that did not exist. On the contrary, the reproach of our lifelessness caused not the desire to prove competence but the emancipation from rules and from purism, which the master abjured, and the daring that showed in the faultiness he exonerated.

XXVI

The Universidad de Chile's inaugural address, of which we have given such a long-winded account due to its importance in our literary history, appalled all of us supporters of the new school, despite the flattering intimations with which the speaker seemed to approve of our attempts and take part in our intellectual emancipation movement. The illustrious rector proclaimed, on behalf of the University, doctrines that eventually went greatly against the grain of this evolution's natural purpose, which, as we stated earlier, consisted of society freeing itself from the prejudices that, like dogmas, reigned in the old colonial civilization. The spokesman for wisdom in our country was placing the tablets of the old law ahead of new hopes. His profession at that time was a power that shielded in its patronage all the old traditions that enchained the human spirit, the independence of which we wished to win. How to fight him at the apex of his glory and his victories? How to assert the small successes that had been garnered? We needed to resign ourselves and wait, working always to pave the way for a future we then believed nigh, and which nevertheless even today is far off.

We said nothing in the press, but we argued with the master, taking advantage of the honor we had in being his disciple at the same time we were colleagues in a State ministry, for he occupied the head clerkship of Foreign Relations, and we, that of the Interior. The opinions in his address were for a long time a compulsory topic in the calm conversations we had daily after work was out. Indeed, one of those opinions, to which we still have not done justice, led to disagreements of notorious consequence, and thus we will tell its story, though summarily. It is the story of historical writings.

Apropos of what we had stated in our address to the Literary Society about the good fortune we South Americans had in reaping the benefits from European civilization, being prudent in imitation, it had been written that we ought to accept a synthesis of that civilization, but without including in any way under that rubric its philosophical systems, nor the moral and political conclusions still subject to examination and discussion. Nevertheless, Mr. Bello rejected that idea in his address to the University, expressing that he had not understood its meaning, for he thought they were seeking to present the philosophy of history as a synthetic product, in order to eliminate the study of history itself, replacing it with the former, and placing them in opposition. "But I am not certain if I am mistaken," he stated in his address. "The opinion of those who feel we should inherit the synthetic products of the European enlightenment, excusing us from examining their credentials, excusing us from analytic procedure, the only means of acquiring true knowledge, will not find many supporters at the University. Respecting others' opinions as I do, and reserving only the right to discuss them, I confess that abiding by Herder's* moral and political conclusions without having studied ancient and modern history, for example, would seem as unsuitable to me for fostering knowledge as would be adopting Euclid's theorems without having done the intellectual work of proving them. Gentlemen, I look on Herder as one of the writers that have been of most service to humanity: he has given history all its dignity, developing in it the designs of Providence and the destinies to which the human race is called on earth. But Herder himself did not intend to supplant the knowledge of facts, but to illustrate them, explain them; one cannot even appreciate his doctrine save through prior historical studies. To substitute deductions and formulas for them would be to present a skeleton to the younger generation instead of a living transference of social man; it would be tantamount to giving them a collection of aphorisms instead of laying out the moving, instructive, picturesque panorama in full view, a panorama of the institutions, customs and revolutions of great nations and great men."

No one has maintained, in speaking of the synthetic products of the European enlightenment, that it was suitable to educate the intellect to accustom it to think for itself, to accept unreflectively the conclusions of just any philosophical system; and if the Argentinian writers had recommended the study of the philosophy of history in Vico and Herder, they had not rejected, as far as we know, the study of history itself, nor had they spoken of that study apropos of the synthetic products of European civilization, placing it on the level of these products. Mr. Bello becomes carried away in the confusion from which he suffers, for by himself accepting Herder's bogus system, he seems to discard the study of the philosophy of history and give preference to the study of the historical chronicle and narrative.

We, who did not accept Herder's theory, nor any another that was based on the assumption of a necessary and immutable evolution of humanity, without the freedom of man playing the least part, do not agree with the rector that Herder had given history all its dignity, developing in it the designs of Providence; for we do not believe that the human race on earth was condemned by the Divinity to fulfill a certain destiny independently of its own actions and freedom. But we concur with Herder on the need for the study of the philosophy of history, as well as on the possibility of writing philosophically the particular history and that of an era in a given nation,

---

* Johann Gottfried von Herder (1744–1803), German philosopher and litterateur. —Ed.

or that of any of its social phases. Mr. Bello doubted this possibility, holding that what could be done was philosophize or moralize about events and men, when writing the narrative history of a nation; for, in his judgment, one matter is the general science of humanity, which is called the philosophy of history, and another is the history of the events of a race, of a nation, an age, without the former leading us to the particular philosophy of the latter as we maintained it. Mr. Bello established a difference between the philosophy of history and events, and believed that the first priority was to make a chronicle of the details, the narration of occurrences, then to deduce their characteristic spirit to appraise and judge them according to their circumstances, in which he invested all philosophy and historical science: so in his view, there were as many philosophies or historical sciences as there are judgeable events.

These constant and at times lengthy discussions induced him doubtlessly to enjoin us to write the first historical Memorial to be submitted to the University; and to commission us for the task, as we have related on another occasion, for since the University should keep surging ahead, it fell to us as a revolutionary to provide the prod.

Let us recall here our ideas on history, our system, which we can vindicate as a discovery that belongs to us, without conceit, for not only did we lay out the plans for it in that first University Memorial, but we have also followed it always in all the historical works we have composed, until giving the philosophical explanation of it we did in the second appendix on *Moral progress* that we added to our *Libro de oro* ["Treasury"] in 1868, and which we perfected in the second of our *Lecciones de política positiva* ["Lessons in Positivist Politics"], published in 1874. This is an event in the literary history of Chile and that of Spanish America, which future historians will surely appreciate for what it is worth, and therefore we ought to record it.

Before 1868 the author of these *Memoirs* was unaware that Kant had considered history a natural phenomenon, in a treatise that Littré made known in his book on August Comte published in 1864, assuring that until then he was unknown in France.* But reading Vico's *Principles of a New Science* in 1840, and then Herder's *Ideas on the Philosophy of History*, we had rebelled against both men's theories, for no other reason than that they were founded on a supernatural concept of human history. Both, starting from the assumption that the human race is governed in its historical evo-

---

* Immanuel Kant (1724–1804), German Pietist metaphysician and transcendentalist philosopher; Maximilien-Paul-Émile Littré (1801–1881), French Positivist, lexicographer, and associate of Isidore-Auguste-Marie-François-Xavier Comte (1798–1857), French founder of Positivism. —Ed.

lution by providential laws, build their systems by dispensing utterly with the conditions that constitute the independence of human nature. The immortal Vico* believes he has found in history the last word of Providence, the law that has reigned and shall continue reigning over humanity everlastingly; this law consists of the three ages that he calls the divine or age of idolatry, the heroic or age of barbarism, and the human or age of civilization. In this tight circle are enclosed the past, the present, and the future; humanity revolves endlessly within it, for each social evolution revives barbarism. Thus humanity forever begins its path anew, guided by God and fulfilling His will, as Bossuet† had assumed also shortly before in his *Discourse on Universal History*. Furthermore, Herder, without squeezing humanity into a necessary and immutable evolution, assumes it is guided by the hand of Providence, and is constantly changing in an endless struggle with itself and against the material world.

In these theological conceptions of history, the freedom of man and its progress disappear as an exclusive product of its activity. Resultantly, his responsibility too is nullified. There is no philosophy in history, and history cannot be the science of humanity.

We adhered then to the definition of *science* that Falck‡ gives in his *Introducción al estudio del derecho* ["Introduction to the Study of Law"] or *Enciclopedia jurídica* ["Juridic Encyclopedia"], wherein he states that science is "an aggregation of truths of the same order, or of notions that, for their relationship to a single object, are linked in such a way that they stand for a single corpus of doctrine and form a unit." And we reflected thus: if there is philosophy in history and therefore history is a science, it must necessarily be also that the events that form human evolution are not a supernatural phenomenon subject to irrevocable or providential laws, for in that case history cannot be the object of an aggregation of truths forming a corpus of doctrine, since each historian will understand and interpret those laws as he will, and determine in his own mind what is truth. On the contrary, for there to be science in history one need believe that human events are inter-

---

* Giambattista Vico (1668–1744), Italian rhetorician and philosopher, best known for his monumental *Principi di una Scienza Nuova d'intorno alla Comune Natura delle Nazioni* (1725), a landmark work that inspired the systematic study of human history. —Ed.

† Jacques-Bénigue Bossuet (1627–1704), French prelate and famed orator. —Ed.

‡ Possibly a reference to Antoine Reinhard, Baron Falck (1776–1843), Dutch statesman and man of letters.

connected natural phenomena dependent upon human action and will; thus, to describe the aggregation of truths that through their connection to a single object, which is humanity, form a corpus of doctrine or of the philosophy of history, it is imperative to study the relationship those events have among themselves and with man's actions, or rather, with all his faculties.

This was the concept that guided us in the composition of our *Investigaciones sobre la influencia social de la conquista y del sistema colonial de los españoles en Chile* ["Investigations on the Social Influence of the Conquest and the Colonial System of the Spaniards in Chile"], the title of the first historical Report submitted to the University, on the first anniversary of its founding, September 1844. Thus it was that in the introduction preceding the work, we did not think twice about setting forth with all the boldness of a firm conviction the following conclusions, which we could only demonstrate laconically, adapting to the nature of an academic discourse:

1st. That the reasoning is erroneous that, starting from the contemplation of a supreme power that, acting constantly, normalizes everything in the immense chaos of ages, deduces that it is logically necessary to believe in historical fatality.

2nd. That since Herder recognizes as he does that the Divinity has imposed other limits on man than those that depend on time, place, and his own faculties, and that spontaneity is inherent in his nature, it is logical to recognize too that humanity is much nobler in its essence than those who, like Herder himself, imagine it bound in its course to providential laws, as blindly as is matter to its own laws.

3rd. "Society possesses that sovereignty of judgment and will that constitutes in the individual the ability to forge his own welfare and exaltation, provided he not trespass against justice. . . . Still, I cannot deny that weakness, ignorance and other mishaps that are not anomalous in the history of the world, and which are difficult to avoid, often weave the misfortunes of nations, despite the latter's resisting with all their might the blow that brings them to their knees; but this same consideration is the very thing that persuades us of the urgent need society has to take its preservation and development into its own hands, availing itself not only of its own resources, but also *of the lessons that experience* provides it, studying humanity in its virtues and in its aberrations and vices, with an eye to gleaning from its very study the preventive of evil, or at least the way to neutralize its effects. So where is those societies' experience found? Where are its precepts stored but in history, in that holy repository of the centuries, in that tabernacle that encompasses all the splendor of civilizations that time has cast, all the wisdom that the catastrophes of the human race contain?"

4th. "The human race has in its very nature the capacity for its perfection, it possesses the elements of its happiness, and no other than it has been given the faculty to make its own way and promote its development, for the laws of its organization form a clavichord that man alone can play to draw harmonious sounds from it. With a view to knowing those laws and appraising them in their natural outcome, he must open the great book of his life, in which it is set down in indelible characters that the constant alternation of well-being and misfortune in which the centuries have elapsed is not the fateful work of a blind power that drives him from event to event, nor the inevitable consequence of whim, but a natural product of those laws, of that order of conditions to which his nature is subject. He will see also that if in the physical universe the causes that act as laws for him evolve spontaneously to produce a necessary outcome, the same process is not at work in the moral universe, for man has the power to initiate the development of his laws or to avoid it through the freedom of his actions, as suits his happiness. Humanity *is not nor has it been what it could have quite been, were the circumstances of time and place paid heed*, but what it had to be, paying heed to the use that the men who have ruled and led it made of those circumstances: humanity has an active part in the orientation of its fate, for were that not the case, its freedom would be an insulting lie, its dignity would vanish, and the idea of justice could not exist in the world."

This last clause contained the categorical denial of Herder's and Vico's theological theories, and despite how much the first of the Argentinian writers, on the one hand, presented us with the example of Michelet, who adopted those theories; and on the other hand, Mr. Bello objected that Niebuhr also, writing on the origins of Rome, and Savigny,* compiling the history of Roman law, recognized the providential laws in the order of events, we persisted in our doctrine founded on the freedom and progress of humanity; upon expounding it in the introduction, we added an excuse in a note to the above clause: "I may perhaps be dubbed bold for departing from the foundations of the brilliant theories of more than one genius of the modern age; but I beg pardon for this if it be a breach, and I request license to use my freedom of thought. I do not believe in historical fatalism, as some wise souls conceive of it."

Otherwise, applying our system to the study of our own history, to prove that the philosophy of a nation could be written, we studied, in the body of that Memorial presented to the University, the events of our colonial age in light of the ideas that had produced them, in order to judge them by our system's criteria. But if we attended to the ideas of the age, we also took

---

* Probably Jules Michelet (1798–1874), French historian, professor at the Collège de France; Barthold Georg Niebhur (1776–1831), German historian and philologist; Friedrich Karl von Savigny (1779–1861), German jurist and historian, founder of the historical school of jurisprudence. —Ed.

into account sentiment, which gives rise for the most part to events, so we did not accept the theory of Hegel's* historical school, which assumes that social events are invariably the work of the idea or the spirit. Starting in our system from the principle that the human race has the capacity for its perfection, and that no other race than it is provided the ability to manage itself and to promote its development, since in essence it is free and thus responsible, we ended up recognizing that it also has the duty to correct its forefathers' experience in order to assure its future, as one can see in the fourth of the transcribed conclusions. This leads us naturally in the survey of our historical antecedents to examine how the Spanish civilization proceeded in the conquest and in colonial organization, in order to understand its workings and influence in contemporary society, and especially in the revolution of our independence, with a view to correcting that civilization in what elements it has in opposition to the adopted democratic organization. Short of resolving philosophically and historically the social situation of our nation at the time of our independence, we cannot know the results of that great revolution, to say nothing of the direction it ought to be given to complete its trajectory. We need to construct our democratic civilization, and to do that we should single out what is to be destroyed of the old one.

When we read in Mr. Bello's manuscript the appraisal we made of those events, according to our philosophical criterion, the wise teacher pitted against us a reflection by Du Rozoir, in his excellent study of the *Historia considerada como ciencia de los hechos* ["History Considered as the Science of Events"] that the *Dictionnaire de la conversation* publishes, and which we had read together. In judging the rational and pictorial or descriptive school, the writer says this: "Furthermore the two schools have their pitfalls as well as their advantages. Beside the drawback of not evaluating events at all, one finds the danger of judging them poorly; and there is no worse guide in history than that of certain systematic philosophers who seek not to see things as they are, but how they square with their system. To these I would cry with J.-J. Rousseau: the facts! the facts! This misapplication of reasoning and cleverness, for which even Tacitus was reproached, can be applied to virtually all the seventeenth- and eighteenth-century historians."

We rejected this observation, in the first place, because we did not make history in the capacity of rationalists, like Guizot, Thierry, or Sismondi,[†]

---

* Georg Wilhelm Friedrich Hegel (1770–1831), German metaphysician and philosopher. —Ed.

† François-Pierre-Guillaume Guizot (1787–1874), French historian and statesman; Jacques-Nicholas-Agustin Thierry (1795–1856), French historian; Jean-Charles-Léonard Simonde de Sismondi (1773–1842), Swiss historian and economist. —Ed.

judging each era, each event, each man, according to the cases and the special idea that they suggested to us, seen in the light of our political or religious opinions; in the second place, because neither did we dispense with the facts, nor try to mold them or adjust them to fit our system, but on the contrary, we needed to see them as they are in order to know their interrelationship, and the relationship they have with the state of thought and feeling prevailing in the age in which they occurred; in the third place, because to evaluate events, we did not have a subjective, metaphysical, or theological system, as Hegel, Vico, Herder, or Michelet had, but an experimental criterion, founded on human nature, on its laws of freedom and perfectibility; and thus we did not run the risk of having a judgment for each case, and far be it from us to have incurred in the deadly error of ignoring human responsibility, of excusing crime, of vindicating or glorifying a man or an event, for which the former might have worked or the latter might have been verified according to the circumstances of their age, or following a certain prevalent way of thinking.

Mr. Bello wrote two critical articles on our Report in the *El Araucano* on 8 and 15 November 1844, with a completely different opinion, for he excuses Spain its conquest and colonization of America, for they did what everyone did in their day, and they proceeded in a way consistent with their circumstances, their ideas, and their great power.

Nevertheless, he ignored almost completely the matter of the philosophy of history, for he hardly made mention of our system, to testify to its originality, or rather, its eccentricity. "Mr. Lastarria has risen up to a height in his investigations," he stated in his first article, "wherefrom he judges not only the events and men that are his special focus, but the several systems that today contend for prevalence in historical science. Braving burning issues of metaphysics relative to the laws of moral order (we were most distant from metaphysics), *he does battle with general principles that for many centuries were the world's belief and that we see copied by eminent writers of our day.*" He later made this other allusion to our system: "This gloomy and despairing dogma of fatalism against which Mr. Lastarria protests, is at bottom much of what is speculated today on the fate of the human race on earth. Acknowledging man's freedom, *it sees in history a science* from which we can derive valuable lessons so that *the course of governments and nations* can be guided by them."

Yet we were satisfied that the teacher of teachers, the highest representative in Chile of letters and sciences, merely made mention of our theory, not assailing it or using it in any other capacity than that of charging it with running contrary to the general principles that had for many centuries been the world's belief and which we see copied by eminent writers of our day. This served to indemnify us against the spirited attack that the distinguished Argentinian writer Piñero had directed against us, assuming the role of spokesman for his countrymen, in Valparaíso's *El Mercurio*, of which he was the editor.

In the issue corresponding to 30 September, the kindly and learned editor had written this condemnation of our theory: "We respect the author of the Report's freedom of thought; but forgive us for saying that the wholesale adoption of his doctrine *would eradicate the dignity of man and the idea of justice could not exist in the world*." Yet to reach this conclusion against a doctrine that in point of fact vindicated reason, therefore recognizing the responsibility of the human race, and which adopted as a criterion of justice and truth the development or perfection of the human faculties and freedom, the writer from *El Mercurio* only counterpointed our theory, by way of refutation, the conclusions of Vico, Herder, and Michelet, which we rejected. Feigning an opposition that does not exist between freedom on the one hand and reason and justice on the other, to stress Herder's incomplete views on the triumph of reason over the heart, and of his ever-growing activities to produce order and justice, Piñero found in that law the hand of Providence leading the world from its inception to the place in which it is found today, and exclaimed with Herder: "Here I bow humbly before this description of the designs of Providence for my species in general, for I recognize in it the *plan for the entire universe*." Furthermore, since the writer assumes that Vico knew how to reconcile the principle of freedom with the existence of a divine Providence that conquers all, that rules all, and leads humanity, he falls into the conflicts of this antinomy, and seeks to escape from them by citing these words of Michelet's, who he believes has found the yardstick of truth in the "[c]ommon sense, or rather, the unthinking judgment of a class of men, of a nation, of humanity; the general agreement of general meaning, of the common sense of nations, which is what constitutes the wisdom of the human race. Common sense, everyday wisdom, is the rule that God has given to the social world." We knew this opinion from Vico's commentator and translator, and also knew that Lamennais found the touchstone of truth in universal accord. But we had not been able to accept these vague remarks as a criterion, nor could we understand how an abstraction like common sense could aid in the discovery of truth, since everyone defines the term after their own fashion and finds it where it suits them. Thus we had taken as our standard of judgment in philosophy the one that the illustrious Argentinian writer discarded for Michelet, not noticing that we will know more certainly if there is truth and justice in an idea or principle, in a fact or event, by examining whether or not they are in consonance with freedom and the development of man, more than by ascertaining how common sense assesses them; God could not have handed that down as a rule, nor could anyone, to the social world, since the good of this world consists of its preservation, the development of its faculties, the extension and intensity of its life, and the use of its freedom to seek out this good, and not in what the common sense of nations thinks or feels.

We scarcely need say that with such ideas, *El Mercurio*'s editor wrote literary criticism vehemently, denying all our judgments on the history of the conquest and the Colony, taking sides with the conquistadors and colonizers for the place they held in the history of the civilization of their age. He believed that the conquests that civilization made, *shown the way by the finger of Fate*, should be judged according to their circumstances, and that it did not follow *to call the sixteenth century to account, given the nineteenth century's enlightenment*. This all-justifying doctrine was the one that the rector of the University used also two months later to refute our judgment, and likewise the one that has prevailed among our historians in defense of and even in admiration of sixteenth-century Spain for its conquests and regime in South America: its civilization both decrepit and resistant to democratic progress, even the enormous injustices of peninsular despotism:

> "Su atroz codicia, su inclemente saña,
> Crimen fueron del tiempo, y no de España,"

> ["Their inhuman greed, inclement rage,
> T'were not crimes of Spain, but of the age,"]

as Quintana stated, conforming to the historical school of absolution and accolade, which ignores the duty to inform the generations what they are to condemn and correct in the civilization they have inherited from their forebears.

XXVII

This accurate narration reveals the failure suffered by our theory on the philosophy of history and the attempt to apply it to the study of our national history. We did not even have the support of the Argentinian writers, who had supported us greatly in our literary revolution begun in the 1842 address. To the contrary, to free us from an ignorant error, they had opposed our theory by explicating it as the theory of historical fatalism; and even, abjuring the relative criterion of Vico, who believed the rule of the social realm was what was considered *just by the universality* of the human race, they taught us that the true criterion of the truth lay in *common sense*, as Michelet believed. Later the country's foremost literary authority, and perhaps that of all South America, presented us to educated opinion as a reckless individual who went up against the general principles that for many centuries were the world's belief and that the most eminent writers of the day defended.

That was more than what was needed to ruin a philosophical foray, and to stop an author in his tracks who was a young man barely having begun forming a school, whose chances for success were not good. What is strange about the eternal oblivion in which not only our theory was shrouded, but also that Report which, in being the first one arising from the statutes to be submitted to the University, is today not even considered a historical work? Has not a historical work been seen in this present year of 1878, written by one of the highest officials in public education, who, enumerating the historical Memorials submitted to the University, disregards the former so much so that he fails to even allude to it?

The 1844 fiasco, we confess, overwhelmed us. We did not in fact know any writer who had thought as we did; and though at that very time August Comte was finishing the publication of his *Cours de philosophie positive* ["Course in Positive Philosophy"], we did not have the remotest news of the illustrious philosopher's name, nor of his book, nor of his system on history, which was ours; nor do we believe that there was anyone in Chile who did, for however much it strikes us now that the editor of *El Mercurio* would end his criticism by giving us advice, in which, by a kind of second sight, he classified us in the future positivist school by telling us: "Continue in the *positive* vein that you have managed to give your studies, do not be dragged down by despair," etc.

Henry Thomas Buckle* had not yet written his admirable *Historia de la civilización en Inglaterra* ["History of Civilization in England"], with a viewpoint and a doctrine that amazed Mr. Bello twenty years after that age for the similarity it bore to our theory, which had been viewed so suspiciously by the teacher. He himself introduced us to Buckle's work, drawing our attention to several overlapping points of doctrine, especially in the way it judged Spanish civilization, and congratulating us for the strength of conviction with which, in spite of everything, we had upheld and applied our theory.

Herder's translator still had not completed his philosophical maturation in order to write his profound *Historia de la Revolución Francesa* ["History

---

* Henry Thomas Buckle (1821–1862), English historian. —Ed.

of the French Revolution"], about which E. Pelletan has just pronounced this judgment:

"Until then," he states, "historians (except for two or three, Michelet being the first) had seen the revolution in a man or in a party; one carried the coattails of Mirabeau's frock, another Lafayette's, another Vergniaud's, another Danton's, another Robespierre's. Quinet saw only one man in the revolution, the revolution itself. He accepts, recognizes and admires only its spirit; in the concept he sees the immortal part of the revolution; as for the rest, a pure jolt, a mere accident. It could be or not, it comes from time and returns to time; time has swallowed it up."

"Others have written with great talent, for it is one more triumph of the revolution to have enticed all the great men, all the strong of spirit: Thiers, Mignet, Lamartine, Louis Blanc, Michelet.* Others, we stated, have written the visible history of the revolution; the invisible history remained to be told, a history we could call the physiology of events."

Notwithstanding and even though in 1844 Quinet was, like Michelet, a philosopher who was not yet studying social physiology in history, nor the relationship between events and society's frame of mind, but rather events and providential laws, he had nevertheless been more lenient toward our theory than were our teachers and colleagues. Francisco Bilbao had presented him, on our behalf, with some Chilean works, among them the University Memorial, and the wise professor, who then gave his lessons in the Colegio de Francia on *Christianity and the French Revolution*, in his eleventh one made various citations of our *Investigaciones* ["Investigations"], calling this writing *distinguished*, and was kind enough to send us the installment that contained that lesson, as well as the following letter:

Sir: I was obliged to point out in the work, whenever I could, all excellent points; through this work I have gotten to know you. The occasion does not allow me to say more on the subject; but it is my hope to make amends for this excess of laconicism by expressing my high regard for the works that you have been good enough to send me. Allow me, if I should not ever see you, to extend my hand to you most cordially, from one side of the world to the other. Receive the expression of my most honorable sentiments.—*E. Quinet.*—Paris, 17 June 1846.

---

* Louis-Adolphe Thiers (1797–1877), French historian and statesman; François-Auguste-Marie Mignet (1796–1884), French historian, associate of Thiers; Jean-Joseph-Charles-Louis Blanc (1811–1882), French socialist leader; almost certainly Jules Michelet. —Ed.

When this word of encouragement reached us from old Europe, which was an unexpected treat for us, owing to the kindness of Francisco Bilbao, our friend and dear disciple, we were still studying our theory. Far from abandoning it, though the entire press in Chile was fatalistic in history, we were more confirmed in it through the studies we were doing of Krause's philosophy applied by Ahrens* to the study of law, and based on the very laws of freedom and progress that we took as the foundation of the philosophy of history. Indeed, Krause, in being the first of the philosophers to recognize and establish the laws that humanity obeys in its development and in its progressive course through the complete use of its *free will*, in other words, its freedom, considers those laws providential nonetheless, in the sense that since absolute, infinite freedom is an attribute of God, all finite beings created by Him are endowed with the faculty to develop for the good, with the difference that this freedom is limited; and in the knowledge of when an evolution is necessary in human development, Providence works a revelation in the superior spirits so the progress comes to pass, giving humanity a second wind to venture out in new directions, and this divine intervention in history is a constant.

We who start from the idea that human forces, including freedom, that generate the development and perfection of man, are natural phenomena, leaving aside their origins, cannot accept that doctrine; even when we accepted that these forces had a divine origin, from the start we had negated and contradicted the theological theories that, by virtue of this divine origin, allege that the historical march of humanity is the work of Providence; for in our view there is no basis for positing that God, the absolute cause of laws likewise absolute, is assiduously discharging these laws, enforcing them and changing them in the continuous governance of humanity. We admit with Krause and Ahrens that man's purpose consists of the development of his faculties, that the intelligence and the emotions react to produce this development, that freedom is the reigning power; but we consider the workings of these forces in the preservation and development of natural life incompatible with a constant intervention of the divine power. And we were confirmed in this judgment upon seeing the futility and inefficiency of the efforts to survive that Herder's school still exerted.

We had just received the *Curso de filosofía de la historia* ["Course on the Philosophy of History"] that Altmeyer produced at the Universidad de Bruselas; the author declared that to develop the work, he put the ideas of Herder and the lessons of Schlegel and of Hegel to the utmost use. The dis-

---

* Karl Christian Friedrich Krause (1781–1832), German pantheist and writer; Heinrich Ahrens (1808–1874), German jurist and writer. —Ed.

tinguished professor, as if to confirm this statement, did not hesitate to establish right off that "the philosophy of history is the *revelation of the divine spirit in history*"; and despite recognizing that "all phenomena of individual development on earth in time are manifested only to the senses and to experience, from which it follows that history is a *purely experimental science*, which cannot be separated from real events, from facts," he added forthwith, "that the philosophy of history is in no way the knowledge of individual facts as such, but rather the knowledge of eternal being, and of the eternal laws of the development of life in time; for only through this means does life see history."

The aspiration to unite German pantheism with science can only fall into contradictions, for it is not scientific, it cannot be experimental, which is purely theological or at the least metaphysical. But the professor from Brussels, a disciple of Herder and a great admirer of Krause, wished to reconcile in historical development, which is a natural phenomenon, the free actions of human forces with providential leadership; for he stated that "we should never forget that the world, *ruled by the diligent providence of God*, is the theater in which man's rational freedom unfolds." He believed that the two schools, or rather two parties in the domain of the philosophy of history, could be recognized: the one that has man as the absolute self-ruler, independent of all ideas of divine leadership, and the other that seeks the distinctive character of man in his likeness to God, and renders unto history as its only object and purpose the rehabilitation of the divine image and the successive advancements of this rehabilitation.

This distinction, which had come as a tremendous surprise to us since we did not then know the philosophy of August Comte, and we did not therefore know that there was a school founded, like our theory, on the independence of man, served as the basis for Altmeyer to undertake a conciliation of the two camps, and he did so through incurring in abstractions and contradictions of a metaphysics so unintelligible that we again forsook the task of understanding the *providentialist* school, for however much the Brussels professor, fearing that his metaphysics would drive many away, like us, stated that he "hoped his metaphysical language did not terrify anyone, since German philosophy had been discovered in the style of French thought through Victor Cousin."

Meanwhile our University, which on its second anniversary had accepted heartily the Memorial on *Las primeras compañas de la guerra de la independencia* ["The First Campaigns of the War of Independence"], which don Diego José Benavente had submitted to them, and in 1846 the one García Reyes wrote on *La primera escuadra nacional* ["The First National Squadron"],* as-

---

* Diego José Benavente Bustamante (1789–1867), statesman, author of one of the earliest historical works on Chile and the wars of independence (1844); Antonio García Reyes (1817–1855), writer and editor, author of the first history of the Chilean navy in the independence era (1846). —Ed.

siduously fostered the studies of the history of Chile, with the exclusive purpose of fixedly clarifying and determining the facts. The School of Philosophy and Humanities, in which the activities of that body were concentrated, at the same time that it adopted in April 1844 a new Castilian orthography, which in 1845 established the rules to which the accentuation of the words of the language must be adjusted, also discussed and approved our primary education organization plan; it also sought to pull out the manuscripts relating to national history from the dust of the archives, with a view to publishing them, and established historical topics for the composition of works to be awarded prizes in the annual contests.

In 1847 M. A. Tocornal* was to submit the official historical Report, a man who had set out to write the detailed history of the events occurring during the inauguration of the *first national government*; and since the School of Philosophy had assigned for the theme of that same year's competition some point of Chilean history, we ventured a second essay, applying our system, in the hopes of continuing to write the complete history of the independence revolution if this version was received more benignly than our *Investigaciones*; and accordingly we anonymously submitted our *Bosquejo histórico de la constitución del gobierno de Chile durante el primer período de la revolución desde 1810 hasta 1814* ["Historical Outline of the Constitution of the Chilean Government During the First Period of the Revolution from 1810 to 1814"]. This work contained five chapters: Constitution of the Government in 1810 and 1811, Documents of the High Congress of 1811, Constitution of the Government in 1812 and 1813, Constitution of the Government in 1814, Conclusion.

The reporting advisory Committee, comprising Messrs. Varas and García Reyes, awarded the prize to the work, for the single reason that it had "the indisputable virtue of recapitulating the regulations, bylaws and decrees that were issued in the early days of the revolution to organize public power, as well as of illustrating them with timely commentaries and critical reflections, and of appreciating with acumen the ideas that most powerfully influenced public figures of that age." But the committee refrained from pronouncing any judgment on the accuracy of the facts that served the author in founding his doctrine, and on the opinion that the writer manifested on the nature and trends of the political parties; for that he needed to know the acts and the practical outcome that they have produced in the destiny of events. "Lacking that individual knowledge of the facts," it stated, "lacking a panoramic view of events, people, dates, and the entire

---

* Manuel Antonio Tocornal Grez (1817–1867), jurist and statesman, author of a significant work on the first Chilean national administration (1847). —Ed.

material train of history, it is impossible to trace general outlines without running the risk of giving excessive room to theories and to partially disfiguring the truth of what happened. This drawback arises in works like this Report that consign the fruits of the author's studies and do not provide all their background they have used to form their judgment. The Committee feels inclined to wish that first and foremost works be undertaken which are geared mainly toward clarifying the facts; the theory that illustrates these facts will arrive at once with a sure step on known ground."

Our system had not evolved at all in the three year's time since the first Report. But if the condemnation the 1847 Committee heaped upon it was kind, it lacked for justice. Those who read our *Bosquejo* ["Outline"] will see that we did not dispense with the facts to create doctrines or abstract judgments, let alone disfigure them to mold them to theories. On the contrary, we faithfully set forth the events, citing their proofs; and if we left out details, it was merely when we judged them needless or insignificant. Mr. Bello himself acknowledged in one of his articles on the work that "the *Bosquejo histórico* is, as its title states, a strongly historical work; but then again," he adds in fairness also to the Committee, "it may be true that on certain points and assessments it leaves one wanting for testimony of the facts." The rector forgot, in betraying, like the Committee, his hunger for facts, that Du Rozoir, criticizing M. de Barante's method, thinks that "history written with such prolixity of intimate detail would fill entire libraries, and in the end would never be accessible to most; for the better part of readers demand from the historian more than artlessly presented documents, the ordering and summation of the facts, for they prefer to find of their own will an established opinion, leaving it to their discretion to accept or change it."

It was not, then, the *material train of history* that was lacking in our work, and if the Committee pointed to this lack, affecting ignorance that we contemplated the events in all their truth, in order to judge them, it was because it did not accept our philosophy. It preferred details and minute ascertainments to general outlines, and feared that the latter could set the stage for theories and the disfiguring of truth, not because it had to lodge a single objection to the reality of the events we were judging, but because it assumed that our judgments were not the result of a set criterion based on the laws of human nature, but on *theories* that did not fall in line with a certain spirit of conventionality founded on the prevailing expedients and interests.

XXVIII

The Committee's report was, in our view, as much a result of the predominance of the wise University rector's old opinion on the philosophy of history as an echo of the resistance that the educated opinion of the age put up against any far-reaching innovation in the realm of scientific and literary speculations. Was not our text on public law in those very moments a victim of that resistance? Had it not made a triumphant appearance in *El Crepúsculo*'s condemnation three years previously? The professor's freedom to teach was still a utopia, which was possible to attain only with guarantees and provisos. The old Spanish civilization was still represented in the new University, not only by the priest who had condemned our *Elementos de derecho público constitucional*, but also by many of those who, like the rector, were more concerned about the advancement of public education; in the case of a theory as advanced as ours about the way to write history, we incurred the disapproval of the top writers of the day: among the Chileans, García Reyes, Varas, Sanfuentes, Tocornal, Benavente, the whole University; and among the Spanish Americans who provided us with their intelligence, don Andrés Bello, García del Río, López, Sarmiento, Alberdi, Piñero, Peña, everyone with no other exception perhaps than the eminent writer Juan María Gutiérrez, who denounced as we did the system of historical justification and rehabilitation, out of regard for the time in which the events occurred, and he did not accept fatalism.

We well understood that the triumph of our ideas was the work of time and perseverance, and we did not rebel, nor even grow disquieted, by the official rejection of our doctrines. We trusted in the future to win the freedom to teach, and though we had the presentiment that the former idea would not find a school, and that our *Investigaciones* and our *Bosquejo* would be consigned to oblivion, we continued impassive in the struggle. What we did not foresee then was that thirty years later we would find ourselves forced to talk of ourselves and our actions in that struggle to reestablish the truth of events.

Yet the few literary friends that concurred with our opinions did not remain calm. Jacinto Chacón took up the defense of our work and adorned it with a prologue that explained the advantages of our doctrine, of our method, and above all drawing attention to the fact that the *Bosquejo* was a constitutional history in the style of Hallam's* book on the constitution of

---

* Henry Hallam (1777–1859), English civil servant and constitutional historian. —Ed.

England; so the informing Committee had no reason to require the author to become a mere writer of chronicles, in order to relate the facts, like Guicciardini* in the infancy of science, for that was not his purpose. When the book was published at the end of December 1847, Mr. Bello rushed to the defense of the Committee, refuting our friend's ideas in *El Araucano*; at the same time that the extensive praise he published separately of the Report on The First National Government, in which M. A. Tocornal had made a meticulous chronicle of the 1810 movement, in a brief assessment he unjustifiably found fault with our *Bosquejo* for being inexact. Chacón replied and the *El Progreso* editorial on 29 January 1848 set the wise writer right on the reproach he made of our inexactitude, and explaining our silence in that interesting polemic over our doctrines that was catching fire, he justly called us an "unpretentious writer, tolerant of heart, who takes an unaffected look at the opinions being voiced and the judgments rendered on his work's merit."

Actually, we have never given the lie to the friend who said the foregoing, for we have also looked on his critical judgments of our books appreciatively, though they be unfavorable, never having contradicted them. But on that occasion we felt the need, almost the duty, to take part in the debate to shed light on and defend our doctrine. We did not do so, for our teacher was completely in the wrong and our close relationship with him prevented our reproaching him for it in the press. Today his opinion belongs to history, relegated to *Opúsculos literarios y críticos* ["Literary and Critical Treatises"], published in 1850, and we calmly can point out, though delicately, his mistake.

Mr. Bello forsook historical fatalism in his articles, and made not the least mention of his old adhesion to Herder's doctrine. But neither did he reveal a fixed idea of the philosophy of history, for now he was having a worse guide lead him, someone more deceitful than that eminent theologian, Victor Cousin, who, sipping like a hummingbird in order to eclecticize, at one point believes the philosophy of history is the philosophy of the human spirit applied to history, at another he reduces it to the science of moral and social laws, separating in distinct assumptions the man of society and the man of humanity, and considering humanity itself independently of the influences of place and time, as if it were possible, logical, scientific, to study it as an abstract entity, and not in its reality, as a natural whole. Alongside this generic conception, Mr. Bello, led always by Cousin, acknowledged another philosophy of history, "as concrete science, that from

* Francesco Guicciardini (1483–1540), Florentine historian and Papal statesman, author of a twenty-volume history of Italy (1561, 1564). —Ed.

the facts of a race, of a nation, of an age, the particular spirit of that race, of that age, are derived, not unlike how from the deeds of an individual we deduce his nature, his character."

This eclecticism leads the teacher, in his polemic with Jacinto Chacón, to assume that the author of the *Investigaciones* and the *Bosquejo histórico*, and that he who defended him as the writer of a constitutional history, dispensed with the facts, and wanted "to derive from the general laws of humanity the history of a nation." And to thunder his strictures against such nonsense, he did not rely on his own authority, but invoked that of Du Rozoir, Thierry, Sismondi, Villemain, demanding the fair-minded and trustworthy study of the facts, and even that of Barante, whom he quoted: "We are tired of seeing history transformed into a meek, wage-earning mercenary who lends himself to all proofs one wishes to get out of him," words that harbor a categorical condemnation of the very system that Mr. Bello wished to present as true philosophy of history, to wit, the system that seeks to make concrete science of each particular history, judging, according to the history's particular circumstances, each nation, each race, like one who judges the character of an individual, and making of history a docile sophist in order to get out of it the proofs that are sought by drawing inspiration from a purely individual spirit, opinion, or interest.

This was exactly what we had rejected since we formulated our doctrine, founded on a criterion deduced from the laws that govern human forces in historical evolution; and never, but never, had we believed or set forth that, in applying this criterion to general history or the particular history of a nation, to study its philosophy one could do away with a precise knowledge of the facts, let alone seek to deduce history and the facts themselves from the knowledge of those laws. What then were the University Committee and their distinguished rector seeking by the one preferring historical writings that merely presented the account of events, finding obstacles and dangers in the philosophical study of the events of an age that we had offered him; and the other protesting against the philosophy of history, considering it opposed to the history of facts, as *general science*, and reducing it to the special judgment of each case, as *concrete science*, deduced from each individual history? Why condemn so forcefully the true philosophical history, which, founded on the study of events, on their connection and their relation to the mental and moral state, judges them according to their conformity or opposition to the laws of progress and freedom that regulate the historical evolution of humanity, without considering this evolution as naught but the effect of irrevocable or providential laws or of divine predestination? Why prefer and foster only picturesque narrative or the chronicle stripped bare of the facts, when these forms and the former could be cultivated simultaneously, and the study of all of them could be sponsored by the University? What else are the historical Reports, what are we creating by writing these *Memoirs*, if not the account of events we witnessed, judging them at the same time philosophically by the yardstick of our own doctrine, applied in the *Bosquejo histórico* which raised so many contradictions, and in those *Investigaciones* that were so scorned, and which still are by the chroniclers that have organized under the University's tutelage?

Mostly what we cannot comprehend is the fact that the University and its wise rector consider philosophy what the latter called concrete science, reducing it to the judgments that each historian makes of the facts of a race, of a nation, of an age, from which he derives its spirit, *not unlike how from the deeds of an individual we deduce his nature, his character*. This is the way to write history, which Altmeyer, among others, calls *reflexive*, "or in other words the application of reason to history, one of the faultiest known." "The writers in this school," added the professor from Brussels, "twist round the facts every which way to bend them to their model and disguise them with the clothes of their day. . . . The same observation applies to the history called pragmatic (that of practical conclusions), which has a taste for little moral and political axioms à la Ségur, and for little experimental truths à la Anquetil, an unfortunate method that has lead astray so many fine spirits of the nineteenth century," etc.

Had we taken part in the polemic in those days, we would have cited this passage, in which Altmeyer, refuting the very individuals who assumed that the philosophy of history sets out from speculations conceived *a priori*, exclaims:

> The answer is easy. The philosophy of history is the science of the source and of the development of the life of humanity, the source and development that correspond to the same phases of the life of man. I ask you: Is there anything in that that impedes the facts? The only thought that philosophy brings to history is that of reason: the latter maintains that it is the intellect, and not chance, which rules the world, and wishes to know if history has followed, if it follows, if it will follow, a rational path, in accordance with human nature and the designs of the universal spirit that breathes in all beings, from the smallest blade of grass to the star hidden in the solitudes of infinite space. Still I ask you: Is there anything in that that is incompatible with the facts? We take those facts as they are, we do not twist them in all directions to make them produce what they do not contain, we do not bend them to our narrow perspective, to our petty

judgments, to our selfish interests, to our evil passions. To our eyes there has formed a historical school in Belgium whose intentions are a mystery to no one. *This school recoils in horror at everything that remotely or intimately touches on philosophy*, and it is they who one can rightly reproach for deliberately falsifying history, for planting dangerous ideas in it, for supporting a system hostile to freedom and progress; for having conceived the rehabilitation of Phillip II and the scaffolds of the Duke of Alba; for having girdled with a halo of love and veneration the miserable and degrading reign of Alberto and Isabel, and the administration of all those high-living Spanish and Austrian despots for whom our country was but merchandise, a currency for trade. Inventors of this politics of corruption and degradation that has lead to ruin, to the forgetting of all the noble sentiments that set our great forebears apart!

If only such a spirited apostrophe to the situation we are recalling had not had such a suitable application! These were the very doctrines, trends, and paths that showed the way to future historians who then were standing against our philosophy; and those doctrines, that trend, are those that have prevailed. The criticism of the numerous historical works that have been published in Chile by the magistery, under the sway of the ideas upheld by those who were afraid of our philosophy in 1844 and 1847, do not date from this period; but if one looks into any of them, one will find to what extent dangerous ideals prevailed, as well as the systematic hostility to freedom and progress, the rehabilitation of our oppressors, the small moral and political axioms, and the arbitrary criterion of the regime that has ruled everything in the last fifty years, almost always unwisely, ofttimes immorally, at turns oppressive and small-minded. The few historical books that have come out of that camp are perhaps the least praised, the most forgotten.

The results obtained in the second attempt to apply our doctrine forced us to drop our goal to write the history of the independence following the same plan; but somewhat later, when we had definitely confirmed it with new studies in the doctrine, we ventured to apply it to a history of liberal reforms in Europe and South America. Amid the vicissitudes of fiery politics, and seeking to shorten the bitter hours of exile, or of persecution, lacking books, often lacking all tools in our support save our embattled theory, we wrote the *Historia constitucional del medio siglo* ["Constitutional History of the Half-Century"], a historical review of the advancements of the representative system in Europe and South America during the first fifty years of the nineteenth century, which we published in Valparaíso in 1853. We believed we had elected a neutral ground for making a more fortuitous attempt than the previous ones at our way of profitably studying history, and as completely unconnected as we were from the University's mission, from politics, and even from the literary center, we hoped that that system was not pursued once again. In fact, the neutral ground was so well chosen that no one paid any attention to the book in Chile, except our venerable teacher, who, in the Report he submitted to the University Council in March 1854, informing with due praise on the historical works that don José Víctor Eyzaguirre, don Miguel Luis, and don Gregorio V. Amunátegui had submitted to open competitions, works that for the facts and the curious news they compile deserved his high praise, he brings in our book, which had nothing to do with those competitions, and accorded the following courtesy: "That book," he states, "probably will find no small amount of readers that *will protest against some of the political doctrines* the author holds; but this work, like everything that flows from his pen, bears the seal of lively thinking and stylish exposition." Upon remitting his Report to Valparaíso, he kindly told us not to take that passage as a critical judgment of the book, which had inspired such lively interest in him, for he proposed to publish a study of it, which he never did. Doubtless his vast intelligence, which some time ago had widened the narrow horizons in which the spirit of an age that was winding to a close had imprisoned it, accepted new views then, and set the stage for the conversion that came about in 1864, when the old teacher, amazed at the analogy of our system that Buckle had just used in his *Historia de la civilización en Inglaterra* ["History of Civilization in England"], which he brought to our attention, conveyed to us emotionally and affectionately his hearty approval of our historical works. Ah! It was our turn to be included together in one of those moments of transition when the high representatives of the waning age, still full of vigor and authority, must clash with the precursors of the coming age, who rely only the reflected light from the future!

Still, although that English historian's remarkable work, and other Spanish American writings, mainly the *Ensayo sobre las revoluciones políticas* ["Essay on Political Revolutions"] by J. M. Samper, afforded us the greatest satisfaction, practically a victory, that we were not alone on the road we had laid out for ourselves since 1840 with our doctrine on the way to write philosophical history; we certainly did not end up seeing the same doctrine formulated by a European writer except in 1866. While in Buenos Aires, we picked up *L'État et ses limites* in a bookstore and read it for the first time, a book, which Edouard Laboulaye had brought out the previous year. On one of its pages, the following passage shocked us, drove us out of our head we should say, causing us to shout *Eureka*!:

There is nothing more ingenious than the ideas of Vico, of Herder, Saint-Simon, Hegel; but evidently in spite of their brilliant parts, these ambitious constructions do not rest on anything. Across the spectrum of those irrevocable forces that drag humanity toward a destiny from which it cannot flee, where to place freedom? What part of action and *responsibility* is left to the individual? A great deal of energy is wasted mulling over the problem instead of solving it; but what do these poetic chimeras matter? The only thing that concerns us is just what is not said. If one wishes to write a philosophy that can admit science, one must change one's method and return to observation. *It is not enough to study events*, which are but effects; one must *study the ideas that have produced them*, for ideas are the causes (we would add also sentiment) and *only in them does freedom appear*. When the *genealogy of ideas* is traced, when we know what education each century has received, *how the experience* of those who lived before *has been corrected and completed*, then it will be possible to understand the course of the past and perhaps predict the course of the future. . . .

Then we wrote our *América*, the contemporary history of the democratic movement in this world of the new humanity, of the new synthesis that is attempted here as a platform of future civilization; and upon examining the political doctrine of that celebrated professor, we transcribed the same passage, recalling in a note on page 92 that that very theory had been the one that, conceived by us twenty-five years previously, and formulated in the introduction to our *Investigaciones* three years later, had led us in the composition of that historical work, the *Bosquejo histórico* submitted to the University in 1847, and of the *Historia constitucional del medio siglo*, published in 1853; and we could add that of the *Juicio histórico de don Diego Portales* ["Historical Judgment of don Diego Portales"], published in 1861, and of the same book in which we made that revelation. But then we declared that we were not seeking to recover possession of our creation, resigning ourselves to believing, with Laboulaye himself, that the political writers do not have the good fortune of the poets, "for their works shrink in time, insofar as their ideas become the patrimony of all; and they even become forgotten and unknown by the generation that has appropriated and echoed them, losing sight of the first one to reveal them."

Why then do we appear today recording the precedence and originality of our doctrine? It would be enough of an excuse to observe that in these *Memoirs* we have proposed to draw out our acts, our efforts in the intellectual development of this country, from the shadows of oblivion and injustice, for as the first rector of the University, we can attribute to ourselves *without pretension the attribute of an old fervor for spreading the healthy principles and industrious dedication with which we have pursued some branches of study*, if today we had no more powerful reason we are going to explain.

Despite a tenacious and assiduous study of the social sciences, which, as is plain to see, can never be well served in countries that are far away from the great center of letters and sciences, on account of a lack of books, of inspiration, of outlets, and even of treatment of scientific speculations, we did not manage to read August Comte's *Filosofía positiva* ["Positive Philosophy"] until 1868. We know how slow-going the course of a book is, and how much more so that of a great work is, that of a philosophical system! But before taking up its study, which is immense and liable to daunt the most tempered of spirits if one is not ready, we tried to read attentively that thick, profound study by Littré, entitled *Auguste Comte et la philosophie positive* ["August Comte and Positivist Philosophy"]. In this reading we went from surprise to surprise: it was a revelation for us.

On page 43 we found this passage, which stopped us in our tracks:

> At the moment Mr. Comte took the path that was to lead him to such heights, human knowledge was not sufficient to produce positivist philosophy. It lacked a considerable quality of which I wish to speak: the *notion of history considered as a natural phenomenon*. A natural phenomenon is one that depends on a material substance and a force, and as I have stated, we do not know any other kind of phenomenon. Here in history, material, the *substratum*, is the human race divided into societies; force is represented by the aptitudes that are inherent to societies, and whose foundation is the condition that scientific notions are accumulative. As long as that is not acknowledged, history does not appear as a natural phenomenon; the *substratum* is known, which is the human race, and the force that makes evolution is not: then the conception of history is theological, if one believes it is ruled by a supernatural will, or it is metaphysical if *a priori* principles are accepted to explain it, taken not on material but on spiritual views. Distancing theology and metaphysics from history, Mr. Comte discovered the sociological laws, and then, guided by these laws, mapped out social evolution. This is a lasting monument, however far the new historical studies are carried, studies that confirm it and will continue to confirm it. . . .

On page 182, this other passage appears, which surprised us no less:

> Leaving aside the particular facts, which are found through wisdom or through good luck, what might one mean by *discoveries* in the realms of history? Discoveries are the explanations that demonstrate *the correlation of social systems with the mental state and the connection of these systems*. From this point of view, Mr. Comte's work is an ever-unfolding discovery, because for the first time, human development is established in its circumstances, on the twofold condition of being always tied to the mental state and of continuously offering an intimate connection between what has gone before and what follows. Under this general discovery are aligned infinite particular discoveries. I could easily cite some very important ones . . . [their enumeration follows].

One can ask the South American writers who have performed the feat of cultivating some science and taking it to new levels, in this New World with virgin jungles and without libraries, with towering mountains and without teachers, with portentous riches that neither reach nor aid those who study, one can ask what could have been the impression these revelations would make on us, revelations made by one of the great intellects that represent all the human understanding of our age. Only they can understand it.

Had we not begun just when August Comte was in action, when the press had barely begun to publish his immortal work, which reached Chile only long years later; had we not started out from identical concepts to found the philosophy of history in South America?

That teacher of those in the know, as they call Littré, imitating Dante's *il maestro di color che sanno,** had accomplished a prodigious feat in considering history a natural phenomenon, taking the human race as the material of this phenomenon and its aptitudes as the force, to withdraw from Herder's and Vico's theological concept, and from the metaphysics of the German philosophers, to establish sociological laws, to discover the correlation of events with the frame of mind of their respective ages and their interrelationships. And if that was a great discovery in the center of the great European civilization, it did not come to our attention until twenty-eight years after having set out from the same concept to formulate a like doctrine; after having written, in accordance with this doctrine, five historical works

---

* Aristotle. He appears in the *Inferno* (IV) in Limbo and elsewhere, and is referred to as "the master." —Trans.

that already were somewhat famous in South America, and of which some were known as well in Europe.

That is the motive that inspired the idea of narrating the progress of our doctrine, for it can vindicate a place in the intellectual movement of our continent, and in wresting it from oblivion, the honor of our literature moves us more than the aim of winning accolades for ourselves.

XXIX

We need to complete the scene we are sketching of the period from 1843 to 1849 by recalling the literary newspapers that served, at the same time they represented, the intellectual movement begun in 1842. The progress in the scientific and literary press had been truly miraculous beginning that year, considering our circumstances and relative to our background; but it was not steady but rather intermittent, and rose or stopped in proportion to the prompting it received. When this impetus was the natural effect of the evolution in progress, the literary output increased, and when the literary movement was reigned in by the conservative reaction, it unquestionably diminished that output in no time. We have already mentioned that in 1843 twenty-four serious works were published, half of which were devoted to teaching and to the spreading of knowledge. We are not counting official works of course, nor the special-interest works like juridical defenses and others. In 1844 the number of works rose to thirty-eight, in the following year to forty-eight, in 1846 to eighty, and thus continued the increase in books in subsequent years, except 1847, when it should be noted that at least one-fourth of the works were reprints of foreign belles lettres with which our presses came out, which offers proof of how widespread was good taste and the fondness for reading.

Let no one be surprised that we are returning our attention to this astounding progress, since it confirms the truth that the movement begun in 1842 brought in its wake the social emancipation from the concerns of the old regime and a generous freedom of judgment and of the word, results that were strengthened by the agreement struck in early 1843 to work for intellectual development. However, we must note that neither this agreement nor this effort were united in their motives or in their ends; for although all wished for intellectual progress, not everyone served it in the same way, hence the intermittence of its trajectory, certain inconsistencies, and even certain clashes of varying aspirations.

The old regime boasted powerful representatives, which although, as we stated before, had not snuffed out the emancipation movement at its inception, thereafter they slowly took it over and directed it down a path quite opposite the one its promoters had laid out for it. The government fostered public education; but just as the creation of the University had established in law the basis for the rector to proclaim a confessional teaching, science, literature, and even morality, it also favored all the institutions that the clergy and its adepts founded, no longer merely to educate the youth following the University's command, but following the plan by which jesuitism managed to form a certain order of interests and doctrines that would run counter to the interests and principles of modern civilization and the democratic system. Public opinion, lacking sufficient education, devoid of established ideas and defined goals, followed only a feeling, that of the need to foster intellectual growth; it lent its favors, its applause to all efforts, to all enterprises and speculations, all acts that in some way served this need. Neither did the molders of opinion in this sense know how to tell the progressive movement current from the retrogressive one, and regardless of how liberal their efforts were, they served both, not noticing that they were contradicting their own aspirations, except in the cases where some violent shock to both tendencies or some daring, oppressive reaction wound up warning them that the independence of the spirit was in danger, or that freedom was violated.

This was more or less the state of affairs from the middle of 1843 to 1851. Those of us who at the beginning of that year worked deliberately and logically for intellectual emancipation were precious few, and we lacked support to take on in any way the social powers that represented the old regime: our efforts had to be reduced to propagating sound principles, to teaching, avoiding the raising of anxieties, which abated for no other reason than the fact that until then we had taken pains not to excite them.

We needed to go on with the literary movement, because it alone could change ideas to achieve social regeneration; to this effect we persisted continuously in publishing a newspaper that served this movement. Finally, Juan N. Espejo and Juan José Cárdenas, whom Cristóbal Valdés soon replaced in the task, were able to found a press, and on the first of June 1843, we published the first issue of *El Crepúsculo*, a monthly paper devoted to letters and sciences. We set up the editorial staff with the most enthusiastic of the Literary Society youths: J. N. Espejo, Cristóbal Valdés, Francisco de P. Matta, Andrés Chacón, Jacinto Chacón, H. Irisarri, Santiago Lindsay, F. S. Asta-Buruaga,* and Juan Bello, the rest being contributors. Don Andrés Bello joined our enterprise, promising us one article per issue, and we bargained on the collaboration also of his sons Francisco and Carlos, and that of Madam Mercedes Marín del Solar.

In the first year, the publication came out regularly and with the evergrowing favor of numerous subscribers. The twelve issues of the year formed the first volume, in which there were nine articles on philosophy and two on literary history by Mr. Bello, apart from his celebrated imitation of Victor Hugo entitled *La oración por todos* ["Prayer for All"]; several original and translated poems by Irisarri, Madame Marín, Lindsay, Francisco, Carlos and Juan Bello, Andrés and Jacinto Chacón, and Asta-Buruaga; four novels on national matters, biographies, and studies on matters of social and political interest by the other writers, and F. Matta's literary and theater criticism.

El Crepúsculo's trajectory was brilliantly fixed, and promised to be long, peaceful, and advantageous to the literary movement. The first issue in the second year concerned the background, but the second brought the newspaper to a tragic close owing to official charges against the article *Sociabilidad chilena* ["Chilean Civic Responsibility"], published by Francisco Bilbao. The history of that accusation has been an oft-told one, and we will not try to repeat it; but the value of that writing in the history of our letters is not known, for however much its political importance is known.

Bilbao was a contributor to *El Crepúsculo*, but he had not written until then, excusing himself with the assiduous and persevering studies that he did to settle his ideas, which were found in perfect anarchy since he had stopped believing in Catholicism, as he himself maintained. He was a fiery poetic spirit, but his poetry shone like a manifestation of the unblemished mysticism that shaped the heart of his feeling: he could not help being a believer, and lacking his old faith in Roman Catholicism, he took refuge in the Gospels to condemn that faith, and sought to sate his mysticism in the messianic metaphysics of Lamennais and other theological socialists. He was our disciple and at the same time that of Mr. Bello and López as well, the latter of which, according to his biographer, was the one who had taught him the most in the true science of philosophy. Perhaps that is why he could never break him free, at least in those days, of being a fatalist in

---

* Francisco Solano Asta-Buruaga Cienfuegos (1817–1892), Chilean educator, lawyer, orthographer, and public figure, studied at the Instituto before attending the University, historian of Easter Island (Isla de Pascua), and compiler of a geographical dictionary of Chile (1887). —Ed.

history, like Herder and Vico, of taking common sense as a criterion of truth and justice, à la Michelet, or the universal record according to Lamennais; nor from being eclectic in philosophy with Cousin, although shortly thereafter, in Europe, he became his adversary. He wanted science to fill the void which the absence of Catholicism had left in his spirit, and avid for beliefs, sought a *scientific religion*, at every turn asking himself Voltaire's question:

"*Qui suis-je, où vais-je et d'où suis-je tiré!!*"*

He could not stop thinking of efficient causes and final causes.

His great intelligence having been disciplined in these metaphysical abstractions, Bilbao acquired the habit of generalizing and of expressing generalizations through absolute propositions in the biblical forms of Lamennais, priding himself on an enigmatic style, which he called apocalyptic and which gave leeway to his fellow students to misrepresent him, which forever provided that noble, jovial character with topics with which to parade the gymnastics of his subtle talent and his admirable facility for aphorisms.

Thus is the philosophy and thus the style with which Bilbao formulated his first serious work, *Sociabilidad chilena*, which was to win him a great deal of celebrity. In the introduction to the writing, Bilbao's mystic side asserts that in the transitory ages of civilization, men decline "when they are short of the vivifying breath of faith"; but that in the middle of this guideless desert, social events make the chaos of his intelligence disentangle, "because a spark of the universal pyre illuminates it: brotherhood. . . ." Life is the "incomprehensible admixture of the sublime and the ridiculous, of *fatalism* and *freedom*." The author asks life to account for what it has done and for what it promises, and believes that reason shall form a *new synthesis*, stimulated by those spontaneous calls to brotherhood.

Here we clearly establish the philosophical point of departure: loss of faith; another mystic conception arrives to take its place, brotherhood, this feeling that is the weakest of social instincts, which certain metaphysicians have wished to raise up to the status of law, that is, to the fundamental condition of public and political life. Once this foundation is built, the philosopher asserts that life is the admixture of fatalism and freedom and proceeds to seek the new synthesis, which he considers as still *undefined*.

In the conclusion to his writing, Bilbao formulated that new synthesis as the basis for future beliefs, for he alleges that that aphorism of the philosophers is still in force for the organization of modern society, the one that they said in observing the formation of primitive society: "the organization of society is the consequence of the organization of beliefs." His log-

---

* "Who am I, or what see I and where do I come from?" —Ed.

ical procedure is the following: "Our entire obligation," he states, "is the ascertainment of the LAW. Thus, our task in the political and religious sphere is to accept whatever indestructible facts we acknowledge." Then he establishes the facts thus:

"The freedom of the individual as a body and as a thinking thing. This is a fact." "The equality of my fellow creature insofar as he is another temple wherein God likewise has deposited freedom. This is another fact." "Freedom and social equality, that is, for everyone: SOVEREIGNTY OF THE PEOPLE. That is another fact."

"Freedom of the divine conception, that is, religious democracy. That is another fact."

"Freedom and political equality, that is, democracy properly speaking. That is another fact."

"The awareness of free law, which provides for its own defense and propagation in order to make free individuals of those who are not, that is, the right to civilize or increase the sons of the Divinity. That is another fact."

"From these facts emerges the basis of the future system of beliefs. They are few, but incontestable. They are indispensable. Therefore, they must become the basis of the *future religion*."

From them derives this consequence: order, religion, and politics. Order lies in the precepts of universal morality, which he listed with certain reservations. Religion is reduced to these bases: (1) *Thou shalt love the Creator*, who for the author is *a human being*. "The creation of freedom," he stated, "is in my view the proof of divine freedom. Divine freedom is the individualization of the Creator." (2) *Love thy neighbor*. In his view, "fraternity is a principle and a feeling. Love in the community is necessary: That is the *unassailable foundation of democracy*." As for the politics that derives from those facts, it was reduced to the freedom of cults, to the elevation of all individuals to sovereignty, for through representation the proletariat would declare its right to knowledge, *education*, and its right to possession, *property*. Moreover, he sought the abolition of the Senate, for, since it represented conservative interests or the aristocracy of property, in both cases it seeks to preserve inequality; also the abolition of the death penalty, since responsibility is relative and all penalties should be corrective, the death penalty does not extol responsibility nor does it correct it, and thus it is unjust.

We have expounded with full fidelity the philosophy of *Sociabilidad chilena*. The author recalled it some years later in one of his subsequent works, stating that "that writing was a projection of the eighteenth century, cast by a juvenile soul." In fact, there was the symbol of the new faith that the 1789 French Revolution inspired, writing on its banner: *liberté, egalité, fraternité*; with the difference that Bilbao, following the socialists of the subsequent age, made of politics and religion a necessary duality; and he wanted freedom of divine conception to be the essence of religious democracy, just as that of freedom and equality in politics was that of democracy as such; and at the same time for both ideas to have the social meaning that Rousseau gave to them, considering them not as rights but as the power to self-govern, like the absolute power of the people, like its *sovereignty*. One more difference: Bilbao associated that concept of old-fashioned freedom with the sovereignty of the people, which he had learned in our lessons, considering it the expression of individual rights, for in various passages of his writing he endowed it with these rights, and also simultaneously gave it the divine character that the German metaphysicians ascribe to it, considering it an emanation of infinite freedom, an attribute of God as an infinite human being.

The true projection of the eighteenth century lay in the process that Bilbao developed in his writing, before applying his new synthesis, to our Catholic and feudal past, to our revolution, to the governments that had understood it or impeded it, to the government and to the Conservative Party that reacted against it and that reestablished and backed the Spanish and Colonial past. In this process he took as its criterion the ideas from our literary and political school in Chile on the need to develop in society and politics the principles of democratic revolution, reacting against Spanish civilization, against the entire colonial past, in order to regenerate our society and found our future on new ideas. But, persisting with his historical fatalism, he nevertheless judged with just severity the last regime and the current one, demanding responsibility of its supporters; upon issuing his judgments and new ideas that were to serve as the bases of a new regime, he did so in metaphysical formulas that clouded the true notion of freedom and progress, the only laws of regeneration, and with the theological illusions of a believer and subjective visions of a persistent spiritualism.

XXX

The foregoing suffices in order to understand that Bilbao's work was not ready to have influence either on the literary movement or on the political philosophy of the new Chilean school. In clashing with all the traditions of the old regime, and therefore of the old literary school, it neither satisfied the new one nor corresponded to liberal aspirations, for its metaphysics and its mysticism taught nothing and promised nothing, and added nothing new other than presenting under a strange and indefinable form a process that had occurred a hundred times before, each time with greater clarity to the ruling party, and which was repeated in every way against Catholicism since the last century. Thus the writing would have passed only as an essay that revealed a talented writer, and which affirmed freedom of thought as a matter of course, a freedom we were winning, if at the time the district attorney's office were not occupied by an impetuous youth, who prided himself on being a rabid representative of the old regime and who made a show of being an open partisan of the ruling oligarchy and daring servant of all strong power. Two days after the publication of number II of the second volume of *El Crepúsculo*, the interim district attorney charged Bilbao's writing with being blasphemous, immoral, and seditious. This accusation set off the work's celebrity. This work would have been neither read nor understood if not for a small number of the two hundred subscribers to the paper; but with the accusation and the subsequent seizures of the few remaining copies, they needed to run another edition that did not meet the demand. In the ten days the process took, everyone read *Sociabilidad chilena*, and the prevailing thought was that the accusation ought to be suspended as pointless and contrary to government policy, since the latter had neither inspired it nor had a hand in it. This was accurate; since he who writes these lines had resigned the post he held in the Ministry of the Interior, basing his action on the accusation in the literary newspaper of which he had played such a large role, Minister Irarrázaval gave him evidence of the government's nonparticipation in the matter. But since the minister deemed it impossible to have the accusation withdrawn, we insisted upon the resignation, which we postponed three months, yielding to the minister's demands, and proving our separation before that time period, while the head of the ministry took on the vice presidency of the Republic in October 1844. The determination to avoid judgment, be it by withdrawing the accusation or by denying him a place in the first jury, deeply disturbed the recalcitrant.

They were already disturbed when *Sociabilidad chilena* was published, on account of the fact the widespread condemnation that an uncle of the work's author, who was a chapter curate at the time, had stirred by raising objections to the obsequies for the soul of the illustrious Infante, who died two months earlier, a service which his family intended to hold. The publication of that writing coincided with the attacks the liberal press aimed at the clergy for the same reason, and the prosecutor intervened in support of the interests of religion against blasphemy. When the determination to attack the district attorney's proceedings appeared, and it was seen that *El Siglo* sought to exonerate and defend the accused in correspondence that toned down the writing with the author's healthy intentions and relevant virtues, as well as in the editorials that Matta wrote, criticizing the work and presenting it as the expression of an individual opinion that did not reflect the thought of *El Crepúsculo*'s editorial board, thought that Matta said "is the expression of the intellectual anarchy of society"; then, we say, the division between the ministry and the political circles that supported the government grew ever more pronounced. The old conservatives on the one hand, and the moderates and liberals on the other, joined battle and shook up society; but it is not true that this agitation came from the ruling class and spread to the people. The conservatives spoke on behalf of religion and the endangered social stability, controlled opinion, and took the accusation to its utmost consequences. They went so far as to have the University Council join the persecution, resolving to have the author of *Sociabilidad chilena* expelled from the Instituto Nacional and of all institutions of public learning; this was accomplished through one of their leaders, Mr. Egaña. What is most deplorable and shameful, they had the Supreme Court order the book containing Bilbao's writing to be burned by the hangman's hand.*

* Here is that remarkable judgment obtained through the prosecutor's efforts.

"Santiago, June 27 1844.—Not being determined by the law of 11 December 1828, nor by any other at all, what ought be done with the condemned printed books in competent judgment, the petition of the distinguished party has no substance; excepting his right to appear where it is fitting for the purpose of preventing the evils that he indicates. Silva."

"Santiago, July 2 1844.—Whereas and considering: 1st. that being a necessary consequence of the condemnation as immoral and blasphemous, which has been pronounced by a competent authority against the second issue of *El Crepúsculo*, in the part entitled *Sociabilidad chilena*, which is not to be read or circulated; 2nd. that by the stipulations of law 14, title 24, book 1 of Laws of the Indies, the authorities are empowered to collect the writings that attack the Catholic faith, it is declared: 1st. that the lieutenant constable and the notary of the suit must go to the press where the condemned paper initiated, and to the other places where it is sold, and bring before the first instance judge all extant copies; 2nd. that likewise appear before aforesaid first instance judge the proprietor of the press and its employees, that under oath they state how many copies were printed and account for those unalienated copies in existence, and the place in which they are found; 3rd. that the same judge give orders to the post that all copies of the aforementioned second issue of *El Crepúsculo* be retained and remitted to the court; 4th. that the order be given all press owners banning the reprint of said issue; 5th. that when all copies of the work are gathered before the first instance judge, the article *Sociabilidad chilena* be sepa-

If the accusation alone would have vaulted the work to fame, the jury's and the Court's condemnatory verdicts erected the author's altar of glory, and set in motion a persecution that unfortunately for the progress of the liberal cause in Chile was not to play itself out until the days of that tireless champion of social regeneration. Bilbao, with the foresight of genius and the arrogance of his fiery character, prophesied his glorious future, stating these words before the court: "Two names, that of the accuser and that of the accused, two names intertwined by historical destiny, and which will live on in the history of my country. Then we will see, Mr. Prosecutor, which of the two will make off with posterity's blessing. Philosophy too has its code, and this code is everlasting. Philosophy assigns you the name of retrogressive. So, fine! An innovator, that is what *I* am! Retrogressive, that is what *you* are! . . . " The prediction could not fail to come true, for the irate bursts of hatred from the servants of the old regime have forever sown the coming glory of their victims, and have played a part in the triumph of truth and of freedom almost more efficiently than have the efforts of those who sustain them. Posterity honors and glorifies the author of *Sociabilidad chilena*.

And rightly so. Bilbao was a great patriot and a great writer. His name figures prominently among the writers from the republics of the Pacific and of the River Plata, which he traveled through in his long exile. His style was perfected, losing by degrees the aphoristic and axiomatic intonation, and becoming the clear, transparent, concise, vehement translation of the expansive spirit of a great thinker, a profound philosopher, and above all a passionate heart, ceaselessly and unrelentingly devoted to the service of the liberal cause, to the regeneration and progress of his country and of the entire Spanish American homeland.

However, it is worth noting the influence of Bilbao's early studies, and the persistence of the early tendencies in his spirit. Among his works, there is one that is most remarkable as a philosophical conception, as sublime

rated from the above-mentioned issue, and that it be burned by the hand of the hangman, duly noting this in the record and returning to its owners the scientific part included in the newspaper alluded to above. The appealed writ is revoked and returned." Signed and sealed by Messrs. Vial del Río.—Novoa.—Echevers.—Ovalle y Landa.

The jury members that condemned Bilbao's writing belonged one and all, through their political backgrounds or through their connections, to the extreme splinter-group of conservatives. They were: don José Vicente Izquierdo, don Juan José Gatica, don Vicente León, don Diego Echeverría, don José Antonio Palazuelos, don José María Silva y Cienfuegos, don Pedro José Barros, don Juan de la Barra, don José Pedro Guzmán, don Juan de la Cruz Larraín, don Francisco Valdivieso y Gormaz, don Bartolomé Prado, and don Juan Miguel Riesco.

and irreproachable criticism, and as a plan that is well laid and better enacted: we are speaking of his speech on *La ley de la historia* ["The Law of History"], delivered before the Liceo Argentino de Buenos Aires in November 1858. We have never read a more complete description, nor a more philosophical and high-minded criticism of the theories that consider the historical evolution of humanity as the work of fatalism, of the will of God or of providential laws. Bilbao defines history by saying: "*History is reason judging memory and projecting the future's obligation*"; he considers the philosophy of history the statement of the law of human development, arguing that "all systems developed to set forth this law, from Saint Augustine to Hegel, from Bossuet to Herder, are diverse aspects of the absolute fatality incarnate in the movement of nations."

Then he expounds upon and judges the main conceptions of the philosophy of history: the pantheist, which is that of Hegel, taken up afterward by Cousin and plagiarized straightaway by Donoso Cortés* to flesh out the absolute in the *infallible* and *impeccable* Roman Church; the Catholic conception, which is that of Bossuet, which he founds on the Judaic tradition, and that of Vico, who sees in every nation a divine inspiration revealed in its own dogma; and the naturalist conception, whose author is Herder, who finds the law of history in nature bound to providential laws. "If we pay heed to the moral outcomes of these philosophical systems, which have held sway and continue to do so in our century," Bilbao states:

> we can see the justification of success from all vantage points, the adoration of force, the veneration of all the evildoers that have lorded over nations, but on the condition that they had been great in evil. Such doctrines still rule, unfortunately, and weaken spirits. Eclecticism, dogmatism, the sanction of the status quo, form the spirit and consecrate the facts as law, rebellions as decrees of Providence. Partial histories of modern nations only corroborate that noble doctrine of the *philosophy of history*. The Middle Ages, all conquests, the Inquisition, Jesuitism, the Saint Bartholomew's Day Massacre,† all horrors past and present have been coups d'état from the Divinity, measures foreseen *ab eterno* in his infinite wisdom. And even South America has been over-

---

* Juan Francisco María de la Salud Donoso Cortés (1809–1853), Spanish writer and statesman. —Ed.

† 24 August 1572 (et seq), in which French Catholics attacked and killed Huguenots. —Ed.

run by that plagiarism of the European fate. The conquest of South America, the extinction of races, the servitude of the Indians, the slavery of the blacks, anarchy, and even the monstrous despotisms of the Americans themselves have been acknowledged as providential necessities. How strange is it that after this teaching, and the influence of these doctrines in the history of all the ages, man should lose heart, give up and surrender in the arms of fate or indifference? When have we seen more scandalous apostasies than in our time? What does that justification of the facts, of success, mean, save humiliation in the face of force? How can we be surprised at that tremendous face slavery dons, which is the degradation of the soul, the blessing of the scourge, the adoration of the evilmonger? . . .

Upon reading this just condemnation of those doctrines, one imagines that Bilbao in 1858 forswore that historical fatalism which he had helped bring to fashion in Chile in 1844, when the political press repeated daily the word *fate* to explain all social and political phenomena; when the rector of the University, in criticizing the Report in which we rejected that philosophy to vindicate as bases of human evolution the law of freedom and progress, he accused us of attacking the general principles that for many centuries were the world's faith, and declared that the mournful, desperate dogma of fatalism was then at the heart of what was thought about the destiny of the human race on earth. But that is not the case: Bilbao only took one step forward, as did at the time Michelet and Quinet, whose authority he invoked, placing them at the head of the modern regenerative movement; for he would always remain a fatalist.

The contradiction could not be hidden from his lucid genius, and he tried to get round it by having recourse to entirely metaphysical solutions, which of course solved nothing. He considered humanity "the physiological organism that has its roots on earth and its history in the animal kingdom, and the spirit, which *receives immediately from the infinite Word* the communication of the spark, the vision of being, the harmony of law, and its fate." From this theory is derived the dualism of fate and freedom. "Fate is the law of bodies"; he stated, "freedom is the law of spirits. The solution to the problem is to make fate free and rule by the free element, and freedom to be regulated to the supreme end." With these premises he goes on to find the law of humanity in obligation, and formulates the same doctrine of the philosophy of history that we had established in our 1844 Report, with the single difference that he disfigures it with his mysticism and his fatalistic metaphysics. Here are his words:

Therefore the matter of the philosophy of history boils down to knowing the obligation of humanity, and the nature of being that that law should fulfill and approach the end designated by God himself.

Now the positing of the problem is simplified thus: what is the obligation of humanity?

The obligation of humanity is the complete possession of law and the development of all its faculties in harmony with itself, with society, and with nations.

The idea of law corresponds to the idea of freedom, and the idea of development to the pursuit of an end, to that of bringing an ideal to fruition.

The matter can be simplified. The ideal is the perfection of the human being. The perfection of the human being is the absolute mastery of the universal spirit in igniting universal freedom in everyone.

We can, then, go another step further and say: the law of history is the conquest of freedom in conscience, in facts and in the universality of men.

Armed with this principle, you can descend to the arena of the past and rouse the centuries from their tomb, to question the meaning of their actions.

Let us remove now the concept of the absolute from this formulation of the problem, and nothing will remain as the foundation of the philosophy of history save the laws of freedom and progress that humanity duly complies with in its historical evolution, as we had stated in 1844. This is the truth in its simplest expression and there is no need to seek out any solution to *make fatalism free and ruled by the free element*; for, as the speech's author himself states, "the doctrine of fatalism, despite its pretensions to absolute theory, is but the doctrine of empiricism or experience elevated to a system," and is not a scientific theory, provable by practical observation.

But in Bilbao's same important speech we find another more perceptible trace of the influence of the early studies of the author of *Sociabilidad chilena*; for with the same method of abstraction that in this writing appear as metaphysical entities, embracing and interpenetrating with a mystical connection the law of history and the sovereignty of the people, which is but the power to constitute the State; sovereignty with reason, reason with law, law with freedom, freedom with the republic, and infinite perfection, and all with the imperative of the Creator who is made manifest in individuality and fraternity, which in turn are also other metaphysical entities.

Here is the passage to which we are referring, with which we will finish the study of the mystic metaphysical system of that remarkable writer:

> Therefore the vision of the law is the sovereignty of the people, and here is where you will see the unity of thought that inspired this speech. The law of history ultimately is identified with the sovereignty of the people, the sovereignty of the people with reason, reason with law, law with freedom, freedom with the republic on earth, and the *incessant perfection in the extrasensory worlds of the spirit*. To establish the sovereignty of the people we must, then, establish the sovereignty of law. What is law? Law is the *imperative of the Creator*, which establishes impenetrable individuality and perfectible *fraternity*. Impenetrable individuality is law. Perfectible fraternity is obligation. Law or freedom is the identity of all thinking beings. Obligation is the development of that universal freedom. These are the radical conditions of the good. This is the vision of law that, in setting forth the sovereignty of reason, sets forth the parameters of the nation's sovereignty.

XXXI

The excesses perpetrated by the conservative *pelucón* party as punishment for the author of *Sociabilidad chilena* and his ideas marked the first act of repression against the intellectual emancipation movement pioneered in 1842, and confirmed the fears that had dissuaded us from doing battle with silly preconceptions by spreading new ideas. The few of us who served logically the regeneration of ideas and the independence of the spirit suffered a painful disillusionment, and we paid quite dearly for the false hopes under which we labored in supposing Bilbao's writing, which repeated age-old attacks in an abstract and inaccessible way, would not stir to revolt the archfanatic ruling class. After the accusation we noted that this class was inclined to clip our wings and seize control of the intellectual movement to drive it down the path opposite to the one we had cleared for it.

That was not the worst of it. At the heart of that persecution carried out with as much fury as childishness was a revelation that dashed all hopes and dreams of organizing a Liberal Party in politics. The rift, which we stated before existed in a latent state in the heart of the ruling class and in the cabinet itself, surfaced now, and proved totally ineffectual with the reformist element that might serve as the center of the new party. The Minister of the Interior and his friends had not even been able to avoid *El Crepúsculo*'s accusation, nor even moderate the angry impulses of the University Council and of the Supreme Court, which unashamedly had revived scenes typical of the darkest hours of the old regime. Society had still not progressed enough to have an opinion independent of the ruling powers that would serve as the foundation for those of us working for reform. Had we continued publishing the ill-fated *El Crepúsculo*, we would not have had readers, for even the intellects most unfit for philosophical abstractions thought they had understood Bilbao's writing, and saw in that newspaper a corrupting element, laying the blame for it not so much on the editors as on the Argentinians, whom many years later Mr. Amunátegui still called corrupters of the public judgment.

In this situation we took exile in *El Siglo*, the liberal daily that Espejo and Santiago Urzúa had founded, and which they published since 5 April of that year of 1844 with the cooperation of *El Crepúsculo*'s editors and mainly that of F. Matta. This young man, departed prematurely, was full of vigor and daring, and was in those days a philosopher like Bilbao, only without the mysticism; saturated in the mists that still formed the horizon of French socialism, he sought to explain all social and political phenomena with Vico's fatalism and Michelet's generalizations, the latter man of which he was a great admirer. Matta and Bilbao were disciples of Mr. Bello, but they had profited more from his metaphysics than from his literary taste and artistic forms. Both undertook a journey to Europe after *El Crepúsculo*'s accusation, and the latter changed undoubtedly less than the former with the five years of European education they had; for Matta returned to the Chilean press, not to write as a philosophical fatalist, nor to express socialist abstractions, but to make his mark as a political writer noteworthy for his biting style, impetuosity, and above all for the singularity of his political credo; for by appearing to be a partisan of the liberal principle, he violently attacked the liberals who were determined to organize a party that served democratic reform, and fought in defense of the Conservative Party, resorting to a certain political eclecticism that had the nuances and variants of the banner raised by Benavente and the *Filopolitas** in 1835.

---

* The *Filopolitas* ("Friends of the People") were dissenting Conservative Party leaders who published *El philopolita*, a journal of the mid-1830s, containing opin-

El Siglo additionally served since its foundation as an agency for beginning poets and prose writers who still were lacking the propriety and refined taste of those who contributed to *El Crepúsculo*. Nevertheless, among the former, Eusebio Lillo was a standout right from the first poems he published in *El Siglo*, and more so after a timely hymn to independence, which won the prize in the competition the Literary Society held that year. The students from the advanced courses at the Instituto had brought back this institution, in the tradition of the early founders.

Since Matta stopped collaborating with *El Siglo*, the management and editorial duties of the newspaper were left to Espejo. This young man had a most outstanding character, free of deceitfulness, naive, forthright, and loyal, and he was not a philosopher. He had an exclusively political training and professed an enthusiastic devotion to the cause of democratic reform. His wisdom and powerful intellectual understanding made up for the deficiency of his studies; but in expression, since he did not have a disciplined literary taste, he was habitually emphatic, and although the declamatory tone of his writings satisfied the average reader, he lent himself to attacks by the Argentinian writers, who then were beginning to serve the faction of the pure conservatives. Still, the most experienced polemicists, especially in the political battles in the following years, had to crash all the time against the indomitable valor and chivalrous arrogance of that zealous defender of the principles and interests of liberal reform.

Espejo yielded the enterprise and the management of *El Siglo* to those of us who, as we have stated, took them on in the hopes of vigorously serving the organization of a new Liberal Party. It has been stated already that this hope was frustrated when the course of events brought the old 1828 liberals to the ring, who with their persecutors and conquerors of 1830 engaged in an unequal battle in which the modern liberal element disappeared, and the outcome of which could not help but be advantageous to those who, possessed of absolute power, presented themselves also as generators and protectors of social and political interests that had managed to congeal starting in that year.

El Siglo having been eliminated, the new liberal propaganda was confined to teaching at the Instituto. But the second period of the Bulnes administration began by removing the conservatives from the government, a faction that in the short span of sixteen months had left very deep tracks in its wake, including the ill-fated press law of 1846, and the surrender of power to conciliatory ministers who aspired to rule without a dictatorship.

ions opposing the reelection of Joaquín Prieto Vial to a second five-year presidential term. —Ed.

New hopes for reform and for a liberal system sprouted then, but never bloomed: the political principles and interests of the Conservative Party predominated in the ruling class, and above and beyond having its support in the administrative organization that had been calculated to maintain them, it doubtlessly relied on the country's opinion, powerfully thrust in its favor by material interests, which demanded a strong government to support it, mainly by the Valparaíso business community. The ministers of conciliation, furthermore, had neither the courage to react forthrightly against those principles and interests, nor the necessary aptitudes to consolidate a new Liberal Party, so their political actions were impeded and uncertain; and if they dared seek support in new men and new interests, they did not therefore give up the old ones, and called them at every turn to their side.

Meanwhile the literary movement was paralyzed, and the suspicions born of that quite colorless political situation reached it and robbed it of all impetus. The year 1847 was remarkable in this respect. According to our notes, the press only published four didactic works, of which only Mr. Bello's Castilian grammar is worthy of memory, apart from two translations and four original books, one of them the Report on Santiago's waters by Mr. Domeyko,* and another on field guns and light mountain artillery, submitted by A. Olavarrieta to the Ministry of War. Rectifying now these notes in view of Briseño's *Estadística bibliográfica* ["Bibliographic Statistics"], we find that alongside the special-interest publications, twenty-one reissues appeared, almost all novels and opera librettos; none of which we had taken note, for if the reproduction of similar books revealed a certain taste for leisure reading, it was nevertheless not proof of the continuation of that great literary movement from years previous.

The prostration that year was the effect of political agitation from the previous year and stemmed also from the stance that the Conservative Party had assumed with respect to intellectual development three years previously in the memorable condemnation of *El Crepúsculo*, attempting to burn ideas and the independence of the spirit by the hand of the hangman. The literary movement was not yet flexible enough to resist such reversals, which moreover were supported by the persistence with which the University served that same stance, adopting a restrictive course that in that year of 1847 took them so far as to accuse our constitutional public law text, through a Presbyter from the Law School, of both atheism and Protestantism at the same time, and of condemning through the School of Humanities our doctrine on the philosophy of history. What to do in such a

---

* Ignacio Domeyko (1801–1889), Polish-born scientist and poet who became rector of the University of Chile in 1876. —Ed.

bind? Admit defeat and give up the work of ten years, whose precocious fruits had fed our hopes, announcing that in our fledgling society there was a yearning for progress and the aptitudes appropriate to reaching it? That would have been the most comfortable and advantageous thing, but meanwhile we needed to abandon all hope of regenerating ideas, all plans to prepare the advent of the democratic system, surrendering as a matter of course the leadership of intellectual development to the retrogressives, and the progress of the new regime to the slow course of social events.

The new-school youths proved to be discouraged and harbored practically no other hope than that the ministry of conciliation back the literary movement and reestablish the erstwhile work under its aegis. Nevertheless, we were still planning the publication of a third newspaper, trusting yet in the progressive aptitudes of society; and to test the waters, we took to doing a third publication, preparing a small book with the title of *Aguinaldo para 1848 dedicado al bello sexo chileno* ["Christmas Carol for 1848, Dedicated to the Fair Sex of Chile"]. The printer was Andrés R. Bello, toward whom we pledged to furnish the funds, with him committing to publish a monthly *Review*, if the test run turned out well. We had more than enough material, for we only needed to publish as our part of the bargain a verse introduction entitled *El aguinaldo* ["Christmas Carol"] and two little novels, to make room for a legend by Juan Bello, with the title of *La espada de Felipe del Atrevido* ["Philip the Daring's Sword"]; for the poetic composition *A Peñalolén* ["To Peñalolén"] by his father don Andrés; for several poems by Lindsay, Espejo, by Andrés and by Jacinto Chacón, and two prose works by González and Asta-Buruaga. The results exceeded our hopes, for the public received the book like a memory of past glories, like remembrances of old absent friends, and showered it with praise.

The future was once again secure, since we still enjoyed the patronage of opinion, which had greatly favored the movement begun in 1842. In March 1848 we launched the prospectus of the *Revista de Santiago* ["Santiago Review"]. Subscriptions were not long in coming and immediately offset the cost of publication. To maintain this publication we had the assistance of Cristóbal Valdés, Marcial González, Jacinto Chacón, and also the monthly article Mr. Bello had promised us, as well as the collaboration of the young writers whom we could motivate with the importance of our new endeavor. The assistance of Mr. Bello in these times was of great efficacy, in addition to being generous and reliable. When the downcast, dejected, pensive, and wise old man heard the story we told him of our disappointments and setbacks, of our hopes and goals, he had risen from his seat visibly moved, assuring us with an effusion entirely alien to his ways that we should count on his cooperation and that he was resolved to helping us, to following us in our crusade, in our publicizing, with no thought of the dangers. This had enlivened us and confirmed the idea in us that the teacher was now disavowing the old traditions of which he formerly was the jealous guardian.

The first issue of the *Revista de Santiago*, published in April 1848, was received with accolades that revealed immediately that its acceptance was popular, for it responded to a generally felt need. The entire press of the Republic hailed it with the greatest enthusiasm, and Valparaíso's *El Comercio*, in one of the two articles that its editor devoted to it, the eminent Argentinian statist General Bartolomé Mitre,* expressed himself thus: "We have no knowledge of South America currently possessing a more interesting paper in terms of tone, writing and tendencies, as well as the respectability of some names that are included on its editorial staff. Only the Chilean press in this part of the continent has preserved its dignity, to the point of providing first-rank South American literary luminaries an honorable forum in their publications. How many newspapers in fact are published in South America with works signed by names like Bello and Lastarria?"

Of course, we had the invaluable cooperation of writers who offered the advantage of being known already, such as Ramón Briseño, Eusebio Lillo, and Hermógenes Irisarri, the latter two poets that had performed their first feats of arms, garnering a household name for themselves for their inspiration, their proper style, and for the refined taste and artistic talent they displayed.

Alongside these poets and others who had reaped the laurel previously, such as Andrés and Jacinto Chacón, debuting in the *Review* were Floridor Rojas, who distinguished himself instantly for his beautiful verse translation of Ponsard's *Lucrecia*; José Antonio Torres, who later drew so much applause for his prolificacy and for the gaiety and drama of his inspiration; and finally the lyric poet *par excellence*, Guillermo Blest Gana, who for his exquisite artistic taste and the transparency and gentleness of his sentiment, awakened enthusiasm for poetry and affection for the bard who played such a sweet-toned lyre.

Among the *Review*'s prose writers, youths such as Lindsay, Santiago Arcos, and Fernández Rodella began then to come on the scene, contributing interesting writings; the Amunátegui brothers began their career as well, men who have given so many glories to our national literature, Joaquín Blest Gana and Juan Bello, who later won an eminent place among political orators and among the wisest and most proper writers. These four adolescents, as they were then, were the most assiduous contributors to the

---

* Bartolomé Mitre (1821–1906), Argentine statesman, military leader, and historian, fled the Rosas dictatorship, lived in Chile, Peru, and Bolivia, and served as president of Argentina, 1862–1868. —Ed.

Review, and it is worth noting how since those days they revealed the seriousness of their studies and the admirable endowments of their spirit for the cultivation of literature and for historical research.

But among all those enthusiastic and selfless youths, who set out to construct a national literature in the moments in which the effort begun in 1842 nearly was failing, the untimely departed Cristóbal Valdés deserves a special recollection; and let us do so by transcribing, to set it down in writing here, a part of the biographical article we published in Valparaíso's *El Diario* in 1853, the year of his premature and grievous loss:

> The year of 1842, we stated in that writing, was remarkable in Santiago for the literary activity that emerged almost spontaneously and with neither antecedents nor stimuli to produce it. A large group of youths distinguished for their culture, their manners, for their fine literary voice, and even for their physiognomy, came almost improvisationally to breathe life into the aged society and to impress a new seal and give a new orientation to the customs and to the taste of the good Santiagans, who until then were not accustomed to rousing from their habitual slumbers except for the political events that occurred from time to time and by accident.
>
> These youths were brought up right there in the seclusion of their school cloisters, and owed the novelty of their inclinations and their ways only to the severe study of good doctrines and the practice of a morality founded on principles different from those that hitherto comprised the source of concerns handed down from the Colony.
>
> A very vital role was played by one who stood out among those youths for his kind, likable physiognomy, for the ease of his ways, for the spontaneity and sincerity of his wit, and for his determination to rise through assiduous diligence toward proper studies.
>
> That young man was Cristóbal Valdés, whom death has taken from us after a prolonged and painful illness, acquired from his serious and constant devotion to letters.
>
> The late-lamented Cristóbal had been called to the bar on 21 October 1841, when he was scarcely twenty years of age, and to general acclaim had made his first forays into the court of justice. A *cause célèbre* brought him awfully soon to the high court of the Republic, the case that formed around the Maurelios family, which, as sole inhabitants of the island of Juan Fer-

nández, had tried and executed an Irishman, Osborn, who tried to seditiously resist the authority of that tribe's patriarch. The Maurelioses having been condemned by the Valparaíso judge, it fell to poor Valdés to defend them before the Supreme Court. The young man secured a more favorable sentence for his clients, managing through the spirit and brilliance of his defense to earn the congratulations in chambers of that strict Chief Justice, to the wonderment of everyone who knew that the latter had never offered congratulations like that.

At the time Valdés was also busy giving lessons in the humanities in some schools in Santiago, to the great advantage of his disciples; and his circumspection was such that, in spite of his tender years, the first school for young ladies in existence then, headed by Mrs. Cabezón, placed him in charge of a good deal of the teaching of her pupils.

Valdés devoted himself then to the study of law and of belles lettres, and the theaters in which he displayed the precocious flowers of his talent were the forum, as well as a literary newspaper we schoolfellows published with the title *El Crepúsculo*. Some pages of a novel and a biographical look at the well-known Manuel Rodríguez, hero of the independence, were the most noteworthy of the output from Valdés, who brought that publication to light.

Later, in 1848, when the *Revista de Santiago* appeared, Valdés had stopped work on light studies, and thrown himself passionately into the science of political economy, without leaving his lawyering profession, which provided for his father's abundant family.

Valdés was a constant contributor to the *Revista*, and in all the issues that comprise the three tomes of this important newspaper are found the articles entitled *Estudios histórico-económicos* ["Historic-economic Studies"], signed with his name.

The twelve articles that make up the series of these *Studies*, which include approximately 200 pages of the *Review*, constitute a serious work that would be quite liable to establish the fame of a writer, had its author flourished elsewhere. The style of the work is rather didactic, lacking for no grace, owing to the fondness with which Valdés always sought elegant and flowery forms to express his ideas. The language is generally proper and the phrasing meticulous.

Valdés shows in these *Studies* an erudition most uncommon in a young South American. Assisted by the French, English, and Italian languages he possessed, he could devote himself to the reading of the great wealth of books he had obtained for himself on economic matters; well-versed as he was on the history of Spain and South America, he could judge with noble discrimination the Spanish-American financial institutions.

The purpose that Valdés proposed in his *Estudios histórico-económicos* ["Historic-economic Studies"] is too weighty: he sought to reach a "profound knowledge of the socio-economic improvements that are best suited to South Americans," and to this end he felt it necessary "to study what we were under Spanish administration." But first, he said, outlining the plan of his work, "we will present a comprehensive and general picture of the history of economic science in Europe, to find out how it conformed to the progress of humanity. We will have a glance at what this science was among the Greeks and Romans, proceeding by turns from the invasion of the barbarians to Charlemagne, and finally to the Crusades and the Italian republics, which had already tested the most ardent issues of science and wonderfully increased their wealth and power, then to arrive in Spain, under whose power a spirit full of faith and enthusiasm was to present it with the patrimony of a new world.

The carrying out of this vast plan was lucid, and Valdés never lost sight in his work of the practical tendency that we South Americans should give to economic studies. "The study of economy in our country," he stated, "should have a practical rather than scientific bent. We need to conduct them on the sterile surface of things and not with the flashy pomp of theories. We must use the analytic method and start from the facts and the elements of society in order to derive the theory that suits us: to employ the synthetic method and to apply theories derived from other facts to err at every step, is to create a social monster. The South American republics, for their geographical position, for their industry, for the role they are called to play in the immense drama of humanity, must have a new system of economy, for they have very little in common with Europe in the branches of their administration, in the production and distribution of their wealth."

Elsewhere in his work he strenuously condemns the remedies that have been attempted in South America by taking them from the doctrines and institutions of modern Europe. "The largest questions of economic science," he stated, "those that are the order of the day in the Old World, cannot have any application or influence for the time being in our country. The best distribution of labor, the poverty of the working class, the highs and lows of manufactured goods, the freedom of trade, are matters that if their resolution occurs among us, it is purely out of an obligation of sympathy or antipathy, according to the principles we profess: but not because of our industry, in the mass of our wealth, in the heart of our society, in short, because our laws, our administration, will always be the same."

Valdés ended his work "with the satisfaction of having covered and analyzed one by one all the elements of which the political, economic, and social administration of the South American colonies was made up, and the principles that preceded them in the history of humanity." But the fruit of his arduous labors remained relegated to the pages of a book that very few will have occasion to read, and that perhaps will pass unnoticed by those for whom it was meant. Sad is the state of those who, like the departed author of the *Studies*, spend their finest days lighting with the torch of science the path that we South Americans are hard at crossing in darkness.

But since we are not attempting to write the analysis of one of Valdés's most important works, we will simply write the brief recollection we have just done, to then move on to consider our friend in the public posts he occupied.

The Santiago Court of Appeals numbered him for a long time among its court reporters, and all the members of that court are witnesses to the delicacy, refinement and skill of his execution.

In 1849 he was elected reserve deputy by the administrative district of Elqui, and in that capacity attended the Chamber a few times. The situation at that time was difficult, especially for a young man like Valdés, who was making his debut on the political scene. But his characteristic moderation and steadfastness in the principles he professed saved him from the danger in which he found himself thrust. Although he was considered among the most respected members of the opposition party, he never engaged in unpleasant matters, and was wise enough to take active part only in issues of general interest. In a normal situation, Valdés would have had more room to put his knowledge to best use for the country, from the post in which he had been placed, and would have stood out as an exemplary deputy. . . .

The importance that the *Revista de Santiago* assumed with the writings, by and large excellent in form and content, that all these writers contributed, resonated in the press throughout all of South America; above all it was an efficient aid to lending coherence to the literary school that came to be with the movement of 1842, the school that from the first was able to serve as the active hub for the organization of the new Liberal Party. The spirit that the writing of the articles inspired, even the very tendency of the poetic compositions, and mainly that of our monthly reviews, which always were reproduced by the national press and that of neighboring republics, were headed toward producing the regeneration of ideas, serving the independence of the spirit, and spreading and instilling love of the principles and interests of a democratic reform in our institutions and political practices.

The results of these efforts were not long in coming, for actually the seeds that the *Revista de Santiago* had helped to cultivate had been germinating for some time. The conservative reaction of 1845–1846, which seemingly had extinguished the new liberal school's movement, had been fleeting, and only put that movement in a latent state; so the discouragement in 1847 was unfounded, nothing other than fanciful cowardice, as born out by the fact of the intellectual progress's having resurged in full swing as soon as we published our *Aguinaldo* and the *Revista* just after it. The acanthus was brimming with sap and life, and we needed only to remove the surrounding foliage that weighed it down for its beautiful sparkling greenery to grow.

At that time an error was being repeated under which improvident governments constantly labor, administrations that do not know how to distinguish the facts that pertain to the regular order of social development from those than upset it, to favor the evolution of the former and choke off the latter, if possible, from the start. The recalcitrant Conservative Party reorganized with the support of the weak and shortsighted ministry of conciliation, which was destined by its conditions to continue the modification work begun in 1843 by Minister Irarrázaval; and this ministry allowed itself to be defeated by the Chambers of Congress and by the recalcitrants' press, failing to make use of the new liberal element to promote its growth. Still, the intellectual progress represented and served by the *Revista de Santiago* had regained its bearings and marched onward toward reform, organizing itself and prepared to take over the controls, since the moderate conservatives who also aspired to serve reform were relinquishing them.

These were the factors that determined two well-delineated currents of public opinion in that situation: one, which doubtless was the strongest, wished to reestablish absolute power in government, that power that had its roots and its life in political and administrative organization founded and consolidated by the old *pelucón* party; the other, which was the least cohesive, sought to change that organization to limit its power and give the nation its political rights, its legitimate participation in self-governance. Both currents clash in the 1849 elections, and when represented in the Chamber of Deputies, do battle, to the detriment of the latter. This conflict, however, hoists the banner of democratic reform and keeps it waving until falling with it in the civil war to which it was led by the tenacious and blind persistence with which the conservatives tried from the first to close off all roads to reform, to cut short all discussion with violence, and to stop the old regime from changing by using the ordinary means of a parliamentary government.

During that conflict in 1849, the *Revista de Santiago*, with the nobility and dignity befitting a literary publication of its stature, maintained the principles and the interest of political reform; but at the end of that year it had to yield ground, pressured by conservative influences, which took advantage of the publication of an article on customs in the issue that ends the third volume to deprive it of resources, from which the reformists could not find a way to remove it.

We have stated previously that in 1841 and 1842 the so-called articles of customs had been in vogue, Larra's *Fígaro* serving as the model for those who practiced this genre, among which Vallejo had excelled for his astuteness in depicting the ridiculousness of the situations he chose. But we had sought to give the essays in this genre a social inclination, preferably criticizing stale concerns contrary to democratic civic responsibility in which new customs should be included, for the *Historia de la ciudad de Nueva York desde el principio del mundo* ["History of the City of New York From the Beginning of the World"]* was more to our liking as a model than the *Fígaro*; in the former book, Washington Irving had exploded his compatriot's pretensions to nobility. In *El Semanario* and *El Crepúsculo* we had published some sketches of that nature. At the end of 1849, when the two parties in contention for the ascendancy of their ideas were delineated to a fare-thee-well,

---

* The work's full title is *A History of New-York, From the Beginning of the World to the End of the Dutch Dynasty. Containing, Among Many Surprising Matters, the Unutterable Ponderings of Walter the Doubter, the Disastrous Projects of William the Testy, and the Chivalric Achievements of Peter the Headstrong, the Three Dutch Governors of New-Amsterdam: Being the Only Authentic History of the Times that Ever Hath Been Published.* Written under pseudonym Diedrich Knickerbocker, 1809. —Trans.

and when the liberal element was organized in the heat of battle and the agitation produced by that gigantic development, we thought it timely to write an article geared toward condemning character flaws, antisocial habits, evil passions, and anti-democratic concerns, and we wrote in a demonstrative style appropriate to the circumstances, for effect, the *Manuscrito del Diablo* ["Devil's Manuscript"], which we published in the last issue of the third volume of the *Revista*.

The conservatives took the article as an insult to society, and on behalf of the national honor that they alleged had been sullied, repeating the accusation that worries have always hurled against him who censures them, propagandized to take the *Revista*'s subscribers away and intimidate its editor. The newspaper stopped press, and though Fernández Rodella sought to replace it with *El Picaflor* ["The Hummingbird"], this literary paper only survived a brief time; and the editor had to reestablish the *Revista de Santiago* four months later, in order to take advantage of the rightful fame that publication had earned.

The *Revista*'s second series ran from April 1850 until the same month in 1851, under the leadership of Francisco Matta, who was back from his long trip to Europe; but he no longer represented the principles and interests of the new Liberal Party, because his director, preferring for the Republic's administration the pursuers of that disjointed party, wished to form a separate liberal movement, instead of working within the organic unity of the great democratic cause. Four years later, Guillermo Matta, the valiant poet of the new synthesis, who has greatly ennobled the national literature with his brilliant works, followed the tradition of the *Revista de Santiago* and published from it a third series, in which the most outstanding writers from the first one were included.

Since the latter had gone out of print in 1849, its founder concentrated his efforts on the political movement, and involved in the revolutionary whirlwind of 1851, ended the evolution that had begun with teaching in 1837, at least with the satisfaction that the new seed had been planted in good soil. No less than forty writers had assisted in attending to the far-reaching influence that *El Semanario* in 1842, *El Crepúsculo* in 1843, and the *Revista de Santiago* in 1848 had in founding the high press in our country, in the consolidation of the literary movement, and in the diffusion of liberal ideas. Except for only five of those writers, all the others began to make a name for themselves in those publications; many of them came into their own there, beginning their careers as prose writers or poets, and acquiring the due fame with which afterward they were able to maintain the luster of the national literature, whose existence dates to 1842. The literary future of this beloved country was assured, the independence of the spirit was proclaimed as the basis of intellectual development, and the liberal doctrine was founded on solid underpinnings. Political reversals doubtless could pervert or dull the effects of these new active elements, but extinguish or overcome them, never!

END OF PART ONE

PART TWO

The Circle of Friends
of Literature

I

It is 1859. Ten years have passed since we put an end, in the third volume of the *Revista de Santiago*, to that fruitful literary revolution that had roused the intellect and opened up new and vast horizons to it, and which had laid the foundations of a national literature, with the help of many distinguished contributors, in addition to the contributions which by contrast were made by those who more than once sought to stand in the way.

But everything has changed in these ten years. Although the literary movement has not been extinguished, for it was impossible to destroy its sources or starve its expansive force, its tendencies have been misplaced, and even its doctrines were distorted. Conservative politics lorded over everything, brought back to power with the spirit and ways of its best days, and its seal appeared stamped on all manifestations of social development. This reaction in politics reestablished the old regime in all its splendor, and in undoing the regenerating work that had made such strides in the fourteen years from 1837 to 1850, also brought a vigorous revival to the ideas, feelings, concerns, and anti-democratic habits of the old Spanish civilization. In 1861, attempting to characterize the first reaction brought about by the *pelucón* party, we alluded to the one that appeared in the decade we are discussing now, in these views that we cannot change today, despite the objectivity with which we are regarding the facts.

"The government was powerful," we stated, speaking of that of 1835—: "its inflexible, systematic, and resolute course had surrounded it with prestige and terror, and the strong organization that had taken hold in all the hierarchies of its authority had clinched its victory and that of its party once and for all. The four years that passed from Portales's separation from the ministry until 1835 had sufficed for his successors to consummate the task begun by the former, and to raise the *pelucón* party to the fullness of its rule, the zenith of its power. *But the colonial reaction had not yet completely run its course*, because in the very heart of the ruling party it met some resistance: it *was to reach* its full splendor later (from 1851 on), when, with the greatest naturalness and without the least opposition, temples were erected to the founder of the colony (the chapel of the Cruz colony) in the capacity of introducer of religion and of having been such a great conqueror; when the public was taken with miracles worked in a minister of State's house;* when the same general secretary of the reactionary party, canon Meneses, ascended to the pulpit to sanction with his sacerdotal words the swindles that were perpetrated against the holiness of a lay brother;† when finally the official press brazenly proclaimed that 'the Conservative Party's basic mission is to reestablish *the Spanish spirit* in civilization and in civic duty, to fight the socialist spirit of the French civilization.'"‡

Alongside these developments, which are truly remarkable, political history will gather many others equally characteristic, to prove the complete triumph of the reaction of the Spanish past in that era, which nevertheless was one of growth through the increase of the country's wealth. But this prosperity did not come about from that reaction, but rather served to support and further it. After the political disturbances of 1851, fatigue and disillusionment on the one hand, and the need for work on the other, stimulated by the incentive of handsome profits that mining, agriculture, and trade yielded due to fortuitous circumstances, made the nation submit

* In 1852 there was much talk of the truth of a miracle of Bardesi, servant of God, in the house of the Minister of Culture, and the press in general relayed the fact unremarked.

† Fray Andresito. Also a record on the same issue as the sermon, entitled *Vida i hechos marabillosos de Fr. Andrés García, hermano donado de la Recolección franciscana de Santiago* ["Life and Marvelous Events of Fray Andrés García, Lay Brother of the Santiago Franciscan Retreat"], by E. N. was published in 1855 by the National Press.

‡ *Juicio histórico de Portales* ["Historical Judgment of Portales"]. The newspaper that advocated the reestablishment of the Spanish spirit was *La Civilización*, and its thesis was repeated, applauded, and explained by the Valparaíso *El Mercurio*.

to the domination of the absolute government all aspirations to social regeneration and political reform that had cast it headlong into the grievous crisis caused by the tenacious resistance with which the ruling party had thwarted and stifled those aspirations. A phenomenon quite common among the lower orders, that of the utopian vision, from which even educated people suffer when they do not stop to ascertain whether what their imagination accepts as real on account of seeming so, really exists, made that prosperity and the contentment and satisfaction proceeding from it be attributed to the strong government. Public opinion came out, then, in support of that order that was so valuable to the *pelucón* party, and which so admirably consulted the industrial interest, above all that of foreign trade, which demanded nothing else but security for its profits, though at the cost of the moral progress of the country in which it went about its industry of buying low and selling high.

Meanwhile independent intellectual development did not partake of that prosperity. History and statistics bear out the decline in which, as the institutions of Jesuitic instruction progressed, public education was run by the State, beginning with primary education, which still lacked the law that was approved in 1850 and stayed in effect until 24 November 1860, when it finally attained its authorization, after a revision that lasted three years. We have no need of repeating that history, but included in the aims of these *Memoirs* is making mention of the prostration in which literary production had fallen on account of the same reaction influences, which had paralyzed the literary movement that had expanded its activities to such a great extent in 1849.

These influences had already reached their full extent in 1855, and taking the *Estadística bibliográfica* from the five years that passed up to 1859, one notices that with respect to the literary production being extremely scarce, most of the original works are on matters of some ephemeral interest, or special-interest monographs, like primary education texts and works in the humanities, save for rare exceptions. The booklets of this latter kind abound, as do translations and reissues, owing to the fact that the adepts of the ruling political interest were exploiting the favor that the government granted this sort of work, in support of authorized instruction and of popular libraries, a new institution to which a great importance was attached, and which in practice never was justified for the very reason of its poor organization. But that favor was given with so little discernment and was exploited so unintelligently, that the results served no purpose, nor did they contribute then nor thereafter to literary development. Proof of the injustice of the assistance is found in the fact that they received many teaching texts that had been disapproved by the University, and in the fact that those that earned their approval were so wanting in merit that even if they wound up being used, they soon were discontinued; and proof of the dim-wittedness with which most speculators served the popular libraries, is that the reissued works or translations were not books appropriate to the education of the people, nor were they suitable to instill a taste for reading, but doctrinaire works or reflective histories like those of Guizot, classic biographies like those of Lamartine, and other books of serious works and even false doctrines. That lack of intelligence reached incredible extremes, such as, to cite but one example, that of reissuing a poor translation of Prescott's *Conquista de México* ["Conquest of Mexico"], which the firm of the *Revista de España, Indias y el Extranjero* ["Review of Spain, Indies and Parts Foreign"] published in Madrid, printing on the cover "Chile, Indies and Parts Foreign Edition," because the Spanish edition said "*Revista de España, Indias y el Extranjero* Edition."

As for the number of these publications, the *Estadística* gives us this result: in 1855, fourteen original works, including eight textbooks and some poetry; thirteen translations and republications, among which there are five opera librettos; in 1856, twenty-three originals, including seven texts, and fifteen translations and reprints; in 1857, twenty-one originals, among which there are five texts and some short poems, and the reprints and translations reach seventeen; in 1858, there are twenty-five originals, eleven of them are texts and two national novels; reprints and translations, twenty four; in 1859 twenty-four original works were published, thirteen of them are educational texts, two novels, one of poetry and a code project; the reprints and translations amount to twenty. This tally betrays the prostration of literary production of which we speak, for if we deduct the forty-four little textbooks that have been published in the five years, it leaves only sixty-three original works, mainly circumstantial publications and books on issues lacking in literary interest.

But what proves incontrovertibly that this decline was the natural consequence of the victory of the conservative reaction, which, governing absolutely in politics, ruled the entire society despotically, is the tremendous growth that book production, pamphlets, and official works of exclusively religious and ecclesiastic interest reached in that era. It would appear to be a revealing fact in itself that in that five-year period only sixty-three secular works had come out of the country's intellectual labors; but when alongside this figure the *Estadística bibliográfica* notes one hundred sixty-four works of exclusively ecclesiastic interest, we must needs recognize that the latter was the predominant interest, such that it was actually the one that registered the most growth under the reaction's rule.

These one hundred sixty-four productions of ecclesiastic literature are broken down by year in this way: in 1855, thirty-three; in 1856, twenty-one; in 1857, forty-two; in 1858, thirty-six, and in 1859, thirty-two.

II

Nevertheless, the example of the previous age still acted as a stimulus, for not only did the reaction follow it by seeking the protection of the press to serve their own interests, but also the independent and regenerating literary movement made new attempts from time to time to rehabilitate itself and make its declarations through the press. Its progress, granted, was intermittent, for it lacked the vitality to overcome the reaction, and it followed a crooked path that at times wandered off and lingered; but in each of its tendencies it enriched literary production, and won over new workers to swell its ranks. The times were cloudy and dark, but at intervals would appear some ray of light of the new spirit that showed them the way, as happens on a stormy night when the wind rakes back the clouds to bring shining stars into view, auguries of fair weather.

The theory of the unity of social progress was upheld naturally, in spite of the powerful tendency by the reaction to reestablish the moral order of the old regime. Owing to the reaction's support, all the interests of the active order had been developed, and consequently a material progress was at work that made one forget moral interests, or rather that wished to subdue them in order to stifle the independence of the spirit and the aspiration to freedom, two threats to their peace of mind and their pleasure. Yet the task was impossible. Considerable progress was not made in one sphere of social activity without this change producing analogous progress in the others. Therefore the endeavors that despotism supported by material progress makes to stifle freedom are invariably fruitless, imprisoning the moral order in certain dogmas, in certain traditional rules, or in certain artificial doctrines: moral progress perpetually frees itself and tends to develop comparably to material progress, all the more so when previously it has found its bearings in the independence of the spirit, as had happened here from 1837 to 1850.

Thus we see the traditions previous to 1850 persistently appear in the reactionary age under discussion. No sooner had the *pelucón* party reinstalled itself in power with its whole train of extraordinary authority, exiles, and persecutions, seeking to stanch the wounds and sop up the tears from the civil war by using terror, than a new writer surfaces who, free of the commitments of battle, stayed two years, until 1853, at the Valparaíso *El Mercurio*, fighting against the restoration of religious preoccupations and defending the true interests of industrial freedom, which is in danger in the hands of the speculators and the merchants, who not only put up opposition to that freedom, but also to the writer who denounces them. That novel writer who already revealed a subtle genius blessed with vast education, a correct, vivacious, polished, colorful style, and a fertile art rich in forms and dazzle, is Ambrosio Montt, who later developed those remarkable gifts to the great benefit of the cause of freedom, that of letters, and the glory of our parliamentary oratory.

In 1855 Guillermo Matta reestablished the *Revista de Santiago* and kept it alive during the second half of the year with the collaboration of don Andrés Bello and a few from the 1848 and '49 staff, who, like the rest, had not been forced to roam abroad or outside the capital due to political causes. In this new series of the *Revista*, some writers who, though they had debuted in the political press, or had at their disposal a torrent of deep-fetched knowledge, still did not have the notoriety they won since then.

The one with the most experience among these writers, by virtue of his studies and even his age, was Francisco Marín, who later so often served the liberal cause with his words, as a representative in the Senate and in the House of Deputies. Thus he got a late start on his career as a writer, like Vauvenargues, with whom he has so many affinities: for his benevolence, his Christian piety practiced against all the temptations of incredulity, his physical and moral grief, and even as a sentimental moralist, which hovers between theological mysticism and the metaphysics of the Encyclopedists. With meticulous language and an easy style, he laid out his pages in the *Revista* on the need for the religious principle. But, though he had not been a warrior like that illustrious friend of Voltaire, Marín had the courage to gain his entry in the press by publishing a letter in which he vindicated the Liberal Party against the attacks of the *pelucones* and for the first time took aim with vigorous censures at the ruling power, fearless to disturb it at the height of its victories.

In the same literary publication Alberto Blest Gana began to make a name for himself as a novelist. He had just begun in this genre with us, and fortunately the small essays that had been done, though they lacked any real worth, were not reactionary, in the sense of digging up timeworn, antisocial concerns, or of restoring outside interests in democratic civic responsibility. Alberto Blest Gana followed the same course to cultivate the modern novel, which, in the expression of a judicious critic, is "the one that depicts contemporary society and fleshes out the ideals and sentiments that motivate our century; the one that to the dramatic interest of events unites the sociological interest produced by the accomplished portrait of the characters and the social interest engendered by the issues raised in them; the one that profitably substitutes the old epic and presents with startling truth and brilliant colors the complex life and shaken conscience of this society."

The novelist that was emerging, and who has earned in our incipient literature the highest ranking for his powerful descriptive talent, for his precision in describing our ways, for his accuracy in sketching characters, earned accolades from the first; for, shunning implausible situations and outlandish adventures, and placing himself wholly in the service of regenerating ideas and ways, he possessed the art of painting his domestic scenes with such honesty and sobriety, works that never failed to ring true to life, though they might otherwise lack dramatic movement, brilliant color, and the general interest that the grand historical or social situations inspire, or the great moral issues that stir the modern world.

Side by side with these writers, the poets Pío Varas Marín, Martín José Lira, and Adolfo Valderrama appeared in the *Revista*, though with light-weight compositions; they later gave ample demonstrations of their poetic talents. Also appearing were the prose writers Francisco Vargas Fontecilla, Domingo Santa María, M. A. Matta, and Barros Arana, who had already been introduced a year earlier with the publication of the first volume of his *Historia general de la independencia de Chile* ["General History of the Chilean Independence"].

This third series of the *Revista de Santiago* ended in short order, despite its director's having vowed that it would not die "*of consumption for lack of subscriptions*, since it is provided with sufficient funds to support it." Perhaps they were overtaken by the asphyxia that in the atmosphere of all despotism overcomes independent spirits.

This phenomenon, so often born out by history, was at work then as well, as the statistical data we have presented on literary production in those days attest. What is certain is that this publication, run so brilliantly by old and new writers alike, among whom figured the Spanish man of letters Eduardo Asquerino, did not manage on this outing to produce more than eighty pages.

But the absolutist government had a Caesarean whim. It thought doubtlessly like Augustus and the Napoleons that it was necessary to protect letters and have writers, since the new political situation distanced those who previously had created and honored our literary progress. But it did not make Reports nor write books, like those Caesars, nor even form a doctrinaire school that, like that of Louis Philippe, falsified the representative system and led philosophy astray with a false eclecticism of convenience. This work was done and the French doctrinaires imposed their counterfeitings and mistakes as laws of sociology. They simply published a *Revista de Ciencias y Letras* ["Review of Sciences and Letters"], which came out a year after the demise of the *Revista de Santiago* in 1857, and which in four installments, brought out in the afternoons, contain major works from the eminent foreign professors that were in the service of Chile: Messrs. Domeyko, Cour-celle-Seneuil, Philippi, Moesta, and Pissis. Asta-Buruaga, a public servant like the foregoing, also published therein his important descriptive statistical work on Costa Rica and the Central American republics, and apart from three or four anonymous articles, there appears a critical assessment of Father Martínez's *Historia de Chile* ["History of Chile"], written by Barros Arana, and interspersed in the scientific news pages, which are the best embellishment of that *Revista*. Belles lettres did not catch on in the paper save for the long dull cantos of Sanfuentes's *Teudo o Memorias de un solitario* ["Teudo, or, Memoirs of a Recluse"], a kind of diary in which the hero sets down in labored verse his day-to-day impressions, and which that poet's most impassioned critic, Amunátegui, considers an inferior composition to the others that have flowed from the same pen.

The *Revista de Ciencias y Letras* was not, then, a manifestation of the national literary movement, nor did it help pull it out of the paralysis in which it was mired. But if conservative policy was powerless to create anything to replace the new school that erstwhile had formed, doubtlessly it fostered writers of textbooks and translators of work for popular libraries of which we have made mention previously, backed education and the studies that encouraged the development of the old traditional school, and nobly had its interests represented and defended in the press through *El Ferrocarril*, a daily founded in the final days of 1855, which later earned, through sensible management, the first place among those published in Chile.

Moreover, the ruling party not only made its presence felt in sciences and letters through the public employees that maintained the *Revista*, and in conservative doctrines through the paper to which we have just alluded, but also kept under its sway all institutions of public education, dispensing its favors only on certain official literature, closing the doors of the University to those who were not its supporters, and aspiring to subject to its dictatorship even the independent associations that arose protected from the public spirit that the liberals nurtured beyond the reach of power.

The Colegio de Abogados ["School of Lawyers"], organized in Santiago in 1856, was a victim of this aspiration at its inception. Its promoters had the goal of adding luster to their profession through study, and foregoing involvement in political parties, they invited the attorneys that were active members of the government party, which, wishing to serve politics more than the goals of the institution, had the party bylaws submitted to Supreme Court approval. The government, consistent with their tyrannical policy, approved those bylaws with modifications that placed the association under its dependency, and of course distorted it in a way the organizers found unacceptable. The institution of the Colegio de Abogados was a failure from the start.

Another incident was to happen with the Sociedad de Instrucción Primaria ["Society of Primary Education"] that the liberals organized in Santiago to work for the spread of popular education. The Ministry of Public Education's report in 1853 had shown 8,982 pupils attending 186 schools, and 5,433 attending 94 municipal schools. These two figures added to that of the pupils attending 18 conventual schools and 273 private schools produced a total of 23,156. Meanwhile, in 1857, according to the following year's Report, 35,364 pupils had attended public and private schools; so the increase in students in five years being very slight, there were still 249,125 children ages seven to fifteen without primary education, for according to the statistics addended to this Report, there were 284,489 inhabitants in the Republic of school age and status.

Moreover, the 1853 Report pointed out that most of the pupils in attendance at the schools only learned to read and write, that they did not amount to half the total of those who learned principles of religion and arithmetic very incompletely, those who were educated in some other branches of knowledge reaching at the most a sixth. Another subsequent Memorial provided the fact that there were no more than thirteen advanced schools, in which anything more than reading and writing were taught. In light of these facts and believing sincere the demands those official documents made on the cooperation of the citizens to foster primary education, it occurred to some liberals to spend their time organizing popular societies to set up schools and in this way pave the way for the independent action of the citizens to govern and serve this social interest for themselves. As 1856 drew to a close, the Sociedad de Instrucción Primaria de Santiago ["Santiago Society for Primary Education"] already had several schools founded and run with its own funds, and worked on organizing the same institutions in the principal cities of the Republic. But the tyrannical policies of the *pelucón* government, fearing fallout from this independent movement because of its absolute domination, hastened to take control of it in the provinces, initiating the formation of analogous societies through its employees, and, in accordance with the Council of State, for which purpose it issued in Concepción a decree of 1857 that served as a template for the other societies. Article 5 of this bylaw established that the governor of the province was a member and ex officio chairman of the board of directors and of the society, and that the municipal school inspection committee and the members of the board of education named by the University would form part of the same. This intervention by the authorities in popular societies of primary education, detracting from the nature of the institution, not only hampered the Santiago society's actions in the provinces, but also sapped the life from the purpose in this way, and those that studied during the course of that intervention never worked, nor did they have any other session than that of their installation.

Nevertheless, the Santiago Society for Primary Education was able to resist the influences of the invading policies, and in the 1857 civic celebrations it presented in a general meeting a glowing status report on the miraculous benefits it had secured during its short life. In that session it approved the moral education plan we submitted to it with the title of *Objeto de la Educación Social* ["Object of Social Education"], to do our part toward the common goal of that noble institution, and on that blueprint, to meet the terms of their commission, we put together the *Libro de Oro de las Escuelas* ["School Treasury"], which in March of 1863 the University approved for use as a textbook in the public schools.

III

Around that time the general state of affairs began to undergo profound changes. The inflexibility of the ruling party had endangered, if not the stability of the government itself, at least the tranquillity of its absolute rule; for not only had it kept the ire of its adversaries burning, but also alienated the regard and the interest of the very *pelucones* who in the previous five years had supported it. The former had harmonized public opinion by dint of the dignity and patience with which they had endured persecution and exclusion, which made them appear as victims and not as impassioned partisans of a political cause: the latter presented themselves authorized by the sympathy their efforts for conciliation naturally elicited, which, according to them, were the only reason to spur them to take action in opposing the government.

The latter, moreover, when seeing that the hatred its erstwhile policy had inspired was turning now into a tie that bound together the *pelucones* who had vaunted it, yielding to its retrogressive interests and its aversion to reform, to the liberals that had fought it in the name of democratic principles, it was to change the system substantially. Before, it had neglected to seek the support of its authority in the country's opinion, founding a policy set up on the harmony of the large interests and on respect for freedom; and the new situation forced it to appear no longer as an absolute, retrogressive power, but as a *national government* that defended principles and freedom against the *pelucones* and the public order against the former liberals. This evolution was the sign of emancipation for all opinions and the beginning of a new political face and of new events. Despotism cannot fail its logic, without losing its way: the day it begins to make concessions is the first day of its downfall.

This was the cause of the intellectual movement that began to develop in the years after 1857, in all order of speculation, while on account of other causes, to which the policy that had dominated was not totally unconnected, a complication in the interests in national affairs began to take shape, bringing in its wake the economic crisis of 1861.

The realm of religious concerns suffered the first attacks of free examination, owing to the efforts made by the Curia to piously present a woman suffering from hysterical fits as possessed by the devil. A writer calling himself a competent doctor published a book in Paraíso entitled *Carmen Marín o La endemoniada de Santiago* ["Carmen Marín, or, The Possessed Woman of Santiago"], in which he compiled all the reports submitted ex professo to the archbishop on the sickness from which that young lady suffered, and subjected them to medical scrutiny.* Shortly thereafter, the eminent doctor and naturalist D. Juan Bruner brought out in the capital a medico-psychological monograph with the same title or *El Demonio de la naturaleza y la naturaleza del Demonio* ["The Devil of Nature and the Nature of the Devil"], in which he fought with science the pious hoax that claimed the devil walked among us, taking possession of the hallucination-deluded who did not take care to attribute to their hallucinations a celestial origin, like Santa Rosa de Lima.[†] The press of the day and the entire society discussed the case, and the discussion was favorable to the open examination.

Political interest otherwise emerged full of life, drawing on its freedom of thought, since the government was apologizing for not having respected it before for the sake of pleasing the old *pelucones* that were separating from it now to join forces with the persecuted liberals. Several political newspapers appeared in all the provinces. The liberals founded a press in Santiago, and

---

* We have knowledge leading us to believe that the author of this anonymous work is Dr. don Manuel A. Carmona, an 1828 liberal.

† Saint Rose of Lima (d. 1586), Isabel de Santa María de Flores, a Dominican Tertiary, noted for mystical visions, canonized in 1671, first saint of the New World, patroness of America. —Ed.

in July 1857 began publication of *El País*, a daily that under Barros Arana's editorship brilliantly upheld the doctrines and interests of the party that had remained outlawed for six years. The *pelucones* unaffiliated with the government imitated the example, and the following month founded another daily with the title *El Conservador* ["The Conservative"] to defend its new cause, in the writing of which the now-distinguished men of letters, Blanco Cuartín and Sotomayor Valdés, began their career as conservative writers.

Both writers have remained true to the cause they then defended, and the logic of their faithfulness carried them to the difficult task of seeking always to reconcile the doctrines of their old devotion and the ideals of the old regime with the demands of modern society and the principles and interests of the democratic system. But both stand out for the loftiness and moderation of their writings and for the literary gifts that place them among the most notable contemporary writers.

These writers' stance squares with the hue of the retrogressive party that began to define itself in that age with the new denomination of Conservative Party. One year before the noisy splintering of the ruling party that give rise to this hue, by the middle of 1856, the disintegration of its constituent parts had begun, with the triumphant separation of the ecclesiastic element, which, serving as the axis of the *pelucón* party since 1830, had also been the most solid support of the 1851 administration's defense. The gestation had been long, but since it was multiple, as the physicians call certain fetal gestations, the miscarriage incited by the jolts and shocks of that time brought triplets into the world, which wound up taking part with different names in the political scene, though with practically identical looks.

The existence, albeit brief, of a distinctly retrograde party is understandable, for it is natural that the interests and convictions of the old regime, which still endure, be defended against social regeneration and political reorganization that tend to destroy absolute power, which constitutes the strength of that regime, and install democracy in its place. It is even understandable that a moderate Conservative Party appear in countries like France, where centenary, immemorial tyranny, of all social powers—monarchy, Church, aristocracy, capital, customs, and concerns that today are anti-social—have engendered those freaks of modern ignorance called socialism and communism, and that seek to supplant the principles of the modern republic with outlandish errors, or a mere "semocracy," or with the leveling by personal conditions of the laws that make up freedom. Then the existence is logical of a moderate Conservative Party that, not retrogressively, defends the principles of civilized society against such folly. But in a country like Chile, where all the political circles that sincerely serve political and social reform, have that reform consist of the more or less complete triumph of all the rights that constitute individual freedom, the conservatives who go by the name of moderates seek to delay that reform can have but an ephemeral, sham existence, accepting it in part, and defend the principles of civilized society, which are none other than those that are based on those same laws, which they recognize and claim, and which at times also defend, not against nonexistent socialism, but against the liberals that serve an identical end.

That abortive evolution of 1856–1857, effected by the retrogressive ruling party, continued and developed by circumstantial agreements or personal political interests, wound up creating a certain political literature or, more accurately, a literary sophistry, which, applied thereafter by the writers from the two offshoots of the retrogressive party, the national and the conservative, in twenty years' time succeeded in misleading political judgment, falsifying history and the liberal doctrine. The middle-of-the-road writers, with one foot in the old regime and the other in the liberal system, contrived to claim the freedoms that they needed for the time being, provided they could reconcile them with the interests of the timeworn cause they regard sympathetically and even defend like skilled attorneys. This determination leads them to twist the meaning of the true rights that sustain those freedoms, and to maintain their misrepresentations with the brazenness that in their furious despair the pure and forthright defenders of the old regime used. A new political idea of this type, which endeavors to fit modern progress and democratic principles in old traditions and dogmas, boasts dazzling mirages and can do no less than lead astray that common, popular aspiration for reform that exists; all the more when the transitory situation, symbolized by that new ideal, has been maintained by the concessions that the liberals have made with it for the sake of serving the interests of the moment, forgetting the true liberal doctrine that they represented formerly, and splintering therefore into a few more factions in addition to the three conservative groups appearing in 1857.

We have stated as much already, and we ought now prove with new facts that our most constant desire had been to maintain the unity of the Liberal Party through the purity of its doctrine and the homogeneity of its interests. The publication we made of our *Constitución Política comentada* ["Annotated Political Constitution"] in the *Revista de Santiago* had no other purpose when in 1855 this literary newspaper appeared for the third time. Moreover, the separate edition of that book we published in 1856, when the battle between the clergy and the government was heating up, squared with the goal of reminding the liberals who had professed it of the doctrine of the reform of our political institutions, and who at that time were beginning to get on well with the archbishop and his solvent demands, tired as they were of persecutions and hostilities from the government that had put them to flight in 1851.

We were deluding ourselves then, trusting in the power of the truth to bring men together, and we fancied that by presenting in a corpus the just doctrine of political reform contained in that book, the transitory interests born of a fleeting situation, interests that led the liberals to form alliances with the retrogressives to attack the government, would not prevail over reform. And when the archbishop took an openly rebellious stance against the State, disobeying the Supreme Court's verdict that, against his ecclesiastic censures, supported the canons who because of a dispute with the sacristans had incited an *a divinis** persecution, we took the defense of the power of the State in the Valparaíso *El Mercurio*, which its editor in chief, the distinguished Venezuelan writer Hilarión Nadal, supplied us to show the liberals that he was siding with the State, and did not fall in with the seventy clergymen that had organized the *Canterburian* league against the appeal to force that the laws allow in the courts of justice for those who were victims of ecclesiastical despotism.

Still, the dissolution of the elements of the ruling party went on from those events, and the liberals reconciled themselves with the conservatives outside the fold of the government in order to organize the opposition: such an alliance led naturally to a profound change in liberal doctrine and the annulment of party interests. It was necessary to oppose it. Right from the start we imagined that to that end a history of this party would be of service, one that recalled its brilliant though short campaign, and its sacrifices and sufferings in honor of the liberal cause. But such a writing ran the risk of giving rise to protests and recriminations that were hazardous at that time, and contrary to the purpose of presenting the doctrine of reform in all its purity, and to stimulating the solidarity and respect it deserved. It was more accurate to stress the vivid memory that the illustrious glory of the party then was forming, the memory of the parliamentary debates of 1849. That was the tradition of its doctrines, of its aims and system; in the judgment of some liberals who shared our interest, it could be to great effect, to avoid inconsistencies and dangerous deals, to place a summary of those aims where the party could see it, to remind them of their platform.

That was the origin of the book that we published in 1857 under the title *Proyectos de ley y discursos parlamentarios* ["Bills and Parliamentary Speeches"]. Its purpose was made known with the utmost clarity in the introduction.

---

* Arguably, Lastarria is coining a term for a form of persuasion, in the *argumentum ad hominem* mode. Rhetorically, this type of argument, it would appear, entails an appeal not so much *from* authority—an argument that can incur in a fallacy—but *against* it in support of a hypothesis or conclusion. In short, the position for State-controlled education set its proponents against God Himself. —Trans.

There we declare that, as in the documents in said book, the country's resources and needs are assessed in a liberal sense, and the path the political ideas and principles followed, appears mapped out in them. Alluding to the new *Conservative* Party that was then appearing, we stated that it occupied an intermediate position between the elements that make up the colonial spirit and the Liberal Party; but that, since it has its main support in the former, it never upsets them, always acquiesces to its demands, and only reserves its might, its conservative efforts, and its coups d'état to struggle against the latter and annihilate it. "This very true observation," we added, "leads us to the conviction that the Liberal Party can have no other mission than *that of defending its principles* against the attacks of those two powerful enemies, to realize its goals at some point; and therefore we believe *that all merging or alliance with them is impossible, and that any bargain is a step back in the liberal system's progress.*"

But the purpose of this publication was not understood, let alone fulfilled. The Valparaíso *El Mercurio*, in a weekly literary review published on 27 April 1857, spoke of that purpose, having it consist of our proposing to *present the pure essence of a certain few political principles to which the interest of the Republic is linked*; but with deplorable skepticism, he went on to show an opinion diametrically opposed to the fact that the Liberal and Conservative Parties' political objectives were irreconcilable: "Mr. Lastarria wishes to fix the boundaries," he stated, "of the parties that unfortunately some time ago have divided us, determining each one's place and making each party's presence felt through its principles. In still-backward, novel, and impassioned republics like ours, where personality and egotism have taken root deeply, there is always danger in stirring up the parties and it is more of a holy errand *to attempt to merge them.* But it will be said that their merging is impossible, for one cannot amalgamate the good with the bad, nor intermingle darkness and light. On this point we need to clarify. Let us talk of truth. In Chile there are no principles. There are only partisans. . . ."

The poet J. A. Torres, who wrote this, did not believe that conservatives and liberals had principles, and advocated for their merging, for both were personalist parties. Perhaps he was right in the sense that personal interests prevailed over principles, but this was the objective we were rejecting, and the one that newspaper and the entire liberal press ought to have condemned as well, for it is no holy errand to favor the development of the motives of self-interestedness in politics by thwarting the collective interest that is founded on truth.

The publication of the *Comentarios de la Constitución de Chile de 1833* ["Commentaries on the Chilean Constitution of 1833"] by Manuel Carrasco Albano belongs also to the political press movement begun in that age, which grew by leaps and bounds in 1858 on account of the elections of representatives and aldermen being held that year, as well as the repressive stance the government once again assumed. Carrasco Albano, a young man who died before his time, from his early debut gave outstanding proof of his lofty spirit and his sound judgment, had followed in this work a plan that was historical through and through, and thus different from that of our *Constitución Política comentada* ["Annotated Political Constitution"], and had earned the Law School prize because of that showing, not without protest from some conservative professors, who no doubt feared that book contained doctrines contrary to their political interests.

Though the interest that inspired Carrasco Albano to compose his important work was purely literary, the publication had a political character because of the circumstances in which it was written. The events of 1858 had given coherence to the liberal press that was calling for constitutional reform. The daily entitled *La Actualidad* ["The Current Age"], which had replaced *El País*, and which Barros Arana and Sotomayor Valdés published starting February of that year with the cooperation of several liberal writers; the weekly featuring illustrations and caricatures that Barros Arana and Sotomayor Valdés ran starting in July under the name *Correo Literario* ["Literary Post"], and *La Asamblea Constituyente* ["Constitutional Convention"], which shortly thereafter gave us Vicuña Mackenna,* A. C. Gallo, the two Mattas, and I. Errázuriz, served the noble end of the reform of the Constitution, which two liberals had proposed to the Chamber of Deputies on 22 July, and which had been rejected after two days by the majority who therein served the government's policy against liberals and conservatives.

A large club with the name Constitutional Convention had also organized to work for reform, and though the initiative for the latter appertained to the Liberal Party, the idea was seized upon with fervent enthusiasm by the youths who through their conservative connections had been in the government's camp until the disbandings of 1856 and '57 that occurred in the ruling party; and the conservatives themselves, who in the opposition wished to preserve the traditions of their party, lent their sympathies to certain limited constitutional reforms.

This development of the political press found its limit in the declaration of the state of siege that the government issued in December of that year, and by virtue of which a ministerial decree ordered suspended the publication of the Valparaíso *El Mercurio* and *El Ciudadano*, and of *La Asamblea Constituyente*, the *Correo Literario*, and *La Actualidad* in Santiago.

---

* Diego Barros Arana (1830–1907), Ramón Sotomayor Valdés (1830–1903), along with Benjamín Vicuña Mackenna, fathers of Chilean historical writing, popular among nineteenth-century thinkers. —Ed.

IV

The resurrection of the political press we are recalling was at that time a true manifestation of the literary progress achieved through the efforts exerted up to 1849; parallel with it appeared also, as fruits of the same progress, several widespread productions of a purely literary nature, which advertised the fact that art still had life amidst the agitation of political interests.

The seed had taken root at the cost of that forbearing, laborious ten-year harvest; though the hurricane that began building in 1850 strew the foliage and parched the early buds of the nascent plant, and it had no sun to nourish it during the long darkness of the storm that raged on for six years, its roots stretched out and took hold firmly in fertile ground. There are trees that, finding no life in the inclemency of their environment, concentrate the power of their sap to produce downward growth for themselves, as there are gramineous plants that live a long time under the snow, growing in their roots and gaining strength.

There was, then, no need in this recollected age to undertake the task of creation. The previously begun literary movement existed, and even though it seemed to meander due to the exigencies and interests of the ruling party, its spontaneous and independent manifestations, though rare and short-lived, revealed that the spirit that had inspired it had life. In 1857, the celebrated poetess doña Mercedes Marín del Solar sung of her country on the occasion of the advancements made by the Sociedad de Instrucción Primaria ["Primary Education Society"]; Guillermo Matta brought to light his canto *A la América* ["To America"]; Guillermo Blest Gana, his beautiful little poem *La flor de la soledad* ["The Flower of Solitude"], and Sanfuentes, his *Teudo o Memorias de un solitario* ["Teudo, or, Memories of a Recluse"]. Among several inaugural addresses to the University, of note are that of Santa María for its zeal in justifying his predecessor's stance, absolving General Freire in the political process that lead him to training Portales, and for his wisdom in treating the scientific issue on the retroactive effect of laws; that of Gregorio V. Amunátegui on the study of foreign languages and literatures, condemning the extensive development that was given to the study of Latin and demonstrating the need to replace it with the study of Spanish; and that of Varas Marín, which contains a remarkable biography of the illustrious late dean of the School of Humanities, don Ventura Blanco Encalada, in which shine the modern spirit and the idea that the

Spanish American colonies are emerging also from this condition in the intellectual order. Finally, in La Serena, *El Eco Literario del Norte* ["The Literary Echo of the North"] appeared in May, a scientific, literary, and historical newspaper that managed to publish eighteen twelve-page installments that do not lack interest.

In 1858 the fiery repercussions from the political press did not manage to kill the literary enthusiasm of Guillermo Blest Gana,* who on the one hand brought to light his historical drama in four acts and in verse, *La conjuración de Almagro* ["The Almagro Conspiracy"], and on the other founded the *Revista del Pacífico* ["Review of the Pacific"] in July in Valparaíso through the backing of its editor, don Santos Tornero, who, as proprietor of the typographical establishment and bookshop of the Valparaíso *El Mercurio*, lent a generous hand to the literary and liberal press, and who has distinguished himself to a considerable degree for his efforts in promoting the intellectual progress of his children's country. From the beginning of the year, the same firm published *El Album*, a critical and literary weekly edited by the Argentinian writer don Juan Ramón Muñoz, which folded after the ninth issue. In La Serena a weekly literary, industrial, and customs newspaper appeared, surviving quite some time, with the title *El Cosmopolita* ["The Cosmopolitan"]. The novel was cultivated by José Antonio Torres, who published his *Misterios de Santiago* ["Santiago Mysteries"], and by Alberto Blest Gana, who separately put out an edition of *El primer amor* ["First Love"] and of *La fascinación* ["Fascination"], which he had published in the *Revista del Pacífico*. Social issues likewise were popular in *Porvenir del hombre o Relación íntima entre la justa apreciación del trabajo y de la democracia* ["Future of Man, or Intimate Relationship Between the Just Appreciation of Work and of Democracy"], by don Pedro Félix Vicuña, a book that, although outside the literary movement, is worthy of note in that it proves the rebirth of vitality in those days and shows through its spirit and its views the moment of transition which the metaphysical ideas of social and political organization of the old liberals were entering. The University also contributed to the new intellectual momentum with the publication of the brilliant, official historical Report that Domingo Santa María† presented the year before on the *Sucesos ocurridos desde la caída de O'Higgins en 1823 hasta la promulgación de la Constitución dic-*

---

* Guillermo Blest Gana (1829–1905), poet, dramatist, novelist, playwright, diplomat, and statesman; older brother of Alberto Blest Gana (1830–1920), military engineer, statesman, diplomat, and author of the major Chilean Bildungsroman of the nineteenth century, *Martín Rivas* (1862). —Ed.

† Domingo Santa María González (1825–1889), Liberal Party leader, diplomat, statesman, president, 1881–1886. —Ed.

tada en el mismo año ["Events Occurring Since the Fall of O'Higgins in 1823 Until the Publication of the Constitution Ratified In Said Year"].

This excellent publication was part of a series along with *La dictadura de O'Higgins* ["The O'Higgins Dictatorship"], also an official Report that in the University formal session in December 1853 don Miguel Luis Amunátegui had presented, both works completing the history of one of the most interesting periods of our political organization. This Report, seemingly written with the veiled purpose of drawing a contrast between the age to which he refers and the moments the liberal cause is eclipsed when the work came out, therefore had a political nature that at that time cast a shadow over the great literary merit and sound philosophy that thereafter were recognized in him by those who consider it the author's masterwork. That of Santa María, no less brilliant for the coloring and liveliness of his style, for the correctness of judgment, for the liberal principles, and republican enthusiasm, had openly the same nature as political writing; but it doubtless has true historical merit, for its research and for its animated narration with which it managed to lend interest to events subsequent to the O'Higgins dictatorship, though in the judgment of Joaquín Blest Gana, who judged the work in the *Revista del Pacífico*, that animation fell outside the restrained gravity of historical compositions.

But let us not overlook the contrast that, on account of their number, these remarkable independent works formed, works which revealed the strength of the new spirit of our literary movement in those days with the exuberance of the official and ecclesiastical literatures. The former had produced, in the two years we are discussing, more than forty publications, among them texts, translations, and reprintings; works of religious interest had reached forty-two in 1857 and thirty-six in 1858. Thus the *Revista del Pacífico* had a far-reaching importance at that time; the publication ultimately bound together the literary tradition, which had revived for a fleeting spell in 1855 in the third series of the *Revista de Santiago*.

In the new arena opened by Guillermo Blest Gana, our old workmates reappeared: Blest Gana himself, Miguel Luis and Gregorio Víctor Amunátegui, Joaquín Blest Gana; Barros Arana, Alberto Blest Gana, Martín José Lira, Guillermo and Manuel Antonio Matta* continued their valiant careers; and appearing as new contributors to the literary movement were

---

* Guillermo Matta Goyenechea (1829–1899) and Manuel Antonio Matta Goyenechea (1828–1892), brothers, statesmen, and publicists, who like so many others named herein studied at the Instituto, opposed Montt's autocratic policies and by helping restore liberalism to national prominence, contributed to the rise of the Radical Party in the 1860s. —Ed.

Daniel Barros Grez, José Antonio Donoso, René Moreno, and he who is to-day the most prolific and powerful upholder of the glory of our literature, B. Vicuña Mackenna, who had already made his mark in the political press.

Of the latter, the young military engineer don José Antonio Donoso, who died at a tender age, regrettably for our letters, was the one who drew the most attention from the intellects of the age, for the originality of the themes in which he exercised his genius, for the facility of his style, for the eccentricity and frankness of his moral opinions, and his critical judgments on social ideas and conventions. In reading his writings one notices that these gifts were unquestionably acquired by studying his model, which was Rabelais. Donoso had suffered the deviation to which the majority of the imitators of Rabelais have fallen victim: that they have lacked the noble judgment of Montaigne and of Voltaire.* Donoso had learned from Rabelais to be a freethinker; but without a defined ideal, without a set standard of judgment, he fell in the most fruitless skepticism; and lacking talent for ridicule and for the shrewd perception of his teacher's satiric spirit, he poorly imitated the intellectual profligacy and crudeness of language with which the latter made tolerable his venomous laugh.

But the first appearance of the *Revista del Pacífico* was fleeting: it fell in December of that year with the state of siege that eliminated the entire independent press. Its director had had to take a forced journey abroad on account of political events. But that first volume of the *Revista* contains forty-eight historical and literary pieces, all of which are testimony of true intellectual progress.

V

When the revolutionary storm that was unleashed after that state of siege had passed, that tempest which kept the country in grievous

* François Rabelais (1483?–1553), French satirist, author of *Pantagruel* (1553) and *Gargantua* (1535); Michel Eyquem de Montaigne (1533–1592), French essayist, author of *Essais* (1571–1580, 1588), whose work still has a profound influence on Latin American letters; Voltaire (François-Marie Arouet, 1694–1778), French satirist and novelist, author of *Candide* (1755). —Ed.

alarm and awash in tears and blood during the first months of 1859, it was to be expected that independent literary production would disappear and that the entire intellectual movement would be reduced, like before, to the sphere in which official and ecclesiastical influences reigned. And thus it would have happened, unquestionably, as the great number of didactic texts, translations, and reprints that appeared that year under government sponsorship demonstrates, and the more than thirty works of religious interest that were published, had not an event as fortuitous as it was unexpected happened.

That occurrence was the appearance of *La Semana*, a news, literary, and scientific newspaper that began publishing on 21 May, when it had not been even a month since the cannon rumbled from the last battle of the civil war, when still could be heard the detonations of the last rifle shots of a rebellion, whose disorder revealed its grassroots origins and gave it the character of a protest by the country against the absolutism of a repressive government. Who was to offer the consolations of literature in those moments of intellectual and sentimental pain?

Two children! Yes, the Arteaga Alemparte brothers were adolescents judging by their age, but men by the power of their intelligence when they founded that literary newspaper. They had just returned from Peru, where they had grown up, sharing with their honorable father the sorrows of the long exile this distinguished army veteran had suffered in serving the liberal cause. They were therefore ignorant of the passions of the moment, and could aspire, as the mission statement in *La Semana* states, to represent the thriving life of society, and "to set up their newspaper in the medium of art and science that was dawning on our horizon, to turn their columns into the annals of their growth and progress." They relied on the collaboration of many writers, soliciting the support of all those in Chile who paid tribute to literature, and wanted their paper to be "a contest open to all talents, as much for those who are just emerging as for those whom age and study have matured, where all opinions are acceptable, where all ideas are promoted, without adherence to dogma, without reservation, with independence and good faith."

In fact, *La Semana* was from then on, until June 1860, the representative of the independent literary movement; in it we collaborated with the Amunáteguis, Barros Arana, Joaquín and Alberto Blest Gana, Carrasco Albano, González, Irisarri, Martín Lira, Sotomayor Valdés, and several other youths that there made their first literary trials. The newspaper's editors skillfully maintained the publication's interest through their many in-depth articles. Their powerful synthetic, abstract spirit, their inductive power, and their admirable power of expression made them fit to handle well all issues they took on, and guided always by a noble love of justice and truth, they used the wealth of their knowledge in the service of the new ideals and modern aspirations of society. The two brothers had still not set themselves apart in terms of style. Their writings seemed works from a single pen, for the one who is today a famed journalist, Justo Arteaga Alemparte, did not used the clipped and profound style that typified him, acquired through the habit of concentrating vast and complex concepts in a single sentence, to say everything in brief, lapidary forms; Domingo Arteaga Alemparte had still not reached the high position he holds among our first-rank writers and orators, not only for his stylish, correct phrasing and his clear, concise, and elegant style, but also mainly for the vigor of perception manifested in the precision and logic of his thought.

The founders of *La Semana* had the glory of causing a true literary stir, for during the first trimester their newspaper was an unforeseen revelation of the vigorous intellectual development that had been maintained in spite of the political interests that had predominated and concerned the public spirit. It seemed that, wearied of the struggle and despairing, the old-school writers came to seek the ineffable solace of literature, and that the example of the founders of the newspaper brought new adepts that, like them, were inspired only by their love of literature, and were free from the agitation of the age. Later, Donoso and Barros Grez reappeared in the columns of *La Semana*, Vicente Reyes and don Ignacio Zenteno made their debuts as prose writers with a lively style, and alongside the well-known poets Irisarri and Lira, constant contributors to the paper, Luis Rodríguez Velasco, Domingo Arteaga Alemparte, and Eduardo de la Barra offered in it the first fruits of their muse; don Camilo Cobo and the late-lamented, likable Rafael Santos, who became so remarkable for his fluent versification and comic wit, gave splendid evidence of their expertise in the art.

Also Blanco Cuartín, in spite of being listed among the *La Semana* contributors, published during that time the first installment of his *Poesías*, separately in a 100-page book, and in a different volume, two legends entitled *Blanca de Lerma* and *Mackandal o amor de tigre* ["Mackandal, or, A Tiger's Love"]. Blanco Cuartín, a satiric, comic, and tender poet, not only was possessed of the same poetic endowments as was his father, don Ventura Blanco Encalada, but also the same devotion that the latter professed to the restorers of good taste and purity of language, which raised Spanish letters at the end of the last century up out of the prostration in which the high-flown imitators of French poetry had left it. His poetry had, then, different models, other tendencies, and varied taste, than the school that had already formed then in the translation and imitation of Victor Hugo and Lamartine. The Spanish literary tradition was already forgotten. Very few were those who preserved it, and among the new poets there were no imitators of Moratín, Meléndez Valdés, Cadalso, or Quintana. Blanco Cuartín did not continue to publish his poetry, having devoted himself to studies in philosophy and medical sciences, and later to the simple task of journalist, in which, putting his vast learning to use, he earned deserved renown. But he did not neglect to hold the old place he had attained among the national writers, bringing out excellent work on occasion, in which the beautiful gifts of his spirit, though shackled by old ideals and worn-out traditions, have excelled on account of the rich forms of his style and the charms characteristic of his exquisite wisdom.

VI

The fourth issue of *La Semana* gave notice of a book notable for its artistic forms, which, though published in Paris, was to enrich the repertoire of our essays, though it was outside our literary movement and a far cry from the ideals and aims of this movement, in terms of the liberal opinion of the age in Chile. We are referring to the *Ensayo sobre el gobierno en Europa* ["Essay on Government in Europe"], by A. Montt. Echoing that opinion, *La Semana* stated:

> The material in this book is European, its author South American. . . . *Balance*, or rather, the unity of the sword; *Christianity*, the unity of faith; and *opinion*, the unity of judgment and of customs: these are the three foundations on which rests that admirable monument called civilization or *unity of Europe*. These are the words with which the author ends the first part of his book, thus presenting in brief a curious and surprising enigma, for the ideas and reasoning that preceded it decipher it but halfway. In truth, the conjunction of the sword, the empire of faith and the influence of opinion are three not very homogenous elements that constitute more powers that are ill-disposed to be reconciled with one another. . . . The second and also the final part of the *Ensayo* analyzes the agents of Eu-

ropean civilization, which the nature of preponderant races classifies naturally in two great sections: the Latins and the Anglo-Saxons. . . . On this loom the author has woven his work with acumen and skill. In reading it, one is not hard pressed to see that he is a sophisticated writer, full of wisdom and good breeding. . . . In Mr. Montt's observation in the countries he has visited of the most constant and general facts that make up contemporary life, he has taken pains to reconcile one with the other, and summarizes in its entirety the raison d'être of the European civilization. Impassioned of fact, which infrequently one declines to substantiate, remote from law, which does not always harmonize with fact, he grants to the former the power of the latter, and is deceived with reality . . . . Reality, nevertheless, also has its optical illusions, and it is easy to be dazzled with the splendor of its victories. . . .

In fact, Montt's clear mind had fallen victim to the fascination produced by the great disorder the Second Empire caused in sociological ideas. This fascination also blinded the nations in which the French influence reigned, though in reality against the constant protests of all the sincere liberals of Spanish America, who waited to see that great disorder end with the ruin of the ominous power that maintained it.

The social and political situation in Europe was then, and is now, just as August Comte had described it in 1841: a transitory situation between the breakup of the old regime and the reorganization of a still-indeterminate system, and that could not be defined, in our view, save through the just conception of the "semecratic" synthesis, as we have demonstrated elsewhere.* Such a situation could not bring unity to a disharmonious civilization reduced to ruin by those two contrary tendencies. In that profoundly confusing situation, according to that philosopher, the two simultaneous movements of political dismantling and social recomposition that characterize the modern European societies have had to go slowly and blindly, because the old regime can still hide its powerless decrepitude, using the appearance of their power to seize up political progress, while the modern social elements still lack the unity to affirm their ascendant course. But, though this fundamental situation may be common "throughout the many parts of the great European republic, there is among them nevertheless a very pronounced inequality, as much with respect to the more or less profound decline of the old regime as the more or less complete preparation of

* *Lessons in Positive Philosophy*, Lesson 2.

the new order. From these two points of view, the main differences ought to have proceeded from the general direction that the national influences have given the temporal concentration of the two stages of modern evolution, according to which it has stopped on *monarchic dictatorship*, ordinarily supported by the Catholic spirit, or in *aristocratic dictatorship*, almost always in combination with the ascendancy of Protestantism. . . . The servitude of the aristocracy of necessity had more radically destroyed the old political system than what the demolition of the monarchy had done in England; at the same time, the direct transition from the predominantly Catholic situation to complete mental emancipation had become eminently favorable to the decisive growth of French intellects, so fortunately preserved from the dangerous inertia that the Protestant transition ought to have imprinted on English spirits. . . . "*

But the Second Empire, continuing the tradition of the First, with all the greater facility since it had not been interpreted by dictatorships camouflaged with the name of constitutional monarchies from the restoration of Louis Philippe, believed it had stopped the wheel of fortune, organizing a democratic despotism under the dictatorship of an emperor. But the attempt in no way altered that deeply entrenched battle between the old regime and the modern reorganization, for however much the flashes from the stupendous imperial superstructure dazzled, and however much, as Comte observes, our feeble intelligence is always willing to settle for the least appearances of organization to save itself the noble efforts the conception of a new order demands. The Empire gave everything order, from the welfare of the people, to material progress, to equality, making that the goal behind the social reorganization movement. There was an attempt to head off political decay by organizing a strong, paternal power backed by the Catholic faith and on the balance of the great European powers; and to avoid the fall of the absolute monarchy, and the triumph of individual and social liberty, the farce of races was exploited, staged by Louis Philippe's doctrinaires by making up a Latin race with the mission of upholding the old regime, and another with the fate of conquest and that of spreading incredulity abroad.

The political and social reorganization of the Spanish American republics, which had embarked on their normal path with the abolition of the monarchy and the aristocracy, and the exercise of all individual and social liberties, clearing up all confusion that makes the European situation uncertain or unclear, and giving the two simultaneous movements of political dismantling and social recomposition a forthright, optimistic course through discussion, had nothing to gain from the developments and rigor

---

* *Cours de philosophie positive*, Lesson LVI and LVII.

mortis of the old regime in Europe. This is why the *Ensayo* was seen as a book alien to our interests and aspirations, and as the delusion of a noble mind, which had infected the author of the critical prologue that introduced the work.

Juan Bello, who had written that prologue, rejected his friend's views, and declared that the book was not a course in constitutional, representative, or despotic law. "You all must not look in it," he stated, "for doctrines, systems, theories; it is on the contrary an indictment of political ideology. More than principles, laws, individual guarantees, public freedoms, it speaks of facts, of things, of situations: peace, order, the general welfare are for Mr. Montt the prime attributes of all well-governed societies; the form of government, its more or less perfect organization, the greater or lesser sum of privileges granted to the citizen are of no account to him save insofar as they help to promote or thwart those fundamental ends." Nevertheless, that was all the political doctrine of the Empire, and the critic seemingly does not condemn it, since in manifesting that in his view it was not fitting that the author, in a parallel between England and France, give preference to the former, exclaiming in convincing words: "Of course there does not exist in France the political freedom there is in England, for its current government is nothing less than representative, and neither does it have the consecration of longevity and of an entirely spontaneous consent. But at last it exists, and no one shall make so bold as to deny either its present stability or power, nor the incomparable administration, the strong order and progress it secures for society."

That is the error of logic incurred by those who study past or contemporary history on the false doctrine of the reflexive school, the doctrine that under the pretext of judging events according to the circumstances of time and place, making concrete science, as don Andrés Bello wished, the facts are twisted every which way to adapt them to their mold, and to justify and reinstate all deformities from history past and present. If the authors of the *Ensayo* and of the prologue had judged the events in their line of sight with the criterion of the laws that govern human nature—freedom and progress—they would have seen that those social phenomena, being as they were the complex results of historical situations and human actions, were not in keeping with those laws nor adjusted to the situation and progress of the society in which they occurred; for that situation claimed from the power that ruled it an intelligent direction that singled out the events whose evolution should favor those that it was necessary to oppose and stifle from their inception, in the service of freedom and progress.

This is the true criterion of sociology, a criterion that has guided us in judging the events we are recalling and in applauding or condemning all men who we have come across in our career, including dear and admired friends like Ambrosio Montt and Juan Bello, never taking into account their actions for or against our personal goals in order to judge them. If this had been the motive of our reckonings on this or other occasions, we would resign ourselves to being considered an insufferable fool; and this very day we would acclaim the *Ensayo sobre el gobierno en Europa* ["Essay on Government in Europe"], not only because its author never has placed obstacles in the way of our political and literary goals, but also because we are certain that those goals are his as well, and that the orator that today graces the liberal parliamentary tribunal, the man of letters who does not separate art from the independence of the spirit, to wit, A. Montt, would not write that book with the ideas he favors today.

Aside from all this and continuing our *Memoirs* on the revelation that *La Semana* had made of the vigorous intellectual development that existed, we will repeat that in that age there was no need, as there was seventeen years before, to undertake a task of creation or of leadership. But it *was* necessary to associate all those active elements that were scattered, to give them unity and strength for the aftertime, and to assure our literature a productive existence. And thus we have to once again plague with our vanity those who reproach these *Memoirs* for what to the French is charming in Montaigne's *Essays*, namely, that in each line one perceives the man beneath the author, for that moralist, in the view of the critics, had lived his work, so to speak, instead of composing it. But the fact is we are not writing history, but composing our literary memoirs, compelled, as we have stated a great many times, by those who have passed us over, if they have not glorified others with our services; in this genre of writing, as Blair states and as students of rhetoric know, the author is not subject to the unvarying dignity and gravity of the historian, and he can speak of himself aboveboard and stoop to informal anecdotes; for the only thing demanded of him is that he be lively and interesting and especially that he provide useful and curious news.

And since the news we have to give now is that of the organization of the *Círculo de Amigos de las Letras* ["Circle of Friends of Literature"], which was due to our efforts, we have to speak of ourself for the simple reason that the author of that useful institution was none other than us, as proven by the testimony of *La Semana*'s editors, who would not let us lie, because for all their uprightness, they have not always treated us benevolently.

The 27 August 1859 issue of *La Semana* included the following in its feature article: "It was also the Sunday when the inauguration of a literary circle took place, which tonight gets its efforts underway. To provide for scholarly men and literary aficionados a headquarters that supports and nurtures its efforts with the exchange of ideas and identity of its goals, this is the modest aim toward which this fledgling association inclines. It is Lastarria to whom this thought and its fulfillment is owed, which did not fail to shore up the most stellar and warranted reputations in our literature. Today knowledge and talent have open access to the lists in which their paladins will come to receive accolades and laurel leaves, and to encourage emerging talents by their example and with their advice, and neither are these neophytes excluded from these tournaments of the intellect."

Actually, all men of letters had understood our intention to join together, without discrimination as to background, conditions, political affiliations, and only in the interest of the national literature, all those who felt moved by the love of learning; to share our ideas, our scientific and literary study, in a friendly private gathering. The association had been inaugurated in a smashing fraternal banquet on Sunday, 21 August, of which the *La Semana* article makes mention.

VII

As we finished the first part of these *Memoirs*, we stated that in 1849 the literary future was secure, provided that the independence of the spirit continue to be taken as it had been, as the basis of intellectual development. But when the Circle of Friends of Literature was set up ten years later, the situation was similar to how it was in 1843, while not everyone served that development in the same way; for even though the number of those who were working to keep its foundation intact was greater, the powers representing the old regime had regrouped and strengthened their weakened power, and public opinion, no more educated than they were at the time, indiscriminatingly favored all intellectual movements, be it sometimes in the sense of the regeneration of ideas and social recomposition, sometimes in a sense retrogressive and contrary to those ends.

There was, then, an urgent need that the association of men of letters of diverse backgrounds and principles meeting out of a purely literary interest have tolerance as a fundamental principle if open discussion was to be had, and that it give priority in its attentions to the critical study of facts and ideas, of doctrines and systems, to exercise practically the independence of spirit and to love it. These aims, intimated at first, discussed and well understood later, were ably served by all those who had the constancy to maintain the association for many a year, leaving those who did not find in it the repository of their ideals completely at their leisure to break ranks, and for those who found their place, to join.

Right from the first meeting a lively interest arose for that genre of scholarship, for Marcial González having presented a remarkable critical assessment of the *Tratado teórico y práctico de economía política* ["Theoretical and Practical Treatise on Political Economy"], written in French by Courcell-Seneuil, and translated by Juan Bello at the government's behest, a book that had just arrived for use as a University text, a discussion on utilitarianism was taken up, prompting the young Manuel Miguel, who was to be sent to an early grave, to write a luminous dissertation on the principle of utility in its subjective nature.

In that first conference it was agreed that a contest in celebration of 18 September 1859 was to be held, and to that end a jury was impaneled to judge the compositions and to award the prize, which was to consist of worthy and appropriate books. In the meantime the sessions continued to spark a growing interest, due to a study by astronomer H. Volckmann on the oldest documents in human existence, proven by the astronomical observations of the Egyptians, the Indians, and the Chinese; due to a brilliant description of nature in Ecuador that Joaquín Blest Gana read; due to the survey of public housing in Chile in colonial times, with which don Miguel Cruchaga made his debut; due to another physiological study by Dr. Valderrama on pain and the soul, and also to several poems, among them Irisarri's splendid ode, *Al sol de septiembre* ["To the September Sun"].

In the session of 30 September the reading of the jury's report and the works in prose and verse that were entered in the contest was held before a teeming, enthusiastic crowd, which lent solemnity and great interest to the event. We shall reproduce, as historical documents, that report and the prize-winning poetic compositions, omitting the prose writings, which now are not as useful as the former in evaluating the literary progress.[*]

---

[*] In the journal that was published to make all those works known, an advertisement was placed regarding the organization of the Circle of Friends of Literature, which ended thus:

"To finish this notice, we will give the following roll of the individuals that to date are members of the Circle: "Messrs. Benicio Alamos González, Eulogio Allende, Gregorio Víctor Amunátegui, Miguel Luis Amunátegui, Domingo Arteaga Alemparte, Justo Arteaga Alemparte, Francisco Solano Asta-Buruaga, Eduardo de la

The selected jury having met on Monday of this week for their
commissioned purpose of judging the compositions submitted
to the Circle's open competition, it proceeded to read six works
that had been entered. Three of these met the conditions of the
topic in verse, and the other three were related to the theme in
prose. All of them, save one that proved utterly unfit for consideration, are estimable for more than one reason, and offer gratifying proof of the intellectual activity that is stirring amongst
us, in spite of the disturbances arising from political battles and
from the discouragement attending a dearth of stimuli.

The Circle's invitation, of course, aroused the intellect of
scholarly men, and yielded as its harvest three cantos *A la independencia de América* ["To the Independence of America"],
of uncommon merit, and two prose Studies in which the proposed question, *Was the Revolution of the Spanish American*

Barra y Lastarria, Manuel Blanco Cuartín, Guillermo Blest Gana, Joaquín Blest
Gana, Alberto Blest Gana, Ramón Briseño, Juan Bruner, David Campusano,
Manuel Carvallo, Manuel Carrasco Albano, Camilo Enrique Cobo, Melchor
Concha y Toro, Miguel Cruchaga, Vicente Cruchaga, Ramón Elguero, Federico
Errázuriz, Juan Nepomuceno Espejo, Manuel Salustio Fernández, Marcial
González, Miguel María Güemes, Jorge Segundo Huneeus, Hermógenes de Iris-
arri, Gabriel Izquierdo, José Victorino Lastarria, Santiago Lindsay, José Bernardo
Lira, Martín José Lira, Justo Florián Lobeck, Francisco Marín, Marcial
Martínez, Guillermo Matta, Manuel Antonio Matta, Rafael Minvielle, Manuel
Miguel, Ambrosio Montt, René Moreno, Ramón Morel, Manuel José Olavarri-
eta, Sinforiano Ossa, Vicente Padín, José Pardo, Demetrio Rodríguez Peña, Luis
Pereira, Santiago Prado, Manuel Recabarren, Vicente Reyes, Luis Rodríguez Ve-
lasco, Nicanor Rojas, Salvador Sanfuentes, Vicente Sanfuentes, Domingo Santa
María, Manuel Antonio Tocornal, José del Carmen Troncoso, Adolfo Valder-
rama, Pío Varas, Francisco Vargas Fontecilla, Emilio Veillon, Aniceto Vergara Albano, Benjamín Vicuña Mackenna, Hermann Volckmann, Ignacio Zenteno, José
Zegers Recesens.

"After this publication was done, the following individuals, among others, were
incorporated into the Circle: Messrs. Barros Arana; Blanchet, Adriano; Castellón,
Carlos B.; Cifuentes, Adbó; Errázuriz, Isidora; Gallo, Pedro León; Gallo, A. Cus-
todio; Murillo, Adolfo; Rodríguez, Zorobabel; Santos, Rafael; Sotomayor Valdés;
Torres, José Antonio; and various distinguished foreigners residing in the country
or visiting, like don Federico Torrico, don José Antonio Lavalle, don Manuel María
Rivas, Mr. Luis Larroque, and don José María Santibáñez."

Colonies a Necessary or an Accidental Event? is discussed and answered with fine-tuned insight. The third composition in prose having strayed from the theme, it was excluded from the running.

In the compendious ruling that is to be made of the five remaining works, the Circle will easily appreciate their respective importance and the place that consequently the jury has assigned them. If it is honorable for this body to render their verdict on such outstanding productions, its task is not therefore the less arduous or perilous. So only after a considered examination and comparison of the works was it decided to place them in ranking order as shown below.

Out of the compositions in prose, the one carrying an asterisk for its counter-sign and this quote by Monteagudo for an epigraph: "The Revolution of the American World was the development of eighteenth-century ideas," is the one the jury feels more deserving of the proposed prize.

The author of this Study begins by establishing that the independence of South America was no accidental occurrence triggered by a momentary cause, but the inevitable result of the course of human events subjected to the law of progress, which is the logic of history. The simultaneous uprising of the Spanish colonies against their mother country and the tenacity of the struggle that followed it, prove, in the author's view, that that revolt was but the fruit of the secret forces at work, long years before, in nations placed under identical life conditions, and the success of so great a battle, the only success possible, for it was but the necessary effect of an irrevocable cause. Where did this cause reside? In the incessant progress of the human spirit, which raised on the ruins of the old world the edifice of modern civilization, and has made this civilization travel a long road sown with difficulties and reversals, which produced in succession the feudalism of the early centuries, the absolute monarchies of the following centuries, the Reform and revolution in England, eighteenth-century French philosophy and the revolution, the independence of North America, and finally our own. This indefinite progress, set down in history, which is humanity's itinerary, waged in its course the emancipation of Spanish America, and if the latter managed to be delayed a few years or thwarted on the first attempt, it was to come into its own sooner or later, necessarily, inevitably, as was its destiny. The author identifies, then, the independence of South America as a necessary and inevitable fact.

In the extensive development the author has given to the proposed topic, the jury has been able to recognize clearly the copious abundance of his knowledge, the astuteness of his research and the exactitude of his assessments and reasonings, endowments enhanced by those of a refined, elegant, and colorful style. In this way, the substance and form of the Study have led by mutual agreement to tip the scales of our judgment in his favor and award him the prize.[*]

The second Study in prose, which has as its epigraph: *Regna fluunt; series nova rerum surget et ordo,*[†] is recommended as well for the facility, purity, and brilliance of its style, to the degree that the jury did not hesitate to declare as worthy of runner-up.[‡] In the first part of it, the author holds that the Spanish American emancipation was a consequence of the eternal laws of development to which nations, like individuals, are subject. Nevertheless, at the same time he agrees on the need for South American independence, he finds in the fact of our emancipation only the effect of a random accident. There is, then, a contradiction in these two judgments in the Study, a contradiction that luckily is more apparent than certain, and perhaps arises only from the author's not having formulated his convictions with sufficient precision, nor defined clearly the part in the South American revolution pertaining to circumstantial causality, to the opportunity that made it break out at a given time, and the opportunity that was only the effect of a cause both originating and real.

Each of the three compositions in verse that were entered is a work worthy of the proposed theme.

When the jury took on itself the arduous task of evaluating them, it certainly did not think it would be so fraught with risk and difficulty, even though they all have outstanding virtues and features that impede a rapid verdict.

In one shines ardor and inspiration. This work, which was submitted anonymously, perhaps may have earned another

---

[*] Its author is Joaquín Blest Gana. [It probably was submitted anonymously. —Ed.]

[†] "Royal powers pass; a new line and succession of affairs spring up." —Trans.

[‡] It was written by J. Bernardo Lira.

place than the honorable mention it received, had it been written in a more difficult meter than the one its author chose, and had it not been excelled by others in its plan and its execution.*

The work earning the runner-up spot carries the epigraph *Patria y Libertad* ["Country and Freedom"]; it is an ode in which the author proves he is equal to the grandiose theme proposed. The versification is correct and easy: fresh ideas and new poetic concepts adorn it, and perhaps it would have sent tremors through the jury's judgment had not some carelessness in the choice of rhymes rendered it inferior, in our view, to the work that garnered the prize.

This is the one that has only a mark for an epigraph. Its author has divided his work seemingly in three parts. The beauty of the immense part of the globe called America has swept him away; moreover he has described in beautiful strophes of outstanding poetic merit the privileged soil that was to be discovered by the immortal Genoese. In this lovely description the author has showcased his verbal graces and fluent versifying; to correctness he has wed elegance and freedom, which are so difficult to combine.

He has done no less justice to the intrepid seafarer, the noble matron, his protectress the renowned Isabel I, archetype of sovereigns and of women. The author has wished to adapt himself to the story, and without straying from the path that it has set out for him, he reaches the colony and in robust verses describes its importance and enumerates its shortcomings, salvaging them with the sound judgment with which the immortal Quintana removes them from Spain's blameworthiness to have them accrue to the times.

It seemed to us that the author had absorbed the reading of excellent models: his intonation put us in mind of the masters of the language in compositions of a nature similar to the one that so forcefully compels our interest; and upon hearing it said that it would not be he who

" . . . arroje impuro lodo
Sobre su propio nombre: el nombre godo,"

[" . . . slings impure mud
On his own name, the name of Goth,"]

* Its author, Martín Lira.

247

We thought we heard the Duke of Frías when he says to the children of this Spanish America:

"Y ya del indio esclavos o señores
Españoles seréis, no americanos."

["And now of the Indian slaves or masters,
Spaniards shall you be, and not Americans."]

For our poet recalls with pride that he descends from that race of Cortezes and Pizarros and Valdivias, for that land that, speaking through the peninsular bard, has stated the following cannot help but be very Spanish:

"Que ahora y siempre el argonauta osado,
Que del mar arrostrare los furores,
Al arrojar el áncora pesada
En las playas antípodas distantes,
Verá la cruz del Gólgota plantada,
Y escuchará la lengua de Cervantes."

["For now and always the daring argonaut,
Who shall defy the rages of the sea,
Upon weighing the heavy anchor
On the far-flown antipodal beaches,
Will see the cross Golgotha planted,
And hear the language of Cervantes."]

And how beautiful those verses are with which our poet sings of emancipation! Leaving the past behind, he contemplates the America that awakens and rouses from its slumbers, that plunges into war, that battles and overcomes, and accompanies its victory with vows of eternal blessedness.

We did not want to quote from this most beautiful of compositions, for it must be appreciated in its entirety: it would be cheating the readers of the pleasure they will experience in reading it entire.

We state the same for the other works. In each of the three compositions in verse, aficionados of this type of work shall find much art to recommend them, much to praise and quite little with which to find fault, unless the critic wishes to exercise a strictness and harshness that are not appropriate here.

We shall not finish before relating that through a strange coincidence, in more than one of the compositions we have examined, a moan of distress was loosed regarding the sad panorama that the immense territory his race populates offers to one's gaze. Everywhere devastation, everywhere civil war, everywhere vengeance and mass killing! Unfortunate souls! Whither do we go? Perchance to death?

The poets weep, the poets demand peace for the country, and like the author we have been discussing, they raise their hands to heaven to implore the Supreme Maker that He have pity on our ungodly lot, that He quell the passions

> Con que sus hijos crueles
>   Atizan a anarquía
> En constantes civiles disensiones,
> Porque dé en su clemencia
>   A la América toda
> Paz, unión, libertad, independencia.

> [With which his cruel children
>   Stir up anarchy
> In constant civil strife;
> And that He give in His clemency
>   To all America:
> Peace, union, freedom, independence!]

Santiago, 29 September 1859. —*Hermógenes de Irisarri.*—*Manuel Carvallo.*—*Gabriel Izquierdo.*— *René Moreno.*—*Domingo Arteaga Alemparte.*

To the Independence of America

For José Pardo

FIRST PRIZE POEM
Dedicated to don J. Victorino Lastarria

> Prodigal nature poured down
>   Its most precious gifts;
> It regaled with splendid beauty
>   The regions of the Indies.

Flowers of both zones
        Its vast fields bedeck;
Mamoré and Amazon
        Fertilize its far-flung plains.

Midst mountains, the shady Apurimac
        Unleashes a torrent;
And a face of burnished silver
        The Bío-Bío puts forward.

Eternal snows on the steep summit
        Of the lofty Andes;
In their reflections the celestial fire
        Sheds its burning rays;

And with the selfsame rays in the skirts
        It caresses and shelters,
Midst valleys jeweled a-plenty in emerald,
        Exhaustless tassels.

Here the plunging cataract
        Carves deep river-beds;
And nigh unto them the aromatic breeze
        Whispers among the willows.

A gentle stream is born amidst the crags
        And in its crystals bathes
The banana tree, the coconut tree, the cherimoya
        And the sweetest cane.

The colt salves its indomitable pride,
        When from its waters he drinks;
While to the vicuña and the alpaca,
        The snow lends solace.

The trees engird the hills,
        Clustered in the thickest throng:
Walnut, oak, pomegranate,
        Cedar, ilex.

A thousand birds of splendid plume
        With harmonious trill

Send quivers through
        The foliage of the dense mountains.

The trees, flowers, fruit
        That man most prizes,
The pictorial charm of fowl and beasts
        Of climes most hostile,

The immense continent of America
        In its spaces encloses . . .
The hand of the Omnipotent Lord
        Rested o'er the earth.

A whimsical net of tangled mineral lodes
        Unearths its treasure;
Among the unworked cuts in its fissures
        Shine silver and gold.

Haughty, the sea smashes and devours
        The reckless keel:
But when reaching the fertile shore
        It collects itself and lavishes affection.

An azure, diaphanous, splendent sky
        An aureate disk enhances;
And like a giant, transparent beacon,
        It harbors an embarrassment of riches.

Prodigal nature poured down
        Its most precious gifts;
It regaled with splendid beauty
        The regions of the Indies.

        Arcana of eternal providence,
What audacious language dare interpret you!
For nations robust of intelligence
Peopled the marvelous region,
In vile leisure, in dishonest indifference,
Brought their shameful life in its train;
And each race, each hierarchy
Had a different idolatry.

Of noble ambition and guided by faith,
In rough-hewn ships, fragile vessels,
Fearless, loyal sailors plunged boldly
To the sea.
More than sailcloth and rigging, outfitted
With harquebuses, swords and shields.
God elected Columbus the leader,
And, instrument of God, he led them.

Of the furor of natural forces
The poor storm-beaten caravels,
At the mercy of the violent onrush
Of the angry waves; their lines
And sails tossed by the winds,
Loosed in tatters and shreds;
Incessant misfortunes and perils
The daring navigators met.

Lacking compass, bearing, guideless
Save for the holy inspiration that defends
Such temerity and daring,
Columbus drowns the nascent doubt,
Squelches the betrayal that then was rearing its head
Among the coarse and cowardly people;
And with his strength and confidence
Returns hope to their hearts.

Mixed with waves and foam
Are proof of land not far-off,
Unknown fruit, white plumes,
Grasses that grow only on the shores.
Until the thick impenetrable sea mist
Reveals the longed-for truth;
A new sun anxiously is craved,
And the new sun holds out disappointment.

A tenacious blot dimmed by the horizon
One morning finally is descried.
A splendorous sun washes o'er the ships
As thicker now, the shadow is made out.
No question remains: a magnificent mountain

Breaks the smooth surface of the sea;
It stretches out into wide and fertile lands;
That shadow was . . . The New World!

Sublime, unfading was the glory
Of the Conquest. If lowly covetousness
Oft-times tarnished the victory,
If clumsy ambition and sordid greed
Gave pages to the sad history
Of mourning, blood and barbarous injustice;
So much shame and repugnant deeds
"T'were not crimes of Spain, but of the age."*

Of Isabela no cruel memory stains
The glorious exploits. Noble matron,
Paragon of humility, pure, simple,
In her holy piety what the Catholic queen of Castile
Strives for
Is not to fit to her temple another crown,
But to support idolatrous nations
With the faith and cross of her pennants.

Let us consign to eternal oblivion
Scenes of disgrace, of vengeance and horrors
That the battle poisoned; the hyenas
No longer glut their mutual fury.
They left your veins desiccated,
America, and your flowers and fields.
And that period of bitter memory
Left centuries of deathly lethargy in its wake.

Lethargy, indeed, servitude does not last
Nor vile slavery; sooner may my tongue
Knot up in my throat
Than a single expression issue to disgrace
The far-off land
That enriches the rivers Tagus and Guadiana.

* Hendecasyllable by the famous Spanish poet don Manuel José Quintana [1772–1857 —Ed.] ["Su atroz codiciz, su inclemente saña / Crimen fueron del tiempo y no de España."]

May my humble songs
　　　Not be worthy of popular acclaim,
If to deserve so noble a prize
One need praise vile passions.
　　　He who from the common people seeks
　　　Homages and crowns,
Brings revilement and outrage on himself,
　　　Curses hard colonialism
　　　　　With hollow words,
　　　　　And slings impure mud
At his own name, the name of Goth.

The radiant dawn
　　　Will shine more purely
With holy freedom and independence,
　　　Not by contrast with the dark shadow;
She consumed Spanish America
　　　With flashing scintillations;
She, with no shade to dim her light,
Could shine alone, and shine alone she did.

Its proud head the Chimborazo
　　　Raises among the great
Inaccessible masses of the Andes,
Revealing no secrets in its harsh,
　　　Tetric outlines,
Which harbor candescent furnaces
　　　In their bowels of everlasting fire.

If to its face perhaps an electrified
　　　　　Burning fantasy
　　　To the region of the ideal is lofted,
　　　　　And lends likeness
To its well-known forms;
The bare boulders heaped together
　　　On its towering summit
　　　Sit like a titanic crown;
And the same colossal mountain outlines
　　　An Immense Mausoleum
For immeasurable royal burial:
　　　O sleeping giant

From the larger planet detached;
But without the least sign that shows
        He might awaken
        From his deep sleep,
And in waking, throw the world out of orbit.

And woke he did! And the fire compressed
        In his burnt-up breast,
With a dread-sounding death rattle seething,
He bursts from the crust that confines him
        With a horrendous boom
That shakes up heaven and earth.

Thrust out by satanic forces
        From its crater gush
        Burning, raging columns
Spouted at the stars.

        In its disastrous brilliance
        The entire universe
        Seems swallowed up
In a giant, voracious, unquenchable inferno.

. . . .

        Neither did America reveal,
        In its impassive indolence,
                Its lethargic slumber,
That at the sound of the magic voice of independence,
        The whipped lioness
Would one day rise up with pride,
Robust life-forces welling in her;
And when she lifts aloft with her powerful arm
The noble banner of the free,
Prouder than the very Chimborazo,
        Her children would become
        Dauntless heroes
Their spirits moved for such a heroic mother.

        Ay! For the cry has resounded! Like a shot it rings;
It criss-crosses the American continent

255

Like an electric spark; the banner
Of independence or death is raised;
     Spirited warriors
    With their hearts defend it;
      Steel is bared;
   And on the wings of glory
From victory to victory,
    They reconquer the homeland,
And carve their names in history for all time.

Noble champions in the heroic fight,
    How bravely you perished!
    You who wrote
In your own blood the deeds
Of that undertaking: those that hard luck
    Took to strange lands;
   And those that to slow death
Brutal disappointments condemned.
Oh, venerable shades! If the Eternal
Were to let you hold up your head
    From the frozen tomb!
   If you could see the beauty
   Of withered America!
   On its pure brow
The deep imprint of bitterness unspeakable!
    Ay! how you would shed
   From your hollow eyes
Grievous tears of deep sadness,
    Ay! how you would pray
To the Supreme Maker to have mercy
   On your ungodly lot,
   And to quell the passions
With which his cruel children
    Stir up anarchy
In constant civil strife;
   And that He give in His clemency
   To all America:
Peace, union, freedom, independence!

To the Independence of America

For Eduardo de la Barra

WINNER OF THE PRIZE FOR FIRST RUNNER-UP

Country and Freedom!

Oh, were it given me
To sing as I would wish
My lire would be the first
To celebrate you, America:
      On it I would sing
In strong hearty tones
The great Columbus, the scion of glory,
The favorite son of history;
      And from the sun I would claim
      Its splendent diadem
To crown your brow, o Washington!

And you, Virgin of the South, lie humbled,
howling under iron tyranny?
See how the vile chain snaps
And the eagle of the north rises up.
      America, arise,
      Prepare your cohort,
For the glory of the day shines for you.

May flaming zeal spring to life in your breast,
And from the dust where you lie buried
Your downcast face ennobled rise.
But, *ay*, you do not harken to my voice,
Which in virtue and in valor lack,
You are the plaything of an oppressive race.

I wish for martial Tirtes'* lyre,
For I feel, inspired, my veins afire.
Volcanoes of my country

---

* Seventh-century Greek poet who wrote poems honoring Spartan soldiers.
—Ed.

Accompany my song
In irresistible, formidable tones.
"War!" cry the mountains with a terrifying din,
"War!" they echo; the torrents, "War!"
They go on clamoring with dreadful thunder.

Indignant, the colossal Andes
    Light their lanterns,
Burning fire rages in its caves,
And threaten to hurl an impetuous
    Torrent of lava
    O'er the powerless people
That knows not how to be free and powerful:
    At the dread noise
    The Virgin awakens,
    The giant rises up,
Shatters her chains, and the earth
    Trembles under her heel.

The free wind, proud, repeats
    The blows of steel
With which She strikes the booming shield,
Calling her children to war.
Her voice of freedom sounded on the River Plata,
And echoed through the Andes,
Stretching from pole to pole in a flash.

The nations regard her in ecstasy:
When from nascent America is heard
the sublime oath: "Death or
Recovery of their lost freedom,"
    They applaud wildly
    And shout "onward"
To the triumphant young America.

At the first echo of the sacred voice,
The oppressors of the Europe of old
Shook on their worn-out thrones:
The wilds of Switzerland resonated
    with peaceful sounds;
The echoes wandering on the winds

Carried a germ of hope and life;
And even the heroes of Poland and Greece,
The old heroes of the lost age,
In their tombs, too, were touched;
And the chains of the French colossus
Were dashed to bits, shattered!

Buenos Aires is free. Under its sun,
        In the high ranges
The young tricolor, splendid, waves;
        With free men the phalange
        Is surrounded, triumphant,
And like an enormous boulder come loose
From the summit rolls, unstoppable.
Triumphant, it reaches the stunned world,
Repeating "Victory and Chacabuco!"

Like a mighty evergreen oak of lofty top
That, unforeseen, comes crashing down
O'er its smoking trunk, damaged from a lightning rod,
        So too tyranny,
        Which with its black mantle
Shrouded our sun of freedom,
        Accursed and execrated,
It was felled by the bolt of Maipo,*
        By holy fire.

From the sublime and marvelous instant
In which at the voice of the Divine Maker
        You emerged from the void,
To be free like the condor
Was your destiny, Chile.
And if once in the dust of the past
        You moaned, imprisoned,
You were reborn forever triumphant,
Like the sun that today hides in the west
To shine the brighter tomorrow,

---

* The Battle of Maipú (sometimes rendered "Maipo"), 5 April 1818, one of the major independence confrontations; the other being Chacabuco, fought 12 February 1817. —Ed.

Its beaming face noble and held high:
And just as that sun on its course
    Scatters o'er the globe
The black clouds that obscure its chariot,
    So you, if a foreign nation
Should seek to profane your soil,
Sound the trumpet, and at its throaty call
Bare at once the forbidding steel,
Your banners unfurling in the wind.
Your children will fly to your defense
And if there is one, a single one that does not turn up
To watch o'er the tricolor flag,
May that shameful coward die!

    Beloved country of mine,
    If cruel fate
Again eclipses the day of freedom,
    Recall your past,
    A monument of glories,
Recall the oath to be free;
And if, oh disgrace!, you should wish to forget it
And therewith stain the sacred banner,
Chile, unworthy will you be to be Chile
For you are not the Chile of the past.
    And then avengers,
Fulfill your duty, noble mountains,
Wild beasts shooting burning, destructive cataracts
Of fire that you bear in your insides
At the perjured nation.
Perish, Chile! . . . But no; 'Tis a lie!
What dared sing my delirious lyre?
    Always noble and brave,
    Oh, country of heroes,
Enough proof of grandeur have you given;
And your rich and splendid past
    A future portends for you
Wreathed in bliss and happiness
. . . .
Three damsels rise up,
Tender, radiant, loving, beautiful
From the heart of the mighty Orinoco.

Fresh laurels adorn their hair,
In their hands shines the bloody steel;
"Colombia is free, her chains are
broken," echoes their battle clarion.

. . . .

      Colossal like the Andes
      Bolívar rises up,
      And the proud Hispanic banner,
Its tracks made with daring step;
And Ayacucho and Junín lay a new crown
Of green laurel leaves on Belona.
      America is free now,
      Oh venerated fathers,
Rest well, for you are avenged!
      Despots fell
By God and Justice censured,
And with disgrace and blemished honor marked,
Went behind the oceans to hide.
On the summit of the high Andes,
Full of majesty, full of glory,
      Freedom shows herself.
New banners at her side wave;
And on aureate harps, sublime of tone,
Accompanying her victory songs,
Nine graceful nymphs flank her,
Bearing green crowns of laurel.
And with the world looking on, she tenderly
From her noble, extraordinary throne,
Of a sudden looms up large, and with a gigantic hand
      Threatens the tyrant,
Etching INDEPENDENCE AND FREEDOM
On the sphere of the American sky.

VIII

The Circle held two other literary competitions, one to the memory of Salvador Sanfuentes, the other in homage to the abbé Molina, on the occasion of the erecting of his statue, having obtained brilliant results with both. Although these battles of talent were not necessary to stimulate literary work in that era, in which all men of letters devoted themselves in competition to establish our literature, they contributed withal to strengthening such great spirit, and lent considerable importance and interest to the association's endeavors.

In both competitions, the Circle assembled a jury to examine and serve as judge on its own, and to choose the prize-winner; having held various conferences, in which reigned a high degree of impartiality, a remarkable independence of assessment, and moderation in the discussions that revealed tolerance and fellowship.

On the occasion of the death of Sanfuentes in July 1860, the Circle aspired to render a worthy homage to the memory of the first of our new poets, the constant collaborator in our literary progress, devoting to it a eulogy composed from a biography that Domingo Arteaga Alemparte wrote, from the lyric that Eduardo de la Barra performed at Sanfuentes's tomb, and from the poems that were presented to the poetic competition that was organized. Three members of the Circle entered the contest: Messrs. Olavarrieta, Valderrama, and Rodríguez; the former's composition won first prize, and Valderrama's, second. All the poems were published in the third volume of the *Revista del Pacífico*. Here are the two prize poems.

To The Memory of Don Salvador Sanfuentes

For don Manuel José Olavarrieta

WINNING COMPOSITION

In funereal concert
A nebulous din spreads, aching,
From the waves that, peaceful, kiss
The banks of the harbor
To the snowy-faced colossus,

And from the southern sea to the desert;
For now the virtuous and upstanding magistrate,
The poet who one day
Like a proud swift-wheeling eagle
Through the ethereal regions roamed,
Spread his wings, craned his neck
And sadly exhaled his last breath.

But death in vain
From the throne of mist on which he dwells
Shoots with cruel and daring hand
The fatal arrow
Into the heart of the noble citizen
Who was engaged in serving his country;
Who, though his voice be snuffed out, and too the fire
That one day fed his life,
From it he no longer has need of
That which his mind has already produced;
And clothed in glory,
His eternal name shall live on in history.

Thus is the man, for the tutelary angel
Of Chile is in black mourning;
Thus the patriot for whom all of Chile
Is saddened and moved, and a note
Of profound grief is raised aloft.
His hallmark was love of country,
Freedom his favorite song,
Justice his law, faith his guiding star,
And the future, free of granite walls,
Limitless, bottomless,
The field where his thought lived.

Indeed, from the high summit
Where his creative genius shone,
He saw a thousand nations lift up their heads,
Shaking off the dust that hid
Their former power and greatness;
And he saw rise up from the shadows too,
From the vast forests that adorn
The soil of Columbus, one hundred nations, one hundred more,

Greeting the Old World
Making their way, united the ties of brotherhood,
Marching toward a prosperous future.

But, alack! He does not spy Chile
In the place her destiny prescribes;
And a burning teardrop slips
Down his cheek as he looks breathlessly upon
His country coming from a distance.
He slumps his head down to his chest
And heaves a painful sigh of regret;
For he loves his country so!
And he looks on in pain and dejection
At how far Chile is from first in line.

But the genius ne'er loses heart or strength;
And a moment later, his tears dry,
Serene of gaze, the bard rises up;
And so, like the resplendent rainbow
Is wont to appear as a sign of fruitful days ahead,
Inspiration shines upon his brow,
For the time has not yet come
For the drama that in his mind's eye he stages,
And the glorious history of the past
Of the invincible Arauco, today in ruins,
Unexpectedly offers him a thousand lessons
That will inspire union and love of country
That lack in Chilean hearts.

Yes, illustrious Sanfuentes, you knew
That to be great a country waits in vain
If instead of union and freedom, only
selfishness and ambition rule:
And thus you wanted
In your heart to seize from your brothers
The fire in which you burned,
At long last look upon your sovereign Chile
From the other sphere.
And therefore you turned back your gaze,
Magnanimous Sanfuentes,
To the indomitable nation for which three centuries

Of bitter war
Against the Spaniard were not enough
To wrest precious freedom.
And what better example
Could you show to your brother
Than that of the unconquered Arauco,
Where in each of its children
Freedom looked to erect a temple!
And another noble idea you had
Like your great and beautiful inspiration:
To break down the barrier that divides us
From that uncivilized, warring race,
Inspiring sympathies for it,
Recalling its exploits and glories.
But, alas! Ne'er did you have the chance
To see your country regenerated;
For the more radiant
Noble inspiration shone,
The accurst daughter of the first sin
Let fly into your breast the poisonest arrow
Which shadow lengthened o'er your countenance.

　　　But rest in peace, sleep easy
The dream of death, for your noble, happy Chile
Will see the day,
The day not long in coming,
In which freedom is not a word
But a fruit beautified by the bard
*To awaken man to his grandiose purpose.**

　　　Sleep in peace, and fear not
That oblivion e'er will flap its wings
Above the cold tomb
That covers the bed wherein
Lies your magnificent head.
Genius and virtue are deathless for all time;
Your own essence is of the undying spirit,
For it is a spark
Of the uncreated, eternal mind;

* Verses by Sanfuentes.

And a breath of virtue
Of He who made the firmament rise up from the void
With a single Word.

Fear not oblivion, no, Sanfuentes,
For even the crude, ferocious Araucanians
When they curve their necks to the soft yoke
Of Chilean laws,
And call us brothers,
For you they will ask our children,
And far and wide will search out
Your gravestone
To send up a fervent prayer,
And a burning tear
To shed on it in your memory.

To The Memory of Don Salvador Sanfuentes

For don Adolfo Valderrama

SECOND-PRIZE WINNER

What is that sweet hazy melody
That sadly lingers round
And pervading the shady jungle
Whispers a grieving sigh
In the language of my land? . . .
'Tis not the susurration of the wayward wind
That whorls among the whimsied branches,
'Tis not the smitten turtledove
Who intones her songs of love
For her distant mate;
The tone is sadder
Than the heartfelt notes
The swift wind brings our way.
Look there: on that solitary tomb
There is a sonorous lyre,
Over it an angel is batting his wings of gold
And from its strings bursts forth a supplication . . .

It is the soul of the genius who, tearful,
Has us hear in honey-toned vibrations,
On his own crypt
The echo of his final songs;
It is the soul of the genius who has fallen silent,
And who, as it folds its most powerful wings
Leaves on its soil, bathed in tears,
A famous name: SALVADOR SANFUENTES.

The cold tomb swept you up in its breast,
Mighty poet,
Horrible death served you the poison,
The last swallow of this heinous world;
But in vain it hopes
To take haughty delight in its victory:
There are two pure deities whereto it cannot attain,
Its insatiable vengeance
Shall do no harm to those divine deities . . .
Genius and virtue are forever!

Your cold frame can rest in peace,
For genius cannot be wrapped up in a shroud;
And the vile arrow of horrible death
Cannot o'ertake the author of the Campanario.

What's that, Illustrious SALVADOR? Did you not see
That faithful work
Marked on your countenance
The history of your beautiful poems,
And that the soul's ardent inspiration,
After collecting glorious victory,
Would sleep in the cold tomb? . . .
Indeed you knew, but more did you try
To live on in the memory
Of glorious history
Than to live in the world in which you lived;
You shall not die, generous poet,
Illustrious magistrate,
And when from the luminous throne
On which you sit
You lay eyes on my country,

You will see an old man, grizzled of hair,
Taking your children to your cold tomb
To tell them what their father was.

Be not astounded by the din that reverberates
From the upright mountain
To the bellowing falls,
Which with its foam of brilliant silver
Blankets the boundary of our horizon:
It is the country that weeps
Over the unfortunate death of the poet
And with restless gaze
Seeks your creative intelligence;
The woods of Chile are moved,
Because your soul-stir stopped
The branches break off
When they are shaken by the wind,
Or wracked by voracious flames;
It is the raucous uproar of the volcanoes,
Bawling titans,
Which raise their shoulders
To illuminate your royal funeral
With the colossal burning firebrands
Of their red rubble.
Sleep in peace, SALVADOR, rest,
For if cruel death
Shot its traitorous arrow,
Your lyre still rests on your tomb;
And the soul of your brave spirit,
Ranging o'er its chords,
Shall eternally be echoing
A melodious tune in our ears.
Under the somber cypress
It recalls your magnificent head,
Which on the very rim of the cold vault
From your immortality life springs.
Rest in peace, safe
In the depths of a cramped tomb,
For when the judge of the eternal heavens
Sees the efforts of your conscience
And the sacrifices of your heart,

God Himself will confirm your judgments.
Rest in peace, independent poet,
Songbird of my country,
For the laurel leaves that adorn your ample brow
Ne'er shall wither, and for evermore
Shall live on with your ardent imagination.

The poetic competition held in honor of Molina awakened keen inspiration in the lovers of the muses, and among the many compositions that were submitted, the Circle gave preference to four to be examined; their authors were Messrs. E. de la Barra, M. J. Olavarrieta, Arcesio Escobar, and A. Valderrama. Those that won the prize were the following.

Ode to Molina

For Eduardo de la Barra

FIRST-PRIZE WINNER

> Molina, your country has not forgotten
> your name nor your glory!
> —B. Vicuña Mackenna.

From the united nation to holy inspiration
I lift up to you, Molina, my feeble song:
Feeble, but free as the sun that rises,
And free as the nation that extols you.

Art sculpts bronzes to your memory,
A worthy tribute to fame deserved;
And like an emblem of sublime glory
The sun encircles them in its burning flame.

And when it's westered, tumbles down,
Lending the Andes its final reflections,
It goes far, far away, to come to rest
On a humble, venerated tomb.

That is your gravestone, Molina,
And the sun's majesty bows before it!

And from its high seat
Perhaps seeks to breathe burning life
        Back into the already prostrate brow
Where once thought shone;
Your thought, which scattered
Glorious light among the thick fog
That covered America.

And death snuffed out that intellect
That had been so battered by adverse fortune,
But not his renown or his learning.
His diadem of splendorous glory
Of pointed thistles is full,
For misfortune always waylays knowledge,
Always does traitorous fortune bind it up in chains!
And the heart of the country, so highly prized,
        does not hold your mortal remains!
A country as ungrateful as it was beloved,
And so bemoaned by you in its absence!
Wretched Americas! Knowledge on your soil,
Patriotism, are doomed to banishment!
Of how many glories
Do you retain but wan memories!
But so much safeguarded renown
Will shine as clear as the light of day!

The age in which they came
Is passing, and an age of justice arrives
That, devoid of rancor in its tombs, fails.
The age in which they came
And triumphant merit appears.
. . . .
You, too, noble wise man, from the bitter cup
Of banishment you drank,
And honors from your century you earned
And the acclaim of cultured Europe.
After a long, sad, stormy journey
In Italy your heels came to rest,
        For Chile recalls in you
So much beauty, so much misfortune!
        Oh, wretched nations!

Both sweet freedom lost,
captive Chile, and Italy prostituted!
Equal in valor and mischance,
And their histories in fallen grandeur.
What remains to them? Their beauty alone!
But a memory of glories gone!
No, for you saw patriotism one day
Raise bold your valiant brow,
You saw your country free and powerful
Calling itself independent to the world;
But you did not see the rising sun of Italy!
Roaming amidst its regal monuments,
Witnesses of noble deeds gone before,
Frail remains among so much ruin
With parasitic ivy crowned,
You conjured up the shades
Of the crumbled Roman empire, a wonder of the age.
Mute they remained in the fruitless dust,
Your elated burning fancy
Saw only Arauco the she-warrior.
        And with profound knowledge
Of this supremely unknown soil,
The rich cloak you showed the world.
        And too you told
        With simple eloquence
In the harmonious language of the Tuscan*
The glories of the indomitable Araucanian.
Delighted, Europe listened to you,
        Applauded your words,
And offered you a chair among its wise:
And the echo that reached America,
        Glanced off the Andes,
Through all its vast regions swept
        And filled its spaces.
And as a great man of Bologna among great men
Your renown reached your native soil:
And the people to repay your efforts in kind
Erected statues to you: not like those

---

* Dante Alighieri (1265–1321), Italian poet, author of *La Divina Commedia* (100 cantos, 1307). —Ed.

That are mounted for only shame,
For they carry the odious seal of the factions;
    Marbles that dishonor,
And that to mad vanity are built!
The day will come when the people turn up,
Great and terrible, to deal out justice,
And in their mutinous vengeful waves
Reduce those carvings to dust and do violence to them!
Like them will fall wrongdoing and crime,
And virtue and genius will be in their glory;
    Their chains will burst,
Their true heroes are ennobled,
And marbles for them are raised,
    That only with the slow blows
    Of time will be no more.

But what matter! Perennial is that glory
Of the heroes that the nation reveres,
And your vastly educated name, Molina,
Is written in the nation's memory,
    And inscribed there in the great
Inaccessible summits of the Andes.

There your free spirit roamed,
And found the beauty of virgin America
In its sublime majesty.
Your thought grew noble there,
    And as it haughtily wrested
Secrets from the giant masses,
    In splendent codes
From God whose name you saw everywhere.
Before Him you went down on bended knee, wisely,
And His Name infinite in grandeur
    Your lips whispered:
    Audaciously your thought
    To his throne ascended,
    And Omnipotent God
Poured light down o'er your brow!
You rose up powerful and majestic
Like the cedar of sacred Lebanon.
And to the kingliness in you, nature

Rendered homage!
The royal eagle let loose a savage cry
For you, as lofty it swayed
From the blue sky among the tenuous lace:
The crash of the fast-flowing torrent,
As it hurls down in frothing waves,
    Hushed as you passed,
And the afterclap of the burning volcano echoes.
The ray that burst in the clouds
    Your brow illuminates;
    And to your voice responding
O'er vast spaces roved
The raucous thunder, roaring slow.
And that sublime and terrifying concert
Given off by the immense mountain range,
'Twas the echo of the angel of the Andes.
    Of the angel who said:
"Hail, immortal genius!, glory be to thy name!"
And all of creation echoed "glory be!"
In magnificent notes.
And burning now in holy fire,
It echoes too my humble song
That goes out to your memory:
Hail to you, spirit of my country!
As your immortal soul, so is your glory!

To the Memory of the Naturalist Don Juan Ignacio Molina

For Manuel José Olavarrieta

SECOND-PLACE WINNER

Guardian angel of my country,
Spread your airy wings,
Fly fleet to the region of day,
And bring my cold and fainted soul
A spark of the holy flame
That inspires the eternal song of the cherub.
For now the country wishes
To extol the deserved glory

Of he, he whose illustrious scions
His history relates;
He who dies in tears
On faraway soil
For die he cannot with his gaze fixed
On the clear sky of Chile.
And I want to join my voice
To those harmonious tones in acclaim,
And which rushing winds
To the fertile valley, to the mountain, to the hill,
The echo sweeping away my songs,
Carry off, moaning, the name of Molina.

      The scene in which you play your part is grandiose:
That of my country in grand nature!
And to go with you to the heights
Of the snowy mountains, where only the condor
And the eagle make their nest,
And then descend to the deep valley
Following in your footsteps,
One needs your sublime inspiration that diminishes not,
And powerful lungs.
Ah! That is why I want
A spark from that holy flame
That inspires the cherub's eternal song.
Behold, it is he: alongside the torrent
Whose howling foam bursts through
Among the boulders of the rugged terrain,
Whose mist paints the setting sun
Scarlet and blue,
He contemplates there its deafening roar
And follows its path with his eyes
So that he can go down then to the plain
Where it now is a tame little stream,
And pluck the fathomless mystery
Hidden in the simple flowers
That are born on its two banks.
On the snow-capped crest of that mountain
That rises up higher than high,
Look upon him there too, like a shadow
Dimly silhouetted against the horizon.

But I do not know ..., my gaze is not enough
To bring me to you, oh great Molina!
Even to be able to guess the secret
That your joy-filled heart
Wrested from the dark-brown rocks
That toward the abyss are leaning,
Or from the condor that late buried
His proud neck in the ethereal azure.
More strength, more breath do I need
To follow where you bend your steps;
May your spirit come to urge me on,
I wish to ascend to the summit as well
Of the haughty giant of granite,
And from the wall of rock itself
That burning ray and storm insult,
And in whose deep chasms
The proud eagle hides his nest,
With you to sound the black abyss;
And to see the expression on your wide brow
When your head grazes the clouds
Sent swiftly streaming
By the sibilant wind,
You feel that the thunderclap bursts
In bellowing tones,
To measure the mettle of your soul
Then carry off your thought enrapt.
Indeed, immortal Molina, all of that do I wish,
But not because I seek
To be first with you in your glory:
For in vain I did try
To raise my spirit to the heights
To which yours, Molina, rose,
Much as I requested strength and fervent ardor,
Beseeching the heavens.
Ah, if I wish to forever hold uppermost
Your immortal figure in mind,
It is only, Molina, because I yearn
For my song to be worthy of you.
Pure blue transparent gauze
Stretches from the chain of the snowy Andes
To the peaceful ocean,

Like a vaporous, delicate veil
That wraps around the hair
Of the innocent maiden who seeks
To half-conceal the charms of her heaven,
And the playful little wind unfurls
To reveal to us all the delights
That her shame and shyness deny us.
That exquisite veil
Strew a thousand of the purest glittering gems
And a thousand rays of light playing o'er it
Which a splendorous sun
Scatters by the handful.
Ne'er does vaporous mist cloud o'er
The delicate ink of its brilliant blue,
And each star with great beauty
Shines its clear, sharp light upon it.
Chile's sky
Shelters the riches that it hoards up
In the valley, in the jungle and the mountains,
Where first the purest rays of dawn
Are painted;
It is a sky like none other.
For nature wished to show
Its beauty, pomp and lushness
In my country, a second paradise,
The source of idylls for my soul.

Snowy range rises
'Til touching the clouds with its face,
And one hundred hills lay at its heels
All across the continent.

From their deep gorges
A thousand rapid torrents issue
And forming the most beautiful of falls,
Descend quickly to the deep valley,
And carrying their crystals to the sea,
Cross the plain.

The rich blanket of flowers and emerald
Covers the vast and fertile plain,

While from the mountain on the flat slope lying,
There where the placid stream murmurs,
Laurels, lingues, evergreen beeches
And countless oaks
Show off their bulky branches.

A thousand innocent birds
Of varied plumage
Conceal their respective appeals
From the forest in the splendid foliage,
While other ones endowed with speech
Cross the meadows in song,
And in majestic, measured flight
Others too soar up
Until vanishing into heaven's blue.

That was, great Molina, the holy temple
Where Our Lady of Chile,
—You were full of admiration, full of charm,
Your brow bowing down
In fervent prayer—
At your door looked upon you one day;
And turning her gaze aloft,
Your soul's desires understanding,
Sends up your prayer, and smiling
Out of love and tenderness,
says, "You may enter the temple where
Your soul seeks to know your God."

And you crossed its threshold, Molina,
And Chile showed you its horizons:
The ocean, its long-ranging beaches
Littered with sea-shells and coral;
The mountain, its viscera;
And the volcanoes, their unfathomable mystery.
Like a tireless pilgrim
You crossed o'er mountain and plain,
You listened to the bird sweetly trilling
In the thick of the forest,
And bending your daring step
To the towering face of the colossal Andes,

Where the deep precipice did not daunt you,
You took in, marveling,
The magic, splendent panorama of Chile,
And on the very rim of the dormant volcano
You worshipped the Almighty.
For there is no one who, when seeing the wonders
That nature offers everywhere
Does not fall to his knees
To worship Him who on His works has impressed
The seal of power and grandeur.
And you rose up and went on roving
O'er pasture, woodland and hill,
Collecting a thousand leaves and a thousand flowers
Of peregrine fragrance and beauty.

And traveling on, you stemmed the flow
Of the raging river,
And refreshing your face in its crystal
You looked into the secret
That with tenacious persistence
It hid in its silvery waves.
And you call to your sight
The nimble birds
And the restless fish,
Who in the deeps hide their scales,
To wrest from them their every secret.
And everything is laid bare at the gaze
Of your clear, deep mind,
For it is light radiated
From the uncreated light
Of the Being who with a thought
Made existence spring from chaos.

The invariable laws that sustain
Exploded worlds
That wheel across the firmament on high;
The mysterious forces that contain
In the insignificant sand of the beaches
The violent rush
Of the waves of the liquid element;
And those that wrench the grass and foliage

Of the wilds and the fertile grasslands
And the vast plain
To later lay out in spring
A new mantle of flower and verdure,
And dress the forests in new vestments:
Everything, everything, Molina, do you analyze
And everything your spirit raises up to God;
For everything in its perpetual movement
Do you hear, Molina, that sublime is sung
A mysterious hymn
That from sphere to sphere
Echoes on and on the name
Of He who is the first cause of all being.
But, woe! when your voice
After joining with that song
Raises up in praise
To the thrice-holy throne of the Being,
From your native soil
Fortune snatches you away howling
Nevermore to see the pure sky
Under which your cradle rocked.
And in one nation and another you find yourself
A pilgrim, without a country, nowhere to call your home,
And making your way, without direction or destination
And without a homeland!
Other nations in vain offer you
Their hills, their skies, their mountains,
How somber and sad they seem to you,
For they do not sway
In the horizons of your own fatherland.

But, woe! it no longer is your lot
To gaze again upon the enchanting
Image of your seductive country,
When as the sun sets in the west
Its purest face
Turns carmine of hue,
As if by chance it feared
That as the monarch of the heavens came down
To the regions of a new dawn,
It were to remain suspended in the sea,

Looking on in ecstasy
The delights that, timid, it would
Hide beneath the veil
That stretches blue across its face.

　　　And to Italy finally you turn your gaze,
And Italy, Molina, gives you
A second country,
Where your virtue and your knowledge are displayed,
And wherefrom you, sighing,
Send Chile a gift,
Your magnificent *History*
Worthy of Chile and worthy of your glory;
And your sun is buried in the west.

　　　That was, great Molina, your career,
To worship your God from the heights,
To contemplate Him in the plain, in the meadow,
And in the trill of the bird in the thicket;
And then with your good-bye and final sound
From foreign shores
To erect a monument to your country.
So, in appreciation
Today, Molina, the country, moved,
erects a statue;
So, reverent,
A free nation, its proud face
Bowing at your feet,
Sheds gentle tears of admiration,
And the tutelary angel of Chile sings
The sacred hymn of immortality.

IX

The productive, happy activity that *La Semana* and the organization of the Circle of Friends of Literature had awakened aroused a quite marked interest in Valparaíso, where Jacinto Chacón, jointly with his brothers and other learned men, including several distinguished foreigners, like the eminent French republican deputy M. Adolfo E. Gent, the Spanish doctor Roselleo, M. Feuillet, and M. Desmadryl, founded the Sociedad de Amigos de la Ilustración ["Society of Friends of Education"], with the purpose of spreading knowledge in the branches related to letters and social sciences. Chacón himself at once reestablished the *Revista del Pacífico* starting 1 January 1860, so that Valparaíso, according to the prospectus of this second series of this newspaper, had a voice and representation in the country's literary movement. "Finally," he added, "the passion for literature is expansive and impartial, and it impels us to consecrate our days of idleness and solace to these literary labors where budding creativity showcases its gifts, and wherefrom true talent prepares a career for the future."

The *Revista del Pacífico* reappeared at a most opportune time to fill the gap that the cancellation of *La Semana* had left in the ranks of newspaper publishing; from that point on it continued to be that representative of the literary movement, which already had two hubs of activity in Santiago and Valparaíso.

The workers' activity in those centers presents an extraordinary fact that history can do naught but look upon with veneration, even astonishment. To what stimulus were those industrious and tenacious collaborators in our intellectual progress responding? They were not responding to a political interest, nor could they aspire to official rewards or sponsorship, since, coming from different and conflicting approaches, they were forced to leave aside political issues to keep the peace, and since the government, whose interest was trained on a thorny situation, had neither time nor the desire to foster the pursuit of letters. Neither were they seeking the ineffable satisfactions that stimulate the spirit of he who devotes himself lovingly to teaching, for they were not teachers, but students who could scarcely find the few stolen moments from work they had to perform to earn a living and provide for their families. And could glory whet their ambition, or could the hope of material gain stimulate their activity in a nation that was still awfully far from being in a position to honor and enrich its writers? They responded only to their love of study, without the nobility of this sentiment waning either because of some men's thirst for fame nor the ambition of others to forge a national literature. "There is a divine spirit deep down in the nature of man," stated the editor of the *Revista del Pacífico* in 1860, in reference to this, "that drives him to unrewarded goodness, that stirs him to the investigation of truth for the mere pleasure of finding it, and that inspires in him a love for the noble sentiments of humanity and toward the grandiose scenes of nature, for this is the condition of his being, sensitive to the impressions of what is good, of the truth, of physical and moral beauty."

The literary friends of letters held the interest of the Circle of Santiago conferences for some years, presenting excellent studies on different and vast topics, and literary compositions that today bestow honor on our literature.

Miguel Luis and Gregorio Víctor Amunátegui cultivated literary criticism, and aided the cause of spreading good taste and refinement with their *Juicios de los poetas hispanoamericanos* ["Judgments of Spanish-American Poets"], which, collected later, made up an interesting volume known throughout our America. The critical studies were without doubt the most appropriate to the goals of the institution, and therefore warranted preference: outstanding ones included Moreno's on several Bolivian poets and prose writers, D. Arteaga Alemparte's on the works of Sanfuentes, Moncayo's on those of the Ecuadorian writer Herrera, Briseño's on Espinosa's philosophy, Blanco Cuartín's on the history and advancements in philosophy and medicine, and another on the mutual influence of international literature, mainly Spanish American.

These regular contributors to the Circle not only wrote literary studies, but also presented, among other writings, a critical analysis of *La política del libre cambio y transformación económica de la sociedad inglesa* ["The Policy of Free Exchange and Economic Transformation in English Society"] by Cochut; and a remarkable historical investigation on France's invasive foreign policy. Rodríguez Peña, an Argentinian émigré, had become Chilean through his distinguished wife and children, and through a burning interest in all our progress. A servant of the country, as director of the nautical school, secretary of the marina in Valparaíso and head clerk of the ministry of that department, he had been at the same time a writer for newspapers and a contributor to literary newspapers. He was a thinker of wide-ranging education, and though he did not excel for disciplined taste and irreproachable correctness, his literary styles were fluent and readable, and revealed his noble character, securing him the sympathies that he knew how to earn with his pleasant interaction and unfailing joviality. He died early, but left noble memories in the Circle of Friends of Literature, and in the nation to whose progress he devoted the activities of the best stage of his life.

Historical criticism, history, and studies on contemporary Spanish-American society gave topics to monographs that were very notable for their content and for their form, such as Barros Arana's works on the chroniclers of the Indies from 1514 to 1793, on the discovery of the River Plata by Díaz de Solís, on the ancient history of Peru written by Sebastián Llorente, on the Spanish iconography of Carderera, a study on the life and writings of the historian Caro de Torres, and his life of Ferdinand Magellan; also works such as Moncayo's diverse studies on the status and situation in the republics of Venezuela, New Granada,* Ecuador, Peru, and Bolivia; and the descriptions of nature and of the customs of the Ecuadorian republic by Joaquín Blest Gana, and Vicuña Mackenna's biographical articles.

Alongside the critical studies in literature and history that gave our literary movement in the era the seriousness and importance that for some time had vanished, and that fortunately it retained later, the Circle of Friends of Literature can put forward a great number of works of imagination and poetry that enrich our literary repertoire and that honor Spanish-American literature. Alberto Blest Gana presented there several of the novels and different studies of customs that had earned him the fame he deserves for his acute perceptiveness and regenerating spirit. Valderrama, the Circle's most steady collaborator, the satiric and humorous poet who so closely follows the masters of the Castilian gay science; Irisarri and Pardo, who, for their genius and propriety, were worthy of the renown of classic writers; Guillermo Matta, the deep thinker in verse; Arcesio Escobar, Eduardo de la Barra, Blanco Cuartín, Olavarrieta, Campusano, Santos, Varas Marín, D. Arteaga Alemparte, Rodríguez, Pedro Lira Caravantes, all garnered the acclaim of the Circle for their numerous original poems; Pedro León Gallo earned sincere approval for his extensive and polished translations of Victor Hugo; and Emilio Bello, reading many unpublished poems by his illustrious father, don Andrés Bello, earned a position there that he was able to hold with his own compositions.

All these poetic works, like others published by Messrs. Aniceto and Jacinto Chacón, Villar, Vicuña Solar, Hurtado, Barros Grez, Astorga, Caravantes, and Torres Arce, in the *Revista del Pacífico* offer testimony to the great strides that our literature made in those years. The most notable poets had already forsaken the Zorrilla school: they did not consider poetry the art of coloring, of forms that enchanted for their tinsel and filigree, of the beauty of gardening, whose subtleties reveal nothing to thought: they followed the road paved by those who in 1848 made of the art a tool of regeneration, and in general aspired to write by thinking and beautifying noble ideas and lofty sentiments.

Poetry proper, which is the most difficult form of literary art, and that cannot employ all intellects because the consortium of intellectual endow-

---

* Name the Spaniards gave to Colombia. —Trans.

ments that make up the poet, is nevertheless the favored literary manifestation of youth. This explains the abundance of poetic works in our early literary essays. All youths sung because they were at the age in which the affective faculties prevail; but many hung up their lyre for good as the rule of noble instincts began to decline, and they declined as well as poets. Quite rare are those that remain so amidst the struggle for social life; and in spite of the contrasts of a turbulent existence both material and moral, they maintain the afflatus taught by the sublime art of manifesting in numerous and proper verses the state of the spirit stirred by a philosophically conceived and developed idea or by a feeling.

What happened to those who were poets is what has happened to humanity under a constant law. A positivist writer, Bourdet we believe, determines the law this way: "Real progress is an invincible tendency that leads us to equate our destiny with the immanent laws of the world. It is not so much a question of reaching a great number of sensual satisfactions as of settling on balance and justice, considered as the foundation of our individual and collective evolution in the world and in humanity. A society in which instincts alone, whatever their name may be—industry, war, religion, art—will of necessity have two periods, one of ascension and another of decline. But posit in this society the participation of the faculties of reflection, of judgment, comparison, justice, and you will see a social face in which man will triumph absolutely over his animal nature to attain the eternal youth of all that is good and beautiful."

Thus he that sings inspired only by the noble instincts that prevail in the early age will rise and fall, until breaking his lyre and giving no thought to it thereafter. But he will forever remain a poet if, having the talent to translate the state of his spirit in a genuine and beautiful way, he poses also a living notion of what is right, good, useful, and beautiful, a notion that, philosophically oriented, can triumph over the concerns of his age, the mischances of life, and even the heavy amount of work necessary for survival.

The poet triumphs, then, over animality and acquires an eternal youth, which enables him to sing the inspirations of feeling, as well as those of the intellect. Nothing is outside of his powerful art: nature and creation, humanity and society, individual and social instincts, concrete or abstract contemplation, inductive or deductive meditation, all can be turned into the inspirational numen that sets fire to his soul and gives artistic character to his prodigious expressive faculty.

If this is the truth, it is erroneous to suppose that modern poetry excludes feeling from its realms, and everything that is not scientific and moral meditation. All that the age demands of poetry is that it not collide in its songs with the dominant aspiration, for that is exactly what it imposes on all art. Heretofore the aspirations of societies in our civilization were molded by the rule of religious faith and by the traditions of the past; and now art wished to represent history, depict the present, foretell the future, yet had to be always religious and always traditional.

Today is another matter. The rule of religious beliefs is weakened, and all the traditions that form the baggage of the old regime run contrary to social justice, for they hinder the activity of freedom and progress, which are the laws of humanity. Modern society, moreover, does not want sickly visions, for it can lose its way as much with the school that seeks only the beautiful, finding it in the new, as with the other that seeks to find it only in the conventional good, not in the good that by the law of human development, which the properties or forces of humanity obey, consists of conserving and extending life, but in a certain relative good defined and imposed by sectarian rules and by dogmas imposed on the faith of the believer.

The times in which the ideal of faith and tradition were the law of art, then, have passed. The paintings of Rafael and of Murillo do not charm us today for the feeling or tradition they represent. They are admired for their human, real, plastic, or relative truth that heightens them, like *The Divine Comedy* is admired only for its regenerating spirit of truth and virtue, of justice and freedom that extends through hair-raising, hellish scenes, sad or placid depictions of purgatory or paradise that the keen imagination and unblemished faith of the author forge.

Modern poetry ought to embody other aspirations. The civilization of the age demands of it that it undisguisedly and logically serve social recomposition, bringing about the new order; it wants it to embellish the new ideas, condemn tyrants past and present, sow with flowers the rugged warpath that society follows to hasten its future. It must sing of feeling, which never will fail to be an inspiration for art, and let it sing the smitten man, and whenever the halo that his loves radiate are not obscured by the clouds of the supernatural, of the bizarre, of the phony or antisocial; like the nature-lovers can sing, but à la Bryant, without disfiguring it with a forced and affected sentimentalism, or à la Emerson, who with his simple idylls has acquired in British* literature the high rank of writers who think and make their readers do likewise. Let it sing religious sentiment, as it sings in More, Pope, Montgomery, Longfellow, without contradicting the new ideals and even praising the souls that profess another faith. Let the moralist intone his *doloras*,† but without clouding his morals or distorting

---

* *Sic.* Emerson was North American. —Trans.

† Short, sentimental philosophic poem associated with Spain's Ramón de Campoamor (1817–1901). —Ed.

the truth, like Campoamor, through shocking vices or absurd traditions from a past age, through false apothegms of antisocial philosophy. Let Byron's burin carve its luminous and profound scenes of sublime passion, but let not skepticism befog its sheerness nor muddle its clear light. Let science also strum the sonorous lute, revealing its laws to the world and to humanity, but never perturbing its pure harmony with the discordant notes of a dark metaphysics, as is wont to happen to the most Attic of the thinker-poets of this America, the correct and austere Arnaldo Márquez. What profound truth this statement by Quinet contains!: "The writer of today who is inspired by traditions, only because they have been thrust upon him by the past, is not the writer of this century; he that believes in the metaphysical illusions and the abstractions not revealed by positivist observation, is not the writer of this century; he that doubts and destroys, dominated by skepticism, not seeking truth, not drawing close to nature, is not the writer of this century. . . ."

Here we come to what we wish to observe in the poetry of the time to which we are alluding. Those who cultivated art studiously not only distanced themselves from the colorist school, as Zorrilla's can be called, but also took pains to not see beauty only in the new and bizarre, nor only in what certain precepts take for good. The Circle of Friends of Literature, carefully cultivating good taste in literature, lent its acclaim to a notion more generic and true of the beautiful, the useful, the good, and the just, as born out by, among many other works, the prized compositions from the contests, which we have transcribed above, for no other reason than to define the moment in which this poetic progress begins, owing to that useful association.

Moreover, the Circle contributed not only to the progress of critical and literary studies, for many of its members were devoted to treating philosophical and scientific topics. Outside of the above-mentioned works by González, Cruchaga, and Miquel on theoretical and practical questions of political economy; by Volckmann on the antiquity of the world, and various others we have neglected, Francisco Marín wrote on the future of democracy in our America, Manuel Carrasco Albano on freedom, apropos of the book by Stuart Mill;* Dr. Fonck on the geography and orography of the province of Valdivia, Dr. Padín and J. A. Torres on the institution of public foundling hospitals to favor population preservation, Dr. Murillo on advancements in natural history, on artificial lactation and vaccination; the late-lamented Gabriel Izquierdo, the distinguished mathematician, on the

---

* John Stuart Mill (1806–1873), English philosopher, economist, and utilitarian, author of *Principles of Political Economy* (1848), *On Liberty* (1859), and *The Subjection of Women* (1869). —Ed.

influence of the seasons on man's faculties; and José Ignacio Vergara, a translation of the Seguin Report, titled *Reflexiones sobre las hipótesis de Laplace* ["Reflections on the Laplace Hypotheses"]. Finally, scientific interest never waned in the Circle's conferences, through the dedication of the fertile mind of Adolfo Valderrama, who at the same time he was presenting important professional works, like his *Estudios* ["Studies"] on prostitution in Santiago, on the predominant diseases in La Serena, on medical sciences and literature, he was delighting audiences with his admirable biological and physiological works, like *La flor en el reino vegetal* ["The Flower in the Vegetable Kingdom"], *El dolor y el alma* ["Pain and the Soul"] or the connection between the soul and the human body; *the Ensayo filosófico sobre la muerte* ["Philosophical Essay on Death"]; the *Páginas de mi diario* ["Pages of My Diary"], on the causes that superstitious beliefs maintain in magic and witchcraft; *Opresión y sensibilidad* ["Oppression and Sensibility"], which is a study of character; *El juego y las afecciones del corazón* ["Play and the Diseases of the Heart"], *El fastidio* ["Ennui"], *Sueños, genio y locura* ["Dreams, Genius and Madness"], etc.

Thus that congregation of industrious, self-sacrificing workers, though confidential and operating in a private home full of candid and sincere friendship, acted as the center of the literary movement, and profitably helped the independent intellectual development of the country. In five consecutive years of work, the Circle of Friends of Literature, by giving approval, stimulation, and accolades to the budding spirits, like those who had already earned their place in literature, made its beneficent activities felt indisputably in the high-minded path that literary and scientific studies took, in the propriety and good taste of literary composition, and in the preservation and development of a press that worthily represented the intellectual advancements of the country.

X

Progress in national literature had a life of its own in 1864. The philosophically artistic manifestation, by means of the words, ideas, and sentiments of the country, its needs and interests, its aspirations and advancements made in the speculative order as in the active order, had able and skilled masters to maintain the honor and glory of the generation that, at the cost of sacrifices and self-denial, had invested its country with a literature that was progressive and able to consummate its evolution in the times ahead.

But this very fact entailed dangers that still could spell its undoing. One must apprehend the exact circumstances of that historical moment to gain an accurate picture of the trajectory and nature of our literature.

Social events are not exclusively the result of preceding historical phenomena, nor are they the exclusive work of laws that govern human nature: they are rather the aggregate outcome of historical situations and human actions. The philosopher who considers them only from the first perspective runs aground on Bossuet's and Vico's providential fatalism, or on Herder's fatalism of nature, or on that of the logic of the situation, or the mental state of a few positivists; contrariwise, the philosopher who has them depend on the idea or on the spirit, as Hegel does, or on the nature of the individual, as Bentham does, opens himself up to building, like these two men, a social science grounded on the general laws of humanity, dispensing with history, and having no recourse to it save to verify those laws.

The occurrence of which we speak, the existence in 1864 of a national literature, albeit incipient, progressive, and capable of completing its evolution, is a social event that though depended on historical events that were taking place from the moment of our independence, favoring the intellectual movement, it was mainly the result of the efforts, of the activities of a group of men who, obeying the laws of freedom and progress that govern humanity, were ahead of the time in which the mindset of the country would naturally produce it: and therein lay the danger.

Such an occurrence is not unusual in history. There are social phenomena that flow naturally from historical precedents and that, aided by the slow action of laws that rule human nature, wind up coming about as a logical result of the mindset of their age. But there are many that, also following the logic of historical events, do not wait out the course of these latter developments, and are carried out ahead of their time through the actions of intelligent men who find themselves in a position to take a synthetic, already-formulated idea and carry it through. Intellectual activity is a more powerful lever than the logic of events and is, in Stuart Mill's witty phraseology, what moves the ship and not the steam, which is only the driving force. The event of which we speak was not in fact in the country's mindset: it was the work of a social faction that was relatively much more advanced. Were this not the case, the national literature would neither have managed to become independent of the dominant old traditions and beliefs, nor would it have embarked upon a progressive evolution, able to be completed in the future.

The reason is clear. In 1864, note well, the literary movement was no longer subject to the intermittences of the first age, when all those who wanted intellectual progress were not serving it with unity of motive or purpose, as we stated in several passages in Part One, and especially the beginning of chapter XXVIII. Now not only was the phalanx of writers infinitely more numerous, but more convinced, more logical, because there was really unity among those who supported the progress of an independent literature. The continuous and fertile activity of the Santiago Friends of Literature and the Friends of Education in Valparaíso, the beneficent influence of the literary press, skillfully maintained by *La Semana* and the *Revista del Pacífico*, and even that exerted by the political and liberal press, had been able to promote the cause of our literature, owing to the profound change in policy that had begun to take hold in the regions of power after the internal strife in 1859. Without this change, the efforts of those agents would not have been as effective.

Nevertheless, if the independent literary movement was no longer to be intermittent, it still had to pass the rough test of battling the countercurrent of the conservative school, which five years after 1864 was still consolidated. In twenty-five years, jesuitic education had yielded all its fruit.

The State's activities in public education had continued since 1843, building on the foundation that the constitutional law of the University had indicated, and which served the illustrious Mr. Bello for proclaiming in his inaugural address, as rector, a confessional teaching, and a confessional science, literature, and morality. Outside of the branches of theological and canonical studies that are included in the courses, what Kant calls *theosophism*, instead of philosophy, was taught, as is taught now in the State schools, and a true scholastic theology instead of natural law. The clerical schools, which under the headship or inspiration of the founders of ultramontanism, which, as we stated (Part One, chapter XXIII), had been organized in 1843 with the Instituto Nocturno and the *Revista Católica* ("Catholic Review"), all had adopted the jesuitic teaching plan to spread doctrines contrary to the principles and interests of modern civilization and the democratic system. And yet they were not only sponsored by the government and meticulously assisted by the University Council, as the numerous agreements that appear in their proceedings attest, but also were the ones preferred by the well-to-do families for their children's education, and even by the heads of family that were most incredulous or of dissident beliefs.

The Jesuits from the French reform had established schools in Valparaíso and Santiago before 1844, but in this year the government resolved to send members of the old Society of Jesus to Europe to commission them to serve Indian missions; and to evade the law that had expelled them, it resorted to not allowing them to found communities. "Naturally," stated the Report by that year's Minister of Culture, Mr. Montt, informing Congress of this unique measure, "they have been permitted to live *in conformity with their constitutions*, but not to form communities. For the objective for which they are called, the latter was not necessary, nor could it be *conceded to them*, even if the government had wished to, for *the law that excluded their order from the ranks of allowable associations was in force*. Another member of the same institute has left Santiago to survey the missions of the province of Valdivia, and data are expected from him that will facilitate the new regulations the government is considering."

In the Report from the following year the Minister of Culture related that that initiative had failed, since the Society of Jesus demanded as a necessary condition that it be recognized as one of the country's authorized associations; but the Jesuits soon began to establish themselves in the Republic, and making full use of the advantage of living in accordance with their constitutions, though not *in communities* in observance of applicable law, they founded schools in which they nonetheless lived communally, but as teachers of youth; and they built cloisters and great temples, as adjuncts of the same schools, to live as an authorized association before the law that forbade it. And they made no mystery of this, for the proceedings from their main house in Santiago were published under the name of the *Colegio de San Ignacio bajo la dirección de la Compañía de Jesús* ["San Ignacio School Under the Directorship of the Society of Jesus"].

That law was openly violated through the subterfuge dreamed up by the government; but in the 1854 legislature an attempt was made to put an end to this irregularity through another law, whose bill the Senate began and approved, authorizing the existence in Chile of the Society of Jesus. The bill wound up held over in the Chamber of Deputies, perhaps for being unnecessary, given that the Society of Jesus was not in need of such authorization to exist and to educate the youth with the support of the government, which, moreover, had authorized for itself in a 15 January 1852 decree, the establishment of the Capuchins, who had been abolished in Spain in 1835, for no other reason than for being the community that most faithfully copied the model of the institution of Saint Ignatius of Loyola.

After twenty years, a large generation of both sexes had been educated in the clerical or lay schools or nuns' academies that follow the plan of enslaving the spirit and habituating it to a mental gymnastics that distances it from the truth; that plan in which, in Quinet's expression, proven by the facts, "everything is spectacles, solemnities, academic jousts, and spiritual duels. Who would believe," he adds, "that thought was taking not the least part in its numerous literary occupations, its artificial rivalries, its exchange of writing? This is the miracle of Jesuitic teaching: absorbing man in an immense circle of tasks that produce nothing; to entrance him with smoke to separate him from glory; to hold him nailed to a point, in the very moment when he feels swept up by all the trappings of a literary and philosophical movement!"

In 1868, that generation formed the active militia of the new *Catholic Party* that was organized under the government's protective wing, to hold up the doctrines and declarations of the *Syllabus* as an ensign and credo, which still had not been elevated to dogmas, as they were subsequently by the Vatican Council. The Pérez administration, which originated in the Montt administration, had reacted since its inauguration against the political party that its progenitor represented, allying the interests of the conservative splinter groups that had separated from the latter in 1856 and 1857, and bolstering itself with the Liberal Party. The latter, as we have stated, had sympathized with these splinter groups starting in those years, and had hastened to place itself side by side with the new administration, with the illusory purpose of making it serve the liberal principles, but having to give in and make concessions to preserve the unity of this hybrid fusion, and therefore was unable to produce anything stable or definitive.

This situation could not help but profoundly change the course of liberal progress in politics as well as in letters. In fact, although through the government's fusion policy, which generally was moderate and respectful of rights of personal freedom, that progress had not come to a standstill, and the system of compromise and conciliation among competing interests which that policy had to obey, introduced disarray and even anarchy in the principles and doctrines of the liberal cause.

This anarchy manifested itself in the divisions of the Liberal Party and in all courses of action taken by the politics dubbed with the name of liberal; but it merely appeared in a latent state in the literary movement, and did not become apparent at first blush. The very servants of this progress were its victims, unbeknownst to them, and they thought they were serving the independent intellectual development, the regeneration of ideas and the freedom of the spirit, when in their writings or teachings they perpetuated retrogressive traditions and theological or metaphysical illusions.

The press reveals that the national literature had a life of its own after 1864, as we asserted at the beginning of this chapter. Disregarding the numerous official publications, those of private interests, or of associations of all sort, which were many, for the spirit of association had already spread, the number of publications of social, literary, or scientific interest may be calculated in this way, following the statistical data from the second volume of Briseño's *Estadística bibliográfica* ["Bibliographic Statistics"].

In 1865, there were III works, of which 24 deal with ecclesiastic interests. Among the secular works, the didactic prevail, reaching 23, and the scientific, no less than 18. In history and biography, there were 7; in poetry, 8. There were 13 novels, all translations and republications. The remainder were on various matters.

In 1866, 84 were published, of which 20 were didactic and 4 scientific. History had 5, poetry 9, and of the 8 novels, 5 were original. Those of ecclesiastic interest only amounted to 7, and the rest were on various topics.

In 1867, the works amounted to 125, 22 on ecclesiastic matters. The didactic reached 29; the scientific, 9; those in history and biography, 14; the poetic, 8; novels, 14, but of these only 2 were original. The remaining 29 were on diverse topics.

In 1868, 123 appeared, of which 13 were on ecclesiastic matters. Those on diverse issues reached 59, while there were 18 didactic works, 8 scientific works, 9 in history and biography, 13 novels, almost all translated and only 1 original. Poetry works dropped to 3.

In 1869, we had 117 works, 20 of them on ecclesiastic matters. The didactic reached 25 and the scientific, 16. In history and biography there were 9, and on miscellaneous topics, 31. There were 14 novels, including 2 original ones, and only 2 works in poetry.

The majority of all these publications were tracts, monographs, brief and compendious treatises; but in general all of them reveal scholarship, strong method, and artistry, or at least care in forms and correctness, qualities that are characteristic of an already-mature literature, if that is what the artistic manifestation in words of the ideas and feelings of a society is called. As a matter of course one notices that scientific and sociological compositions prevailed, reaching nearly half each year, or a trifle less, of works published; for not considering that most of them that deal with various issues are serious works of social and political studies, those in the sciences numbered more than 200 in the 1865–1869 quinquennium, teaching and history and biography.

Meanwhile, works of descriptive literature, works of poetry or the imagination, were out of proportion with those works in social and scientific studies, and originality is lacking in them; for in five years only 25 original poetic works and 1 translated work, and of 62 novels published, only 10 are put forward as original.

This can be explained in many ways. Yet, leaving aside consideration of the fact as a special phenomenon of physiology, produced or modified by natural influences, it is true that the tendency manifested in the studies concluded depended on the social and political status of the men of letters, men who, not given to histrionics nor having reason to seek out glory and profit through compositions of pure imagination, were concerned, on the contrary, with the serious interests affecting their political or personal situation. They therefore wrote on social or political matters, on sciences or teaching, history or philosophy, for the interests of the moment or those of their personal status forced them to focus their attention on those topics; and they were not inclined by taste, nor did they have the time nor the motivation, to prefer imaginative compositions. The latter, moreover, would not have been a literary manifestation of a social necessity, for the European novels that were imported and those that were reprinted here or translated to fill the idle moments and satiate the emotions of the readers of this genre of works, sufficed.

These observations are even-handed and do not only explain that fact in the moment to which we are referring, but also now and as long as it lasts. But in that most serious and high-minded literature, the mindset of the age and the political situation were represented. The former because in it prevailed the stationary, the traditional, the conservative element that backward-thinking education had revived and bolstered, and the latter because the writers that had represented and sought to represent the innovative and progressive element appeared in anarchy, for their political situation divided them, and forced most of them to appease the conservative and retrogressive interests.

The independent literary movement was no longer systematic, it lacked a unifying center and had no representation in the press, for since the *Revista del Pacífico* ended in 1861, no independent literary newspaper had been able to assert itself, and those that appeared under the titles of *Mariposa* ["Butterfly"], *Correo Literario* ["Literary Post"], *Revista Ilustrada* ["Illustrated Review"], *Revista Literaria* ["Literary Review"], etc., had a fleeting existence. The Circle of Friends of Literature had gone on recess starting in 1864, and the publication that was organized in Valparaíso had ceased operations when the *Revista del Pacífico* stopped press. So that movement that had so greatly contributed to affirming the independence of the spirit, to spreading the literary art, forming that phalanx of writers that had brought coherence to a national literature, did not have in the latter anything more than a half-hearted part and was blinded by a special-interest, partisan spirit.

Meanwhile, the conservative element, which was strong in the power wielded by the State and the Church, which ruled public education, and which set their sights on controlling opinion as well, was faithfully served in the political and ecclesiastical press, and had organized their representation in the literary press. After an exclusively literary weekly newspaper, which the writers of this school sustained in 1865 under the title of *La República Literaria* ["The Literary Republic"], the political society of Amigos del País ["Friends of the Country"] founded *La Estrella de Chile* ["The Star of Chile"], a scientific, religious, literary, and also political weekly review, aimed at serving the Catholic Conservative Party. This newspaper appeared in 1869 as the country's only literary forum, while the writers that cultivated the art entirely independent of factions and dogmas had to resort to the political dailies to publish on occasion their productions aimed at serving the independent intellectual development.

XI

To this point we have attempted to determine all the circumstances attendant to that era, and now we will proceed to explain how we resumed our activities in the literary movement, reinstalling the Circle of Friends of Literature in 1869, regardless of the fact we had not stopped collaborating with several publications, published here and abroad, toward intellectual development. Those who do us the honor of reading these pages, believing they are inspired by vain pretension, will forgive us, since the plan and purpose of these historical *Memoirs* oblige us to inconvenience them with our presence in the events; for it is not possible to make of these an exact narration without noting the work that then was undertaken to put a stop to the anarchy that regrettably separated the old workers from our literary progress.

After a prolonged absence in the service of the Republic, upon returning we found ourselves forced to battle preferably against that political situation, in which the liberals sacrificed the organization and the future of their historical party, blinded by vain delusions; for they considered one of the Conservative Party splinter groups a liberal body, merely because it reacted against the policy of the other faction calling itself national, and hoped, through its alliance with the former and with the Catholic circle, to eventually effect reform, which could be naught but fallacious and deceptive, since it was to be based on a compromise of such opposing principles and interests. But since not only the Liberal Party and true political reform, but also literary progress had to come up against the predomination of the conservative circles, the former servants of this progress, who looked on it in pain as it strayed from the path that they had strained to blaze, they imposed the obligation upon us to take once again to our old literary endeavor, to save ourselves from the true backwardness that the victory of a literary standard of judgment based on the traditional and on sectarian demands would entail.

Hence, the reorganization of the Circle of Friends of Literature in 1869, which returned keenly to its old projects. But, alas! The workers who five years earlier competed in talent, selflessness, and industry were no longer included in its ranks; nor was it efficient to dispense with parties and beliefs, which formerly was the basis of our union and brotherhood to work for the progress of our literature. Politics divided us deeply, and the only ones who returned to work were those who were outside of political interests and those who fought against those of the dominant parties.

It was necessary to affirm the existence of the association and extend its activities outside the domestic quarters in which it operated. To that effect it was agreed that public readings or lectures would be held at least once a month, and those given in May, June, July, and August in the ballroom of the Municipal Theater were always attended by more than one hundred fifty people, including even thirty ladies. The novelty of these lectures took hold of the popular imagination, and the press applauded them, promoting productions in prose and verse by Valderrama, Domingo Arteaga Alemparte, Pedro L. Gallo, and Guillermo Matta, who basked in the applause from such distinguished gatherings. But in spite of the fact those felicitous attempts were harbingers of a splendid outcome, the lectures, which had been so well received, were to end for lack of a suitable meeting hall; for the generous permission the Circle had received to conduct its business in that building was revoked.

In the first of those lectures, on 23 May 1869, we performed a reading of the address with which we ushered in the reinstallation of the Circle. It was a veritable platform, in which faithfully translating the spirit and goals of our coworkers, we pinpointed the anarchistic state of our national literature; and tracing the path that we were to follow to save it from moving backward, we also established an independent and positive yardstick for guiding us in literary and scientific composition.

This work is a document correlating with the 1842 address to the Literary Society, and should be included with it. Then an effort was made to found an independent literature, emancipating our literary movement from tradition and from the rule of the literature from our old mother country. In 1869, our needs lay elsewhere: national literature was lively, and after having followed the initial impulse in 1842, despite the roadblocks it faced from society's state of mind, and the resistance that official teaching and the authority of the rector and the University Council presented, after that victory, we stated, it stalled and was on the verge of moving backward under pressure from the triumphant doctrines and interests, amid a political situation that could not last.

It was crucial to reestablish that impulse in all its vitality, reinforcing its fulcrum, which was none other than the independence of the spirit, and indicating the proper criterion that art ought to follow in order to move ahead free of fear, doubt, and dread. That was the end of the inaugural address of 23 May 1869, which appears below as proof of the logical plan to which we have aligned our participation in the literary movement of our era.

XII

Gentlemen:

Nothing could be more pleasant for me than the invitation that many of you have extended me to reestablish the old Circle of Friends of Literature, that modest society that has left a deep footprint on the path of our nascent literature, and whose memory I hold near and dear to my heart. Inaugurated on 21 August 1859, a year of terrible political upheavals, it traversed a period of five years, up to 1864, in which it brought literature a tremendous surge of power, which was not subverted by the momentous and profound changes that then were coming about in our history.

Two literary newspapers were sustained by its works. *La Semana*, which don Justo and don Domingo Arteaga Alemparte published in Santiago, and the *Revista del Pacífico*, which was published in Valparaíso and on which the society worked together starting in July 1860. Additionally, a daily, *La Voz de Chile* ["The Voice of Chile"] adorned its weekly literary review with the poetry that was being read in the Circle. Three literary competitions promoted and brought the society to a happy ending, one in praise of the country in 1859, the second in memory of Salvador Sanfuentes, our colleague, and the third in honor of the abbot Molina. Seventy members had inscribed their names in this fine institution, and lovers of literature in attendance at their meetings were in excess of eighty.

There was never any shortage of enthusiasm to nourish that hub of intellectual activity, in which the youth that appeared on the literary scene met with the encouraging cooperation and accolades of writers who already had made their mark in literature. So that institution that had resisted the evidence that imperils the existence of all the associations not based on a social need or legitimate interest, already had a life of its own; and it did not adjourn except for circumstances entirely independent of the interest it supported.

You all are right to reestablish it: there is no reason to doubt that it will once again be strong.

There is no reason to list for you the host of scientific and literary productions that, born under the fertile shelter of that institution, constituted its treasure and its glory. To sing its praises would be tantamount to burning bothersome incense in your faces. But today, as we reconvene, let us devote a memory to those who have paid their debt to nature, leaving us the memory of their invaluable contribution: Carvallo y Sanfuentes, who by taking part in the foundation of the Circle lent it the support of his name; Rodríguez Peña, a constant contributor, who among several writings left us his memoirs on *La literatura chilena, su nacionalidad, su carácter y su influencia en el progreso y felicidad del país* ["Chilean Literature, Its Nationality, Its Character and Its Influence in the Progress and Happiness of the Country"], and on the *Influencia mútua de la literatura internacional y principalmente de la hispanoamericana* ["Mutual Influence of International Literature and Chiefly of Spanish American"]; Miquel, who after having illustrated with his words the interesting debate that was provoked on political economy, apropos of the critical reception of a work by Courcelle-Seneuil, read to us a brilliant study on *La utilidad en su carácter subjetivo* ["Utility in Its Subjective Mode"]; Padín and Torres, who wrote a very useful work about Mdme. Pastoret's institution, considering the *Cunas públicas como un medio de proveer al aumento y conservación de la población y educación de un pueblo* ["Public Foundling Hospitals as a Means of Providing For the Increase and Maintenance of the Population and the

Raising of a Nation"]; the poets Martín José Lira, Arcesio Escobar, y Pío Varas, who, dead in the flower of their youth, succeeded in delighting us with their beautiful poetry, the first two competing heatedly in the poetic contests, and the latter leaving behind for us his heartfelt ballads and tender canticles in imitation of foreign poets; Carrasco Albano, finally, who, although living, has lost the lucidity from that fine intelligence that burned out its final lamp in his radiant work *La libertad* apropos of Stuart Mill's book [*On Liberty*].

Beautiful souls, radiant with light and zeal, pour down on us, you fellow workers who are still at work! Support our efforts, since you are no longer at our side to support us with your presence!

Indeed, we need encouragement, a great deal of it, to continue at our task, for the deed is vast, and we will not live to see it crowned. What other incentive spurs us on? What laurel do we await, before remaining on the road like our companions? Literature is not yet a center of life, of glory and fortune. It is but a path that we are going to clear by dint of unrewarded fatigue. Let us not delude ourselves, and let us paint the scene as it is, to attempt the task inspired only by awareness of the obligation.

What is the status of the writer in this country? What is so brilliant and praiseworthy about that situation, what usefulness, what advantage? Actually, there are no other motivations than those born of love and study, and the setbacks are many; many too are the drawbacks that stifle and extinguish those motives; therefore love of study must be a true virtue in and of itself, a quite powerful force, so that it too is not extinguished, and can surmount the obstacles that beset it.

A simple fondness for letters cannot abide, a love of truth that is not honest cannot endure a battle, a commonplace propensity to study cannot reign supreme. Thus you see weak spirits yield to the mainstream of interests and concerns, pay them homage, become their footmen, in spite of the fact that alone, in private intercourse, they acknowledge and confess the truth, and even despite their devoting their studies and conferring their respect on it in the depths of their conviction.

The only ones to persevere are those in whom the love of study is an unyielding force, a virtue that does not back down but gains strength in battle, and feeds on the worship of truth, and which triumphs with it and because of it.

And so it is that the life of study is a life of sacrifice. For it to not be so, at least on the animal side of existence, study needs to be a kind of speculation: indeed, speculation into the narrow horizons that the so-called liberal professions have in this country, which barely provide a comfortable subsistence, if any at all; or speculation in the sterile and very narrow sphere of publicity in which social, political, moral, and material interests still move. But what writer can earn a fortune devoted to serving any of those interests, or even earn himself a name that is known beyond his circle?

It is true that in the anarchic state in which all social interests were colliding, due to the crisis in which moral progress is found, literature, which is the expression of society, lacks unity and reveals that multi-front war throughout the entire civilized world. It is true that on account of that very situation, even the writers of genius find insurmountable obstacles to finding uncontested acceptance. How much greater they are for everyday talents, however educated and powerful they may be! But finally, in the great nations, the orbit of influence of each one of those interests is too wide, and its writers find in it a vast compass to fill with their name, and abundant benefits that come to gild their path and repay their toils. But in small nations, which scarcely are beginning civilized life, as is our nation, that anarchic situation of ideas narrows each writer's circle in such a way that fortune and glory refuse to accompany him, leaving him to wrestle alone with poverty and obscurity. Neither education nor the power of intelligence suffices; even genius would not be enough to succeed, to have all of society in one's grasp, to gain acceptance in all the different spheres in which opposing systems have been established, systems that down different paths pursue the respective social ideal and particular truth each has chosen. Today there are no national writers anywhere, at least not in our country. The days are gone when the unity of absolute power brought in its wake the unity of society's aspirations. Literature then, echoing those aspirations, also represented social uniformity, and the writers that most faithfully gave shape to it were as great as kings, and their names rang everywhere throughout the nations. When did French and Spanish literature reach their zeniths? At no other time than in the age of the most crushing domination by the absolute monarchy, an age of wars and despotism, of depraved customs and inhuman acts of violence, an age called the Renaissance in France because, fleeing the social intelligence of that frightful moral cataclysm, it found refuge in science and in the resurrection of the creations of Greek and Latin genius. Writers served and represented that movement, and society, which could be felt rejuvenating within them, crowned them with glory and granted them the power of legislators of good taste.

But with the horizons of the spirit widened and with the light of truth shining down, the darkness was dispelled, the unity of absolute power was broken, and social aspirations cropped up everywhere and diversified, also breaking the unity that hitherto had bound them together like in a bouquet. Literature no longer had a single form, and began to represent the plurality of social aspirations.

This is not to say that absolute power has been more favorable to literary development, for, in producing through the law of contrasts a single aspiration for the truth in an oppressed society, it has also favored the reign of writers who shared that aspiration. Today men of letters are not dictators, they are not the apostles of a new truth, they have debased themselves, they have become commoners in the measure that, the horizons having been clarified, society believed also that it could set off on its way down different roads. But the sciences have gotten out of the sorry state they were in when living at the mercy of absolute power, and literature, which then served a single aspiration, are today the battle artillery that all aspirations employ, aspirations that abound and are in contention in modern society. Thus as literature has widened its domain, the literati have swapped the dictators' crown for the warrior's sword.

The panorama of this situation is frightening, for one does not know how to work free of it. Quinet depicts it with steady hand and vivid color, but keeps mum, as do all, on the cure for such an obvious disease.

"You ask," he exclaims, "why do the nineteenth-century writers not have the sway over the nation that the eighteenth-century writers had? The reason is simple: today, the truest ideas, the most just, cause fear. Before the Revolution, they were aspired to in all quarters. . . . In the eighteenth century all classes aspired to the same truth, they hastened to find ideas, they had a thirst for knowledge. Thus a single writer was the organ of the entire society; nobility, middle class, commoners, all had the same curiosity, the same ambition for truth. Society still being one, it allowed the genius a universal domination.

"After the Revolution, each condition, each part made its own little exclusive truth, outside of which there is no salvation. Do you all express one of those truths? Instantly, you are condemned by everyone who has placed his flag elsewhere. Every degree of wealth and poverty has its system of ideas over which the word and eloquence cannot have the least importance. One entertains such a thought not because it is certain, but because it pertains to such a situation in which it is used. In order to know what men think, I have no need to interrogate their souls; it is enough for me to know in what circumstances they live. From bottom to top, I thus discover all systems of philosophy and belief. Show me your habit, I will know a priori your way of conceiving the order of the worlds, from our planet to the star Sirius.

"This is the nineteenth-century writer's torture. What is more miserable and limited, what more contrary to the freedom of the spirit than to be embedded in one condition, and rejected at the same time by all others? Thought no longer spreads by virtue of its natural form, and there are no longer national writers. How many of a party's great men are scarcely known by others?

"The solution to these difficulties is found in abstaining from thinking, because it is thought that divides us; and the solution for living in peace lies in worrying only about a blend, which neither disturbs nor scandalizes anyone. So men of letters gradually renounce ideas and feelings, which become obstacles, and lock themselves away inside coloring and form, neutral ground, on which life is comfortable for them. Everything that profoundly moves souls ends up truly scaring those who strive for any domination through the art of writing. They begin by standing aloof from thought, as if it were a veritable discredited pursuit; soon they have no need for this precaution: thought withdrawing, on its own it makes half the road, and it saves them the work of fleeing from it thereafter.

"The Revolution is far from having freed the spirit of the French as much as we think. Today there are more conventional and mandatory ideas from which it is not permissible to stray, than there were in the eighteenth century. A writer feels chains that then did not exist. After the earth shook, an enormous dike of commonplaces, of sophism, of opportunistic phrases was erected with great haste, out of impatience or fear, and which no one has examined. One is compelled, moreover, to respect it under penalty of being suspected of wishing to bring on a flood. This threat did not exist for the eighteenth-century writers, who could cast a steady glance at men and at the world. We have replaced sacred things with conventional things. Is servitude any less because it is voluntary?

"In spite of our revolutions, the life of the writer who serves the truth, and does not wish to serve more than the truth, has become more difficult in France than anywhere else in the world. For him to dare, it is imperative he be cloistered from everything, that he renounce everything. This is a conviction that I owe to experience. Can the writers who do not accept such a fate be reproached? That would be cruelty. The majority of them spend the second half of their life retracting the daring truths they had advanced in the first half. . . . "

Is this not likewise the situation of the writers in all modern countries that receive inspiration from France and that have been moved by their great revolution? At least I find in that scenario the condition of men of letters in Chile defined, because in addition to our country's moral situation being analogous, we are testing out a form of government here that favors, more than did the French monarchy, the development of individuality, so that diversity of aims and in systems can make intellectual anarchy more painful. Here not only do parties and classes have their little systems, but also individuals, even those who are least accustomed to thinking and those who are most unaware of the procedure that the intellect must follow in investigating the truth. Who does not feel authorized, because he has the right to render his opinion, to denigrate the ideas of the writers that are not of their favorite stripe?

Our revolution has emancipated the spirit less than has the one in France, and it has anarchized it more, giving encouragement to individual pride to establish itself in its preoccupations and absurdities. If there the spirit runs aground on a vast dike, here one drowns in commonplaces, sophisms, and conventional phrases, which cannot be examined either without being stigmatized by the whole society that lives in that ocean of errors like the fish in the salty sea. All parties, all walks of life, seek in respect and in submission to those errors the triumph of their interests and rulership. Issue forth your free thought in the regions of philosophy or of science, and you will not manage to feel the echo of your words, for it will not be drowned out and condemned without your being heard out; issue forth your free thought in the regions of history or of politics and you will raise a storm; proclaim your thought undisguised, and they will treat you like a madman. There is no other choice: one must stop thinking and feeling, or else think and feel like everyone, as per the accepted rule in the form adopted and consecrated in the party to which you belong, in the social standing you rate, and in the system that authority has dictated.

That is the situation. Could that be also the future you pursue, you who have the virtue of scholarliness and who aim to bring American literature to life? Will you have to worry only about color and form, in order to not frighten, to find applause, with a view to ruling through the art of writing? Will you have to consecrate yourselves to pleasing the common run of know-it-alls, or "talk to them in stupidity for their pleasure,"* adopting those forms in which the independence of thought sallies forth only against moral judgment?

I only ask these questions of you to greater stress the negative. Who has said that those who persevere, that those who have the strength of that great virtue called love of study, can link their heart and soul to the forms sanctioned by the interest of each system, to earn accolades, to earn a weak and fleeting renown within their own clique that will not withstand the first ray of light that the sun of truth sheds on it? No, that coloring, those forms, are not those of art, but of an exclusive system, those of the small relative truth in which each party, each of the sects that fragment society, believes it dwells. That is not art: the first law of art is the truth, positive truth, universal truth, and not dictated or conventional truth.

Fortunately, the tyranny of sophism and commonplaces is not as overwhelming here as it is in France, nor does that diversity of aspirations, which there divides society into factions and diverse truths, here have the same raison d'être. No, the fundamental truth of the Americans is democracy, and that should be the center of all aspirations, whatever the political or social affiliation that characterize them may be. If any man, party, class, sect, that does not have that aspiration, let him be made anathema! Can we obstruct it out of a sectarian, party spirit, an interest either personal or factional, without selling

---

* The line is Lope de Vega's (see part III, chapter 4): "Hablarle en necio para darle gusto." —Trans.

out the country, without giving up our revolution, without imprisoning ourselves in betrayal of the future and the natural development of our civil responsibility?

Democracy, that is the synthesis, the complete entirety, that can give unity to our actions, to our thought, to our feeling. When it forms our universal credo, society will be one again, as it was under the absolute rule of a monarchy, and the spirit will have a universal import: then each social status, each party, each sect will have its moral or material, political or social, interests to defend; but it will not have a small exclusive truth, outside of which there is no salvation, for all will be united in a universal truth, in democratic synthesis, which will be the center of all aspirations, the focal point where they all are to converge to be refined, to legitimize their existence and procedures. Then writers will not abstain from thinking, nor will they suppress feeling, to seek peace and an easy victory in the neutral field of color; for the cause of the factitiousness will not lay in thought, but in the interests being stirred, which can only live and be legitimated under the heat of free thought and under the shelter of the universal truth that gives unity to society and its development.

This, which would be an unachievable utopia in the current state of European societies, in which the human spirit is shackled by the conventions of the authority and the parties that the anarchy of moral progress engenders, is simple in Spanish America and practically a reality in Anglo-American society. There you can observe the unity of social development and the majestic course of their fledgling literature: just as that development moves in a single direction, that of semecratic government, which is the great end toward which all aspirations converge, toward which all parties, sects, and social conditions tend, literature represents at the same time that one-way movement that leaves the spirit full independence, not chaining it in systematic forms, nor in small conventional truths, and letting it trail freely behind positive, universal truth. What nation has produced in this century more eminent statesmen, more distinguished historians, more original poets, and scientists more admirable and practical than the United States? Do you not see how science, sociology, and even European letters are beginning to change under the influence of American literature's inspiration? What does that nascent literature's power, as new as it is stupendous, mean? For it does not yet boast geniuses like European literature, nor masters that in the exact sciences, in social science, and in art, exhibit, like the Europeans, a name that has grounded its fame in a fifty-year domination of the literary art. That means that the freedom of the spirit has found its theater in North America, through the unity that society, and the literature that represents it, have acquired in the democratic synthesis, which unites all aspirations, and which kills off small systems, exclusive truths, antisocial factions, which in Byzantine Europe fetter thought, sterilizing genius, leading talent astray, and promoting only those writers who fulfill the role of sophists or of artificers of a literature that leaves no other recourse but to adopt a picturesqueness, a conventional truth. The unity that the absolute monarchy sought through terror and domination of society is at work in democracy through freedom, which gives life to that fertile union of all aspirations.

We too, with little effort, can impart our literature the same character and the same course. We have the strength that the virtue of study gives: a bit of courage, and the victory is ours. If, as I have stated, our social situation is analogous to that of France, to that of the nations that live in Europe under the rule of Byzantine traditions, the difficulties are not therefore insurmountable, as they are there. That analogy lies in the fact that moral progress here is in a state of anarchy on account of those traditions. But the strength of the latter is more apparent than solid in Spanish America, for they are discredited, since they do not rule because they are true, and they have no other support than sentiment, which daily grows the weaker, and tends to regenerate, seeking its support in democratic progress as the only form of moral betterment.

The proof lies in that here there are no parties that break with democratic progress, that fight democracy. All of them take it as a standard, as the goal of their aspirations, however much some do not understand it, nor accept its truth entirely, committing the error of seeking to ally democratic truth with those traditions, with the enslavement of the spirit, with the events and the feeling in which the forms of the old society are still granted asylum, as with the rules of the recalcitrant and retrogressive life. You see now that the latter is not serious, that it has no raison d'être, and that this ephemeral and transitory situation will vanish on the day in which democratic synthesis is understood by all and loved by all, as the only means of bringing unity to social development.

Here is the work of men of letters, those who pledge their love to study. Lest their efforts not be fruitless, their foremost obligation is to be that of winning and securing the emancipation of the spirit, in theory and in practice, in institutions and in society, in public life and in private, in all manifestations of thought. When that emancipation is a reality, the systems of exclusive truths that yet exist will disappear utterly, those systems that fortunately do not have a real life, but a fictitious one, in our country, nor solid support in the parties' aims and in social conditions. Those aspirations are generally vague, moreover perplexing, for they are lacking the faith that gives possession of the truth. When they understand democratic truth, faith will come; and with it, social unity, that fertile unity that can coexist with the plurality and diversity of moral and material, political and social interests, because all these interests can be served comparably and find their development under the support and rule of democracy. In that situation, there will not be exclusive systems that cannot coexist with some ahead of others, nor will each party have its exclusive truth, nor will men of letters have to give up thinking and feeling in order to pursue a career, taking refuge in neutral forms and in combination. Literature will take the course that it takes in the United States, where there is none of that; but to reach such a state, we need to begin by emancipating the spirit, by returning to thought and to feeling all its powers, all its strength, all its freedom.

On another occasion I have stated quite forcefully of the social sciences something I can repeat here in reference to literature:

"We have to reconstruct social science like the Anglo-Americans have reconstructed it: to blindly accept the European traditions, to continue the errors and concerns handed down to us by the nation that was the most behind of all Christian nations, since it turned into the *last bastion of uniformity* of despotism and pagan ideas about the organization of society and the State; to transplant the dominant historical, political, and moral criterion from European societies to America clearly and without reflection, that criterion that one could call official, since it cannot be extricated from the prevailing principles of order, and that when it goes beyond concerns it is rejected or condemned, or at least is shunned as a utopia or a heresy, it blocks our regeneration, slowing it, leading it astray from its natural course. Let us teach history, philosophy, morality, law, political sciences, not under the inspiration of the dogma of strength, the dogma of Latin monarchy, the *imperium unum* that rules conscience and life in Europe, but under those of the new dogma of democracy, which is that of the future, which is our *credo*, which is the way of life imposed upon us by the rule of circumstances and the conditions that the revolution of 1810, the largest event of the ages after Christianity, brought about and consummated."

Indeed, we must reconstruct our literature. But if I aim to reconstruct Spanish-American literature on the democratic foundation of the emancipation of the spirit, do not think that I have come to proclaim that literary revolution of emancipation that split French literature in 1830 into two bands, the *romantics* and the *classicals*, which became a cruel war and corrupted the true idea of *Freedom in Art*, which was the banner of the former, like the political parties had corrupted the true idea of political and civil freedom starting with the revolution of '89. Freedom in art, literary emancipation, will be the natural offshoot of the independence of the spirit; and just as the latter, which, being the pure outcome of democratic freedom, will never wind up being confused with the waywardness of reason nor the madness of a sickly spirit, in the same way that democratic freedom is not confused with the abuses of law, neither will literary emancipation be able to constitute a transgression of the law of art, which is the truth.

The fundamental law of art is the truth, and therefore Victor Hugo has been able to say that the beauty of art is not perfectible, for neither is the truth. When art reaches the truth, be it in painting or sculpture, in music or in poetry, art only has managed to attain it through the freedom of the spirit to investigate the truth, to express it vigorously and clearly, free of the constraints of any other authority than that of the facts. This is the fundamental doctrine of the literary art, for it does not subject genius to conventional good taste, nor does it tie it down to forms dictated by the whims of schools or of societal concerns, which are suitable only for enabling mediocre talents to come out on top, to rouse an Avellaneda against Cervantes, a Green or a La Harpe against Shakespeare, a Trublet against Milton. It is a fact that mediocre spirits do not gain anything with freedom, which frees them from preventive rules, but rather they run the risk of going astray. But what does literature lose in that? Does it take anything away from their grandeur that there are owls who think they are condors, as long as these kings of the ether can soar?

Art, which in expressive literature is the imitation of nature, and in the scientific, the genuine revelation of the truth, is not simply a revelation of the beautiful, an element of taste or of pleasure, as those who profess art for art's sake assume, but a powerful instrument of social progress, for it is the form of the useful, of the just and true. The great poet I have just recalled says that: "At the point where the social issue has been reached, everything should be collective action. Isolated actions are canceled out, the ideal and the real are in common cause. Art should help science. These two wheels of progress should spin in synch. . . . Thought is power. All power is obligation. In the current century, should this power take a rest? Can this obligation close its eyes? Has the time come for art to lay down its arms? Now less than ever! The human caravan, owing to 1789, has reached a high plateau, and since the horizon is vaster, art has more to do. That is all. All expansions of horizons entail expansions of conscience. . . . Let us raise up as high as possible the lesson of the just and the unjust, of law and of usurpation, of oaths and of perjury, of good and evil, of *right* and *wrong*; let us go there with all our old antitheses, as they say. Let us contrast what should be with what is. Let us shed light on all things. Bring light, you all have it. Let us pit dogma against dogma, principle against principle, energy against stubbornness, truth against imposture, dream against dream, the dream of the future against the dream of the past, freedom against despotism. . . . "

Art, then, is social, universal, for it is the form truth takes. In this sense, there is no literary or scientific work, there is no manifestation of thought that is not subject to art, whatever its nature may be. Scientific and philosophical works need art, like those of the imagination, for if they do not pay mind to artistic form they can become obscure, contradictory and even ridiculous in the exposition of thought.

That doctrine having been admitted, which frees art from arbitrary rules, like the human spirit from authority, the judgment of art, like that of the spirit, should only be sought in positive truth; and to that end we need to classify works of literature.

Nevertheless, we will not make the mistake of classifying them by their artistic form, nor even by their subject matter, because the form cannot be a single one, a classic form, since there is no other law nor rule than the truth; neither can the matter give us the logic of a classification, since it is multi-faceted and unclassifiable. Meanwhile, we need a classification to establish the common criterion that should guide us in the composition and criticism of literary works, because the fundamental strength of literature, which consists of the independence of the spirit, should have a criterion, a light that sets it always on the road to positive truth.

Thus I seek classification in the nature of composition, in that nature that the work receives from the procedure that the free spirit adopts to think about and look into the truth. So I would divide writings into:

Scientific, which are those in which the positive laws of the universe are researched;

Sociological, which are those that have human activity as their objective, those that study the faculties and motives of the individual's activity, the laws of his relationships, of his development in history, in current times and in the future, the general conditions of the moral universe;

Exegetic, those of simple exposition, be it scientific or sociological, and that are aimed at generalizing and disseminating the findings of philosophical investigation in the exact sciences and in social science;

Plastic, those that paint a scene of physical or moral nature, translating a feeling, an impression, depicting a slice of life, a drama, an event in which the complete panorama of a situation appears.

This basic classification admits many specifications, all of which should be supported on the philosophic procedure of the spirit manifested by art. Art is common to all of them, for without artistic form there can be no literary work, whatever its subject matter may be, whatever its scope. For between philosophy and art there is the closest connection: those who scorn form and are negligent of art, expecting it to be enough to look after thought, forget that the latter cannot be understood nor appear in all its splendor when it is presented in a careless, unsuitable and arbitrary exposition: those who give everything to art and to the picturesque, abstaining from thinking or feeling, or thinking falsely, prostitute literature, making it the instrument of errors, of lies, of sophism, and thus, of the perversion of moral progress.

The truth of art is philosophical truth, and the former depends on it. Therefore the spirit needs to investigate truth in a positive way, not led by a theological way of thinking, which assumes imposed dogmas and unproven absolute truths; nor led by a metaphysical way of thinking, which proceeds by attributing reality to abstract, imaginary entities which have no grounding in nature; nor departing from an arbitrary, unproven principle, like that of those philosophers who assemble their system on the false supposition that human progress is a necessary and unavoidable evolution of the nature of humanity, in which freedom has no part; or that of those who accept the idea that every generation has an innate specialty and that it is destined by divinity to widen its physical and moral life, like Virgil, who constructed his *Aeneid* by assigning a providential character to Latin development.

None of the above: philosophical truth should have all the virtues of a positive truth, and the power of art shall consist of revealing it and manifesting it also in a positive way. This is the great standard of the robust literature that is characteristic of a democratic nation, whose intellectual strength should derive all its strength from the independence of the spirit. And do not think that this standard kills feeling; what kills is the straying and the falsity of feeling, not its truth, just as it eliminates error in thought and lends life to its activity.

In this way the rule of composition or of criticism of scientific works, or of the writings that deal with the phenomena of the universe, can be none other than "always support philosophical research or reasoning about positive proofs, and not about negative proofs, or in a demonstration of impossibility, which can be flawed." The basis for reasoning in writings of this sort can only lie in facts proven positively by science.

The rule of composition and of criticism in sociological writings, or works of social science, is that "one should take as a basis for reasoning only the facts founded in human nature and revealed by all the manifestations of this nature." Philosophical investigation and art of this genre of writing should rest always on positive proofs, which give us the test and the attentive observation of the nature of man.

No matter how little we study the nature of man, we understand that he is a being endowed with intellectual faculties, with instincts or affective faculties, and with active faculties; and all these faculties, in the aggregate and in practice, reveal to us a fundamental *tendency* and a *strength*. The tendency is toward increase, to the development of all the latter, therefore there is reason to believe that the purpose of man, that is, his perfection, consists in the complete development of all his faculties, in accordance with the general order of the universe, and to the particular order of each being in that general order, so that the universal balance is maintained. The strength that is revealed in the aggregate and the practice of human faculties in that power we call *freedom*, by virtue of which man selects and uses in all the acts of his life the conditions of his perfection, the means on which his full development depends.

The standard for works of social science originates in the knowledge of these laws of humanity, in such a way that the work that does not conform to this standard is a false, erroneous one, contrary to human nature; for if reasoning does not take those positive laws as its grounding, it attacks the perfection of man or ignores his freedom.

The rule of composition and criticism of exegetic and plastic works is the same as scientific and sociological works, according to the exposition or the painting. If the written discourse is scientific or if the plastic work is a scene from physical nature, its standard lies in the facts demonstrated positively by science. If, on the contrary, exegesis or generalization involves a matter of social science, or if the plastic work is a representation of a feeling, a scene out of life or a social or private situation, its standard lies in the facts of human nature; and if such works be didactic or poetic, they cannot stray from the laws of human nature without pouring out error, doubt, or confusion on the perfection or freedom of man.

This is the general, positive standard of all works of a progressive literature. Those that are not held to that standard can have naught but a false and ephemeral life, they cannot be masterworks, nor are they even works worthy of the progress of a democratic nation, nor can they serve the only goal toward which the independence of the spirit should head, which is social perfection.

Literature should parallel the true idea of the positive progress of humanity. According to this idea, each generation is responsible for its events, for each one has the obligation to complete the experience of previous generations, to correct ideas in the crucible of truth, and not accept blindly the errors and crimes of its forebears; for only in this way can it develop all its faculties, to fulfill its destiny, and take social and individual life to its uttermost intensity.

And how do you all imagine that this can happen if literature, which is the agent and instrument of that obligation that we have to correct and complement past experience, does not have a positive standard to guide it in the investigation and rectification of the laws of the universe and of the laws of humanity? Literature has to be progressive, as is society, and it can never be so without the independence of the spirit, nor can the latter serve that grandiose end if it is not guided by the criterion of laws that run the universe in matters physical and human.

So just because this criterion is positive, literature is going to materialize? No, moral progress has positive truth as its guide; and the imagination and feeling, which are such important parts of developing it, should not be doomed to sing and sanctify lies, or false illusions, or accustomed error in its plastic works. There is more poetry in truth than there is in lies, and an illusion beautified by art has no more worth than the sparkles of a will-o'-the-wisp that dissipates when we draw nigh. Works of the imagination are the very ones most in need of vigorous philosophical investigation, in order to find the truth and represent it, for otherwise they do not co-exist nor advance with humanity; and if the power of their charms or their particulars has merit to perpetuate them as an artistic, but stationary, curiosity, it is because in their proportions lies some dead truth, like that of an Egyptian mummy.

To this end, a writer, explaining the death of the ancient epic, states that: "Epic poems are very unlikely to please one's taste and intelligence, since far from containing the future, progress, and hope, they sing only of the history that is erased, the glories that fade, the missions accomplished, the facts exhausted by experience; to win over their audience, they would need an unheard-of level of superiority in form and a prudent reserve that prevents them from assimilating the past that banishes them with a present harboring new promises. Therefore the true social poems written in verse or in prose are those of Ariosto, Rabelais, Lesage, and among the moderns, those of Eugene Sue* and Victor Hugo, for they have *living humanity as their subject, its emancipation as their object*, without submission to any other authority than that of events."

Only in this way is poetry social and progressive, like science and sociology are, adapting themselves to the laws of humanity, serving its emancipation, depicting its sufferings, its

---

* Ludovico Ariosto (1474–1533), Italian poet, author of the epic 46-canto *Orlando Furioso* (1532); Alain-René Lesage (1668–1747), French novelist, author of *L'Histoire de Gil Blas de Santillane* (4 vols., 1717–35), and playwright; Eugène (Marie-Joseph) Sue (1804–1857), French novelist, author of *Juif errant* (1844–45) (i. e., *The Wandering Jew*), exiled from France for opposition to Napoleon III. —Ed.

deviations, its flaws, and serving its progress and its future through the revelation of the positive laws that lead up to it.

Let us build the progressive literature of a democratic nation, then, on this foundation, and thus will we forge a wide and secure path to the South American spirit, which until today, shrouded in the mists of old and antisocial traditions of anarchic literature from France, has not even been able to serve our moral progress. Allow me to repeat to you what I said of our writers on this score on another occasion:

"There is no South American writer who presents to us in a body of doctrine specific ideas on moral progress, nor positive principles to which social agreements are adapted, nor exact notions that serve as standards for the detailed concepts that the spirit must form about the facts of practical life. The first have illustrated moral and political matters, drinking in their inspiration from French metaphysics, presenting us entities or fictions instead of practical and clear notions; the others have sought to wed that inspiration to theological dogmas, or to doctrines of compromise dreamed up by the eclectic philosophers of the presumed just mean and by the parliamentary statesmen who thought they found the ultimate expression of progress in constitutional monarchy. Alongside all these have appeared positive writers who find the formula for progress in material development, and those who find it in the rule of the principle of authority, or who seek it in the alliance of order and freedom, through a strong authority that is constituted in the physician to the sick man as nation, to administer it freedom by doses, by drops; or that is constituted in the minor's guardian called society, to concede its rights little by little, to make it concessions that that authority alone knows how to measure, that it alone knows how to do opportunely. Other positive writers, finding things past to be devoid of truth, have held fast to justice without defining it, they have proclaimed new principles without demonstrating their truth, they have placed their confidence in the future without deciphering or delineating it: and among the latter there are philosophers who, understanding that the theological way of thinking cannot give us the solution and the criterion for social issues, have vented their rage against religious dogmas and sought to destroy religious sentiment, not realizing that religion can exist without political and moral issues, science, the arts and social instruction, industry, and trade necessarily being ruled and oriented by theological ideas: the religious sentiment and the fundamental idea of religion constitute one of the spheres of the activity of the spirit, which cannot be destroyed; and if moral progress tends to it not dominating the other fundamental ideas, that it not aspire to take the direction completely opposite that of man and society, it should not therefore be denied its freedom, that is, its right, to constitute itself and develop, like all the other aims of humanity. That is the truth that these philosophers have not apprehended, though perhaps if they had, they might have aspired, like others in Europe, to invent a new religion to replace the known ones, which they believed imperfect. The former and the latter philosophers' mistaken aspirations have contributed in no mean measure to rouse religious interests to revolt against moral progress, and to lead religious men astray in a battle in which religion is no longer the union of the soul with God, but a matter of worldly interests. From this frightful chaos of theories and theological and metaphysical doctrines, the speculators, those whom they call the *skillful*, have only profited in America, like in Europe."

Let us do away once and for all with such a perilous situation. Let the criterion of positive truth serve as our oriflamme in this great crusade of the intellect and of freedom. To work, beloved peers! You who have filled my sails so many times in this exhausting journey with the example of your constancy, you who persevere still, and those who begin the work with the spiritedness of youth, brandish that banner faithfully in the triumph of democracy and with the strength that inspires your unshakable love of study! Onward! The emancipation of the spirit: positive truth! That is the mark of victory!

Hear the voice of alarm of the precursor spirit of European democracy, that voice that clamors amidst the still-trembling ruins of the old European monarchy: "Now, all rise, to work, to the task, to fatigue, to the obligation, rise up, intellects! It is about building. Building what? Building where? Building how? We reply: Building the nation. Building it in progress. Building it through education!"

This is the task that lies before modern literature. In it lies its grandeur, its honor, its immortality!

END OF PART TWO

PART THREE
The Academy of Belles Lettres

I

The address we have just transcribed did not give rise to arguments and polemics like that of 1842 had done. The press merely reproduced it or paid it a few tributes. Nevertheless, the literary doctrines it set down as fundamental, or rather, as the course of action that the free development of our literature ought to take, were meticulously studied and debated by the youths who sought to cultivate art independently. And we mention this since for the longest time we were responding to verbal and written judgments on those doctrines, and we passed with flying colors in the assessment of South American writers who, like the eminent Argentine man of letters, Juan María Gutiérrez,* supported our point of view on the characteristics of Spanish-American literature.

Still, the circumstances in those days were not favorable to literary studies, and men of letters found themselves bound by the political duties that the situation imposed upon them. This was extraordinary in every way, because the coalition of conservative and liberal elements in power rendered the Pérez administration utterly powerless to undertake unimpeded politi-

---

* *José* María Gutiérrez (1831–1903), was an Argentine lawyer and writer, and associate of Mitre, first constitutional president of Argentina, 1862–1868. —Ed.

cal reform, which was actually the historical event for which the social drift had set the stage, and which the vox populi had imposed.*

Said coalition lent the ruling class the nature of a veritable center party, one of those in which by its nature are more suitable, in the felicitous phrase of a French statesman, to paving the way for situations than to having a say over them. Yet, since in this party not only did the conservative interests have the upper hand, but also the clerical circle prevailed, they who were born into the fold of the liberals, the latter of which had believed they would shore up their ranks with it to fight the Montt administration's policies, the administration of 1869 could not loyally arrange a new situation.

Thus the Pérez administration on the one hand seemed to serve the reform demanded by national opinion, to make it run aground in the sense that it did no damage to the organization of absolute power, defended by the interests and doctrines of the conservatives; and on the other hand, believing that these interests and doctrines constituted its main strength, delegated public functions to the circle of reactionaries, mainly those at the University and in teaching, which were the duties they most craved. The liberals who were enlisted in the ruling party unconditionally served this policy, either in order not to lose their status, or because they lacked the support to change it. This passive stance stood out against the activity that the reactionary circle was engaged in to back its bold demands; moreover, the administration naturally sought its defenders not so much among the liberals, who were wanting in organization, as among the adepts of the freemason lodges that the clerical circle had organized for making war, in the name of religion, not only against the prerogatives of the State and the social freedoms condemned by the Church, but also against the industrial property of the newspapers that, like *El Ferrocarril* and *La Patria*, were accused of heresy for not defending ecclesiastic interests.

In the throes of such a situation as this, the elections for representatives were held in 1870, and for President of the Republic in 1871, so political interests around that time absorbed the attention of independent and liberal spirits. The new President, informed by the governmental coalition, could not oppose the situation that the latter had brought into being and which constituted its strength and main foundation. If the lofty aspirations of the elect prompted him to free his administration from the reactionary element's interests, as occurred ensuingly, the circumstances of his coming to power forced him then to rule as his predecessor had, and to further the same policy that he had had an efficient hand in founding. The new administration was organized with the elements of the previous one, conferring on the clerical constituent a

* Reference is to the administration of José Joaquín Pérez Moscayano (1800– 1889), Liberal president, 1861–1871. —Ed.

more direct and effective participation, for it gave one of the leaders of this circle the position of Minister of Justice, Culture, and Public Education.

The clerical party from that moment on came to rule Chile, and already being in control of the University and the public institutions of primary school, middle school, and advanced education, it had everything for crowning its victory once it had the Ministry of Public Education at its disposal. Having brought together and strengthened that party under shelter of the moderate liberals and the decided support of the Pérez administration, whom the latter served, it had been able to establish the organization of the ultramontane Catholics in Europe, boasting of its submissions to the foreign power of the government in Rome, of its principles and doctrines of divine right, of its zeal to subject national sovereignty to spiritual sovereignty and civil law to canonical law; and all with the approbation of the government of the Republic, which never had wished to see the danger and the threat that that organization entailed against the freedom of society and against the independence of the State.

The ultramontanes' gospel was the *Syllabus*,* turned shortly thereafter into the canons of the Vatican Council; and the Minister of Public Education, who was the government representative of the interests and doctrines of that party, could only obey and fulfill the declaration of that papal bull that excommunicated and condemned for heresy all who stated and maintained that "in a well-constituted society, popular schools open to children of all classes in the nation, such as in general the public institutions devoted to the teaching of literature, to advanced education and the training of youth, must needs be free of the authority of the Church, of all directive influence and of all intervention on the latter's part; also, that they be wholly subject to the decisions of civil authority, in conformity with the will of the government and following the generally received opinions of the age" (*Syllabus*, prop. XLVII).

This canon would have a faithful observer in the government, and it was expected that all measures taken by the Ministry of Public Education be directed toward establishing the complete monopoly of the ultramontane Church in State-sponsored education, with a view to wiping out all liberal, civilizing influence on the education of youth; for it is likewise a heresy, following proposition LXXV of the *Syllabus*, to imply that "the Roman Pontifice can and should fall in step with progress, liberalism, and modern civilization."

* Reference is to the *Syllabus of Errors*, the Allocution attached by Pius IX to the Encyclical *Quanta Cura* of 8 December 1864. *Quanta Cura* consists mainly of a denunciation of liberalism and modern secular culture and civilization. In it and in the *Syllabus* the Papacy denounced rationalism, pantheism, naturalism, socialism, communism, secret societies, and clerical-liberal societies, and defended the temporal powers of the Papacy in matters of Church-state relations and the concept of one true faith. It is one of the quintessential documents of Catholic conservatism and ultramontanism, hence important to nineteenth-century Chileans. —Ed.

Nevertheless, the reaction could not prevail this time out, as it had before, despite, as we have noted, its still having the means to crown its victory, given that the party that undertook it was a constituent of the government, imposed by circumstance, and since among the rulers there had been no systematic royalists, nor dogmatic or radical liberals.

And triumph it could not, for literary progress had already been consolidated, to the point of having spawned a national literature, in which the new idea had powerful supporters, both of whom were able and knew how to keep it alive. It was of no account that the political party that had served the liberal cause had been virtually vanquished by the forces of conservative and retrograde circles to whom it had capitulated, surrendering to them its banner in exchange for preserving itself as a kind of auxiliary legion. Nor did it matter that after the coalition in the presidential election, they had disarmed the political circles that had waged merciless war on it. The circumstance of the age was still fully standing and operative: *the need for reform.* This was the social and historical phenomenon of the time; and it had been fashioned slowly and patiently by the literary progress, rather than by the parties' demands and dealings. The servants of that progress, asserting the independence of the spirit, had flooded the entire country's outlook with light, and the country had understood and felt that need, freeing itself from the interests of the old regime, which had so forcefully been upheld in the institutions and the organization of the powers that be.

That event holding sway, then, the dominant coalition was forced to take the name of *moderate Liberal* Party, and compelled the ultramontanes to adopt the strategy of their kindred in Europe, a tactic that meant seeking to rebuild their former power in the name of freedom, dubbing even the most absolute powers of the Church with the name of freedom.

By dint of these ploys, the reaction sought to make its way, and through disarming political circles in the first year of the new presidency, scarcely another voice of leadership was to be heard save that issuing from the political and literary centers of the ultramontane reaction. Leaving aside the latter's productions, since, whatever their artistic merit, their aim was not to speak only for a fringe interest in the literary movement, we will recall that the clerical political press pitched a reckless battle against the legal system of the State and of society, aping the tone, gall, and insolence of the ultramontane press in France and Belgium, failing to notice that the same blind violence of their attack hurt the defense of their cause and their attainment of power.

The *Revista Católica* on 8 July 1871, for instance, examining two judgments handed down by the Supreme Court on two appeals, unhesitatingly held that civil law ought hold its peace in the face of the Church's wishes, and issued a ban of the magistrates of the Supreme Court, paving the way for censures and excommunications that the bishops later were to hurl against national representation and the government of their country for not submitting to the foreign sovereignty of Rome. Among other things the newspaper stated that "the superiority of the canons to the civil law code is as evident to Catholicism as much as the Church, in fulfilling its divine mission, *has the authority to reprove or condemn the civil laws* it deems contrary either to dogma, to morality, or simply to *canonical discipline.* Thus does one clearly deduce from the following proposition from the *Syllabus: LVII. Philosophy, morality, and civil laws can and should refuse the authority of God and of the Church.* That obligation to obey the law of the Church over that of the State, which still exists in the civil magistrates, in addition to deriving from the Catholic doctrines we have set forth above, can be corroborated through the very conduct of the Church, which is assisted by the Holy Ghost in matters pertaining not only to dogma but also to overall discipline. In fact, the Church is well aware that the civil laws establish the recourse to force; and yet, it condemns with the severest of its penalties the judges that accept them. . . . So, then, let their lordships the ministers of the High Court say what they will, those among us who voted for the appeal declared in the sentence that we have been discussing, have incurred in an *anathema* reserved for the Pope's jurisdiction, as decreed in the *Apostolicæ Sedis,* which was proclaimed in the Vatican Council. Here are its terms: 'Therefore we declare subject to *latæ sententiæ* excommunication especially reserved for the Sovereign Pontiff's use the following: VI. Those who directly or indirectly impede the exercising of ecclesiastic jurisdiction, be it from the internal forum, be it from the external, and those that with this purpose have recourse to the secular authority, those that seek its commandments, *those that dictate them,* or those that abet, counsel or favor those individuals.'"*

II

Nevertheless, this menacing activity on the part of the clerical press, even though it carried the divine word and defended the interests of the Church, which were so strongly constituted and so openly supported by political power, found the liberal opinion of the country impassable. The

* The Pérez administration had sanctioned and publicly announced on 20 December 1869 a law assisting with 20,000 pesos, for travel expenses, the bishops of Chile that had gone to the Vatican Council to establish this canon, which was put in place to anathematize the Supreme Court, and all the old canons that attack the sovereignty of the Republic.

independent dailies that sought to represent this opinion did not feel the need to discuss the enormous demands that press made; and when they did, they did not persist ardently and even capitulated, through error or affinity with the feigned clerical freedoms, such as with the freedom of teaching in the ultramontane sense, which was demanded and defended in order to monopolize teaching in favor of the Church.

Wonder of the age! Why is the powerful reaction undertaken to reestablish the spiritual rule of the ultramontane Church in modern society so ineffectual? Why do its passionate efforts, its immense divine power, though buttressed by the strength and the despotism of political power, run headlong into that inertia of sorts in which society whiles away, only emerging from it sporadically, and then just to raise its voice, and not to lift a finger? The fact is that this reaction runs up against the truth and against the experience that makes of that truth the patrimony of universal conscience. The Papacy endeavored to establish, under the pontificate of Pius IX, its traditional policy of thoroughgoing domination of society and civil power; but since now, in seeking an earthly empire, it not only came across the sovereignty of kings, as before, but also the sovereignty of nations and the new principles that constitute modern civil society and the independence of the States, it blasted these principles, national sovereignty, the freedoms of conscience, worship, education, and of the press, against all individual, social, and political liberties, their formidable anathema of the *Syllabus* and of the encyclical of 8 December 1864.* And nevertheless the servants of this intruding policy have tried to impose it in the name of morality and freedom, thereby placing itself in a continual contradiction, which they have had no success in concealing with their theological and metaphysical equivocations, even in the eyes of the Church itself, which is more logical and aboveboard in its intrusion, let alone in the eyes of natural law and educated opinion.

In another work† we sought to describe this situation, condensing the impartial observation of modern wisdom in this connection in the following terms, which there will be no objection to our transcribing, the better to explain the reaction's helplessness in the days we are recollecting:

> The Catholic Church—we stated—is indisputably well within its rights for wanting civil law not to interfere with its indepen-

---

* I.e., *Quanta Cura.* —Ed.

† Lastarria, *Lecciones de política positiva, profesadas en la Academia de Bellas Letras* (1875) ["Lessons in Positive Philosophy, Imparted in the Academy of Belles Lettres"] Lec. IV, paragraph II, "El Estado y la religión" ["The State and Religion"], page 103, Paris Edition. —Ed.

dence; but it also demands that that law not regulate the conditions of certain legal functions of civil status, such as matrimony, nor that it support dissidents in their beliefs, nor that it have jurisdiction over the civil actions of the ecclesiastics or over the latter's rebellion against the laws, nor that it fund the Catholic religion; as if civil matrimony, birth, and death, as if the freedom of belief and religion, as if the abolition of ecclesiastic jurisdiction, and as if the cessation of budget subsidies were not a few other necessary consequences of the independence that the Church itself clamors for and of its separation from the State.

The Catholic Church less defensibly wishes to keep its title as teacher of morality, and as its dogmas exclude the freedom of inquiry, it clings to the idea of retaining that of arbiter of truth. Yet therewith it seeks also to completely lord over the spheres of activity of the two fundamental ideas of morality and science, which have the same right as that of religion to maintain their own independence; for social progress would grind to a halt if one of these ideas held sway over another, or if the three were taken under State control. In morality, such an aspiration ignores two experimental truths, that there is a universal morality independent of all religious dogma, and that for that very reason, the morality that all religions teach and practice is analogous; so a religious belief, whatever its dogmatic truth, cannot, without attacking freedom of conscience and also without making an attempt against independence and the development of the moral activity of society, seek to have other beliefs, that man, family, and society not profess or practice any other morality than the one it teaches. In the sciences, that pretension is even more pernicious and impracticable, for, even believing that a revealed religion, whichever it may be, possesses the absolute truth, no believer in good faith can be right in maintaining that this truth is any other than the religious one, and that God, in revealing it, has wished to go against the grain of the laws of human nature, linking intellectual growth to a dogma outside of which physical and moral nature cannot be studied, and with which those that profess it can condemn scientific and sociological truth whose evidence they cannot deny. Religious truths are individual convictions that lack the universal evidence of scientific truths, and that cannot be imposed upon science without stopping intellectual progress cold, and without dealing a blow against the freedom of the spirit, the freedom of conscience, and against equality and peace in society.

Apologists for the new Catholic dogmas stand up for this invading claim in the name of freedom: it is no wonder, since in its special phraseology, all absolute powers attributed to the infallible Church for having sway over the State are termed freedoms, subjecting civil law to its canonical law in order to rule over morality, the sciences, and letters, in teaching and practice. The power to regulate people's marital status, to curb the State's jurisdiction, to subdue all beliefs; these are a few of the Catholic Church's freedoms. The power to dictate morality, to rule the realm of science, are others; and everything that society and the State do to check that invasion of powers is an attack on the freedoms of the Church, oppression that renders it a victim of despotism, leaving it only to lash out and complain by way of defense. Thus the absolute monarchs who have been dethroned by the tides of reform, or who have had to agree to them, thus limiting their own arbitrariness, have also been able to complain of the loss of their freedom to rule over everything. A strange abuse of the word *freedom*, which, although in Greek and Roman civilizations it meant self-rule, and in the Middle Ages, property, in the Modern Age it means only law, it neither is nor can it be other than the use of law. So, for instance, in that vernacular it is called the freedom of education, not the faculty of teaching or learning at will without subjection to preventive or coercive measures, which is a right, for it is a condition of intellectual development, which the State should serve and further, with the exception of State interference, so that the Church replace the State in its deeds, and can renounce all teachings that are not in keeping with its dogma. As a result, freedom is not freedom, or rather, it is not the right but the suppression of the right and the triumph of spiritual enslavement.

The truth of these observations lies in the conscience of all men, and each effortlessly can prove it to be a natural fact. Herein lies the explanation of how that ultramontane reaction, which seemed practically victorious in the politics of that time, was powerless to preside over either the literary progress based on the independence of spirit or the social trend toward reform and the possession of freedom.

In 1872, despite the silence of the liberals that represented this trend, and that no other political party seemed to be at work besides the conservative ultramontane party; despite that public attention was concerned only with industrial and stock market performance, two literary journals came out: the

Revista de Santiago, a twice-monthly publication edited by don Fanor Velasco and don Augusto Orrego Luco, and the *Revista Médica de Chile*, a monthly publication devoted to the cultivation of medicine and the natural sciences, under the editorship of Messrs. Murillo, Philippi, Zorrilla, and Schneider, with the collaboration of Messrs. Aguirre, de la Barra and Lastarria, Bixio, Díaz, Leiva, Miguel, Peña, Salamanca, Silva, and Vanzina. In La Serena a few months previously in 1871, the *Revista Científica y Literaria*, a new weekly journal published by don Enrique Blondel, had appeared also.

This *Revista de Santiago* was not tauted as the continuation of the publication that had put out under the same title three series from 1848 to 1849 and from 1850 to 1855; and to judge by certain particulars that characterized its appearance, it was considered an echo of the moderate liberal footsoldiers of the dominant politics. The circumstances at the time, the editorial tone, and even its language gave the *Revista* unique standing in the history of our literary and liberal progress. The publication did not propose preserving and continuing the tradition of the literary movement, and its editors declared that they would print on its cover the words *Literatura, Artes y Ciencias* ["Literature, Arts and Sciences"] like a comprehensive and indeterminate inscription, or like "*a somewhat flexible motto*"—they stated—that could be expanded or narrowed according to our resources and as circumstances warranted. Under this *rubric*—they added—"we shall include poetry, customs, criticism, biography, and—why not just come right out with it?—we shall also include *politics*, but politics that can keep its distance from the impetuosity of the passions to take up residence in the more serene regions of observation and principle."

Subsequently, the *Revista*, to bring off this plan, featured two political articles. In the section entitled *Miradas retrospectivas* ["Backward Glances"] it unleashed a hailstorm of criticism against subjecting the parties to the outcome of the presidential election, censures that were far from issuing from the serene regions of observation and principle, in a way no more upstanding than that of the plan. "A day on the brink of despair," the article stated, "was succeeded by a day of hope; and if the believers did not sacrifice on the altar of today's idol, at least they did not declare it an incorrigible deity, nor did they judge it unworthy of cautious worship. That caused something of an uproar among the youthful souls, and being youngsters, they were inexperienced; but later it was said that that was the way to practice politics in the republican nations, that the Yankees rip each other to shreds around the electoral table and that once the vote count is in, the hatchet is buried. If this was progress, we ignore it. Above all, we cannot consider it as such. Men of honor do not fight more than once. Afterward forgiving is wont to come, but forgetting, impossible. To make war today only to hobnob tomorrow, to drag another's good name through the mire only to then have the pleasure of polishing it clean, to preach extremes today only to counsel moderation tomorrow, to exclaim today *impossible!* to reply tomorrow *acceptable!*, today a war to the death and tomorrow an unconditional peace, all this can be most wise and very politic, but it is to do as the fishwives in the marketplace do. . . . Hence an intensely expectant situation. The President of the Republic governs amidst an Octavian peace. One group fawns around him; the others would *like* to fawn around him. Among Christian principles peace and harmony reign. Some men have distanced themselves, but they have taken the precaution of staying at a suitable remove that allows them to come running quick at the first sign. The others, the former adversaries, are still distant; but upon hearing how they clear their throats from time to time lest they be left in oblivion, we understand that they do not foresee any insurmountable obstacle in their way. Regrettably, the pretense and power went on as always holding many in the antechamber and a select few in the reception room of his confidence. . . ."

The other political article was entitled *El peor enemigo de lo bueno es lo mejor* ["The Worst Enemy of the Good is the Best Thing"] and aimed to raise to the level of good political doctrine the tactic of acquiescing to conservative demands and backward-thinking interests, a strategy adopted by the moderate liberals to make halfway, deceptive efforts to carry out the reforms for which the country clamored. But the writer's skill did not manage to hide that this tactic, which sought to turn the reforms into compromise settlements, was diametrically opposed to the true logic of all political reform, which can never be useful and advantageous if it is not true and therefore radical. "Those concessions merely reinforce the shortcomings of the spurious regime, and to welcome them just to get something in return is a swindle bringing in its wake only a nation steeped in wrong-headed and depraved practices, instead of habituating it to the truth of the representative system. . . . The political future of modern nations is much better off not practicing the true representative system than taking to one disfigured by the flaws and errors that sully it, for in the latter case they will never understand it, nor have interest or fondness for it."[*]

Thus was the tenor of the *Revista de Santiago* in 1872, and thus was the cause of the poor impression its appearance made on those who kept alive our literary movement's tradition. Out of the country at the time, we got wind at our solitary retreat of the evidence of that poor impression; and if we recall it, to point it out to you readers as a cause of the situation the *Re-*

---

[*] *Lecciones de política positiva* ["Lessons in Positive Politics"], Lesson IX, paragraph III. See Lesson V, paragraph VII, "Reforma social y política, su procedimiento científico" ["Social and Political Reform, Its Scientific Procedure"].

vista was in, it is not to condone those that groundlessly assume that we disapprove of what we did not play a role in, nor because neither then nor now have we failed to appreciate and respect the worthy writers who imparted that character to the publication, but first of all, because we have taken on the task of relating and faithfully characterizing the literary events of our age; second, because despite the tone of the first issue of the *Revista*, we were confident that it would become the rallying point for freelance writers, and to this effect we spurred on our friends.

In effect, soon thereafter the *Revista de Santiago* was the agency of those writers' scientific and literary lucubrations; its founders, especially Mr. Velasco, took a firm and noble stance against the ultramontanes' pretensions, shedding light in well-considered articles on current affairs, like education in State schools, which was in the most danger for the attacks that the clerical writers and the minister representing them in the government launched against it in the name of freedom.

The same overweening aspirations of the clerical party and the daring with which its minister wished to satiate them, cautioned of the common danger to the moderate liberals, who began to react against their own work, seeking to eliminate from the government an element that they themselves had engendered and consolidated to the point of giving it representation in power.

III

A t the outset of 1873, public opinion supported that reaction latent in the heart of the regnant party, and it looked like the erstwhile political coalition of rearguards and liberals was reaching the end of the line. The Minister of Public Education's actions had been a violent jolt to the country's conscience.

The reaction had been accused of having carried off the plan to bring down the national schools and disband public education in favor of clerical education. In the 1 April issue of the *Revista de Santiago*, one of the most distinguished writers of the ruling liberal circle finished as follows the first of his articles on State and public education: "Ultramontanism understands that well," he said, "and it tends its efforts toward it. The press preaches the word and sows it by example. Due to its maneuvering, the Instituto Na-

327

cional has been on the verge of giving in. The provincial secondary schools have its most cordial antipathy. It bolts down not one more seat, nor does it open one more new class in the State schools; but instead all its applause and all its benevolence are reserved for the ecclesiastical institutions that, like that of San Felipe, offer the public a bit of counterfeit science."

The University Council meantime argued heatedly, not vocally but through long written Reports, the issue of school exams. The liberal council members endured government control of all examinations, against all the Presbyterians who represented there the aims of the ultramontanes, who moreover had alarmed the public with a project to reform the humanities course, reducing classes to the topics and the size that an ancient papal bull had stipulated.

In March, the Minister of Public Education had reorganized the Instituto Nacional, placing it under the management of the ultramontanes. There was widespread agitation. On the 26th of that same month a well-attended popular gathering in Valparaíso denounced and attacked the ultramontane minister's actions, and the press in all sectors of the Republic reproduced the lengthy speeches made by the orators at that meeting, which for its importance and seriousness represented the general opinion in its protests.

This stir had awakened in all servants of the unaligned and liberal literary movement the feeling that an organization was needed. We were returning in those days from a grueling pilgrimage in the desert of Bolivia, and reciprocating the sentiment of our former cohorts, we set to task.

But that organization could not be useful, nor serve, as was desired, as a center and support for teaching and for literary art, independent of sectarian doctrines and political interests, if it did not rest on fixed principles that established the norm, the criterion, the blueprint for a true philosophic school. And it was all the more necessary to do it thus, because the ultramontanes' literary organization had a strong foundation in their ecclesiastic dogmas and canons.

This idea was accepted, and on 29 March the *Academia de Bellas Letras* ["Academy of Belles Lettres"] was founded via the following charter:

> Gathering the undersigned, we officially declare that we commit to the founding, organizing, and maintaining of a literary society under the name of the Academy of Belles Lettres, adopting as fundamental statutes the bases we have previously accepted and whose purport is as follows:

> FIRST

> The Academy of Belles Lettres has the objective of cultivating the literary art as an expression of philosophic truth, adopting as

a rule of composition and criticism, in scientific works, its adherence to the facts demonstrated in a positive way by science, and in sociological works and works of serious literature, its adherence to the laws of the development of human nature. In its studies it shall give preference to that of the Spanish language as the foremost element of the literary art, to perfect it, in accordance with its nature, and to mold it to the social, scientific, and literary advancements of the age.

SECOND

The founders of the Academy shall confer the title of such and that of honorary Academy members to the distinguished writers in this genre, and also to unlettered persons that lend some advantage to the promotion of the institution.

THIRD

All aficionados of the pursuit of literature can attend the Academy's private sessions, and deliver lectures in them, without any other requisite save that of being introduced and signed on by a founding Academy member or honorary member.

FOURTH

The Academy will have private and periodical sessions frequently; also, it will hold them in public to give readings or lectures to all that freely attend.

FIFTH

The founding Academy members shall remit, upon joining, a sum of not less than forty pesos, and shall pay two pesos monthly thereafter to form the Academy's fund.

The honorary Academy members shall only pay twenty-five pesos for their diploma.

SIXTH

When sufficient funds are available, the Academy shall pay an honorarium of not less than twenty pesos for each public reading or for each lecture given in public on a scientific or literary topic, whenever the reading or lesson should fall in line with the institution's plan.

SEVENTH

The Academy shall have a President, two Vice-Presidents, a Secretary, and a Treasurer, and with a view to delegating the organizational and procedural tasks, all its members shall be divided into three sections: one for sciences, another for sociology, and the third for belles lettres.

EIGHTH

A special regulation shall describe these bylaws in detail.

To proceed without ado to the organization of the Academy of Belles Lettres, the following agreements have been entered: 1st. To commission don D. Barros Arana and don F. S. Asta-Buruaga to present proposed constitutional bylaws, which the association is to adopt for its functions. 2nd. To appoint a temporary board comprising of don J. V. Lastarria, President; don D. Santa María and don M. L. Amunátegui, Vice-Presidents; don E. Cood, Treasurer, and don E. de la Barra, Secretary. 3rd. To hold private sessions Saturdays at seven thirty at night.—J. V. Lastarria, A. C. Gallo, D. Barros Arana, Miguel Luis Amunátegui, E. de la Barra, Jacinto Chacón, D. Arteaga Alemparte, Marcial González, B. Vicuña Mackenna, F. S. Asta-Buruaga, A. Vergara Albano, A. Valderrama, D. Santa María, Demetrio Lastarria, Daniel Lastarria, Enrique Cood, Pedro Godoy, Benjamín Lavín Matta, Marcial Martínez, F. Vargas Fontecilla.

A few days later more adhered to the basic principles, and were elected founders, in addition to the following as corresponding members:

Founders:

Messrs. Juan de Dios Arlegui, Benicio Alamos González, Ramón Allende Padín, Alejandro Andonaegui, José Alfonso, Manuel Blanco Cuartín, Daniel Barros Grez, José Manuel Balmaceda, Juan Bruner, Miguel Cruchaga, Juan Nepomuceno Espejo, Santiago Estrada, Pedro León Gallo, Eugenio María Hostos, Jorge Segundo Huneeus, Hermógenes de Irisarri, Sandalio Letelier, Pedro Lira, Manuel Antonio Matta, Guillermo Matta, G. René Moreno, Ambrosio Montt, Adolfo Murillo, Manuel José Olavarrieta, Augusto Orrego Luco, Nicolás Peña Vicuña, Santiago Prado, Uldaricio Prado, Baldomero Pizarro, Luis Rodríguez Velasco, Joaquín Santa Cruz, Fanor Velasco, José Francisco Vergara, José Ignacio Vergara, Francisco Vidal Gormaz, José Zegers Recasens, Ignacio Zenteno.

Sponsoring Academy member: Mr. Federico Varela.

National correspondent Academy members: Messrs. Alberto Blest Gana, Guillermo Blest Gana, Manuel Bilbao, Alejandro Carrasco Albano; Mrs. Rosario Orrego de Uribe.

Foreign correspondents:

Messrs. Cecilio Acosta, Justo Arosemena, Manuel Ancízar, J. Antonio Barrenechea, José R. Bustamante, Pedro Carbo, Daniel Calvo, Miguel Antonio Caro, J. G. Courcelle-Seneuil, Aristóbulo del Valle, J. Manuel Estrada, Carlos Guido Spano, Florentino González, Juan María Gutiérrez, Luis M. Guzmán, Claudio Gay, Luis Guimaraes Junior, Ricardo O. Limardo, Vicente Fidel López, Bartolomé Mitre, Pedro Moncayo, Ricardo Palma, Amado Pissis, D. Rocha, Arístedes Rojas, José María Rojas Garrido, José M. Santibáñez, José M. Samper, J. Simeón Tejeda, J. M. Torres Caicedo, Francisco de Paula Vigil.

The Academy used its first sessions to organize definitively. It set down its charter, divided in sections to delegate tasks, and adopted the emblems of its diplomas and seal in this way:

1st. The emblem on the diplomas consists of a shining sun in whose center appears an Isis, or goddess of nature, crowned with twelve stars; she bears in one hand a scepter capped with a terraqueous globe, and in the other an eagle taking flight, and a moon at her feet. This emblem, taken from the theosophy of the Egyptians, represents the universal fertility in the goddess of nature. The sun symbolizes creative power and the crown of stars the path of that star in the Zodiac; the scepter is the sign of perpetual movement of nature in things created and yet to be; the eagle stands for the heights to which the spirit can soar in its free exploration, and the moon placed at the deity's feet represents the infinity of matter and its domination by the spirit. The aggregate of all this in Egyptian arcana heralded a strong showing for the enterprises in which the activity that sows the seeds is linked with the uprightness of the spirit that brings the works to fruition. The philosophical assertion that expressed this thought among them, and that the Academy adopted as a motto for placement above the sunrays, is this: TO ASSERT THE TRUTH IS TO SEEK JUSTICE.

2nd. The emblem on the great seal is a circle of roses bordered by equidistant figures: a man's head, another a bull's, the third a lion's, the fourth an eagle's. These signs, which were the attributes of the Sphinx, mean: the human head, intelligence, which, before taking action, must study the goal of its aspirations, the means of attaining it and the obstacles it is to evade or hurdle; the bull's head, that the man armed with science should have a tireless will and a foolproof patience for opening his mind and making his way successfully; the lion's head, that it does not suffice to have will in order to attain the object selected by the intelligence, but one also needs bravery; and the eagle's head, that caution is necessary until the moment of working with the resolution that soars toward the empyrean.

In the 23 April 1873 session, the Academy was officially inaugurated. Let us consign here the inaugural address for the opening, which was published on 4 May by *El Ferrocarril*, whose editorial carried the following pleasant words of introduction:

"At this time of disgust, in which disdain for noble things is in good taste and even fashionable, it does our hearts good to see there are still spirits that do not jump on the bandwagon and that believe in the future.

"This is what the organization, or we might well say, the founding of the Academy of Belles Lettres, promises.

"Its conception occurs to one of our most indefatigable fighters, Mr. Lastarria, and in a few days it becomes a reality. Its promoter might well say: 'I came, I saw, I conquered.'

"And everything predicts for the Academy a long and full life; for the proposal aims to breathe life into the intellectual activity in our country, providing a headquarters for those who still know how to think and still wish to work for art and science, which are beauty, goodness, understanding, courage for the heart, and wings for the soul.

"We expect that the handful of initiators shall not sow in unrewarding soil. There is a most marked trend beginning to develop in our country toward works of the intellect, which will grow strong the minute it shakes off the isolation and indifference that assail it. The Academy, seeking a meeting place for the noble of spirit, will create among them strength and constancy of purpose, which always bring unity through a common goal.

"What will the Academy be?

"This is what the masterful words of its president will tell us, that illustrious veteran who, after forty years of study, of work, of struggle, of glorious defeats, of cruel pains and all too few victories, today carries on with the ardor, the momentum, the spiritedness, the hope of the youngest. If misfortunes have wracked him, they have also revived him, and he believes today in the future as much as he did on the first day in which he began to serve it. The enviable privilege of noble souls!

"Now, let us lend an ear to Mr. Lastarria."

ADDRESS BY THE DIRECTOR OF THE ACADEMY OF BELLES LETTRES IN THE 26 APRIL 1873 FOUNDING SESSION

Gentlemen:
Organizing this Academy with fifty men of letters, among them the country's most outstanding, has been a few days' work, and was brought off without a hitch.

Let us mark well such an event, whose extraordinariness knows no end, especially if one considers that we have come here from different paths, forsaking the causes that kept us separated, that drove us far, far from the path that, in better days, we had all cleared together.

There is doubtless some higher interest that once again gives unity to our efforts, and that offers us the certainty that the new enterprise will not dissolve as easily as it came together. Life overall is all the more brief the more precocious it is in its development; but there are lianas in our America that grow in no time, and whose shoots nevertheless acquire the strength of the centuries-old tree in which they are entangled, and they live with it to a ripe old age.

If our enterprise responds to a need in our society, if the interest that so easily brought us together is nurtured in the focal point of our great social interests, we should have no doubt that our work will be lasting, or that it will sow seeds, if we do not lack for willpower, and if, when the time is right, we have the heart to oppose the slings and arrows of fortune.

Also, our association has the unquestionable aim of satisfying a social need. The circumstance of all of us having fearlessly and openly adopted the first cornerstone of our institution is proof enough of that; our association, in establishing as its objective the cultivation of the literary art, embraces as a rule of composition and of criticism, its agreement with the facts proven in a positivist way by science, and in sociological works and belles lettres, their conformity with the laws of the development of human nature, which are *Freedom* and *Progress*.

We defined the goal of our aspirations thus because we all feel, understand, and assert a noble truth: that literature should live up to the true idea of the positive progress of humanity. And since the truth has the power to join men together, we therefore have come hastily from the different circles in which we moved to assemble in service to that great truth in the only way possible: by adopting a criterion that, while leaving the independence of the spirit in full force, also guides it and gives it the key to study and investigate the phenomena of the physical and moral universes.

The study of letters and science in democratic nations like the South American ones can definitely not have any other basis for investigating the truth than the independence of the spirit, an independence that constitutes one of the most valuable rights of man, one of the rights or freedoms that make up the essence and subsistence of democracy, for without making them hold fast or without practicing them, in no nation can democracy exist.

Nor how can literature live up to the true idea of the positive progress of humanity if the spirit endure the least bondage, if it were to be subject to some predominance alien to its independence, to any party interest? In a situation of that sort, letters and science would be pure conventions of convenience, and the literature that represents them would be a narrow one, sterile, leaving no choice but to adopt platitudes and received wisdom. A literature like that, fitting only to train sophistic writers and poseur artists, appears periodically in history as a sure sign of the social and political decline of the great empires that have established, as their power base, the unity of death.

In history, that has been the necessary outcome of the attempts aimed to restrict the independence of the human spirit; and conversely, wherever the spirit has been free to study nature, accepting as true only what is in keeping with its eternal laws, there have letters and science flourished, and literature has been able to live up to the true idea of human progress, like in ancient Greece, like in modern Germany, and above all in the American Union, whose literature is now in an infancy more robust, more resonant, and more consistent with positive progress than that of the former nations.

We Spanish-speaking South Americans can and should also aspire to such a literature, and we doubtlessly will achieve it if we place letters and science on a high plane, above that of the momentary interests that divide us, and if we study them only in the interest of truth, of positive truth in physical nature, and the positive truth in the human order, adopting as a criterion of the former the observable proof of phenomena, and as a criterion of the latter its conformity with freedom and with the development of an intelligent being's faculties, which are the two foremost laws of human nature.

This is the legitimate aspiration that serves as our link; this is the social need that has gathered us together; this is the task on which we are going to work together.

Now that the goal of our aspirations is defined, the means of serving it are readily understood: they amount to intelligent work lead by the positive criterion we have adopted. We will not reach this goal, for it is too grandiose to be the work of a single generation; but at least we will have charted the course if we have the firmness of will, the courage, and the prudence to instill a love and understanding of it among those who follow us in the enterprise of upholding this motto, which is that of our society: TO ASSERT THE TRUTH IS TO SEEK JUSTICE.

It is with good reason that we have surrounded this meaningful axiom with the symbols with which the theosophy of the ancient Egyptians represented intelligence, staying power, courage, and prudence; for these are the moral forces we shall set in motion to serve the ends of our institution.

It is not enough for the intelligence to understand the truth for it to reach out and grasp it, and to see that it is accepted. A firm will is also needed for seeking and proving it, for loving it and spreading that love to others, for sowing it and scattering it abroad, getting the better of mistaken opinions only through reason, fighting adverse interests without wounding or exacerbating them. This work of tolerance and love cannot be carried out without courage and prudence. We must begin by overcom-

ing the spurs of our own egotism by rising above discouragement and the setbacks that we come across at every step in a
task removed from the motivations of ambition and greed; for
only thus will we be able to vanquish the foreign obstacles we
will find in our way, and take judicious advantage of propitious
opportunities for asserting the truth.

Luckily, those obstacles are not insurmountable in the present age, at least in the moral order; for the age is one of debate,
of constant aspirations to justice, and errors and lies scarcely
have a shadow of the brute force that in days gone by the
scepter of absolute power held in his hands. Perhaps, or probably, the only serious impediment to our efforts will be the material one, that of insufficient resources for publicizing the product
of our studies through the medium of the press and via public
readings and lectures.

These means of spreading the truth need something that the
men of letters as a rule do not have, and that the princes of fortune could only provide if they were to understand that when
material and intellectual development do not run parallel,
progress stalls, and society in its progression loses the stability
that guarantees its future.

The day we can foster study through recitations and public
readings, the helping hand the Academy can lend to popular
education will be stretched out; and the fruit of our labors,
which elsewise would not leave the private confines of our humble abode, will become public domain, stimulate the intellect of
the youth and offer a new horizon. Then we would begin to derive the satisfaction of seeing our mission accomplished.

We will make it, if we have the unyielding willpower, courage
and prudence to act selflessly, as should all men that cultivate the
natural or social sciences purely in the interest of truth. May the
truth reign! May society assimilate it with that prodigious facility
with which all new truths are assimilated, even forgetting, and often unaware of, the name of the first one to bring them to light.
That will be our victory, though our name be overshadowed. The
new light that bursts forth will not shine the less bright for it.

Yet our work should not be confined to the narrow horizon
that looms before us in the towering Andes. Not because nature
has cloistered and secluded us in the deep hollows of these
mountains, are we any less sympathetic to the cause of democratic civilization on our great continent. We have the obligation

to join forces with those who, like us, work in the rest of the American regions for the cause of moral progress, social regeneration, the attainment of democratic synthesis through intellectual development, which is the first agent of progress, because it is its driving force and rudder.

Efforts all South Americans make in this connection must be parallel and unified, for the social goal is one and the same for all. These nations, born of a common revolution, can each have its own autonomy, but they will never have anything but a single literature, and the scientific and literary advancements of each will be the advancements of all. How could there be a Chilean literature different from the Mexican, or a Peruvian literature different from the Argentinian, if in each of these nations literature has to hold to the true notion of a single positivist progress, common to all, serving a common end, with the same criterion, a single language, equal means, and identical aims?

So, our first priority has to be contacting our brothers in action, meeting them and introducing ourselves, studying their works, judging them by our standard, to bring into our fold those who are agreeable, to become close friends in our goal of seeking positive truth only in the laws of nature, for only there will we find the realization of our goal: American democracy.

As you can see, our task is colossal. It perhaps will be rough going. We may not achieve in our lifetimes any of its lofty results. But when has moral progress been anything but slow and laborious, and yet, when have men who, like you all, carry in their spirit the will to truth, to its teaching and propagation, ever failed to pay their debt of service to it?

We shall fulfill our obligation. At least I shall pay with my constancy in work the debt of gratitude you have inspired in me by showing your vote of confidence in me to guide our work. I have faith in moral progress, and I know from experience that it only gains its sustenance from independent and altruistic efforts by men of letters, however much the latter, at times, have the misfortune of falling out of favor with the social powers that stand opposed to truth.

IV

We must not gloss over the fact that this address elicited from one of our friends a sigh of dismay, or better yet, a friendly admonition, which though it did nothing to detain us in our mission, is unquestionably worthy of remembrance, since it issued from a well-known writer. Blanco Cuartín addressed to us, through the *El Mercurio* of Valparaíso, a letter to dissuade us, assuming that we were out for literary glory and that we were working to return to talent the throne that greed and sensuality had seized from it. In his estimation this endeavor betrays either ignorance of what the world is about today, or overconfidence in the forces of the heart and the mind; and taking no stock in such wishful thinking, he declares to us his low hopes for the future of Chilean letters.

These *Memoirs* object to such an assumption, and clearly show that those who in Chile have worked to assert the study of the sciences and the cultivation of letters in the independence of the spirit and in the truth, have not done it to seek glory, but because they had faith that this is the most efficient means of regenerating ideas, to setting our civilization aright, and to eventually having an independent literature, like the one we had at the time when one of its own champions denied its existence and entertained doubts as to its future. We knew from early on that popularity is not found when it is sought, and that literary glory cannot exist in backward nations, unless one does like Lope de Vega, who, saying he kept the precepts under lock and key and dismissed Terence and Plautus,* exclaims:

> "*Y escribo por el arte que inventaron*
> *Los que el vulgar aplauso merecieron;*
> *El vulgo es necio, y, pues lo paga, es justo*
> *Hablarle en necio para darle gusto.*"

> ["And I write for the sake of the art those deserving
> of the rabble's applause invented;
> The mob is stupid, and, since they're paying, it's only right
> To talk to them in stupidity for their pleasure."]

---

* Imitators of the Greek author of New Comedy, Menander (342–292 B.C.). Terence (Publius Terentius Afer, c. 185–159 B.C.), Roman comic dramatist of north African origin who came to Rome as a slave. He is likely the main antecedent of the Comedy of Manners. Plautus, Titus Maccius (c. 254–184 B.C.). Also a Roman comic dramatist, like Terence he enjoyed great popularity during the Renaissance. —Trans.

This art still can be and is used profitably, but it is no easy task to preserve the glory it produces; nor does glory in their lifetimes follow those who, instead of praising, fight against the errors and troubles of their age, for the writers that are fated to live fifty, one hundred years, or more ahead of their contemporaries, and that seek to beat others to the future, safeguarding it, find only isolation and poverty. Literary glory has light and shadow, and if it is a path to earning wealth in nations where there is literary taste, it is also wont to be eclipsed and vanish when the earning was done only in the service of evanescent traditions, or passing delusions or passions, or errors and systems that disappear in the light of truth.

All this slipped our friend's mind as he reasoned with his customary charm and sparkle on the glory of literature, and above all he forgot that his letter was going to be read by youths avid for learning, not for laurels or riches, and which at that very time was creating a new literary and scientific journal, *Sud América*, in whose first issue appeared the following words: "It has been only a few years since the word *science* reached our shores, and today he who is lacking at least a nodding acquaintance with it dares not confess it." "This generation arises and grows in that climate." "Battles, and uphill at that, remain to be fought. The eternal enemies of progress, ignorance, and preoccupations, will not easily give up ground." "The combatant needs to screw up courage and enthusiasm, which are indispensable to him."

Thus the dismayed voice of our friend, the well-known writer, had the faint ring of enthusiasm and of valor. But let us read outright that remarkable letter. Here it is:

DON JOSÉ VICTORINO LASTARRIA

Master and friend:

I have read and reread the beautiful address you delivered at the inauguration of the Academy of Belles Lettres, and I assure you my admiration grew by leaps and bounds upon seeing you, in spite of your disillusionment, as spirited as ever about the future of our literature.

To believe in literary glory in these times of brutish mercantilism, to aspire to decorate one's brow with the undying garland that ancient Greece bestowed on the sons of Apollo; to work to return to genius and to talent the throne that gold-lust and the unquenchable thirst for sensual pleasures have usurped, are, in my view, an aim, belief, and task that, although reflecting purity and elevation of spirit, clearly demonstrate either ignorance of what the world is in the year of grace we are reaching, or else overconfidence in the forces of the heart and the intelligence.

Let us extend our gaze over the horizon. What role is played to-day by the wise men and literati in France, which still presumes to hold in its blood-stained hands the scepter of science and art? Look back a bit. Lamartine, the divine Lamartine,* as he was called, low-ered himself to humbly beg for alms in exchange for his work, or rather, for his great ideas, for the lofty sentiments that shook hu-manity, leading it down the paths of beauty and to travel with light on their brow and hope in their heart all the vast spheres of free-dom and progress.

A beggar like Homer, he went door to door singing the glory of the country, and the country, personified in Caesar, rather out of weariness than pity, repaid his laments with a stipend that might have pleased a courtesan, but that could only ridicule the philoso-pher and the poet. And notice that the mendicancy of the author of *Graziella* and of *Jocelyn* was the venerable beggary of the muses, the holy misfortune of philosophy. But, what did all of this matter, when France had gold only to support its vipers, to gild the weighty chains of its servitude? Victor Hugo,† more fortunate than his ill-fated colleague, did not lose heart; he confronted the wrath of power, laughed at his poverty, and after having braved the despot, having marked him forever with the stigma of history, took to the skies as a passing swallow and went finally to make his nest on the icy shores of Jersey. What will he do there?

To modulate songs like Ovid to excite the compassion of Augus-tus? No, the soul of Victor Hugo cannot exhale complaints; it is tuned like those scimitars of Damascus, and needs to slice, to cleave its adversaries. He writes *Los castigos* ["The Punishments"], *El hom-bre que ríe* ["The Laughing Man"],‡ etc., but he does not write to in-struct and delight as he did formerly: he writes to slander, to defame, and mocking with the same uninhibited candor the conventional forms as the eternal rules of justice, he ends by furiously tearing from his temples the poet's crown, and stripping bare his brawny arms to volunteer himself as the first boxer of the word and of the pen.

Meanwhile, what say the academies, the gymnasiums, the lyceums, upon seeing their idol-turned-pugilist respecting nothing? Do they cover their heads in ash, rend their clothing, even bemoan

---

* Alphonse-Marie-Louis de Prat de Lamartine (1790–1869), French romantic poet and, in 1848, minister for foreign affairs. —Ed.

† I.e., Victor-Marie Hugo (1802–1885). —Ed.

‡ Hugo, *Les châtiments* (1853), *L'homme qui rit* (1869). —Ed.

that miserable transformation underdone in the giant? Nothing of the kind: they forget, and if some solemn cry restores their memory, they settle for saying with beatific hypocrisy: "Poor Victor Hugo! He finished where he should have started."

If from poetry we move on to history, it strikes us first to inquire after Guizot. And well we should! Where has he been, where is that famous historian? After returning from England he has not set foot out of Paris. Why then not until now, when he has just come out with a new book, has anyone mentioned him? Are his books no longer studied, does European civilization no longer need him at all?

Thiers, who along with Bismarck are the most respectable figures in Europe, would be forgotten also had he not played the role with which happenstance has favored him. Nevertheless, that illustrious old man, neglected until September 1870, had written admirable books, works that might have meant the eternal glory of a seventeenth-century writer. But, why belabor the point, when Villemain, Sainte-Beuve, Droz, Sismondi, Thierry, Philarète, Chasles, Musset, Montalembert, etc., go unremembered in that Paris that was the noisy hub of their fame?

Now, if from French letters we proceed to Spanish, the disenchantment would be crueler still. Without Ribadeneira,* Spain would not even know the names of the literary figures it produced in the so-called Golden Age. And then, how lucky those are who still cultivate letters there! Severo Catalina asks for a job that a journeyman scribbler would turn up his nose at, and Minister González Bravo denies him it, just as Berganza not many years ago refused a young writer a petty office in the Santiago treasury. The old *Friar Gerundio* has lived and continues to live off his fixed income, that is to say, his copper coins, and that does not mean any of Isabel's ministers, who emphatically considered themselves Maecenas't men, nor those of Serrano, who was nothing short of a kind-hearted man, ever deigned to reward him with any honorable position. One must re-examine, as I did with biographical dictionaries in view, to become convinced of what literary Spain is, and even then, how distant we still are from the truth. This says it all: Castelar,‡ who

---

* Pedro de Ribadeneyra (1527–1611), Spanish Jesuit hagiologist. —Ed.

† I.e., Gaius Cilnius Maecenas (70?–8 B.C.), Roman statesman, patron of the arts, especially literature, and friend of Horace, Virgil, and Octavius (Augustus). —Ed.

‡ Probably Emilio Castelar y Ripoll (1832–1899), Spanish statesman and historian. —Ed.

enjoys one of the premier reputations in Europe, cannot forsake, in spite of his complicated tasks, the scanty salary he takes home as a correspondent for the large newspapers of South America. If we think on this, it comes as no surprise that Cervantes, forgetting the haughty dignity of the hero of his novel, as a beggar flatters the Duke of Béjar and the Count of Lemos to ensure himself the meager alms with which he can hardly feed himself.

Outside of Quevedo,* a frequent dinner guest of princes and luminaries, which of those who took part in the Golden Age was not looked upon as lowly dregs? Ah! We must pull our gaze away from that age lest we be ashamed of the destiny of the men of letters. The poets took up their lyre and sung, but in the best of their cadences to God, nature or immortality, they set it down in order to grab hold the rebec† and weary the ears of their patrons with the most cloying of praises.

Returning home after such a long walk, do you not think, don Victorino, that we are still a far cry from the days in which South American letters can constitute its own literature, one that praises not just the country whose identity it assumes, but those who limit themselves to its cultivation?

I understand very well that nations like those of this continent, and especially Chile, can in time boast no end of literati, wise men and artists of note; but what I do not understand is how art, letters, and science, following the route where we are underway, will be able to defeat the thousand foes that beleaguer them. The first is sloth, that spinelessness that we demonstrate for all moral work and that we only break out of on occasion to reconcile ourselves halfway with pride. The second is the lack of stimulus in opinion, which deems as lost all moments not devoted to earning money, and brands as libertines, if not dangerous vagrants, those who have the courage to prefer study to profit, the peaceful satisfactions of the spirit to the crashing blows of the body. The third is the nature of our institutions, those which, however democratic they become, always will be restrictive enough to not lend themselves willingly to the strict examination of philosophy. Letters live only under the benign breath of tolerance, they develop only under the loving fervor of enthusiasm, and even for that we need for the governments,

---

* Francisco Gómez de Quevedo y Villegas (1580–1645), Spanish statesman and prose satirist, known principally for the picaresque novel *Historia y vida del Buscón* (1626). —Ed.

† A three-stringed instrument of the Middle Ages and Renaissance. —Trans.

placing themselves at the head like their patrons, to be able to esteem their priests by calling on them to carry out the great functions that seem to be the resort of those who devote their lives to the study of man and nature.

Long would our toils be were we to go on discoursing upon this familiar topic, and longer still if by delving into the depths of the social state we were to point out one by one the causes that impede bringing intellectual tasks into developmental accord. To make literature, society indispensably must be represented in all its interests, and the artist's brush that paints the national landscapes, like the pen that gives voice to its feelings, aims, and trends, must find countryside, matter, light, air with which to crown its many efforts with success. Not even artificial literature, that literature that forever is copying the exteriorizations of others' lives, as is happening to us now, will form a symmetrical totality in which the moral and physical needs of the nation can be studied as long as it does not wholly conform to the pattern that serves as our guide. Allow me to provide an example. What is poetry in our country? Is it by chance the reflected light of our national sentiments? Is it the aggregate of cadenced notes whose harmony lies only in our spirit? Is it the true language of our passions heated by the burning rays of the sun that melt the snows, toast the golden ears of wheat and ripen early the perfumed grapes of our vineyards? No one would say so because our verses are but watered-down imitations of the Spanish verses. There is wit, tastefulness, inspiration in many of them, but rarely does one leap out that shows originality, that makes one say to the poetry taster (forgive the metaphor): there is Chile with her gorgeous women, her blue sky, her red-flushed clouds, her woods, her rivers, her mountains beyond compare. We love in the Spanish style; we hate, hope, and empathize like the Spaniards do; only our rhyme is original because we use words that no one uses, turns of phrase that recognize no grammar.

Let us turn to history: who are those who cultivate it?

Apart from Benjamín Vicuña Mackenna, Barros Arana and Amunátegui, who are more properly speaking chroniclers, no one as far as we know, from independence down to our day, has deserved the name of historian. I recall that when reading the *Historia constitucional del medio siglo* ["Constitutional History of the Half-Century"] for the first time, I repeated painfully: "After all, Lastarria is the only one in Chile who judges historical events with philosophical high-mindedness, so his narration serves not only to satiate one's curiosity, but also to yoke morality with teaching."

These, then, don Victorino, are the reasons I have for lacking confidence in the future of Chilean letters, reasons you shall not fail to recognize as powerful despite the untiring service that for thirty-three years you have rendered them, and which, it seems, you are destined to render them still.

Nevertheless, how can one not expect something from an enterprise that has you at its helm and that now has fifty keen collaborators? Now that the big question of freedom of education has begun to be understood, if the Academy of Belles Lettres wished to complete the defeat of the academic state and open the way for freedom of professions, which is its logical consequence, their works not only would be thought highly of from the speculative point of view, but also honored and consecrated in the practical realm.

Above all, if the Academy of Belles Lettres grows stronger without more assistance than that of the public, it will be a model consortium of free universities, those that, once acclimated, will render obsolete the state university, which has consumed so much money and has not produced the least benefit for anyone.

I shall not conclude this letter without expressing to you the desire that that beautiful and useful institution of which you are the most worthy director manage to lay solid foundations, attracting to it all the intellects and the generous gifts of fortune in its favor. Finally, my desire is that, as Voltaire used to say, the academy in time will be to the state university what ripe old age is to infancy, what the art of speaking well is to grammar, what the refinement of culture is to the first notions of urbanity.

Master and dear friend, here's to you! To your good health always! Never may your life ebb away, for to it many memories, many interests, many hopes are tied.

So may God prolong your life for as many years as possible, that you may delight in your work for freedom, for which you have worked and suffered so much. The great authors are rarities, the material magnificent; yet your foundational work will end. How I would like to live to see it! I am not old in years, but old in misfortunes and afflictions; for that very reason I naturally am not among those who will have a seat at the feast. Believe that it distresses me to say so. . . . Shake my hand warmly and I will wait!—MANUEL BLANCO CUARTÍN

However, the Academy of Belles Lettres since then was a hive of literary activity, and fortunately is still, despite the difficulties and disenchantments that are rooted in the situation outlined by the letter we have transcribed. It is not yet time to write the Academy's history, and to finish with the information we have accumulated in these *Memoirs*, so that later they may serve the history written on our literature, we will add as documents the annual Reports that recount the society's projects, and accounts of the literary competitions it held.

V

Director's Report

Gentlemen:

We have performed a test both heartening and comforting: the Academy of Belles Lettres has had a year of active, productive life, which assures it a far-stretching future.

A strange movement was afoot at the start of 1873, and all eyes were drawn toward public education. It was believed in danger of being run by political interests and even whims, which tended to worsen the situation, turning the legal dependence it lives in today into disastrous slavery.

But that movement did not lead to any solution, not because the patres familias in this country lacked the ability to organize a public education that could exist outside the political vicissitudes, even when it was not independent of legal management, but on account of the lack of selflessness and of the habits of personal freedom, and more than that, due to the deep-seated habit of surrendering the management of social activity to the powers that be, even in those affairs that by their nature can only be governed by this activity.

Then a few of us men of good will wondered if it would not be possible to organize even one modest center in which letters and science might find the independence that in the nether regions of the intellect guarantees the unrestricted development of its principles and doctrines, and shelters them from splinter-group interests and political mood-swings. A great number of men of letters stepped forward right away to prove that it was possible, through their voluntary and altruistic adherence to the principles of this new institution.

After the initial constitutional compromises, the Academy was constituted with more than fifty members. A large part of these members has devoted unwavering and productive efforts, while the rest have simply lent their support and their loyalty, for as long as they are able to dedicate to it the fruits of their intellect.

This was not the only result of the founding. Around that first hub of intellectual activity, a number of brilliant youths were not long in forming, eager also to lend a hand to the independent cultivation of science. At the time more than two hundred young academics signed as visitors in the Academy's registry.

And as if to show that this healthy movement did not remain indifferent to society's active members, don Federico Varela, an intelligent and hard-working patriot, who has linked his name to one of the industries that have most contributed to the development of public wealth, offered the Academy a sum of money that could facilitate its organization. This philanthropic act, to date unique and extraordinary among those upon whom fortune has smiled, offers a practical example of what the active, affluent set could do in support of intellectuals, who ordinarily cannot contribute to the general progress except through their intellectual powers. Among the latter, we will not fail to mention the name of Mr. Alamos González, also an exception, who subscribed with one thousand pesos for the Academy.

One of the Academy's first points of business was to put together a public readings program, in order to do its part toward developing the teaching and dissemination of knowledge; but the lack of resources and of strong basic principles has been until today an obstacle to making this idea a reality, though we are going to make it work in due course, hoping, through perseverance, to overcome the difficulties. Meantime, the valuable debut that was made on how to contribute through lectures to the scientific education of the fair sex, an appearance that has provided the subject for several Reports of great merit, not only has had a share in elucidating this matter, but also has clarified the rules that ought to be adopted for those lectures.

To a certain degree that debate, like the several different debates that the sociological themes of the readings performed have sparked, have made up for the dearth of readings and conferences in the Academy, for there is no questioning the benefit those arguments have produced in commanding attention and shedding light on matters of true social interest.

The Academy above all can be congratulated for having stimulated the cultivation of letters, even when it still has not been able to make use of the effective resource of public lectures and readings, for their sessions, though private, have always brought together a number of attendees averaging seventy. And not only have the young intellectuals presented their works, but what is noteworthy, we have also been honored with those of two ladies, doña Rosario Orrego de Uribe and doña Lucrecia Undurraga de Somarriva, whose works won sincere applause.

Moreover, the Academy has taken some other steps to promote literary works, among which two are especially deserving of attention: one whose aim is to publish in honor of the redoubtable Bello a book that is the fruit of the cooperation of Academics and visitors, and one establishing an annual contest for those who wish to cultivate dramatic composition. This latter measure has yielded splendid results, seeing as fourteen plays, including dramas and comedies, in prose and verse, were submitted to the first contest. The judging of these works was turned over to a jury consisting of Messrs. Barros Arana, Amunátegui and Rodríguez Velasco, who submitted their report separately, awarding the prize of three hundred pesos, by majority vote, to the comedy in verse entitled *Quien mucho abarca, poco aprieta* ["Don't Bite Off More Than You Can Chew"] by Mr. Rafael Jover. The other vote was for the prose drama entitled *La mujer hombre* ["The He-Woman"] by Mr. Román Vial.

The number of readings performed in the Academy in this first year of its foundation reached seventy-six, of them fifty-nine by Academy members and seventeen by visitors.

Among Academy members, Mr. Matta M. A. has performed seven readings; Mr. Letelier, six; Mr. Barros Arana, five; Messrs. Hostos, Amunátegui, Barros Grez, Lavín Matta, G. Matta, and the Director, three apiece; two each by Messrs. Orrego Luco, Moreno, Rodríguez Velasco, Murillo, Coog, Gallo P. L., and Lastarria D., and one each by Messrs. Arteaga Alemparte D., Valderrama, Martínez, González, Estrada, Velasco, Asta-Buruaga, Chacón, and Santa Cruz.

The visitors that gave readings are: Santa María F., Cegarra, and Larraín Zañartu J. J., two each, and one by Messrs. Dávila Larraín B., Martínez F., Torres Arce V., Ferrán, Zubiría, Murillo Ruperto y Lemoine; we should also add two readings by Mrs. Orrego de Uribe, now a member of the Academy, one sent by Mrs. Undurraga de Somarriva, and a series Mr. José Antonio Lavalle, a distinguished Peruvian man of letters, is passing on to us from Europe.

All these works can be classified by their subject matter in the following order: on geology, one; botany, one; physiology and medicine, five; philosophy, four; speculative and practical politics, ten; political economy, one; history and historical criticism, ten; biography, four; literary and bibliographic criticism, twelve; philosophy, three; education, five; poetry and literature, twenty.

These are the fruits of the earnest labors the Academy has exerted toward worthily discharging its duties. This alone would suffice to justify the intention it had to contact the most distinguished men of letters in South America, and even Europe, which to some extent are interested in our literary progress, if on top of that it were not enough to back this goal to have the desire to bring unity to all the South American writers' efforts, that the cultivation of letters and science in the New World may be built on its only natural foundation: the independence of the spirit.

Fortunately, the literary royalty of our continent and the European writers interests' in our progress have reacted to that goal with signs of real enthusiasm; so the Academy today has no less than thirty-five member corespondents in the South American nations and in France.

Yet, as we mention this commendable progress, we must regret the loss of two illustrious writers that had accepted that title, lending us support that, certainly, would not have been reduced to their names had they had time to show their solidarity: I refer to the historian and naturalist don Claudio Gay, who gave ample evidence of his loyalty to Chile, and to the Peruvian literato don José Simeón Tejeda, who, as president of the Literary Club of Lima, had applauded the ends of our organization.

Additionally, if we focus on the nature of the Academy's works according to their classification, we notice that, although the number of sociological works exceeds that of the scientific, the former have a clearly positive bent, which is indicative of progress. The political works are all special studies of some practical matter; those in history have been generally critical investigations geared toward the discovery of truth, and not simply chronicles, which also disfigure history, as Mommsen* says, for, keeping only to the form of events, they leave their causes in the dark; those on literary criticism have carried out the adopted plan of introducing the South American literary movement; and those in literature have been in large part translations or imitations of the grand masters, while the original works presented are harbingers of a marked trend away from the eccentricity that characterizes the two dominant schools in Europe, the one in search of beauty in the new, though it be outlandish, and the other, which, trying to seek it out in the good, preaches a morality as antisocial as the former; for both only come to man,

---

* Theodor Mommsen (1817–1903), German historian and recipient of the 1902 Nobel Prize in Literature. His most enduring work is perhaps *History of Rome* (Vols. I–III, 1854–56; Vol. V, 1885). —Trans.

forgetting society, and they distort him, either through the madness of the passions, or through the childishness of a sickly sensibility, immolating the intelligence on the altar of a visionary ideal.

To writers of this genre applies that nameless verdict as terrific as it is just: "The writer who in this day and age draws inspiration from traditions merely because they have been thrust upon him by the past, is no writer of this century; he who believes in metaphysical illusions and in abstractions unrefined by positive observation, is no writer of this century; he that doubts and destroys under the spell of skepticism, neither seeking truth nor converging with nature, is no writer of this century."

Actually, when history is written, subjecting it anew to the crucible of positive criticism in order to bring unity to its periods and to study the laws of human development; when by means of the same method one studies physical nature to know its laws and to give a positive value to natural sciences; when philosophy abandons individual speculations and discernment born of one's inner feeling to establish as scientific exclusively what is true in the eyes of a rigorously objective method; it is not rational that literature still persist in seeking its delights in the eccentric or false illusions of individual subjectivity, which seeks to make man in its image and to consider him outside of the laws that determine his relationships and his social future.

There is no fear that the Academy stray henceforth from this path of positive truth if its first forays have held so faithfully to the primary foundation of its institution. What is of consequence to us is never to confuse this foundation with the criterion that the rest of the philosophical schools that in our age consider themselves positivists have respectively adopted, since they have abandoned discernment born of one's inner feeling with which subjective or metaphysical philosophy felt authorized to establish its random assertions as science, at times invoking individual conscience, at others, subjective observation.

All these schools lack a true positive criterion to judge and assess the events and doctrines of the social sciences, and therefore they help support intellectual anarchy, which presently is the cause of the moral disorder and the confusion that reigns in those sciences. So the naturalist school, which rejects the label of materialist, since unlike materialism of old, it does not place moral phenomena under the sway of the laws of inert matter, but nevertheless takes moral equilibrium as its criterion, seeking to reduce to specific laws the harmony of the movements that make up what it calls a moral reality, and forgetting right from the start that the primary law of this reality is free will. What rule will be followed to dismantle and put back together harmoniously that benefic or malefic machine called man? How to lead or modify the course of its sensations, of its images and tendencies, dispensing with its conscience and its freedom? In this doctrine there is no shining principle accessible to all, nor any specific idea other than considering man a fated entity, neglecting the law of his development and of his freedom. The same vagueness and the same specious reasoning occurs in the utilitarian school, which makes the good consist of the useful. But how is the good conceived of separate from the development of man's faculties and relationships? What rule will we have for knowing if all that is useful is good, or to gauge the greatest good for the greatest number? But if these schools leave us in doubt, in the dark, the sensualist school and all the philosophical doctrines that are called experimental, because they invoke the subjective experimental sensation, not only lead us to doubt, but can also lead us awry, while habitually they dispense with the only two laws that rule human nature, that of development and that of freedom. One of the most characteristic exponents of this philosophy in South America, Mr. Ezequiel Rojas, believes he has discovered a new system founded on natural law, which gives to human actions the property of affecting man, making him happy or unhappy. But can a criterion be the demonstration that happiness consists of agreeable sensation, and unhappiness of painful sensation? Could it be that agreeable or painful sensations, happiness or unhappiness, can provide us a fixed, unassailable rule for judging morality and finding the truth of sciences that are founded on individual and social man?

The true positive philosophy, the school that seeks the truth in the analysis of facts through their objective confirmation and through the verification of the laws that govern the physical and moral worlds; that school to which the astounding advancements of civil and natural history of this century are owed, has as its guide the criterion the Academy adopted, taking as a rule of composition and of criticism, in scientific works, their agreement with the facts demonstrated positively by science; and in the sociological and literary works, their agreement with the laws of human nature, which are development and freedom.

This is something understood clearly and precisely, and that lets us know what is being spoken of when the term moral equilibrium is used, an equilibrium that cannot be mechanical, when we hear utility, the good, happiness or unhappiness invoked. The relative, and therefore vague, sense of these terms becomes precise if we reduce it in sociology to the complete development of the faculties and relationships of intelligent beings and the law of freedom that governs that development. Human good can be found only in it, for man cannot fulfill his destiny if he does not develop to the utmost of his intensity in individual and social life, through his free will, which chooses and employs the conditions of his perfection.

The Academy must continue as it has begun, guiding itself by this compass, if it wishes to lend its work a character that has always been lacking in our studies—unity—in the means and in the end. We have been bred in contradiction, hearing in one course of study the opposite of what was taught us in another, studying man always separate from the environment in which he lives and trying to know ancient society, leaving in total darkness the one that cradles us at her bosom. Thus have we ventured out into practical life: devoid of principles, of judgment, and without knowing man, or society, and even without knowing ourselves.

Perhaps this is why so many undertakings made since 1842 to set literary study aright and to give it direction through association, the only effective expedient used in all ages to preserve the sciences, to make them progress and disseminate them, have foundered. From those attempts have emerged many writers in the thirty years that have gone by; but the cultivation of the sciences and the system of studies have not progressed appreciably. Let us be steadfast. Let us follow the flow of the century, armed with the criterion to which the former owes so many advancements, and let us not forget that he who forsakes this criterion of light to blindly follow tradition or to chase metaphysical abstractions unrefined by positive observation, or lets himself be ruled by the skepticism that does not seek truth in nature, is not nor can he be a writer of this century.

REPORT BY THE COMMITTEE FOR EXAMINING
THE DRAMATIC COMPOSITIONS SUBMITTED TO
THE COMPETITION HELD BY THE ACADEMY
OF BELLES LETTRES

Santiago, 9 April 1874.—Mr. Director: The Academy of Belles Lettres, in our judgment, must be congratulated for the outcome of the competition it held this past year to present a prize to the best dramatic composition submitted to it. In spite of this being one of the most laborious literary genres known, and the national talents having done quite little work in it as of yet, fourteen authors, whose works are of fairly high caliber, have joined the fray for the prize awarded.

The three members of the examining committee have read each of the fourteen plays separately.

Having then spoken collectively on the works' respective merits, they were in agreement to declare from the outset that the five following works could not enter the competition with the others; it should be understood that we are listing them in simple alphabetical order:

El hijo abandonado ["The Abandoned Son"]: drama in three acts and four scenes, prose;
El triángulo ["The Triangle"]: drama in five acts, prose;
La huérfana ["The Orphan Girl"]: comedy in three acts, prose;
Más vale tarde que nunca ["Better Late Than Never"]: drama in three acts, verse;
Salustio o fuerza y debilidad ["Salustio, or, Strength and Weakness"]: drama in five acts, prose.

It seems these compositions are primarily essays, and for that very reason, one can easily see that they suffer from fairly serious shortcomings; but, since their authors allow us to glimpse somewhat strong talents, one hopes that if they continue working devotedly on cultivating literature, they will compose more accomplished works.

Superior to the preceding are the five works whose titles we will cite, also in alphabetical order:

El monje negro ["The Black Monk"]: drama in two parts and four acts, verse;
La calumnia ["The Betrayal"]: comedy in five acts, prose;
La conspiración de Milan ["The Milan Conspiracy"]: historical drama in two acts and three scenes, prose;
La mejor espuela ["The Best Spur"]: comedy in three acts, verse;
No hay mal que por bien no venga ["Every Dark Cloud Has A Silver Lining"]: comedy in three acts, verse.

The first of the above-mentioned compositions has not been written expressly for the competition, as confided by its author, but he has submitted it as a work from his juvenilia. The play is set in the eighteenth century in the Tuscan theater. It is involved, romantic, and dark, in the manner of the Bouchardy* school. The versification is in general regular, and at times forceful. Though this drama has interesting scenes, it is regrettable that it did not verge closer to naturalness and verisimilitude.

* Joseph Bouchardy (1810–1870), French dramatist employing intricate plotting and having a decidedly populist, melodramatic flair, often featuring villains who meet their comeuppance for crimes committed. —Trans.

The second work is a comedy of character and of manners whose action occurs in Santiago and in our time. It deals with the efforts and intrigues of two families to marry their fortunes through a rich southern landowner, who comes to the capital unversed in the arts of civilized refinement. The author shows ingenuity and sparkle, and manages to fit in fairly successful scenes; but he betrays inexperience, and has not edited out incidents that hamper or overwhelm those scenes.

The third composition features a plot about the conspiracy that cost the life of Galeazzo Sforza, tyrant of Milan in the latter half of the fifteenth century, in a temple. It is a scaled-down historical description in which love makes no appearance and in which not one woman comes on, a work talentedly sketched through straightforward, lively dialogue. Though the author has studied the history of this event fairly thoroughly, he did not stick scrupulously to it; and we believe that he has not wrung all possibilities from this affair.

The fourth work showcases a protagonist who, ruled by what could be called the passion, or rather, the madness of verse, shuns all feeling for hearth and home and all his family's interests. The action aims to lay bare the choices to which one of his wife's female cousins resorts to bring him back to his senses. To this end, the cousin disguises herself as a man and pretends to be the lover of the poet's wife, until she arouses the latter's jealousy and forces him to offer her a duel. The showdown does not take place, for the truth of the matter is revealed. It all ends with the poet's emendation. As one can see, this plot is utterly unrealistic. There is also more than one occurrence to which the same can be applied. At times, too, the author does not show all the ingenuity one might expect from him. The verse is fluent; some scenes are interesting.

The fifth work is a comedy in which there is an attempt to highlight the advantages of marriages of inclination and the drawbacks of marriages of covetousness. Though it is regularly versified, and though the author shows talent in the depiction of three of the characters he brings out, he has unfortunately failed to avoid the pitfall of the long discourse and of the commonplaces typical of compositions of this type.

In spite of the fact we agreed that the previous compositions are not wanting for merit, we feel they cannot hold their own against the four we are going to discuss, which are given in alphabetic order:

Arbaces o el último Ramsés ["Arbaces, or, The Last Ramses"]: drama in three acts, verse;
La mujer hombre ["The He-Woman"]: drama in three acts, prose;

Los dos amores ["The Two Romances"]: drama in three acts, prose; *Quien mucho abarca* . . . ["Don't Bite Off More Than You Can Chew"]: comic proverb in two acts, verse.

The first is adapted, with slight variations, from the famous Bulwer Lytton novel entitled *The Last Days of Pompeii*, as the author of the drama himself has taken pains to express. The plot has been well handled, and is in general well versified; but it raises the misgiving, which is well worth considering in the present case, of not being original.

The second work develops the theme of which we are going to make the briefest of summaries. Florentina, a poor young orphan, is the only means of support for her sister Luisa. To feed her she masquerades as a man, and obtains from don Jorge, a rich trader from Valparaíso, the job of clerk, which she fulfills with the greatest of zeal. Clara, don Jorge's daughter, believing, like everyone, that Florentina is a man, falls in love with her; and in turn, Florentina pledges her love in secret to Julio, also one of don Jorge's sons. As for Julio, he is in love with Luisa, Florentina's sister. This knotty situation causes the heroine all the grief one can imagine. Meanwhile, Ricardo, another of don Jorge's clerks, a scheming evildoer of a character, prompted by malevolence, pursues his colleague Florentina until managing to have her hauled off to prison under the blow of a robbery accusation. In the end the plot winds down in a way favorable to innocence. Everything is found out and explained. Ricardo is caught stealing. Don Jorge offers his guardianship to the two orphan girls. Julio weds Luisa. So Florentina, paragon of virtue and self-denying heroine, does not wind up rewarded in her love. This compendious exposition allows us to judge the merits of a stage-play that is far from everyday, but it seems to us unlikely that Florentina's disguise would not be detected.

The third work gives a lively presentation of one of those battles between passion and obligation, and in which are featured certain generous spirits in the habit of triumphing over everything before stooping to low behavior. In this composition there is a certain youthful verve that is affecting. If its author carefully cultivates the felicitous aptitudes with which he seems to be endowed, he will successfully avoid the pitfalls into which he has tumbled and will produce works that do honor to the national literature. This drama can be considered a good first attempt.

The fourth work is a comic sketch conceived cleverly and written in remarkably correct language, versified elegantly, and developed with knowledge of the dramatic art. The scene is set in

Madrid, but the author struck upon the good idea of having it appeal to Chileans by relating it to people that have resided in our country and who show affectionate feelings toward it. The main action of this dramatic proverb is well executed. A girl who has four gentlemen callers winds up, by the most natural means, with none of them; and her father is quite right to remind her of the well-known proverb *Quien mucho abarca, poco aprieta* ["Don't bite off more than you can chew"]. Nevertheless, the subplot, the servants' love affairs, which offer a most pleasant scene, is left without a real denouement.

Two of the members of the examining committee are of the opinion that this latter composition is the one deserving of the prize, against the vote of the third, who finds *La mujer hombre* to be superior.

Our cohort don Luis Rodríguez Velasco, who is currently away from Santiago, has not been able to sign this report; but we have proceeded in accordance with him and we are fully authorized to so state to the Academy.

We have the honor of offering our considerations to the Director and the other members of this institution.—*Miguel Luis Amunátegui.*—*Diego Barros Arana.*

VI

OFFICIAL SESSION OF THE SECOND ANNIVERSARY OF THE ACADEMY OF BELLES LETTRES, HELD ON 11 APRIL 1875

Director's Report

Gentlemen:

Today the Academy of Belles Lettres celebrates its second anniversary, but it still has not been able to fulfill all the noble goals that flattered its birth and that were grounds for such gratifying hopes.

It is not surprising, for once the danger stirred by the lively sentiment for the independence of literary pursuit had abated, a sentiment that gave rise to this modest center of writers who wished to take refuge from splinter-group invasions of the spirit and political mood-swings, calm was restored, and with it ended that moment of extraordinary activity.

Though letters and science is still a component of social activity in our country, it is true that the need to complete our knowledge, which is the need that urges individual effort, is not yet enough to create a collective interest; for beyond being generally satisfied by public life, all too few are the men that can devote themselves to it freely and selflessly, and despite having the certainty that their sacrifices will be unknown, if not disdained, and fit only to bring them isolation and defenselessness, maybe even hunger.

I mention this only to point out how deserving the congratulations are that I have the honor of extending on this solemn occasion to those who have been able to persevere in keeping alive this modest center with their intellectual efforts and their personal sacrifices.

This year eight founding Academy members have been chosen: Messrs. Bello, Cuadra, Dávila Larraín, Gaete, Koenig, MacIver, Montt Luis, and Sotomayor Valdés; and two correspondents, Messrs. Lavalle and Fernández Rodella. Thirty visitors have joined as well. Nevertheless, the list of founders has suffered a change, since several have withdrawn, expressing their wish to be relieved of the duties they had shouldered.

The Academy has celebrated this year nineteen regular sessions, with an attendance lower than that of the first year; but, on average, it was not less than fifty attendees, of which three-fourths were visitors. The readings performed totaled forty-four, among them twelve by visitors and thirty-two by Academy members.

Of these, Mr. M. A. Matta delivered six readings; Mr. Barros Grez, three; Messrs. Amunátegui, Allende Padín, González, Lastarria Demetrio, Matta Guillermo, and Orrego Luco, two apiece; and one each for Messrs. Asta-Buruaga, Bello, Carrasco Albano, Dávila Larraín, Lavín Matta, Santa Cruz, Lavalle, Murillo, Montt Luis, and the Director, adding one performed on behalf of the corresponding Academy member from Caracas, Mr. Rojas Garrido.

The visitors that have performed readings are: Garriga, who has shared with us his most beautiful poetic compositions; Lemoine, Montt Julio, Orihuela, Sánchez Massenlli, Vergara, and Zubiría.

All the works, among which there are several of great merit, are distributed according to genre: seventeen in poetic literature, twenty-two in sociology, and five are scientific.

The first were imaginative scenes in prose and verse, mostly original, which we cannot call outstanding for their artistic merit, and that, revealing in general that their authors penned them as a pastime, show that this genre of composition is still very rarely cultivated in our country. Among the second, biographical works and historical criticism abound, which exhibit a sharp-focused investigative spirit; there are additionally six on themes of economy and political science that have the signs of a markedly positive, experimental, and sensible survey, both practical and statistical; one on primary education; another on philology, and four on philosophy, among which two examinations of the philosophical and moral theories of the Eastern nations* are standouts, works with high discernment and free of metaphysical illusions. The scientific works are physiological and medical, all of them of practical utility for our society.

In general, one notes in the studies submitted to the Academy a veritable abandonment of all systemic interest, which reveals a healthy trend toward obeying the first law of literary art, which is the investigation of positive truth without subjection either to conventional forms or to a received truth. We must not lose sight of this trend, in order to foster it and buttress it, for it is the one that behooves the fledgling South American literature, which must rest on the independence of the spirit if it is to serve democratic growth, shunning partiality, systems, and sects: the unity of literature must be sought in freedom. This is the natural result of the independence of the spirit, and its law: the fundamental law of art is truth.

But we need to mention that that healthy trend doubtlessly has some part in the deficiency of our poetic literature. Here there is no taste formed by a certain conventional idea in art, and if it is lacking, it is more than satisfied by the shoddy contrivances the European market imports to us in the form of novels and works of the imagination. Nor is there a small-scale conventional public art that is privileged by some public institution subordinate to the State. Dramatic theater is still lacking, owing to the dilettante furor of the authorities who would rather educate the people through music like they were savage beasts, laying waste the fruit of their contributions in buttering up the ruling class. What then does the youth do, they who feel the inspiration of their burning spirit and their sensibility boiling, seeing that there is glory only for he who cultivates letters and sciences in search of positive truth? Right from the start they understand that to seek it in poetic literature, in works of the imagination, one must work seriously at imitating nature, and this being an arduous pursuit that does not lead to glory, it is better to direct one's energy to scientific studies, which have some recompense. If they do not reckon in this way, and removed from all interests, they pay the first fruits of their genius to poetry, and soon bid their adieu of the muse the moment they enter practical life. In this way the cultivation of serious literature falls nearly always to the neophytes,

* I.e., both East and West Asia. —Ed.

if, by an exception as strange as it is felicitous, the noble passion of art does not endure in some self-sacrificing spirit.

Is this a misfortune or a stroke of luck? Happily, no doubt, our society lacks those first two stimuli, which in the old European societies do nothing more than diminish and disfigure art. But we consider it a misfortune that in a new nation, full of life, all incentive is lacking, even in dramatic theater, to engage in that fertile activity that, via works of the imagination, imparts sprightliness to the spirit, hardiness to independent morality, publicity to lofty ideas, strength of character, nobility, and refinement to family relations.

You believe as I do, and thus you all have devoted a large part of your efforts to creating in this Academy a meeting-place for encouraging the spirit and a wellspring for art. But our isolated determination is not enough. We need the Montyons,* and our mere accolades do not provide the glory that literary art seeks, nor supply the inducements that increase its pursuit.

This year we would not have been able to hold a literary competition without the happy inspiration the respectable Committee assigned to organize the International Expo of 1875. To encourage the national fine arts and to secure its pursuit in that great feast of industry, the Committee resolved to hold several competitions, including one musical one and another poetic, placing the Academy of Belles Lettres in charge of the latter. The Academy agreed on the following rules:

"1st. Two lyrical compositions were awarded prizes: *one hymn to industry and a ballad to fraternity in work.* The hymn is intended as a musical composition that should be played by a large orchestra, and will be composed of a choir and strophes; the ballad will serve as a theme for a song for voices only, and require a marked and cadenced meter.

"2nd. There will be two prizes for the hymn and two for the ballad. The two top compositions will have first-place medallions, and the runners-up, second-place, provided by the Exposition Directorate. Each one of the first two prizes will be increased by the sum of fifty pesos to be paid by the Mayor of Santiago.

"3rd. The compositions will be submitted before 1 April to the Academy Secretary, anonymously and marked with a countersign matching the one on the closed fold in which the author's name is to be found.

---

* Reference is to Jean-Baptiste-Antoine Auget, Baron de Montyon (1733–1820), French civil servant, economist, and philanthropist, donor of lucrative national prizes for outstanding achievements in literature, medicine, science, and "acts of virtue." —Ed.

"4th. The Academy will impanel a jury comprising three of its members to report back on the merit of the compositions, in order that the institution award the prizes by absolute majority of its members present in the session apprised of the matter."

The Academy's invitation has been lavishly honored, as in the drama competition held the year before, for ten compositions were in the running, all of which were submitted for consideration by a jury comprising Messrs. Amunátegui, Asta-Buruaga, and Barro Arana.

These gentlemen have not found among all these compositions but a single one that adheres to the rules of the competition, specifically a ballad for voices only; and it considers that out of the hymns there is no more than one that is worthy of mention. The Academy has proceeded to judgment, and after long deliberation, has accepted the conclusion arrived at in the jury's report on the ballad, awarding the first prize designated by the Exposition Director to the author, who is Mr. Eduardo de la Barra; and as for the hymn to be prized, it has seen fit to extend the contest deadline until the last day of the month, for it entertains hopes that other poets will enter, and that those who already have, will make another attempt, or will have time to rewrite the compositions already submitted.

But, if the Academy has been able to do something this year to stimulate intellectual work, its efforts toward disseminating knowledge have run aground on a certain indifference, which we do not know if results from indolence, or lack of habit, or if the topic chosen for lectures and the person who set out to do justice to it did not awaken interest or strike an emotional chord. Whether one of these causes or all of them occasioned the fact, we cannot fail to find out, though it grieve us, in order that it may be brought to bear on the history of our intellectual development.

It was thought that political science would be a most interesting lecture theme, given that it is a branch of indispensable knowledge that is not included in our public education, since it was eliminated from the University for being a threat to the tranquillity of personal governments' absolute power. Youths that were educated in the last twenty-four years have not acquired a scientific doctrine on the theory of civil society, nor on that of political organization, and in these subjects has but the generally imprecise and incomplete empirical knowledge that makes up the bulk of the practice in the fledgling oligarchic republics that have had trial runs in this part of the Americas. It is true that this empiricism usually holds and holds now the place of science under ordinary circumstances, and that it still reaches the point of resisting it or simply scorning it; but it also serves as a foundation for prevailing absurdities, the tricks of underhanded politics, and, what is more, for chance to rule over law, and personal interests over the collective interest of society.

Nevertheless, the Academy's thought could not translate into a productive reality, since once the initial novelty of the attempt had worn off, the lectures were left practically deserted, and the professor merely had to put his lessons in block letters to hold them off for a more suitable occasion.

It is understandably most awkward for the author of these *Memoirs* to set forth these results here without registering a complaint therein, but instead discharging the duty of faithfully presenting the events he must narrate; but if one considers that he is in the habit of sowing for the morrow and not of harvesting out his portion, justice will be done him in believing that in fulfilling this obligation he completely sets aside his individuality. The proof is that he still is willing to repeat those lectures, undaunted by the risk of meeting with indifference, for he aspires to encourage those who feel equal to the task of facing that same risk.

In this way, and by dint of steadfastness, the Academy will acclimate this type of teaching that is still unknown in our country; and naturally it is with satisfaction that I can tell you there will be new lectures, which, for the importance of their themes and the genial talents of their authors, will pique greater interest.

Another reason motivating us to present you the truth about the results obtained, unvarnished and unattenuated, is the need we have to entertain no illusions about the insurmountable obstacles that all free associations unaffiliated with any concrete special interests must overcome in serving a speculative social interest like that of the independence of the spirit in the study of letters and sciences. We would do well always to remember the symbols with which we have surrounded our motto—those of intelligence, an iron will, courage, and prudence—in order not to falter, though we find ourselves alone.

We have defined the end of our aspirations and the means of serving it, which boil down to intelligent work guided by the positive criterion we have adopted. We will not achieve that end, as I told you on another occasion, since it is too grandiose to be the work of a single generation; but at least we will chart the course to be followed if we are firm of will and have the courage and prudence to instill it in the hearts and minds of those who come after us in the task of upholding our motto: TO ASSERT THE TRUTH IS TO SEEK JUSTICE.

Mr. Director:

In fulfillment of the honorable mission the Academy of Belles Lettres has been kind enough to confide to us, we have proceeded to examine the poetic compositions submitted to the competition held by this institution to celebrate this year's International Expo.

As you know, the competition was twofold; granted that compositions designed to be sung in a choir for unaccompanied voices could be entered, as well as compositions to be sung with musical accompaniment.

We have received three of the first variety with the title *Baladas* ["Ballads"], and seven of the second with the title *Himnos* ["Hymns"]. Having examined all of them attentively, we will express to you the verdict we have reached as to their merit.

Of the three ballads, we award first place, and consider deserving of the prize, to one entitled *A la fraternidad en la industria* ["Song To Fraternity in Industry"], and whose first stanza, which is a choir of children, begins as follows:

"Los cielos se tiñen
De claro arrebol . . ."

["The heavens are imbrued
With a bright red flash . . ."]

The way in which the main idea is developed, the good taste with which the basic traits that characterize industry are incorporated, the fluency of the versification, and its successful pictorial poetic expressions, give this composition an incontestable superiority over the others submitted to the two competitions. We believe, however, that the author can still polish some verses tarnished by minor flaws.

We find one ballad that carries the signature *Escipión* worthy of an honorable mention. In it there is an evenly developed pattern, and pleasant, well-made stanzas.

Regrettably, we cannot render an equally favorable opinion of the seven compositions submitted with the title *Himnos* ["Hymns"]. We would be afraid to digress somewhat pointlessly were we to call attention to the imperfections from which each of these pieces suffers, but we believe it only right to make an honorable mention of the *Himno a la industria* signed *Delio*, in which, although we have not found the conditions necessary to make it eligible for the prize, we acknowledge that it does not lack a certain merit.

This is all we have the honor of reporting to our colleagues in the Academy of Belles Lettres in this regard.

Mr. Director, kindly accept our most heartfelt regard.—Santiago, 9 April 1875.—*Miguel Luis Amunátegui.*—*Diego Barros Arana.*—*F. S. Asta-Buruaga.* Director of the Academy of Belles Lettres, etc.

Canto A La Fraternidad En La Industria

BALADA PREMIADA

Coro de niños

Los cielos se tiñen
De claro arrebol,
¿Quién manda esas luces?
¿De dónde esos tintes que anuncian un sol?

Coro de ancianos

¡Oh! ¡Industria, sabemos
Quién eres, tu voz
Despierta a los pueblos,
Los llama, los mueve, los lanza a la acción!

Coro de jóvenes

Templad nuestros yunques,
El brazo empujad,
Y grillos y espadas
En combos y arados sabremos trocar.
¡Oh! patria, tus valles,
Tus montes, tu mar,
Serán de los libres
Futura grandeza, magnífico altar.

LA INDUSTRIA

(*Todas las voces juntas*)

Yo todos los pueblos
Reúno en un haz,

Empujo el progreso
Y afianzo en el mundo la unión y la paz.
El yunque es mi trono,
La fragua mi altar,
Mi ley el trabajo,
Mi imperio la tierra, y el aire y el mar.

La inerte materia
Yo sé transformar,
Y aduno en mis moldes
La luz de la ciencia, del arte el ideal.
Concentro los rayos
En breve cristal,
Y fundo la lente
Que el fondo del cielo permite tocar.

Yo fijo en mis prensas
La idea fugaz,
Y es chispa que envío,
Creciendo, alumbrando de edad en edad.
Yo tiendo mi alambre
Y al habla ya están
Las playas distantes,
Y así les preparo la unión fraternal.

He creado un potente
Moderno animal,
Caballo en la tierra,
Se lanza a las aguas, novel Leviatán.
Su ijar es de acero,
Su voz de huracán,
Su altivo penacho
Mi reino a las gentes se avanza a anunciar.

Taladro los montes,
Remuevo la mar,
Y cruzo los aires
En frágiles barcas de leve cendal.
Y acaso mañana,
Tras rudo lidiar,
Despliegue a los vientos
Las alas ligeras del águila real.

Mis trojas, abiertas
A todos están:
¡Oh pueblos dispersos,
Venid al banquete de unión y de paz!
¿Buscáis abundancia?
¿Queréis libertad?
¡Seguidme! Yo toco
La diana que anuncia su carro triunfal!

E. DE LA BARRA

Song to Fraternity in Industry

PRIZE-WINNING BALLAD

Chorus of children

The heavens are imbrued
With a bright red flash,
Who sends those lights?
Whence those tinges auguring a sun?

Chorus of elders

Oh, Industry, we know
Who you are, your voice
Rouses the nations,
Calls them, moves them, springs them into action!

Chorus of youths

Tune our anvils, all,
Drive your arms,
And fetters and swords
We will be able to swap for sledges and plows.
Oh! Homeland, your valleys,
Your mountains, your sea,
Someday will be the grandeur,
The magnificent altar, of the free.

INDUSTRY
(all voices)

All nations
I gather together in a sheaf.

I am the driving force of progress
And guarantee union and peace in the world.
    The anvil is my throne,
    The forge my altar,
    My law, labor,
My kingdom, earth, air and sea.

    Inert matter
    I can transform,
    I join in my molds
The light of science, the ideal of art.
    I focus the rays
    On thin glass
    And cast the lens
That allows the depths of heaven to be touched.

    I hold tight in my presses
    The fast-fading idea,
    And it is a spark I send,
Growing, shedding light from age to age.
    I lay out my wire
    And far-flung beaches
    Are then within hailing distance,
And thus I prepare them for fraternal union.

    I have created a powerful
    Modern animal,
    A horse on earth,
It rushes headlong into the waters, a new Leviathan.
    Its flank is of steel,
    Its voice of hurricane
    Its haughty pride
Presses on to proclaim my reign to the people.

    I bore through the mountains,
    I remove the sea,
    I cross the winds
In fragile boats of lightest gauze.
    And perchance on the morrow,
    After a hard fight
    The lightweight wings of the golden eagle
Will spread in the breeze.

My granaries to all
Are open.
Oh scattered nations,
Come all to the feast of union and peace!
Seek ye freedom?
Follow me! I play
The reveille that announces your winning chariot!

E. DE LA BARRA

VII

OFFICIAL SESSION OF THE THIRD ANNIVERSARY OF THE
ACADEMY OF BELLES LETTRES, HELD ON 12 APRIL 1876

Director's Report

Gentlemen:

The Academy of Belles Lettres's labors have been much more productive this year than in the two previous ones; but if we can be glad that through their pursuits it has evolved, we should harbor no illusions about its future. We still have to consolidate our institution's only stable foundation: interest in the independent cultivation of letters and science.

We cannot rely on the future as long as this interest is not collective, as long as intellectuals are convinced it is possible to complete one's knowledge without first strengthening the independence of the spirit, giving it a positive criterion for discovering the truth, so we do not attribute a scientific character to any theory if it cannot be proven by experience.

When this conviction leads to love of study and has awakened a true collective interest, the association will have a foundation, and the Academy's existence will be consolidated. Only the truth can band people together effectively, for sentiment itself and speculative or active interest do not serve as a center of union and cooperation, except insofar as they respectively are a truth or at least a conviction.

In this year now ending, the Academy of Belles Lettres has held thirty-nine sessions, and in them fifty-five readings were performed by Academy members and twenty-one by visitors, in addition to seven conferences or oral dissertations, and some works delivered by foreign correspondent Academy members.

The authors are: Mr. Valderrama, who has read fourteen compositions; Mr. Zambrana, ten; Mr. Matta M. A., eight; Mr. Garriga, six; Mr. Barros Grez, four; three apiece from Messrs. Lavín Matta, Carrasco Albano, and Mrs. Orrego de Uribe; two from Mr. González and the Director, and one each from Messrs. Santa Cruz, Asta-Buruaga, Piñeiro, Dávila Larraín, Allende Padín, and the Secretary.

The visitors V. Letelier, Dr. Peña, Cubillos, Sève, Caravantes, Ferrán, Quirós, J. Lagarrigue, performed one reading apiece; Messrs. Lemoine and A. Lillo, two, and three each from Messrs. E. Barros, Orihuela, and Escuti.

These eighty-three compositions, which reveal fertile effort, can be classified in this way: thirty-six sociological, five scientific, and forty-two imaginative literature.

The first prove that growth, as vast as it is interesting, has come about in studies on the social sciences: general philosophy, rational morality, political science under its two aspects relating to social organization and to that of the powers of the State, political economy, history and historical criticism and biography, have provided the topics for the different works presented in the Academy. All those topics have been dealt with earnestly and in the light of a remarkably positive criterion, which imparts to the studies a bent that is practical and far removed from metaphysical illusions and unscientific theories. Among these studies there were some that were immediately useful, dealing with administration matters, and others of great speculative interest, such as those that served as topics for oral presentations.

This genre of works that we longed to propose as one of the most pleasant and simplest forms for spreading knowledge, has been tried out this year to great effect. The Academy also happily held other lectures that were great motivators, without holding in high regard the many conferences with which the Directory of that free institution of primary education, called the School of Artisans, sparked so much interest; it was to that organization we ceded our reception room to assist them in their charitable pursuit. Mr. Zambrana, whose absence leaves such fond memories in this organization, first delivered three fascinating papers on the social and political status of the Anglo-American colony before its independence, mostly from the point of view of religious tolerance, and on the relations between Church and State in the American Union after the Republic was constituted. Apart from these papers, the same Academy member gave others on the philosophy of August Comte, which aroused a brilliant debate, and elicited dazzling replies from Messrs. Jorge Lagarrigue and Benjamín Larraín.

The attack on positive philosophy brought to our open forum some of the objections with which the experimental school has challenged certain of the great French philosopher's conclusions, neither disregarding nor rejecting the foundations and the criterion of positive philosophy; and he tried additionally to cast aspersions on the latter with the malicious recriminations with which the metaphysicians and the theologians have treated it, thus lacking one of the primary conditions of tolerance, which consists of respecting and not disparaging the opinions of others, using against them, when they are in the wrong, only the means of persuasion, those that never will have an impact if they are girded with violence and decorated with the jeering from which truth flees. But the defenders of the philosophy guiding our studies rejected and explained those attacks, demonstrating the advantages of the scientific or positive method that can be applied to the examination of all material and moral phenomena, without risk of running up against the two inevitable obstacles of metaphysics, which are materialism or idealism. Whenever in studies of social science the facts of human nature revealed through all their manifestations are taken as the foundation of reasoning, and whenever philosophic research and art in this area of studies rest on positive evidence demonstrated by observation of this nature, there is no reason to fear the extremes of idealism, nor those of sensualism or materialism, nor the strayings of which people seek to accuse positive philosophy, and which are but the product of a lack of examination or observation.

As for the compositions commonly called serious literature that were submitted this year, it is fair to state they were superior in quality to last year's. This genre of writings, which in our classification we call plastic, since, heeding the spirit's method, produce a painting depicting physical or moral nature, rendering a feeling, an impression, sketching a slice of life, an event, or a situation, should be subject to the criterion of scientific or sociological works, depending on their respective subject matters. We do not understand modern poetry outside of the laws of the physical universe or those that rule human nature. The relative truth of any imaginative painting cannot endure by ignoring or flauting those laws, nor can there be morality in it if the collective interest of the human species does not triumph, since the poet cannot stray from the laws of the nature of man without dousing the idea of our perfection and of our freedom with error, doubt, or confusion. However great the genius and artistry of a mythological painting may be, for example, it can be of no interest unless it is for the charms of its form; while if, when producing a nature scene or capturing a human situation, relative truth and morality are preserved in an artistic form, genius and art will have accomplished the lofty mission that philosophy of the modern age reserves for the poet.

And this is exactly the trend discerned in the majority of compositions in this genre that have been submitted to the Academy, for which reason we take pleasure in announcing true progress, as evidenced by a large number of poetic works and especially by the stanzas of the beautiful satiric poem that Mr. Valderrama has read to us.

Among those poetic works, those submitted to the competitions held this year now ending are not lagging behind on the new course. As mentioned in the previous year's Report, there was a competition left pending for a *Hymn to Industry*, which had been initiated upon request of the Directorate of the International Expo. In the attached documents appears the report by Messrs. Matta, Arteaga Alemparte, and Valderrama, who were the jury that issued a judgment, and related the outcome of the Academy's deliberations.

Buoyed by the splendid results of that competition, this institution sought to celebrate the anniversary of the 1875 independence with another, and to that end announced the following themes:

1st. An ode in celebration of some glorious event or some personage from national history;
2nd. A strictly historical narrative in prose, also taken from national history;
3rd. A study on the practical effects of political centralization;
4th. An article on ways and manners;
5th. A description of the Chilean Andes.

Only compositions on topics 1 and 4 were submitted to the competition. The committees named, pursuant to competition rules, provided the findings addended to this Report, and the Academy agreed to award the prize to don Manuel Antonio Boz's ode entitled *Al dieciocho de setiembre* ["To Eighteen September"], merely making the submitted feature on ways and manners an honorable mention.

The great movement launched by the works I am reporting on provided the Academy sessions with a regular turnout in excess of two hundred people, which kindly graced us with their company and applause. The indifference we spoke of last year with respect to the conferences we had gotten off the ground, is no longer a danger we have to overcome, though it is true that there is not all the activity on the part of the Academy members that could be hoped for, an effort which they could invest to great effect were they to recall their commitment. But the Academy has been reinforced with new workers, naming as founding members Messrs. Fernando Santa María, Pablo Garriga, Diego Torres Arce, Gaspar Toro, M. G. Carmona, and Ricardo Becerra; and honorary members, Messrs. D. F. Sarmiento, A. Zambrana, Arnaldo Márquez, P. Paz Soldán y Unanue, and E. Sève, all of them remarkable writers and some famous on our continent.

In reporting these nominations there is a memory painful to us, that of the sudden loss of the young Santa María, whom death seized before his time just as the Academy was inducting him to repay the major contributions he had made since the early days of our organization.

Another loss the Academy sincerely regrets is that of don Francisco de Paulo Vigil, illustrious scholar and wise Peruvian writer, who honored our list of foreign correspondent members.

In conclusion, gentlemen, I must call your attention to the circumstance of having finished our annual work with the initiative of a reform that will serve as a topic for our next deliberations. I speak of the bill the Secretary introduced to organize literary circles in Copiapó, La Serena, San Felipe, Valparaíso, Talca, and Concepción, with the duty of extending education through free societies, which they would head according to a uniform plan common to all. This goal and the others encompassed by the reform project are worthy of serious consideration; and if we do not lack for means to see them through, the Academy will rejoice at having launched a robust movement with great results, since it is not to be limited to cultivating literary form, but to support the only foundation of all intellectual progress: the independence of the spirit.

SECOND JURY'S REPORT ON THE POETIC COMPETITION

Director:

In fulfilling the duties of the committee with which the Academy was kind enough to honor us, we have examined the twenty-four hymns that have entered the open competition for poetic compositions in the class devoted to praising industry.

The last seven, or rather, those marked with the numbers 18 to 24, do not withstand the test of a first reading. Faulty in their composition, style, versification, and even in their syntax, there is similarly nothing to recommend their poesy.

The remaining seventeen hymns, considered as a whole, reveal in their authors a fairly thorough and precise understanding of the topic to be treated, and of the metric conditions to which their cantos should conform. In them we notice a fluency of versification, the ardor of fancy, poetic instinct, pleasant thoughts, beautiful images, and at times an inspiration that, spreading powerful wings, climbs to the spheres of exalted poetry.

In our judgment, none of these seventeen compositions meets the necessary requisites to be declared an accomplished work. But among them are found five that, for different reasons, are praiseworthy and deserving of consideration as works of true merit.

We now will list them.

Hymn number 5, whose chorus begins

"¡Salve! ¡Salve!, tu mano derrame," etc.

["Hail! Hail!, your hand pours out," etc.]

is written in consonantal decasyllabic lines arrayed in eight-verse stanzas, in which acute rhymes are mixed symmetrically with grave ones. All its verses have the rhythmic stresses the poem requires and flow naturally and fluently. Its form would leave little to be desired if it were not tarnished by some inelegant or imprecise constructions.

As far as the hymn's subject matter, its poetic interest is sustained by a string of images and thoughts that are fitting to characterize industry and glorify its benefits and wonders. What one may find lacking is a perfect build-up and gradation, the strict linking of its different parts. One colorful and vibrant image is followed by another wan and colorless one, and the energy and liveliness of an early thought are perhaps spoiled by a muddled or inconsistent one that follows it.

Hymn number 8, written in assonant decasyllabic quartets, beginning

"Tu redimes al hombre que lucha," etc.

["You redeem the man who fights," etc.]

is superior to the others for the beauty and appropriateness of its creativity. The poet presents man as prisoner to natural inevitabilities. The former turns his gaze toward heaven in search for assistance and brings redeeming industry down from on high. With its help, the serf becomes king of creation, the slave becomes master.

Unfortunately, the hymn's execution is not up to par with its conception. Though its style may not be lacking in swiftness and charm, it is missing precision and suggestive grace that were necessary to bring vivacity and splendor to the idea.

Hymn number 9, dubbed *patriotic song* by its author and beginning

"Hogar propio nos trajo la guerra," etc.

["The war brought us our own home," etc.]

is composed of strophes of eight decasyllables in which paroxytonic consonants alternate with oxytonic ones. Each of the stanzas is preceded by a chorus different from the first one, which gives the hymn three different choruses.

Its metric devices together with its choice of rhymes evince an intelligent and deft versifier.

To the merit of its versification are added the elegance and liveliness of the style, the poetic charm of expression.

For its treatment of the inspiration and overall organization of the poem, we feel that it does not excel nor even equal the other hymns we are considering. As for the qualifier of *patriotic song*, it is justified by a few graceful stanzas flattering to our national pride, in which the poet recalls Chile's industrial pursuits and advancements.

Hymn number 15 in its versification obeys the laws of iambic heptasyllabic stanzas, in which Leandro Fernández de Moratín lamented the death of the historian Conde. Its chorus:

"Industria, tú que guías
Los pueblos hacia el bien
En su gloriosa marcha
Siempre a Chile sostén."

["Industry, you who lead
Nations toward the good,
Provide for Chile evermore
On its glorious path."]

It is regrettable that that chorus is so poor in rhythm and poetry, for the rest of the hymn abounds in charming verses and beautiful stanzas, among which the following one stands out, a most beautiful strophe and perfectly singable, except for the arrhythmic eighth verse:

"Cuánto vergel oculto
Te guardan nuestros llanos!
Encierra el monte inculto
Metales que en tus manos
Son herramienta, máquina,
Adorno, estatua o riel;
Y en clima suave y grato
Sabrá aquí obedecerte,
Sumisa a tu mandato,
Raza viril y fuerte,
A la opresión indómita,
Pero al trabajo fiel."

[“How many hidden orchards
Our plains hold for you!
The wild mountain harbors
Metals that in your hands
Are tool, machine,
Adornment, statue or rail;
And in a balmy, pleasant clime
It will bend to your will,
Submissive to your bidding,
A race virile and strong,
Untamed by oppression,
But loyal to work.”]

In stanzas of the same meter and combination, though shorter, hymn number 16 is written, which has the following chorus:

"¡Salve! esplendor del arte,
¡Segunda creación!
Tremole sobre América
Tu augusto pabellón."

[“Hail! Splendor of art,
Second creation!
Wave over South America
Your stately flag.”]

There is a good deal of artistry in the composition of this hymn, a work intended less as a tribute to the glories of industry than as a celebration of the coming Santiago International Expo of 1875. Its versification is proper and fluent, its stanzas have feeling and movement, and more than once poetic inspiration shines through in its verses like a flashing light.

The brief analysis we have just offered proves what we stated at the beginning of this report; to wit: that for different reasons the five hymns mentioned are praiseworthy and deserving of consideration as works of true merit.

These circumstances make it difficult to give preference to one over the others. But if the task the Academy has entrusted us extends to that, we deem hymn number 16 the winner, more for its greater adherence to the particular requirements of the proposed theme than for its intrinsic quality.

As we conclude this report, allow us to congratulate the Academy for the results of the competition held under its auspices. It brings us new testimonials of our youth's growing activity and incessant progress in the pursuit of literature.

Yours most respectfully, Mr. Director.—AA. SS.—*Domingo Arteaga A.*—*Adolfo Valderrama.*—*Manuel A. Matta.*—To the Director of the Academy of Belles Lettres.

Himno

(CON MOTIVO DE LA EXPOSICÍON DE 1875)

PREMIADO

Coro

¡Salve! esplendor del arte,
¡Segunda creación!
Tremole sobre América
Tu augusto pabellón.

I

Graves, solemnes cantos
Escuche el firmamento:
De un pueblo el libro acento
Celebre en coro olímpico
Los triunfos de la paz.

Al templo de las Artes
Acudan las naciones:
Sus contrastados guiones

En el soberbio pórtico
Flamean en un haz.

II

A abrirse va el palenque;
Los émbolos se agitan
Y unísonos palpitan
Los pechos y las máquinas
En rítmico latir.

¡Salve! triunfal Industria,
Tu fuego nos alienta,
En tu crisol fermenta,
Obra de nuevos Cíclopes,
Radiante el porvenir.

III

Apréstanos las alas
Del cóndor eminente,
Y en tu taller ardiente
Vigor halle el espíritu
Y el pueblo libertad.

¡Venid, naciones todas!
La luz y la experiencia
Del arte y de la ciencia
En armoniosa síntesis
Amigas desplegad.

IV

Gallardeando ufanas
Los anchos mares venzan
Las flámulas indianas,
Y aporten de la América
El natural primor.

Y al par, lleguen los dones
De aquel tan portentoso,
Tan grande en dar lecciones,
Soberbio nido de águilas
Que el Niagar' arrulló.

V

La siempre sabia Europa
En nuestro templo encienda
Su luz, votiva ofrenda
De sus antiguas fábricas
A un mundo juvenil.

Y el arte nos descubra
Que en la materia inerte
Calor y vida vierte
Para decirle: "¡Lázaro,
Levántate a vivir!"

VI

¡Oh Watt, y Morse, y Fulton!
¡Oh Gutenberg glorioso!
El carro victorioso
Regís, y es vuestro Píndaro
La lira universal.

Leves, divinas sombras,
Espléndidos fanales
De rayos inmortales,
A los obreros pósteros
La senda iluminad.

VII

¡Alzad, y con vosotros
Los ínclitos, los grandes
Guerreros de los Andes
Rasguen sus velos fúnebres
Al eco del clarín!

Llegad al patrio suelo
Donde tenéis altares,
Y ved, propicios lares,
La antes colonia gótica
Cuán próspera y feliz.

VIII

¡Suena a la lid la trompa!
Los émbolos se agitan,
Y unísonos palpitan,
Los pechos y las válvulas
En rítmico latir.

Grandioso el coro rompa,
Y al formidable acento
De máquinas sin cuento,
¡Unase el canto armónico
De un pueblo al porvenir!

E. DE LA BARRA

Hymn

(ON THE OCCASION OF THE EXPOSITION OF 1875)

PRIZE POEM

Chorus

Hail! Splendor of art,
Second creation!
Wave over South America
Your stately flag.

I

Let the heavens' vault hear
Grave, solemn songs:
Let the voice of a nation
Celebrate in olympic chorus
The victories of peace.

To the temple of the Arts
Let the nations flock:
Their clashing royal standards
In the grand portico
Flutter in a cluster.

II

The arena is poised to open;
The pistons are set in motion
And in unison
Hearts and machines beat
In rhythmic pulse.

Hail! Triumphant industry,
Your fire is our sustenance,
In your crucible ferments
The work of a new Cyclops,
The future bright.

III

Lend us the wings
Of the eminent condor,
And in your burning workshop
May the spirit find vim
And the people, freedom.

Come nations all!
Put on parade
The knowledge and experience
Of art and science
Joined in peaceful union.

IV

Graceful and proud
May the Spanish-American streamers
Conquer the wide oceans,
And furnish the natural enchantment
Of our continent.

And equally, let the
Gifts arrive from that superb eagles' nest,
A nest the Niagara lulled,
So portentous and great in imparting lessons.

V

Let the eternally wise Europe
Light in our temple

Its light, a votive offering
From its old factories
To a youthful world.

And let art discover for us
That into inert matter
Heat and life are flowing,
Saying to it: "Lazarus,
Rise up and live!"

VI

Oh, Watt and Morse and Fulton!
Oh glorious Gutenberg!
You are at the reins
Of the winning chariot, and the universal lyre
Is your Pindar.

Slight, heaven-sent shadows,
Splendid beacons
Immortal of beam,
Light the way
For workers to come.

VII

Rise up, and with you
May the illustrious, the great
Warriors of the Andes
Slash their mourning veils
As the clarion call resounds!

Reach the native soil
Where your altars lay,
And see propitious firesides,
The once gothic colony
How prosperous and happy they are!

VIII

The trumpet calls to arms!
The pistons are set in motion,
And in unison
Hearts and valves beat
In rhythmic pulse.

Let the chorus burst out grandiose,
And to the formidable voice
Of machines without number
Let the harmonious song
Of a nation be joined to the future!

E. DE LA BARRA

REPORT ON TWO ODES
SENT TO THE ACADEMY OF BELLES LETTRES

*Competition in honor of the anniversary
of the Independence*

Let us examine scrupulously the two poetic compositions on which
the Academy requests our opinion; but since this report is to be
merely a foundation of argument and since the Academy reserves the
right to reach a verdict on its own on this matter, we will allow ourselves certain expositions that, while they are the reasons behind our
report, also show the point of view from which we chose to judge.

The ode in the modern age has undergone a complete facelift;
the Hellenic ode that was used in most cases to celebrate feasts and
religious solemnities sung alike of the glory of heroes and the
praises of the gods: an eminently lyrical composition, we see in it
the rapture of passion, the forceful impulsiveness of genius, the daring of the images and the harmony of the turns of phrase, wedded
to the forcefulness of the style; but its principal character among
the Greeks was to be always singable. It is known that Pindar is the
highest personification of the Hellenic ode and though Anacreon
and Sappho, who have lent their names to two genres of composition, sung, the former of sweet and tender love and the latter the
ecstasy of a frenzied passion, gave to their compositions a loftiness
and an intensity that enrapture the spirit and place them in Greek
literature as the expression of the most extraordinary lyricism.

The Latin poets did not fly as high, and Horace, an admirer of
Pindar, is no match for his role model's ecstatic ardor and forceful
inspiration, in spite of his culture and elegance. This quite probably
depends on the different civilizations in which the two poets lived,
to say nothing of the individual faculties of both men. Make of that
what one may, the Latin ode was not sung.

Since the most distinguished masters have established their precepts by basing themselves on the study of the Greco-Roman poets, it will come as no surprise to the Academy that we have taken a look, albeit briefly, at the characteristics of the ode in those days.

The ode in the modern age is a composition designed to depict the rapture of passion, everything that can shake the soul and elevate the feelings to the rarefied regions of fervor: thus the ode has few rules; fervor does not reason coldly. The spirit flies skyward on the wings of inspiration, plunges into the luminous ether of images and noble thoughts, and there the poet, in his element, writes an immortal work, or, his wings burnt up by the fire of an air he cannot breathe, falls desolate and tearful to the easy atmosphere of mediocrity, and relinquishes the laurel leaves that crowned the brows of Pindar and Horace.

The Spanish poets, narrowing the realms of the ode more than did the Greek and Latin poets, gave it alternately a heroic, philosophical, sacred or amorous and comic nature. Testimonials of these many forms are fray Luis de León, Fernando de Herrera, don Esteban de Villegas, Meléndez Valdés, and many others; and whatever direction the Spanish bards gave to the odes, they always respected the essential nature that the Greek and Latin poets gave to this genre of composition. Ardor and passion are the essential qualities of this kind of work; the verse should be fluent and harmonious, the images vivid and spirited, the thoughts lofty, the style at once vehement and majestic, the passion deep and ardent; all trivia are banned from this type of composition; one might say without fear of being mistaken, that the ode is the noblest expression of lyric poetry.

As for the meter in which the ode should be written, it is impossible to determine: typically it is rendered in equal stanzas, but they can be composed in several ways; in one instance some stanzas may comprise hendecasyllabic and heptasyllabic verses arranged in different ways, like in Herrera's ode celebrating don Juan of Austria's exploits, in another instance they may be Sapphic-Adonic* as in some odes by Cadalso and the ode to don Esteban de Villegas's zephyr; it is less common to find, in this genre of composition, iambic heptameter. At all events, since the essence of these works is passion and ardor, these compositions are to be short if one does

---

* Sapphic verse is named for the Greek poetess (7th–6th c. B.C.) and refers to a type of Aeolic meter (wherein dactyls and trochees are employed together). The Sapphic stanza comprises three Lesser Sapphic lines and one Adonic, which takes the same form as the last two feet of the dactylic hexameter (six-foot line of long syllables followed by two short ones). —Trans.

not wish to lose steam, as one cannot maintain the spirit for long in the atmosphere of sublime thoughts and images, and because the more surpassing spirits who might wish to attempt such recklessness, would almost always be short of air. This is the standard generally followed by the great masters of Castilian poetry, some of whom we have mentioned and whom don Manuel José Quintana, in more recent times, has had the glory of equalling.

With all this in mind, let us examine the compositions the Academy has done us the honor of subjecting to our humble judgment, and we shall not demand they rival those written by the masters of the art, but that, with an eye on the models, we shall see which comes closest to the difficult conditions required for this type of work.

Two odes, which the Committee is going to examine, were submitted to the Academy's competition. One has the title of *Chacabuco*, in which the author sings the praises of the hero of that glorious expedition, and the other is the ode *Al dieciocho de setiembre* ["To Eighteen September"], in which the poet exalts that day that was so gratifying for the country.

We must confess that, after having read them one after another, with the objective of observing the general outlines of each composition, the vitality and coloring of each one of them, we have not found that loftiness, nor that grandiose tone, nor those fits of ardor that make up the essence and the principal merit of this genre of work; nevertheless, we must acknowledge in both a fluent versification, forceful style, and a certain South American fragrance that renders them worthy of acclamation.

Deepening our study of the works, we see that the first of these odes, entitled *Chacabuco* and beginning

"Para cantar la hazaña
De más eterna gloria," etc.

["To sing the feats
Of most eternal glory," etc.]

falls off in quality at times, and on occasions is careless in form, inharmonious in its verses; we notice that the poet changes meter in mid-composition, doubtlessly to end the work majestically with a hendecasyllable, but fails to notice that this unexpected change somewhat drains the work of its unity and beauty. The preposition with which he begins the ode is an unfortunate choice, and the reader braces himself to hear an argument, which in fact comes: but this could have been avoided had the author wished to begin with the fifth verse, which says

"Sublime inspiración, brinda mi canto."

["Sublime inspiration, invite my song."]

We find most beautiful stanzas in this composition, and some noteworthy comparisons; here is the stanza:

"Jamás fueron más grandes
Los gigantescos Andes
Que el día aquel en que su cumbre hería
La planta audaz de la región de bravos
Que a libertar corría
Pueblos cansados de sentirse esclavos."

["Never were
the gigantic Andes greater
Than that day on which its peak wounded
The audacious soles of the legion of the brave
That rushed to free
Nations weary of feeling like slaves."]

In the ode *To Eighteen September,* the beginning is worthier and loftier, and although the work is not free of flaws, it is made with more artistry and less negligence; the verses are in general fluent and harmonious and the inspiration never flags, perhaps since it is shorter; but we have already mentioned that this is one of the conditions of the ode, which would put the composition in a favorable light. The uniformity of meter in every sense gives the ode a certain unity that leads the reader to embrace in a glance the few but mindful charms the work contains. To cite but a few verses, the Academy's attention is drawn to the following:

"La esclava que abatida y macilenta
Por tantos años soportó la afrenta
De ser de viles amos sierva humilde,
Te vio llegar en bendecida hora,
Cual tras noche de amargo desconsuelo
Se ve brillar el cielo
A las luces primeras de la aurora."

["The slave who, for so many years,
Endured the outrage
Of being the humble servant of villainous masters,
Saw your arrival in blessed hour,
Like after a night of bitter grief
The sky appears shining
In the first light of dawn."]

These verses are fluent and harmonious, and the simile, though not new, is rendered in stylish and euphonic forms: the author has taken pains at the end of each strophe to place a fluent, harmonious verse to sow a pleasant, musical impression in the spirit.

In sum, the Committee does not deem any of the compositions an accomplished work, though it ventures to recommend to the Academy the ode *Al dieciocho de setiembre*, in the hopes that the organization will rectify with its noble judgment and refined literary taste where this humble opinion might have erred.

Santiago, 24 September 1875.—*Adolfo Valderrama.*—*Pablo Garriga.*—*Francisco Solano Asta-Buruaga.*

Al Dieciocho de Setiembre

I

¡Salve día de gloria,
Página la más pura y la más bella
De nuestra joven y brillante historia!
La esclava que abatida y macilenta
Por tantos años soportó la afrenta
De ser de viles amos sierva humilde,
Te vio llegar en bendecida hora,
Cual tras noche de amargo desconsuelo
Se ve brillar el cielo
A las luces primeras de la aurora.
Y tú viste a esa esclava despertarse
Del letárgico sueño en que yacía
Y llena de ardimiento y de fe llena
Romper con fuerza heroica la cadena
Con que atada se vía.

II

¿Qué estruendo pavoroso
Se extiende por los campos y los bosques

Do habitó el indio rudo y belicoso?
¿Qué insólito temblor la tierra mueve?
¿Qué eco es el que repite esa montaña?
¿Qué voz la que conmueve
A la ciudad, al pueblo, a la campaña? . . .
¡Oh día de ventura!
¡Tú escuchaste ese grito que imponente
Voló desde el ocaso hasta el oriente,
Infundiendo fatídica pavura
A la del vil tirano raza impura!
¡Grito de libertad, grito de guerra
Que estremeció la tierra
"Del ancho Bío-Bío al Atacama";
Grito que en varonil ardor inflama
Al niño delicado,
Y que reanima del valor la llama
En el anciano débil y encorvado
Bajo el peso del yugo que lo infama!

III

Tu sol, ¡oh fausto día!,
Que presenció después en cien combates
Que cien victorias fueron,
El valor, la constancia y la energía
De los que patria y libertad nos dieron,
Ora viene a alumbrar, no las legiones
De esa raza de leones
Que con sangre la tierra enrojecieron;
No las rudas batallas do probaron
Las huestes de esos ínclitos campeones,
Que puede más el sacro patriotismo
Que el torpe, asalariado servilismo:
Hoy derrama su luz sobre el progreso
Que la creadora paz, la paz bendita,
Con benéfica influencia
Da al arte, y a la industria, y a la ciencia.

IV

Ese monte, el collado, esta llanura,
Aquella selva umbría,
Testigos de la fuerza y la bravura

De tus valientes hijos, patria mía,
Y que ilumina con su lumbre pura
El majestuoso luminar del día;
Esos campos que Marte presidía
En aquel tiempo aciago,
No de la guerra impía
Demuestran hoy el lamentable estrago . . .
Ceres con mano amiga
Fructífera simiente les prodiga
Y en la colina, el valle, el fértil llano
Regados con la sangre generosa
De tantos héroes, se alza ya la hermosa,
Dorada espiga de dorado grano.
¡Y por doquiera que la vista alcanza,
Allí se ve la mano
De un pueblo libre, grande, soberano,
Que poderoso al porvenir se lanza!

V

Tú, que a la patria mía
Guiaste por la senda de victoria,
Recibe, ¡oh fausto día!,
El saludo que Chile ora te envía:
¡Salve día de gloria,
Página la más pura y la más bella
De nuestra joven y brillante historia!

Setiembre de 1875.

MANUEL A. BOZA

To Eighteen September

I

Hail day of glory,
Purest and most beautiful page
From our young and brilliant history!
The slave who, for so many years,
Endured the outrage
Of being the humble servant of villainous masters,

Saw your arrival in blessed hour,
Like after a night of bitter grief
The sky appears shining
In the first light of dawn.
And you saw that slave awake
From the sluggish dream in which she lay
And summoning courage, her faith brimming full,
Break with heroic strength the chain
That bound her.

II

What dreadful clamor
Rumbles through the field and forest
Where the coarse and warring Indians dwelled?
What unwonted quaking shakes the earth?
What echo does the mountain repeat?
What voice stirs
The city, the nation, to the countryside? . . .
O happy day!
You heard that imposing cry that
Flew from west to east,
Spreading ominous dread through the impure race
Of the vile tyrant!
Cry of freedom, cry of war
That shook the earth
"From the wide Bío-Bío to the Atacama";
Cry that in manly ardor inflames
The delicate child,
And that rekindles valor's flame
In the stooped and enfeebled elder
Under the weight of the yoke that defames him!

III

Your sun, o blessed day!,
Who witnessed thereafter in one hundred wars
That spelled one hundred victories,
The valor, constancy and drive
Of those that country and freedom gave us,
Now you come to light up
Not the legions of that race of lions
That bloodied the earth in scarlet;

Not the hard-fought wars where
The armies of those illustrious champions were tried,
For holy love of country can do more
Than slow-witted, salaried servility:
Today it pours down its light on the progress
That creative peace, holy peace
With charitable sway
Lends to art, to industry and to science.

IV

That mountain, the hill, this plain,
That shaded forest,
Witnesses to the strength and bravery
Of your valiant sons, my fatherland,
And that the majestic luminary of day
Lights with its pure flame;
Those fields o'er which Mars presided
In those ill-omened times,
From the ungodly war
They show not regrettable ruin today . . .
Ceres with a friendly hand
Lavishes on them a bountiful seed
And on the hillock, the vale, the fruited plain
Irrigated with the generous blood
Of so many heroes, the beautiful ear
Of golden grain now is gathered in.
And everywhere one's eyes alight
Is seen the hand
Of a people free, great, sovereign,
Powerful people hurtling toward the future!

V

You who guided my country
Down the path of victory,
Hearken, o lucky day!
To the greeting Chile sends you:
Hail day of glory,
Purest and most beautiful page
From our young and brilliant history!

September 1875.

MANUEL A. BOZA

VIII

Report by the Vice-Director don Marcial González

I

Gentlemen:

Today marks the four-year anniversary of our Academy of Belles Lettres, and having reviewed the minutes from the sessions, I have the satisfaction of affirming that, in the course of this last year, its efforts have not diminished in number or in importance. Within its modest sphere, it has continued serving the development of national literature, as well as the betterment of noble studies; and though attendance by many of its founding members has not been constant, literary and scientific works brought to this hall have never been lacking and must have had some remarkable attraction when more than one hundred visitors, almost all of them young students, baccalaureates in humanities or law, lawyers, doctors, engineers or simple aficionados of the literary art, on every evening of sessions have diligently formed a select audience, which with its enthusiasm and assiduous attention urges on the writers and shows real interest in all things related to the pursuit of letters and science in the country.

In the year in which I am reporting to you, the Academy has held thirty-two sessions, in which seventy-one readings were performed, forty-six by Academy members and twenty-five by visitors. Of the former, eight were by Mr. Letelier and seven by Mr. Valderrama; from Messrs. Barra, Dávila, Garriga, and Gallo, five; from your reporter, four; and one each of Messrs. Asta-Buruaga, Cañas, Lavín M., Montt (Luis), and Matta (M. A.). Among visitors, Messrs. Quirós read four times; Boza, Castro, Escuti, and Ferrán, three; and one by Messrs. Cubillos, Lagarrigue (J. E.), Román Blanco, and Torres Arce. Out of the forty-six readings by Academy members, thirty-eight were in prose and eight in verse, and of the twenty-five from visitors, sixteen were in verse and nine in prose.

Also in the same year seven works from major to minor importance were read to the institution: one by Academy member Blanco Cuartín entitled *Lo que queda de Voltaire* ["What Is Left of Voltaire"]; another by Mr. Arístides Rojas, foreign correspondent, *La supuesta delación de don Andrés Bello* ["Don Andrés Bello's Alleged Denunci-ation"]; another by Dr. Frick, from Valdivia, *Estudio sobre una or-tografía universal* ["Study of a Universal Orthography"]; another by don Jorge Lagarrigue, from Paris, speaking on *El último libro de M. Littré* ["M. Littré's Last Book"]; *Estudio filológico referente al valor de la Y griega* ["Philological Study On the Value of the Upsilon"] by Mr. Mathieu de Fossey; another, *Estudio sobre la vacuna* ["Study on the Vaccine"] by Dr. R. Ortiz Cerda, of Santiago; and some *Versos a Dios* ["Verses to God"] by Mr. Alejandro González, of Concepción. So all told this year seventy-eight readings were performed, twenty-five in verse and fifty-three in prose.

II

In these works I am remarking on that there have been a fair number of exceptional quality. By genre, they can all be distributed thus: eleven in literary criticism; eight in philology; seven in science; nine in didactic literature; ten in literature, such as articles of ways and manners and stories or prose skits; one in general politics and four in sociology. Moreover, heartfelt poetic compositions on diverse topics and of greater or lesser artistic quality have been read, but all show in their authors a taste refined by the pursuit of literature. On occasion the authors read two or more compositions on a single night and that was considered a single reading. Mr. Ferrán read five or six composi-tions entitled *Poesías en prosa* ["Prose Poems"] and they were taken down as a single one. *Estudio sobre la viruela* ["Study on Smallpox"] by Dr. Ortiz, has two parts; it was read in two different sessions and counted as a single reading. The same was done with Mr. Blanco Cuartín's long study, and those of Messrs. Frick, Fossey, etc.

If in writing of this matter I must follow the division adopted in the Reports of the previous three years, the readings for the year in question could be distributed as follows: sociological compositions, twenty-four; scientific, seven; literary, forty-seven; in total, seventy-eight, a difference of five fewer compositions than the year prior, in which they amounted to eighty-three, thirty-six of them being in the single field of sociology, in which now the entire difference lies. Could this be due to the lack of diligent work, or to not having found strong research topics in national sociology?

III

Returning to the readings performed in this forum and, in order that their tendencies may be seen, I will take this opportunity to classify them in detail, stating that works in criticism numbered eleven: by Mr. Dávila, five; by Mr. Montt, one; by Mr. J. Lagarrigue, one; by Mr. Rojas, one, and three by a few other occasional visitors. Works in the sciences, seven: three from Dr. Orrego Luco, two by Dr. Letelier, one by Dr. Valderrama, and another by Dr. Ortiz. Works in philology, eight, including six by Mr. Letelier, one by Mr. Frick, and another by Mr. Fossey. On political economy, four, written by the undersigned, and one in general politics by Mr. Lavín Matta. Eight in literature, five of them by Mr. Barra, two from Mr. Larraín Zañartu, and one by Mr. Blanco Cuartín. Four ways and manners articles: two by Dr. Valderrama and two by Mr. Barros Grez. Five readings by Mr. Pedro L. Gallo on a translation of *El espíritu nuevo de Quinet* ["The New Spirit of Quinet"], and twenty-five compositions in verse on diverse topics, four of them read by Messrs. Garriga and Quirós, three by Messrs. Valderrama, Boza, Castro, Escuti, and one each by Messrs. Matta (Manuel Antonio), Ferrán, Orihuela, and Torres Arce.

Analyzing in still more detail, we will find that the compositions read by Mr. Dávila are all bibliography and tell of books useful to the country. Mr. Barra's on Dante and poetry, considered by type. Mr. Letelier's on philology and medical-legal studies. Mr. Barros Grez's articles on ways and manners like *Los santos de Chile* ["The Saints of Chile"] and *Los llamadores* ["The Callers"], and *Un estudio sobre el verbo Hacer* ["A Study of the Verb 'Hacer'"] with a long narration in which only this verb is used. Mr. Larraín Zañartu's works in literature, like *La hija de Augusto* ["Augusto's Daughter"] and a *Cuento alegórico sobre el gobierno de las finanzas* ["Allegorical Story on Financial Management"]. Your reporter personally has read four studies on economy and civics entitled: *La crisis actual* ["The Current Crisis"], *Más vale cuenta que renta* ["Life's Better as a Debtor"], *Los trabajadores rurales* ["Rural Workers"], and *La moral de ahorro* ["The Morality of Saving"]. Mr. Orrego Luco, three studies on medicine: *Nueva teoría sobre las funciones cerebrales* ["New Theory on Cerebral Functions"], *Literatura médica* ["Medical Literature"], and *Signos de la muerte* ["Signs of Death"]. Dr. Valderrama, five, two in verse, one comic sketch, one article on ways and manners, and another on premature burials. And lastly, twenty-five poetic compositions, four by Messrs. Matta, Cañas, Garriga, and Valderrama, and the twenty-one remaining by visitors and correspondents, resulting in all seventy-eight compositions read: twenty-four sociological works, seven scientific works, and forty-seven artistic, which amount, as I stated, to five less than last year's tally.

If we now state that the lion's share of these compositions reveal productive work not only for the charms of their form, but also because nearly all of them sought to serve the collective interest of society, it will be simple to recognize that such results speak very highly of the Academy. Yet at the same time it cannot but regret the chronic absence of many regular Academy members, who with their talent and education would bring prestige to this organization by taking part in its projects and attending its sessions. This doubtless stems from the fact that letters and even sciences unapplied to a practical end are far from being a career in our country, and also from the fact that the need to acquire knowledge to the fullest is not yet a spur capable of generating collective interests here, nor giving an independent life to an association like this one, which imposes tasks without glory or emoluments. But whether this is the result of indolence or lack of habit, the encouragement that the young people devoted to the pursuit of letters or sciences receive here is enough for all of us to want to see this consortium preserved, and for me, in speaking with you on this occasion, to pay my cordial compliments to the Academy members in attendance, the institution's generous sponsors and the visitors, who with their works and their enthusiasm have been able to keep this small center of intellectual activity in our country thriving.

IV

The Academy's private works in the year in question likewise did not lack in importance. Among them the one perhaps bearing the greatest fruit was the one presented in session 94 by don E. de la Barra, and which, published in a quarto distributed in the previous official session and sent on to committee, had the misfortune of not being related until now. I refer to the project on creating literary centers in the main cities of the country, and on encouraging youths to study and to work, tracing out paths for them to make progress in the pursuit of letters and for them to serve public education in the meantime. To this end he proposed, among other studies, the examination of our night schools for artisans, the better to improve them, and the creation of an institute for women in Santiago, two ideas that have met with the valuable support of the administration and that are today on their way to completion and to yielding beautiful results. Mr. de la Barra, called away to appear at other public functions, will be missed here, but his idea will evolve and I expect we will discuss it in the course of this year.

To encourage literary work and in celebration of our independence, the Academy agreed last August to hold a poetic competition subject to the same conditions as in the year 1875 and establishing the following as the topic: *Una oda patriótica* ["A Patriotic Ode"] and *Una narración histórica* ["A Historical Narrative"], both plots being taken from national history. Four compositions were submitted, two in prose and two in verse: the first ones, *Abdicación de O'Higgins* ["Abdication of O'Higgins"] and *Formación del ejército libertador por San Martín* ["Formation of the Liberation Army by San Martín"]; and the latter two, *Manuel Rodríguez* and *La independencia de Chile* ["The Independence of Chile"]. Only *Manuel Rodríguez* was awarded an honorable mention; as for the others, the Academy gave only a few words of encouragement to their authors in the hopes that next time their compositions gain more acceptance, since the present ones were mere reductions of known historical works and were produced with little research and less artistry.

At the prompting of our current Secretary, Mr. Dávila Larraín, on 14 October last it was agreed to open a new competition whose classifications were a novel and a dramatic composition in the comic genre, with two prizes, one first and the other second class, which would consist of books suited to their object. Six compositions were submitted opportunely to this competition: a novel entitled *Los Altos de Bohemia* ["The Highs of Bohemia"], by Atahualpa; *Isabel*, a comedy in three acts and in prose, by Sinbad; *Escenas caseras* ["Domestic Scenes"], a comedy in three acts and in verse, by Nemo; *La política en Chile* ["Politics in Chile"], a comedy in three acts in verse, by Tres Corazones; *Todo menos solterona* ["Anything But An Old Maid"], a comedy in three acts, in verse, with a sign, and *Un descubrimiento a tiempo* ["A Discovery in Time"] a one-act comedy in verse, having a star as its mark.

Reports have been prepared on all these plays and the Academy is hearing its reading with a view to issuing the corresponding verdict on their respective merits.

V

Throughout this year several people and institutions have given gifts of books to the Academy in order that they be reported on in its sessions. Mr. Asta-Buruaga, on behalf of the Ivison publishing house, from New York, and Mr. Carmona, head of official commercial returns in Valparaíso, have sent a portion of volumes to our library. The Burdeos Geographical Society, the Lima Literary Club, the Romance Language Society, and the Argentinian Academy of Letters and Sciences have also sent us works and newsletters of theirs, and have asked that we cultivate literary relations.

The system of weekly conferences we tried to put in place last year has not managed to yield the harvest one might expect, since there are many roadblocks that hinder the progress of an institution appointed to serving purely speculative interests, such as the cultivation of letters and science following the criterion we have accepted in our bylaws. Such an enterprise does not attract converts nor find ready-made collaborators. To the contrary, it imposes commitments and tasks that are difficult to fulfill, and one requires the full respect due the intelligence and a dauntless resolve to not back down from said respect in this thankless work. Thankless, but in time it should garner rather useful results for the country, if we work selflessly to preserve and foster it.

So we must believe it will come to pass, gentlemen, not only for the need for overall advancement, which is the law of progress, but also for the acceptance that some of the ideas that came to light through us have enjoyed, such as the night schools for adults and literary societies in the provinces and even in public and private schools. The care that all our social classes take today to be educated and the assurance one has that one cannot be a full-fledged citizen without knowing how to write and speak well, will surely see to it that institutions like ours find greater acceptance with every passing day, and that they have a greater number of collaborators, enabling them to more usefully serve society. Our weekly readings by Academy members or visitors do much for letters and even sciences, but they will do more in the future if we persist in our work and widen its scope through public readings on natural history, chemistry, physics, etc., and if the government, without flouting any law, adopts the objective of making elementary education mandatory in Chile, for this is also a supremely powerful medium for making widespread the pursuit of literary knowledge.

VI

Someone has said that, when this last is accomplished, the government diminishes paternal power and encroaches on freedom by disregarding each citizen's rights to do what he please, provided no one else's rights are infringed upon. As I see it, gentlemen, this argument lacks strength and opportuneness, for if the father's power is challenged by forcing him to send his children to primary school, is it not challenged and much more so with mandatory service in the national guard? If the father who is an artisan, rancher, tenant farmer or itinerant laborer in the fields, has need of his sons' work, and therefore he does not rear them like the interest of the Republic calls for, is it not worse that they lack education or that they live in leisure, or spend all their time gratuitously serving as rural patrols or watchmen? But if one observes that compulsory education violates the most holy right, man's right regarding himself, recall the simple reply that the distinguished writer Legouvé* has just made to that objection: "When someone possesses a good that harms others, he is dispossessed of it in the interest of all," he states; "and with equal grounds, I ask that the people's ignorance be expropriated from them for the cause of public utility."

It is evident that elementary education is only designed to give a first fueling to the spirit, without which sustenance the latter will die of starvation: it is like milk for the newborn, a nutriment which sustains it for the time being and prepares the infant's system to receive more substantial nutrition thereafter. But that kind of moral hungering, can it be tolerated in a country like ours, where every man is a citizen and has obligations to fulfill and rights to exercise? The issue is perhaps thorny in principal. Nevertheless, we must not forget that the freest republics, the United States and Switzerland, have declared primary education mandatory, and Prussia has made of their own a military and monarchical state; these are the only nations in the world where everyone knows how to read and write properly. There it is thought that the father does not have the right to fail in his obligations to his son, nor to society, without the latter having the right to intercede at once; for it has been shown that there is no tyranny when the father is compelled to pay a debt that would deprive the son of a necessary resource, and the State of a useful citizen, and that would place the public safety at risk due to the very close correlation that unfailingly exists between ignorance and crime.

VII

I think, gentlemen, that from this deficiency in general education in large part comes the desertion, into which even educated people here retire, of the pursuit of letters and sciences. There is nothing more worthwhile or fitting than young people from wealthy families earning scientific degrees and becoming baccalaureates or licentiates in humanities or law; nothing more right or more laudatory than their visiting Europe and bringing back objets d'art, breeds of useful animals and new tools for agricultural or industrial cultivation. But does the patriotic mission of the man of fortune boil down to only this? Why do young people of leisure forsake the pursuit of letters and the fostering of education, which is the richest

---

* Gabriel-Jean-Baptiste-Ernest-Wilfrid Legouvé (1807–1903), French essayist, playwright, poet, and novelist. —Ed.

source of progress and one of the most beautiful delights of civil life? The independence of the spirit for the acquisition of knowledge is also an excellent gift of nature and must be represented in all nations by the advancement of literature, which is like the mirror of society. And if the field of individual action in Chile has never been as broad as it is now, in order for social forces to be duly balanced in this country, it is necessary that when everything springs up and thrives, literature alone not be forgotten and forsaken by those very people who, owing to the advantages of their station, are the ones most obligated to cultivate and further it.

It has been some time since when one spoke in our country of progress to a man of letters, he would smile sadly, recalling not-too-distant eras, and observe, somewhat pained, that if it is true that schools have mushroomed and that everything in Chile has developed in the last thirty years, letters, however, have stayed stock still for lack of encouragement and enthusiasm from those who should be fostering them. What is, in fact, the field of action, which the theater for literature here? There is none other than the newspapers, and even there, there are few fortunate editorial writers, for bulletins, ephemera, local chronicles, and critical or scientific articles that are published periodically, be it for reasons of the impersonal course of journalism or the marked improvement of the newspapers, they are no longer the hubs of influence and forums of opinion they were in bygone ages. The dailies are read today because of fondness for their doctrines and to know last evening's events, breaking news, playbills, situations wanted, auctions of furniture and real estate, and houses for sale or to let. But between them and the public, the true tie is none other than curiosity, not because the journalist has stopped writing well, but because he does not believe that he does justice to voicing the general opinion and thus he is not listened to with the former public's fellow feeling.

A proverb says "those who are liked are understood with half a word." Yet it seems that in letters, as in politics, friendly ties are growing weaker instead of stronger. Right now there are no parties as such. Count them and you will see that their labors are going the way of the literary labors. The parties, like the works of literature, appear one day only to disappear the next, and form neither a school nor a public, just as the travelers that cross a city do not count as inhabitants. In matters political, I do not feel the same, for I think that the fewer parties there are, the more country there is, the fewer differences of opinion, the more individual interests that emerge derive inspiration and further the overall progress. May God grant that this change come about in the case of literature! I have a soft spot for believing in the ineluctable law of progress; and the simple exposition I have given you of the Academy's works from this year ending today suffices to demonstrate that the love of letters and of sound schooling has not been totally forgotten, and that by persevering in our mission to support this institution and to foster it as a hub of literary activity, we will bestow no small benefit upon our country's intellectual culture.

VIII

It is a rare thing, gentlemen, that when public education in all its branches is on an ever-ascending course in Chile, the pursuit of literature and even nonapplied sciences is practically at a standstill, being thus that it could alone elicit the talent and the everlasting, splendid triumphs and benefits from many of our compatriots. You all know it: there is no immortality greater than that of literature that lives on despite the passing of centuries, nor that of the sciences that are the focal point whence emanate the light, power, and wealth of individuals and of nations. If we neglect them and dispense with their incalculable benefits, is it not obvious that we will move backward or remain lingering in one place on the path of civilization, now that universal advancements shout out to us, *forward march!*, *forward march* forever? When the University and the Instituto and the administration make all manner of efforts to ensure that education be distributed without personal or class discrimination, and that the Republic become a reality in Chile due to the schooling and virtues of its scions, does it not grieve us that acquired learning be left unapplied and that the pursuit of knowledge, for lack of literary or scientific practice, cease to yield the beautiful fruit that in books, pamphlets, or newspapers would put our progress in evidence at home and raise our country's prestige abroad?

It is imperative, gentlemen, that we remedy this ill, and since letters and science are inexhaustible mines of progress and happiness for the ages, we must not neglect them, and every educated Chilean must work, within the limits of his power, to gain all the advantage he can for himself and his country.

But when we study letters to be writers, journalists, professors, lawyers, or mere literati, we study them specifically in their applications, for theory would get us nowhere without practice, just as it would not be enough to know the grammar of a language nor the rules of a literary manual to successfully produce just any composition. No one is unaware of the fact that to write or speak well, one needs to train the pen or the word, and just as from the comparative study of legislation arises the philosophy of law, so too, and proceeding by comparison, does the practical study of literature arise from the philosophy of letters, and man rises to a knowledge of the events and principles that form the writer's science and develop good taste. Thus an Academy like this one provides a true service by stimulating labor and education in all their forms, streamlining literary output, and bringing it to the audience's attention, comparing and analyzing it, and awakening in spirits the keen desire to complete those studies that are the primary basis underlying general progress.

In spite, then, of the lack of encouragement, or rather, in spite of the neglect into which the cultivation of literature has fallen in our country, it is due to the existence of this modest literary gathering-place, gentlemen, that not only do letters properly speaking but also sociology and medicine, public and private law, philosophy, political economy, and virtually all the important branches of national biology have had a neutral testing ground here, and a place to grow. All have benefited from the publicity of our weekly readings, and this is how the Academy has been gradually building up a small repository that symbolizes progress made up until today, so that in time new writers may profit from those studies, and build with them a solid foundation for the future advancements of national letters and science.

Even were that not to come about, I have no doubts that this society always would be deserving of the solidarity of well-intentioned patriotism, since it is not the least of its services to engage the public in sincere studies that are selfless in all concerns, such as partisan spirit. Let us continue then, gentlemen, in the task of nurturing our modest Academy of Belles Lettres, which, from whatever vantage point, is a truly useful creation. And if by furthering and improving literary and scientific works we succeed in giving reason a solid criterion for unearthing truth, content in the certainty that this institution will grow strong, its work will be more far-reaching, and encouraged by the sustenance of progress, will go on yielding ever-greater results for our country.

Conclusion

Thus end the main documents of the Academy of Belles Lettres, with which we bring these *Memoirs* to a close.

We have borne witness to the events of our intellectual growth that have fallen within our sphere of influence in the last thirty-five years, and have sought to stay true, to tell the truth, and to right wrongs. If our character flaws have thwarted our purpose, we shall be delivered of blame, for we cannot be made over again. But as for what we feel to be just and true, following our philosophic criterion, on that we will stand firm, for it is our opinion, deliberately formed and resolutely adopted. Whatever the case may be, whether we have rendered accurate judgments or not, the truth is that these *Memoirs* could end with the utterances with which Marchena closed his address in 1819 on the *Historia literaria de España* ["Literary History of Spain"]: "Thus is the state of our literature, thus the culture of the human spirit in our country. This address is the reply, corroborated by events, to the issue of *whether fine literature can thrive under despotic governments*. Consider the literary state of our nation, compare it to its political state, and the matter is settled."

THE END